Anne Griffin

Using Political Ideas

Using Political Ideas

Barbara Goodwin

Brunel University

JOHN WILEY & SONS

Chichester · New York · Brisbane · Toronto · Singapore

Library of Congress Cataloguing in Publication Data

Goodwin, Barbara
  Using political ideas.
  Includes bibliographical references and index.
  1. Political science.   2. Ideology
  I. Title
  JA71. G66   320.5   81-16009

  ISBN 0 471 10115 *X* (cloth)   AACR2
  ISBN 0 471 10116 8 (paper)

British Library Cataloguing in Publication Data

Goodwin, Barbara
  Using political ideas.
  1. Political science
  I. Title
  320   JA66

  ISBN 0 471 10115 X (cloth)
  ISBN 0 471 10116 8 (paper)

Phototypeset by Dobbie Typesetting Service, Plymouth, Devon, England
Printed in the United States of America

Contents

PART I INTRODUCTION

PART II IDEOLOGIES

PART III IDEAS

Part I

INTRODUCTION

CHAPTER 1

Who Needs Political Theory?

Should men be more equal? Is the state more important than the individual? Can a socialist society be free? Is political violence ever justified? Must we tolerate the intolerant? Can the majority dictate to the minority? Is it right that the rich should also be powerful? Such questions are the concerns of political theory. Although they sound deceptively simple, and susceptible to 'Yes' or 'No' answers, when we try to answer them it becomes evident that each conceals a wealth of disputable assumptions and that the meaning of its key words is also disputable. Furthermore, the answers inevitably express opinions on *what ought to be the case*, rather than describing *what is the case*. Political values and ideals are at stake here, and choices between ideals must be made. *I* may give priority to freedom rather than equality because I think it more vital to human happiness, *you* may judge the opposite. Also, most people are influenced by political ideology, whether they knowingly subscribe to it or unconsciously absorb it as part of received opinion, so not only do the answers to political questions vary according to individual opinion, they also differ with the individual's ideological position.

The practice of political theory helps us to set about answering such questions logically, and to criticize the answers which others give, by dealing with political matters at a more abstract and general level than does political science. Take the question 'Is political violence ever justified?' The constitutional theorist's answer would be an emphatic negative since violence is outlawed both legally and constitutionally. But political theory asks if justification might not be advanced according to circumstance. Does not a repressed minority, denied the freedom to state its case, have a justification for using violence? Does not the validity of that justification further depend on what sort of violence and against whom it is directed? And so on. The usefulness of political theory is that it allows us to consider such problems without always returning to the factual replies of the constitutionalist or lawyer. It frees us to think speculatively and idealistically, instead of being trapped into describing what exists as if it could never be changed. A critical approach rests on the ability to escape from the existent.

3

At first it appears that the 'great' political theorists who appear in the 'Plato to NATO' political theory syllabus are engaged not in criticism but in a permanent struggle to legitimize rulers or governments and to justify the existence of power. Plato looked to absolute justice to validate his Guardians, Christian theologians of the middle ages looked to God's intentions to sanction the rule of kings, while contract theorists such as Hobbes and Locke saw government as founded on the people's rational choice. But Plato, Hobbes and Locke were highly critical of the politics of their own societies and voiced this opposition in their descriptions of government *as it should be*, ideal government. Marx's revolutionary *Communist Manifesto* is often seen as the archetype of critical political theory. Naturally, there have also been theoretical apologists for existing regimes, but propagandists are intrinsically less interesting except to the social historian, and rarely end up on such syllabuses. Political theory, then, is a technique of analysis which can be used to overturn, as well as to uphold. It describes and explains politics in abstract and general terms, departing from fact and detail, which allow scope for the critical imagination.

Political theory may therefore be defined as the discipline which aims to explain, justify or criticize the disposition of power in society. 'Power' is used broadly here: even *obedience* is an aspect of power, for it connotes deliberate self-restraint by citizens who might otherwise resist the government, or acquiesence to a regime. Power essentially lies where resources (personal, economic, moral, ideological, etc.) lie, and operates through inducements as much as through threats and through the withholding as well as the deployment of resources. Sociologists tend to analyse power in terms of individual interaction, as A's capacity to get B to comply with his (A's) desires, but political theory sets these familiar, everyday machinations in a formal power structure. However, even theorists observing the same phenomena may conceptualize the power structure differently: where liberals saw equality and social harmony, Marx saw conflict and oppression. Different conclusions result: for example, a constitutionalist who views politics in terms of institutions might consider that unions should not be politically active, while someone viewing politics as pressure group activity would think it inevitable that they would be. Different conceptualizations of power therefore generate different political ideals and problems.

A critical reader new to political theory might raise the following objection to the subject: surely it would be better to study political institutions rather than abstract ideas or concepts, since ideas must be incarnated in institutions if they are to have any meaning. We can best discover the meaning of 'democracy', it might be thought, by examining the institutions of our own and other democratic countries and extracting their crucial features, rather than by reading Plato *et al*. This raises a fundamental problem which haunts all social science subjects: which comes first, concept or fact, theory or reality? Is there an *essence* of democracy, or is it constituted by a configuration of institutions as observed in Western democracies? This is a modern evocation of the most ancient philosophical controversy: does reality reflect ideas, or vice versa?

This problem cannot be solved here, but it provides an apt opportunity to define some of the mysterious labels which are tied to various arguments in political theory. Plato's view, also associated with Descartes and others, that reality approximates to unchanging transcendental ideas, is labelled *idealist* (not to be confused with the more familiar 'idealistic' which means 'bearing ideals or values'). In social science, the idealist approach suggests that ideas (concepts) and theory precede factual observation. The opposed view, originally associated with Locke, that concepts derive from our observation of physical or material reality, is generally called *materialist* (again, differing from 'materialistic').

A materialist outlook is often associated with the *empirical* and *inductive* scientific method, although not invariably. *Empiricism* requires that the natural or social scientist should first observe reality and then induce a general theory based on a large number of instances or facts. Empiricism is the dominant scientific method in the Anglo-Saxon world. The Greek root of 'empirical' means 'in experience', which suggests that the empiricist lacks preconceptions and is a naïve observer who makes discoveries: this contrasts with the procedure of the *rationalist*, who begins with a pet theory. The conflict between the empiricist and rationalist viewpoints is one of *epistemology*—that is, it is concerned with the criteria by which knowledge can be established and so with truth, falsehood and proof. This debate, although philosophical, is closely related to issues in political theory, as we shall see.

Meanwhile, the objector who wants to define democracy by observing democratic states is still waiting. He is clearly advocating an empirical approach which would supply the general principles of democracy by investigating its organizational features. The obvious drawback is that to analyse the idea through countries or institutions which are reputedly democratic leaves us with no independent criterion to judge whether they are so, or not. And how would this approach cope with self-proclaimedly democratic countries such as the USSR and Tanzania? It has no obvious justification for excluding them from its analysis. To define 'democracy' through a study of existing democracies begs the question of what democracy means. A theory so formed can only mirror observed phenomena, whereas a theory which is to have critical power needs to make reference to the ideal composition of democracy.

The case against the empirical approach to political concepts is well put by Marcuse. He contends that our political vocabulary is becoming increasingly 'closed', with key words being defined purely in concrete, factual terms (for example, 'democracy means one-man-one-vote, the secret ballot, equal constituencies . . .') so that critical usages have become impossible.

Such nouns as 'freedom', 'equality', 'democracy', and 'peace' imply, analytically, a specific set of attributes which occur invariably when the noun is spoken or written . . . . The ritualised concept is made immune against contradiction.[1]

In other words, in Marcuse's view political concepts have become like minor characters in Dickens's novels, each with his distinguishing trait. We cannot imagine freedom without choice any more than we can picture Mrs Gamp without a gin bottle, hence we have a 'one-dimensional' view of freedom. Marcuse also cites research on factory workers' grievances in which the researchers 'operationalized' the complaints, transforming vague grumbles about conditions and pay into specific complaints about dirty washrooms or the financial problems of particular workers. By this device, heartfelt alienation is dissolved into concrete trivia and the critical element of the grievances is vanquished. Marcuse's general thesis is that the 'concrete' approach to political matters deliberately precludes the proper use of abstract concepts as open-ended tools for criticism and protest.

Even if Marcuse's criticism of capitalism is rejected, his point, that the critical dimension is essential to thought and argument, is indisputable. The term 'criticism' is frequently given a pejorative undertone, but in defining criticism as the central task of political theory, I view it in the neutral sense in which Enlightenment philosophers saw it, as the tool by which our reason appraises the social order. Only by taking an abstract, conceptual approach, starting from ideals and a theory, can we achieve an appraisal which is *detached* from existing society, even if it cannot be entirely impartial. Political science and political sociology lack this detachment in many instances, and political theory is important because it offers this perspective.

Such arguments may convince the sceptic that political theory is indeed worthwhile, but he may still doubt its relevance to real life. Is it not an ivory-tower subject of no interest to ordinary citizens, whose abstract and detached approach prevents its influencing the world below? The next few pages are intended to show not only that political theory can sharply analyse current political controversies, but also that even the crudest political argument relies on the fundamental concepts and ideals supplied by theory. Often these are unvoiced, but their role in determining the forms which political argument and *Realpolitik* take is crucial. Consequently, the political theorist has the important task of exposing these hidden mechanisms.

The recent and continuing debate on workers' participation in management which has ensued since the Bullock Report (1977) on industrial democracy appears to concern industrial relations but is really a contemporary rehearsal of age-old arguments as to the best form of government. Advocates of workers' management take participation as a positive good. It increases the number of viewpoints considered, gives the workers the impression that they are controlling their own destinies, increases the acceptability of decisions and emphasizes workers' responsibility to follow management policies. (The idea of workers' representatives on Boards of Directors could in this sense be said to draw implicitly on Hobbes's view that the 'author' or elector has a duty to abide by what his 'agent' or representative decides.[2]) Against this viewpoint, others assert the value of specialist and expert management. The justification of elite government since Plato's time has rested on a division between mental and manual labour. In the context of this argument, workers are said to be obsessed with their own short-term wellbeing, and unable to make the strategic industrial choices which require economic know-how and managerial experience. A Board of experts, managers, and informed outsiders will supposedly make un-self-interested decisions in the interests of both firm and employees.

The two underlying principles in this debate were familiar in classical times, when both government by experts and participation by the people were tried in the Greek *polis*. The former emphasizes the benefits that knowledge and wisdom bring to mankind, while the more egalitarian principle spells out the subjective importance for individuals of having a voice in public affairs: expertise and efficiency or participation and greater satisfaction? These rival values are incommensurable, and cannot be simultaneously realized; a choice about worker participation (or good government) requires an ordering of priorities. A change of priorities, or values, changes the social institutions which embody the values, so the ability to extract and evaluate the old and new values is important for participants in such political debate.

I now turn to a set of arguments based on less reputable principles. It is often argued that immigrants in Britain have no right to be here, even 'third-generation' immigrants, and that they consume resources to which native British people are entitled. Underpinning this assertion is a notion of *'natural' justice*, which deems that being born in a country gives one a special right to its resources, including a right to welfare and a right to work. This is an instinctive or 'gut' conception of justice, hence the epithet 'natural', a term often invoked when rationality offers no support to an argument.

In times when there was little transport or mobility and men lived in village economies which were locally self-sufficient, there was some basis for the view that they had a primary claim to the local resources which they themselves processed and relied on. (But there were also traditions of generosity between communities in hard times.) Now that migration is common and mobility almost universal, at least in the West, and economies are not local or national, but international, how could we substantiate such a claim to natural entitlement? Anyone who maintained that only native Mancunians had the right to work in Manchester or consume its precious manufactures would rightly be found guilty of absurdity. But this patently absurd argument differs only in degree from the claim that immigrants should not work here. The controversy over the notion of patriality in the 1972 Act restricting immigration (now even further complicated by the 1981 Act) made plain the incongruity of the idea of natural entitlement. In what sense is a 'patrial', someone with at least one British grandparent, *entitled* to come to Britain and work? Grandpaternity may be a natural relationship, but it is also arbitrarily chosen—why not cousinhood, or aunthood?—and bears a tenuous link to the right or need to immigrate.

If, on the other hand, there *is* a principle of natural justice, this might equally be cited to support immigration. Most immigration since the Second World War has been a consequence of the colonization which created the

British Empire: the extension of British nationality to inhabitants of the colonies gave them a right, and an incentive, to migrate to Britain. Our present wealth, it could be argued, is substantially derived from our use of those colonies' resources, to which the forefathers of today's immigrants may have considered that *they* had a natural entitlement. Does not natural justice therefore decree that their grandchildren should come and share our prosperity? This argument may be as poor as the opposing one, but it illustrates that citing natural justice to substantiate a non-legal claim against someone is a double-edged process, because the notion of entitlement by birth, geography or similar accident can usually be countered by another, equally 'natural', claim. There may be pragmatic and tactical reasons for limiting immigration, but we should refrain from thinking that such a limitation is necessarily based on justice — despite the fact that no government is ever likely to concede that its acts are *unjust*!

Another topical claim supposedly based on natural justice is the demand of some Scottish nationalists that Scotland should have the revenue from the off-shore oil located on their share of the continental shelf. Leaving aside the breathtaking simplification of the problems of ownership of the world's resources which this assumes, one wonders if any Scot would countenance the obverse argument that Scotland should not benefit from resources located elsewhere in Britain. The fact that Scotland has so benefitted in the past would presumably not be thought relevant to the present claim — proponents of natural justice generally take a myopic or selective view of history when it does not favour their case.

The emotional and intuitive appeal of claims to natural justice is evidently strong, but the concept collapses under analysis. Bentham argued in the eighteenth century that 'natural rights' are nonsense, the only rights being those established in positive law. He would have said that the same goes for natural justice. Malthus wrote, concerning the pauper, 'At Nature's mighty feast there is no vacant cover for him. She tells him to begone.' In one respect, Malthus was right: in no sense does the world 'naturally' owe us a living, even less does a particular corner of the world owe some inhabitants, rather than others, a livelihood. (This is not to say that individuals in society do not have moral obligations to each other.) The fact that such claims have been established by social and legal convention does not make them naturally just. There is no justice in nature, although men have contended against the intractability of the natural world and its imperviousness to their needs by creating the idea of human rights and, more recently, those of 'welfare rights' and the 'social minimum'. But crucial to the idea of human rights is their *universality, every* man's claim to life and livelihood — a claim which 'natural justice' by implication rejects.

Prominent among contemporary political movements are nationalism, separatism, and devolutionism. These doctrines all rest on an ideal of self-determination, and most of all on a notion of the 'natural' geographical, racial or economic unit. The axiom 'what is natural is good' prevails. When we consider how arbitrarily and for what Machiavellian reasons many national boundaries were drawn, especially in colonial Africa or post-1918 and post-1945 Europe, it is small wonder that internecine wars and separatism are now rife. At first, the idea of the natural social unit seems valid, because members of racial or language groups, for example, clearly have salient characteristics which unite them and differentiate them from others. But it is not easy to devise a general political principle on this basis of natural affinity. 'The people's right to self-determination' which created free Balkan states in 1919 also provided justification for Hitler's march into Austria and his invasions of Czechoslovakia and Poland to 'protect' German-speaking citizens. The most aggressive forms of nationalism are often based on a dogmatic assertion of the naturalness of the national unit. In reality, of course, most nations suffer in part from unsuitable boundaries, yet the destruction of their territorial status quos might have worse consequences for everybody, separatists included. In the face of such intractable problems, political theory can at least show analytically that none of the 'natural' determinants — geographical, cultural, linguistic, etc. — are well-founded or universally applicable, and that 'what is natural is good' is a highly fallacious argument. It can also offer alternative ways of conceptualizing such situations which may be more appropriate. In the devolution debate, for example, the more theoretically minded advanced a notion of sovereignty against the idea of the natural nationhood of the Welsh and Scots, although this too was not unproblematic.

The goodness of what is natural is an adage which has not lost its appeal in our highly artificial civilization. In politics, it is used to sanction gut convictions and propositions for which no evidence can be advanced. But the implication that society is as natural as trees and rocks is totally misleading. Certainly, men are part of nature, subject to the same needs and aging processes as other mammals, but society is an artificial environment *not* subject to inexorable natural laws: men *can* manipulate and change society. However fond some politicians may be of the analogy of the Body Politic, society does not function like a living organism. So claims about what is natural in society are misleading, just as it is false to cite Nature as the moral yardstick by which to measure our social arrangements: there is no morality in nature, and not much that is natural in society.

Without overstating its claims, political theory's task is surely to dispel popular delusions of the kinds just described and to expose misleading ideas. In this connection it is relevant to consider briefly the other device so often accorded final authority in political arguments, *human nature*. How often is it said that socialism is impossible because men are naturally greedy (rather than justifiably sick of monotonous work)? In common with other social science subjects, political theory makes suppositions about man's character or motivation, or at least, minimal assumptions about regularities in his behaviour. This is necessary for a consistent explanation of political life and institutions, but such assumptions, whether covert or explicit, hypothetical or well-founded, determine from the start which form a theory shall take.

Mediaeval Christian theorists, convinced of man's original sin and depraved, bestial nature, saw the power hierarchy as the curse of imperfect man: heaven would need no politics. Hobbes, believing in the natural aggressiveness of men, depicted political institutions as barriers against a flood-tide of violence. But optimists of the Enlightenment and after, among them Rousseau, the utopian socialists and various anarchists, viewed man as a *tabula rasa* (blank sheet) at birth, innocent of evil and only corrupted later, by invidious social institutions. In consequence, they envisaged ideal societies resting on man's natural faculty of reasoning and requiring no political or legal control. Some even theorized that in ideal circumstances man could become morally perfect: hence they were labelled 'perfectibilists' or 'optimists' by contrast with the pessimists who thought man irredeemably corrupt.

By contrast with these moralistic accounts of human nature, the fundamental liberal assumption that man's natural behaviour is to maximize his wellbeing seems morally neutral, unless we assume — as many liberals do — that life is marred by scarcity of resources, so that one man's maximization is necessarily another's minimization. This unpalatable implication is often ignored, though many liberals would add as justification that men are naturally competitive (the evidence being that men compete in competitive situations — hardly conclusive!). One modern version of the human nature argument is the contention of some feminists that politics is an all-male activity and political theory nearly an all-male subject because men, the dominant partners in society since time immemorial, have shaped both in the image of their own salient characteristic: aggressiveness. Hence the emphasis on power, competition, assertiveness, and domination, with the correlative, despised 'female' counterparts of obedience, conciliation, and acquiescence. Negotiation and peaceful compromise are regarded as loss of face in politics and political language reflects this contempt.

However, arguments from behaviour do not constitute evidence for there being an *innate* human nature and individuals are surely moulded by institutions, rather than vice versa. Theorists usually derive their generalizations about man's nature from how people currently behave in society: this is by definition socially determined behaviour, so it does not necessarily reflect a fundamental 'human essence'. Vandalism and violence are not proof of original sin — or are they? This debate is a species of the more general controversy as to whether we are formed by heredity or environment, nature or nurture. Different political consequences stem from whichever assumption is made. My own preference is for the environmental explanation, partly because of the scientific evidence supporting it, partly because of the impossibility of even conceiving of a human being *outside* society who could serve as an exemplar of untainted human nature, and partly because it has positive implications for social amelioration. We can change and improve our environment more easily than our genes. Indeed, the most radical and revolutionary socio-political theories date from Locke's inception of the *tabula rasa* notion which entails that man will improve himself if his environment is improved. For this reason, among others, Marxist theorists reject as reactionary the claim that there is a fixed human nature, and argue that the individual is formed solely by socio-economic factors. As this brief account of the 'human nature' debate suggests, we should always beware when confident claims are made about the nature of man.

The arguments of the last few pages illustrate that political theories, ideologies, and opinions conceal a wealth of assumptions and arguments, not always well-founded, which a student of political theory is better equipped to uncover than a bystander. In this respect, academic political theory is more a technique than an end in itself: it cuts sharply through the verbiage and factual confusions of political debate to the core of beliefs and prejudices, and raises such questions as 'Is this assumption tenable?' and 'Do these values really represent what is valuable?'

In common with other philosophical subjects, political theory has various inner logics which need to be exposed and a number of conventions to be inwardly digested before the subject can be fully intelligible and stimulating. Unfortunately, many writers use shorthand to denote familiar sequences of thought or theoretical positions, which confuses or annoys the uninitiated. References to idealism, naturalism, relativism, etc., which bear a wealth of connotations for the *habitué*, have zero, or negative, explanatory force for the newcomer. I shall try to demystify some of these obscure terms. Idealism, materialism, and empiricism have already been mentioned. Most such concepts come in contrasted pairs and are supposed to exhaust the logical possibilities between them. One such pair is *descriptive* and *evaluative*, adjectives used of statements or theories. This distinction was implicit in earlier paragraphs of this chapter where political science, which *describes* reality and builds explanatory theories on the facts, was contrasted with political theory, which analyses and *evaluates* ideas by reference to other concepts and values. Similar to this is the *descriptive–normative* distinction, which may generate confusion for anyone familiar with the sociologist's use of 'normative' to mean 'conforming to a norm or average'. In political theory 'normative' simply means 'bearing or promoting norms (in the sense of "values")', as opposed to descriptive.

The opposition between a descriptive and an evaluative approach is mirrored in the distinction which is often made in political debate between *facts* and *values*. Facts which are established empirically are said to be beyond dispute — as if nobody knew how to lie with statistics, or present a one-sided case! Values, by contrast, are often considered insubstantial and unverifiable, no more than mere opinion and therefore inadmissible as evidence in debate; it follows that an evaluation is merely an expression of opinion. In social science it is now more generally acknowledged that facts are not such innocent entities, since a framework of social investigation dictates *which* facts shall be created, and which ignored. However, political polemics, both academic and popular, are frequently conducted as if facts were facts and values, values, and never the twain should meet.

The fact–value dispute relates back to the choice of methodology in social science: an empiricist approach naturally deals in facts, whereas a theoretical method admits insubstantiable theses and values. (An empiricist approach could not have achieved the Copernican revolution.) Two other terms which also relate to this fundamental methodological division are *appearance* and *essence*. These terms had strongly technical connotations for scholastic philosophers and others such as Kant, but in the present context they denote differing approaches to the analysis of a political idea. The objector who contended that democracy could be defined by studying the attributes of democratic countries was recommending an empirical examination of the *appearance* or the *contingent* or *accidental* characteristics of democratic systems, such as the secret ballot, regular elections, and the existence of at least two parties. The alternative is to consider theoretically the *essence* of democracy, its *necessary* or *defining* characteristics (abstractly conceived) such as political equality and the responsiveness of government to the will of the people. In practice, one approach to political analysis needs correction by the other and the distinction between appearance and essence becomes blurred, but for the purposes of argument they are often presented as irreconcilable opposites, as are facts and values.

The meaning of *relativism* is further discussed in Chapter 2. Relativism is an epistemological position which repudiates the originally Platonic view that objective knowledge is possible. It asserts that there are no final, objective, indisputable criteria for truth, and hence for knowledge; such criteria are relative to time, place, and culture, and knowledge is only valid within the context which generates it. This doctrine would overturn many of the distinctions already made—today's value may be tomorrow's fact, and so on. Thus its effects are sometimes liberating, but relativism can also culminate in total uncertainty or unwillingness to assert principles or positions.

The distinction between *subjective* (personal, individual) and *objective* (impartial, impersonal) often plays a pivotal role in political theory, as when Rousseau argues that in an ideal democratic assembly men would put forward their *subjective* interests in discussion but vote according to the *objective* good of the community, thus becoming part of the General Will. Important parts of Marx's political argument turned on his assertion that the proletariat, objectively the most exploited class under capitalism, had no subjective awareness of its situation, and so had not yet become a revolutionary force. Political theory is usually concerned with the nature of the 'Good Society' and thus, directly or indirectly, with human happiness, and so the subjective aspects of life cannot be ignored by theorists, although they sometimes are by political scientists, especially the behaviouralists.

Political theory is a close relation of moral philosophy. Both are value-bearing and evaluative and although not all political values have moral origins (*tradition*, which Burke valued, and *efficiency* seem to be non-moral) they rely on moral language, since a value is something we would consider *good*, and would prefer to have more, rather than less, of. But although a value such as democracy is primarily political, its supporting values, freedom and equality, are as pervasive in moral as in political philosophizing. This shared area of concern and similarity of language is appropriate, since both moral and political philosophy attempt to define the Good Life, the first on an individual level, the second for the community at large.[3] So the importation of moral terms into political theory is permissible and necessary.

Is the connection between political theory and ideology equally necessary? Evidently, as will be argued, ideology is crucial in forming the political theorist's own view of the world. It would be convenient if we could distinguish clearly between ideology and theory—if we could label theory 'ideological' whenever values and prescriptive and persuasive elements are visible. But many ideological influences affect theory invisibly, pre-selecting which data the theory will explain, and dictating its conceptual vocabulary from the start. Likewise, much theory contains ideological bias without having ideology's express aim of persuasion. So I shall assume that *all* political theory is susceptible to greater or lesser ideological bias, and that a necessary task for commentators and students is to identify and evaluate that bias—and, of course, their own bias. The second part of this book sets out to analyse the concept of ideology and give a critical account of the major political ideologies and the problems which they encounter.

'Political theory' is an umbrella term. It comprehends the persuasive and normative doctrines called ideologies; it also embraces the analytical activity known as political philosophy, which styles itself 'value-free'.[4] Rather than propounding grandiose hypotheses about the nature of political society and the Good Life, this examines the units of which political theory, including ideology, is composed, the *concepts*. Hence it is sometimes called 'conceptual analysis'. Its main endeavour is to 'clear up confusions' which result from inclarity or inconsistency in the use of concepts such as freedom and equality by providing a clear and coherent account of their proper use. This activity often employs the methods established by the school of philosophy called 'linguistic analysis' which flourished in Oxford in the 1950s but is now increasingly challenged or rejected.[5] The other task of political philosophy is said to be to provide generally acceptable definitions of central political terms. These self-ascribed functions also rest on the conviction that even value-laden concepts are capable of a constant and definite meaning. Abbreviated formulae such as 'justice is giving every man his due' and 'democracy means "one man one vote"' summarize attempts at comprehensive, fool-proof definitions which appear to be factual and to describe justice, democracy and so on in terms of behaviour or institutions. But these formulae can easily be shown to be disguisedly evaluative. The attempt to provide such definitive analyses also falls foul of the linguistic philosophers who condemn the attempt to define *values* as ill-founded. Many political philosophers are now sceptical of this search for fixed meanings and argue that political concepts are 'essentially contested'—that is, that their meanings are necessarily disputed and vary according to the meaning of a cluster of related 'contextual' concepts, and are ineradicably dependent on values and ideologies.[6] If no final definitions are possible, it would seem that political philosophy has no useful role to play. But its defenders deny this, maintaining that the discipline deals with problems that are *in principle* open to theoretical solution, despite the contestability of the concepts which are its tools. Part III of this book shows the range of meanings which political ideas can take, and relates them to the ideological contexts.

Newcomers to political theory deserve two cautions. The subject often appears unsatisfactory because it fails to deliver decisive answers to political questions. It can analyse the logic of liberalism and the concept of tolerance but cannot determine whether we should tolerate the intolerant because this requires an ordering of values, which is said to be the task of the committed, ethical individual. Political ideology is an artefact, in which priorities are ordered and values asserted, but political philosophy strives to be a neutral tool of analysis and appraisal — so argue its partisans (although opponents see this neutrality as mere pretence). The 'neutral' approach leads to the unsatisfactorily inconclusive character of much political theory, and its concentration on the secondary or 'meta' level of debate and avoidance of substantive questions. However, not all political theory seeks to be neutral, and the current fashion is for more committed theory which seeks to influence, stimulate and provoke.[7]

The second caution concerns the idiosyncratic way in which political theory proceeds. A case is stated and evidence offered, then various objections are raised and sustained with apparent conviction, only to be elegantly disposed of, whereupon the theorist reverts to a modified version of the original proposition. The process manifests a degree of showmanship, and the reader has the impression of receiving a guided tour of blind alleys, followed by a smug arrival at a pre-determined destination. The reason for this form of argument is that political theory, like other philosophical subjects, originated in the oral, dialectical tradition whose essence was argument, objection, modification, restatement, and so on, and whose intent was to move rationally towards a final definition of a political idea such as justice.

Plato's *Republic*, starring Socrates, exemplifies this method admirably, and the dialogue form was still employed in some philosophical writing in the eighteenth century, long after oral debate had been replaced by printed polemics. The writer of theory, unlike Socrates, has no troublesome Thrasymachus to interrupt and contradict, so he must anticipate, state, and refute likely objections. We might blame the occasional appearance of complacency which this performance gives on Socrates, who usually won the argument. But the process, though circuitous, is one of the explanation and attempted proof rather than flat assertion and so these rehearsals of criticism and self-criticism are vital to political theory.

Although political theorists are typically unwilling to draw political conclusions, readers may rightly wonder what the bias of this book will be, and I should therefore state where its value is intended to lie. We are all, to a greater or even greater extent, integrated in a complex socio-political-economic machine against which there are few weapons except reason, information, and intelligence. The same is true of Soviet citizens and of those of third-world countries, which are willy-nilly enmeshed in international politics and finance capitalism. Our progress to advanced industrialism has created a form of socio-political organization which is neither manipulable nor controllable by individuals or groups and has its own logic and momentum, But our *compliance* is necessary for its continuance and success. Compliance is as much a mental as a physical act: the ideas supporting and validating advanced industrial society must be propagated and internalized. The study of political theory should make us more defensive and sceptical of the justifications of the system which nourish our compliance, and more willing to contemplate alternative political and social forms. This book advocates a critical appraisal of political ideologies, concepts, habits of thought, and prejudices: this in turn may lead readers to consider critically the political behaviour which certain political ideas generate—and even to behave differently.

Notes

1. H. Marcuse, *One Dimensional Man*, Sphere, London, 1968, pp.79–80.
2. T. Hobbes, *in Leviathan*, (Ed. C. B. Macpherson), Penguin, Harmondsworth, 1968, pp. 218–9.
3. The commitment of political theorists to a vision of the Good Life is demonstrated in A. Arblaster and S. Lukes, (Eds), *The Good Society*, Methuen, London, 1971.
4. See Quinton's introduction in A. Quinton, (Ed.), *Political Philosophy*, Oxford University Press, Oxford, 1967.
5. An account of, and repudiation of, linguistic analysis appears in E. Gellner, *Words and Things*, Gollancz, London, 1959.
6. The idea was first expounded by W. B. Gallie, in 'Essentially contested concepts', *Pro. Aristotelian Soc.*, **56**, 167–98, (1955–6).
7. For the controversy over the function of political theory see, e.g., A. Cobban, 'The decline of political theory', in *France Since the Revolution*, London, Cape, 1970 and P. H. Partridge, 'Politics, philosophy, ideology, and J. P. Plamenatz, 'The use of political theory', in *Political Philosophy*, (Ed. A. Quinton), Oxford University Press, Oxford, 1967.

CHAPTER 2

Ideology

'Ideology' must currently be the most overworked word in political discussion. The word has been drained of most of its analytic content and has become a mere label to be tied on doctrines which we dislike. 'Ideological' is rarely used except pejoratively, as a synonym for 'doctrinaire' and 'dogmatic'. But the contention of this book is that all coherent political doctrines are ideological, as is our use of political ideas themselves: if this is accepted, the pejorative connotations of the term must be laid aside. This chapter examines the various concepts of ideology which have developed, and their significance for political theory.

Marx on Ideology

The term 'ideology' literally means 'the science of ideas' but in the early nineteenth century a more critical usage was established: it came to mean an abstract, visionary or speculative way of thinking. While it was Marx who offered the first major analysis of ideology as such, the philosophical problem which gave rise to the notion had been widely debated during the Enlightenment. The problem is that of the status of knowledge. Many previous cultures had believed knowledge to be certain, absolute and objective: Plato thought that there existed in some non-physical or metaphysical dimension Ideas or Forms, absolute truths which served as models which men should strive to realize in society. The knowledge of these Ideas (such as Justice and the Good) was absolute knowledge, attainable through philosophical contemplation. Despite its pre-Christian origins, Platonism influenced the Christian view of knowledge and truth. Mediaeval Christian theology held that truth was God-given and absolute, reflecting the divinely ordained and fixed order of the world. The chief source of such knowledge was the scriptures, although during the Renaissance the experimental or scientific method of gaining knowledge was reconciled with Christian precepts. According to both the Platonic and the Christian views, knowledge 'exists' independently of man or emanates from some non-human source, and so is objectively established. Knowledge is to be discovered, not created, by man.

Enlightenment philosophers, many of whom were atheists, used *reason* as an implement for destroying the prejudices and mysteries of Christianity, arguing that the world was in principle explicable scientifically. A new conception of knowledge resulted: thinking man was seen as the *creator* of knowledge. Kant and Hegel developed theories of knowledge, epistemologies, on the basis of this insight, which abolished the polarity between man as a thinking *subject*, passively absorbing objective knowledge, and the external world, the source and *object* of knowledge. The new theories emphasized the *subjective* aspect of knowledge: thinking man inevitably intrudes himself into his perception of the object which he is trying to know. This had been implicit in Locke's argument a century before that knowledge of the external world is gained through our senses and so is sense-dependent, and subject-dependent: given a different eye structure, the world would appear to us as black-and-white. Kant emphasized that knowledge results from an active process, not mere passive absorption of data, while Hegel's dialectical account of knowledge described the constant dialogue between the conscious subject and the object, each stage raising the subject to a higher form of knowledge.

Marx's accomplishment was to codify the ways in which the social identity of the 'knowing subject' altered his knowledge, and to describe the process of knowing in concrete terms. As a *materialist*, he believed that material causes could be found for all events and phenomena in the world: there were no mysterious or metaphysical events and everything was scientifically explicable, including man. All human thought, ideas, and theories (in general, 'consciousness') were determined by material factors or, more precisely, by social circumstances.

Consciousness is, therefore, from the very beginning, a social product, and remains so as long as men exist at all.[1]

Marx considered that the economic structure of society determined all its other aspects, from social relations and political forms to law, morality and knowledge itself. Each economic system gave rise to the existence of classes in society, and men's knowledge and beliefs were determined not only by the general social context but by their particular class position in society. In propounding this materialist theory of consciousness, Marx challenged the 'Young Hegelians' and, indirectly, Hegel himself, who were, by contrast, *idealists*. They believed that ideas had an autonomous existence and could act as independent causes of events in the material world: the intellect had priority over man's physical existence. Revolutions, even, were made by ideas. Hegel had seen history as the movement of 'Spirit' through the world, realizing itself in different social forms. Marx thought such idealism (not to be confused with 'idealism' in the sense of 'the pursuit of ideals', although the two meanings are related) illusory and philosophically false.

Marx never set out his theory of ideology systematically in one text, but a coherent doctrine can be extracted from his works. Social reality itself is contradictory, Marx held: capitalism fosters two antagonistic classes, the bourgeoisie and the proletariat, whose interests are diametrically opposed, and which will finally come into direct conflict. Ideology is a solution of these contradictions *in the mind*: thus, capitalist ideology may 'resolve' class conflict by emphasizing the common interests and harmony between the classes, or the 'organic' nature of society, but this cannot alter the *real* antagonism between the interests of those classes. Because ideology tries to resolve the irresoluble, it gives an inaccurate and distorted representation of material reality.

The elaboration of this general conception of ideology shows what Marx thought its social functions to be. An individual's consciousness is determined by his class position, his ownership or non-ownership of the means of production, and the social relationships into which he enters as a member of a certain class. Marx gave an account of the genesis of different class viewpoints in economic factors, showing how each point of view distorts reality according to its own interests. His dialectical view of social processes (discussed below in Chapter 4) entailed that in each conflictual situation the opposing classes or groups had their own *partial* understanding of the process: he described the productive process from the viewpoint of the capitalist and from that of the labourer, showing the differences between these subjective, one-sided accounts of the same phenomenon.[2] Because such knowledge was bound up with the knower's class position, it was necessarily partial, an inaccurate representation of the world: hence, it was ideological. For Marx, the only escape route from ideology to accurate knowledge was via a synthetic account which comprehended both sides of the process, as did his own theory, which he designated 'scientific', in contradistinction to 'ideological' social theory.

Under capitalism, the bourgeoisie reinforces its dominant position in the economy by all possible social and political means, including the creation of the state. Ideology is viewed by Marx as a major instrument of repression in the hands of the ruling class, used to deceive subordinate classes about the true nature of capitalism and to perpetuate its own domination. The law, religion, morality, social and theory, and philosophy all evolve or are refashioned so as to reflect the bourgeois standpoint, and they become part of the wider ideology, functioning to disguise the contradictions in society and the grievances and discontent of the proletariat. Although the worker's class position should give him a set of ideas which reflect his own reality, he may instead absorb the all-pervasive bourgeois ideology which misleads him as to his own, exploited state: then, he is said to be the victim of *false consciousness*, which makes him unlikely to rebel against his oppressed condition. When Marx spoke of false consciousness, he did not mean anything so simple as the direct deliberate deception of gullible proletarians by the malevolent bourgeoisie. Bourgeois ideology invades the consciousness of workers through the propagation of common-sensical, seemingly non-dogmatic ideas, such as

'Everyone should pay their way', which establish the work ethic, the consumption ethic, and the ideal of the self-made man, all of which are vital to capitalism. A doctrine of individualism likewise develops which teaches that we establish our personal identity via material possessions, and so, conveniently, extends our desires and needs to keep up the level of demand necessary for capitalism to operate. Everyday wisdom correlates with the behaviour which best supports the capitalist system and established beliefs suppose capitalism to be the 'natural' form of society. Such doctrines permeate the workers' consciousness imperceptibly; also, the better-off they become, the more inclined are they to identify with the bourgeoisie and accept its values and doctrines, thus extending their own false consciousness: Marxists call this process 'embourgeoisement'. Thus, ideology is the gentlest method of oppression, but also the most invidious.

Marx did not consider that bourgeois ideology was always a deliberate distortion of reality: its distorting nature was sometimes merely a consequence of its class origin. The economic theories of Adam Smith, whom Marx admired, fell into this category. Although they were ideological, they were not intended as propaganda to foster bourgeois domination; they merely charted economic reality from the bourgeois standpoint. By contrast, Marx castigated Bentham as a mere apologist of capitalism, whose utilitarian doctrines presented a deliberately distorted view of reality intended to deceive and indoctrinate other classes. Most people latch on to the idea of deliberate distortion as the defining characteristic of ideology, but Marx equally often used it to mean an account of reality which is incomplete and partial and so, incidentally, tends to favour one class. The focus of Marx's theory was, of course, the proletarian revolution. The worker who shares the ideas of the capitalist about the sanctity of private property and the importance of individual rights has misidentified his true interests, so that, before a revolution is possible, workers must shed their false consciousness and develop a consciousness which accurately depicts their exploitation and oppression and shows them their real interests. When such consciousness becomes widespread, the workers constitute a 'class-for-themselves', a class aware of their true situation, ready to take political action. Marx's doctrines were themselves to form an important part of this new class consciousness.

Many sophisticated theories have been built upon Marx's account of ideology, and many controversies stem from it which cannot be examined here, but one question must be asked: was Marx's theory itself ideological? Critics of Marx hope to disprove his theory by showing that it fell into the very category of thought which he condemned. Briefly, Marx considered his own theory objective and scientific, believing it to give a complete, non-partial account of reality and its contradictions, but to the reader it may appear ideological in that it espouses the proletarian viewpoint and attacks capitalism. Lenin argued that *all* class knowledge is ideological, yet he viewed Marxism as a science. Other Marxists do, however, concede that Marxism may be an ideology. The question cannot finally be resolved, for ideological convictions enter into the debate, but according to modern, non-Marxist definitions of ideology, Marxism is unquestionably one ideology among many — which is not to say that it may not be nearer the truth than its rivals.

'Ideology' Since Marx

Marx's theory was one expression of the conviction widely held from the Enlightenment onwards, that knowledge is relative to the time, place, and thinker, or to a combination of all three. This 'relativism' dispelled the hope that absolute truth could be established in any field, except perhaps that of pure science. In this century Mannheim offered an influential account of ideology based on Marx's ideas, although he rejected Marx's political conclusions. Mannheim believed in the relativity of *all* knowledge which, he thought, always originated in the lives of groups or classes, within which certain climates of ideas develop. He defined ideology as an idea or ideas 'incongruent with reality', which have the effect of protecting a contradictory reality, and supporting the status quo.[3] He distinguished *particular ideology* from *total ideology*. The former is a set of ideas relative to a group's particular interests, which promotes these interests and deceives other groups. The ideological weapons used by the bourgeoisie exemplify this. Total ideology is a way of thinking common to a whole society or a particular historical period, a 'world-view' from which individuals cannot escape unless they migrate to another culture — where they will find a different total ideology. The classification of various epochs as 'The Age of Belief', 'The Age of Reason', and so on, reflects this idea of a total ideology or world-view which goes beyond class interests and establishes the form in which all thought, including particular ideology, can present itself. We might say, in trying to characterize the world-view of our own time, that this is the Age of Technology, when all forms of life are subordinated to the technological ethos and subject to efficiency calculations. The machine plays a dominant role throughout our culture, and knowledge is established by scientific procedures. All new doctrines and policies are liable to be evaluated according to technical, not moral, criteria.

Mannheim has been criticized for his acceptance that all knowledge is relative and ideological in one sense or the other (including, logically, his own theory, which is relative to an age of relativism, . . .), an admission which blunts the critical edge of the concept of ideology. If everything is ideological, how can we judge between or criticize doctrines? Even if we eradicate particular ideologies, our thoughts are still trapped inside the total ideology. Mannheim hoped that 'classless' intellectuals would produce a synthesis of non-ideological knowledge, but this aspiration has been generally derided, given the clear allegiance of most intellectuals to one class or the other. Undoubtedly we cannot escape from the dominant ideas or the ethos of our own time and culture, but this fact does not diminish the force of Mannheim's critique of partial ideology, which can, he says, be recognized and eradicated.

Since Mannheim, many Western political thinkers who would reject Marxism have turned nevertheless their attention to ideology. Ironically, whereas Marx and Mannheim both defined ideology as a reactionary phenomenon, such thinkers condemn it for its *radical* tendencies! Foremost among the ideologies which they criticize is, of course, Marxism itself, while liberal–democratic ideas are considered not ideological, but true. Arendt emphasized the deceptive explanatory nature of ideology and its one-dimensionality. 'Ideologies are *isms* which to the satisfaction of their adherents can explain every occurrence by deducing it from a single premiss'.[4] Putnam, a political scientist, defined it more loosely and less critically as 'a lifeguiding system of beliefs, values and goals affecting political style and action'.[5] From the current non-Marxist analyses a number of defining characteristics of ideology can be deduced, which are as follows:

(a) Ideology presents ideas and knowledge in a way which entails certain kinds of beliefs and actions.

(b) Ideology purports to have explanatory power, to make the world comprehensible to its believers, although in fact it distorts the truth by selection, interpretation or plain falsification. (This point rests on an implicit reference to some established truth which ideology distorts — the possibility of which may be an illusion).

(c) Ideology has persuasive force; its precepts often appear as moral imperatives. It tries to harness the emotions by evoking common prejudices and deep-rooted fears.

(d) Modern ideology often claims to be scientific, based on patterns of argument like those of science, or invokes scientific evidence, as the Nazis did in trying to prove Aryan superiority. This helps to give it explanatory force. (Mannheim would say here that particular ideology conforms to the total, scientific, ideology.) Ideology also manifests a spurious coherence and rationality and substitutes itself for superstition, religion and tradition.

(e) Despite (d), ideology is frequently irrational and illogical, when analysed. It reconciles within itself incompatible elements by changing the meaning of words or distorting the facts, so as to present itself as an apparently self-consistent, logical whole.

Evidently, these characteristics were not specified by any friend of ideology! They suggest that it beguiles men away from clear, discoverable political truths. But the existence of such objective truths, especially in politics and social life, is to be doubted according to any relativist conception of knowledge. The pejorative account of ideology which derives from those characteristics need not, however, be accepted. But it is not surprising that writers within the dominant ideology of liberal democracy (which denies its own ideological status) should give a derogatory account of the nature of other doctrines, *qua* ideologies.

The conception of ideology rests on prevalent views of the nature of knowledge. The stronger the doctrine of empiricism, which stipulates that knowledge is constructed on the basis of *data*, the more critical the conception of ideology, which connotes a departure from empirical truth into the realm of theoretical abstraction and distortion. However, in the last twenty years or so, philosophers and social scientists in the West have conceded that the social and even the natural sciences are 'theory-laden' and not purely empirical and objective:[6] in a parallel development, political theorists have acknowledged the evaluative and ideological dimensions of all political thinking[7] and have tried to come to terms with it, not by searching for the 'pure truths' from which ideology deviates, but by analysing the functions and limits of ideology. A number of rival theories have emerged:

(a) Some theorists retain a Marxian view of ideology as an instrument of class rule which vindicates, persuades, and deceives, but use this to criticize communist regimes.

(b) Ideology is seen as a remedy for 'stress': it compensates for the psychological inadequacies experienced by individuals because of social maladjustment, alienation, and personal problems. Thus it is seen as a necessary evil. This *functionalist* account, which explains adherence to ideology because of its uses, does not distinguish between ideologies: all ideologies are distortions, and any ideological commitment is a sign of malfunctioning which, presumably, could be eradicated in a healthy society.[8]

(c) Ideology is explained by its general social functions. It provides solidarity for communities and a basis for authority in newly emergent nations; it can also provide a role for young people in search of identity. Whereas traditional societies bound their members together in other ways, ideology is an important factor in social cohesion in modern, atomistic, fissiparous society.[9]

(d) Ideology, like myth, may perform symbolic functions, reconciling the irreconcilable. (This reflects Marx's view that ideology conceals contradictions, but does not admit that capitalism suffers such contradictions.) Marcuse describes the role of Marxism in the USSR as a ritualized language with a magical quality which obliterates the split between reality and illusion.[10] Geertz argues that ideology can symbolically formulate scientifically unformulable realities and render incomprehensible social situations meaningful. (We should note that *meaningfulness* may have little to do with *truth*.[11])

Many contemporary thinkers therefore concede that ideology need not be immediately dismissed as distortion and deception, but can be explained within a functionalist model of society. This approach wrongly assumes that ideologies are clearly recognizable, self-contained doctrines, espoused by those with special needs and eschewed by the well-adjusted mass of adults in the

West: in other words, these definitions are so contrived as to exclude liberal democracy from the category of ideology and to present other ideologies as temporary, functionally useful addictions which would vanish from mature, Western-style societies.

The exclusion of liberal democracy from the category deserves closer scrutiny. The academic onslaught on ideology emanated from the USA in the 1950s. Ideology was viewed as a root cause of the Nazi and Stalinist phenomena and a contributory cause of the Second World War. MacCarthy's anti-communist purges had removed most left-wing figures from public positions in the States, and the postwar lull made a consensual, bipartisan approach to politics possible in the USA. Intellectually, the dissemination of logical positivist philosophy (which had started in the 1920s in Europe) with its ruling that moral statements and value-judgements were unverifiable, led to a rejection of normative social science in favour of positivist, empirical studies. It was felt that the dangerous 'rule of ideas' was coming to an end, and intellectuals would henceforth participate in government and administration on the basis of their neutral, scientific skills. In the mid-fifties, the doctrine of 'the end of ideology' was put forward by Bell and others[12] and became a symbol of the intellectual climate of the time, which rejected ideological commitment and dispute. Ideology had been, in short, superseded by consensus politically, and by the scientific method academically. As a result, the study of politics was transformed: political theorists adopted methods of 'linguistic analysis' then popular among philosophers, and argued that the subject should not promote values or ideologies but should analyse the *uses*, and hence the meanings, of political terms, neutrally. Sociologists and political scientists meanwhile adopted functionalist and consensus models of analysis, applying both in ways which validated the American political and social system.

The result was that values went underground: covertly, 'objective' analyses upheld the liberal way of thinking. The political scientist Sartori, for example, published an influential study of various democratic states which showed the high incidence of conflict in states with a multiplicity of parties with strong ideological commitments.[13] He concluded that ideological politics was inimical to democracy and that a two-party system was best. Many other political scientists came to similarly neutral conclusions. The value-free 'post-ideological' approach led political theory into an impasse, since analysing and promoting values had been its traditional function. For a time the discipline was almost in abeyance, with political science being sucked in to fill the vacuum. But the Civil Rights, Black Power, Women's Liberation, Student Power, and Anti-Vietnam movements of the 1960s and 1970s in the States showed that ideology and conflict could not be excluded from politics for ever. Left-wing thinkers such as Marcuse and Wolff[14] sought to expose the covert ideological premises of liberal-democratic thought and institutions and others demonstrated that even the most empirical studies were in fact guided by theoretical presuppositions which could not themselves be empirically established, but were *assumed*; such covert values pervaded political science in particular, with its supposedly neutral, 'quantitative' definitions of concepts like consensus, political system, and elite. As the 'end of ideology' vogue itself ended in response to political circumstance, and the 'theoretical' (as opposed to empirical) and ideological nature of social and political studies was acknowledged, there was a resurgence of controversy and commitment in political theory and the subject was restored to health.

Conceptual Problems

The readiness with which non-Marxist thinkers borrowed the concept of ideology and adapted it as a critique of radical theories suggests that such a concept is indeed necessary to political analysis, whether Marxist or not. But the precise scope and meaning of the term is often unclear and non-Marxists do not employ it in the same sense as Marxists. The relativist approach casts doubt on all knowledge, including the status of any theory of ideology and of the discipline which Mannheim inaugurated, the 'sociology of knowledge'. Marx's basic contention that consciousness, and hence knowledge, is historically produced, determined by material conditions, suggests that, while all knowledge is relative in this respect, it need not be ideological: a class may obtain accurate knowledge which appropriately reflects its circumstances and is a guide to political action and truth. On this account, Marxism itself would not count as an ideology, but as true knowledge. But on the other hand, according to Mannheim, objective truth is only to be found in mathematics and perhaps in the natural sciences. Otherwise, all our ideas are to some extent incongruent with reality, and either tend to uphold the existing system (as ideologies do) or to destroy or 'transcend it' (as utopias do). No political ideas merely reflect reality objectively. A different view is held by Western thinkers working within the empiricist tradition who, while conceding the functional uses of ideology, criticize its distortion of 'objective' fact and its secretion of values, which cause people to deviate from the direct, empirical path to knowledge.

In each of these three critiques of ideology, there is an implicit standard of truth against which it is measured: for Marx, true ideas are those which acknowledge contradictions and accurately reflect the class position of the knower. Mannheim refers to 'reality' as some kind of standard; ideas congruent with it would be true, neither utopian nor ideological. For the empiricist, knowledge based on the accumulation of data and induction of general principles without the intrusion of values is true and objective. Marx and Mannheim would acknowledge that truth is relative to time and place, while the empiricist approach seems to imply the possibility of permanent truth.

This book is based on the conviction that in thinking about politics (and studying social science) it is impossible to think non-ideologically or in a 'value-free' way. The relation between ideology and values needs some explication here. Since Weber's influential pronouncements on the social science method,[15] practitioners have felt duty-bound to strive for value-free social science, although Weber himself thought that since this was almost unattainable, social scientists should, rather, seek to make their values explicit and justify them. The suspicion of value judgements engendered by logical positivist philosophy, on account of their unverifiability, gave social science a new impetus towards neutrality. However, while admitting their own susceptibility to value judgements, Western social scientists had to deny that such judgements were ideological, having defined ideology pejoratively. The implication was that values were plucked out of a vacuum and could, as easily, be banished from social science. But clearly all values emanate from some ideological outlook, which need not be narrowly political but offers an interpretation of social life and action and a standard for judging good and bad. Values are symptoms of ideology, including those value judgements about epistemology and scientific method. Thus, the empirical method in scientific studies is connected both historically and doctrinally with liberal ideology, while what empiricists think of as the ill-founded 'theoretical' (theory-informed) approach to social science has affinities with Marxism.

Someone who denies political commitment in arguing the virtues of empirical social science is nevertheless maintaining a value found in the liberal world-view, and empirical studies tend to support the existing form of society because they have no critical dimension. Likewise someone who claims not to have an ideology but strongly advocates the freedom of the individual is voicing a part of liberal ideology, even if unwittingly. People may adopt the values embedded in an ideology without knowing or understanding it as a comprehensive doctrine, especially in societies where the existence of ideologies is not officially acknowledged and isolated beliefs appear in everyday political argument without the supporting justifications which an ideology provides—a procedure which does not facilitate the understanding of politics. While someone who only holds some isolated beliefs cannot be said to be an adherent of an ideology, such beliefs *are* ideologically determined, and we can only escape from one ideology into another. This is another reason why liberals deny that their own beliefs are ideological and deplore the espousal of ideology by others: it damages their conception of the individual as a free and rational being, who chooses objectively between political doctrines on the basis of their manifest truth and rightness.

A major purpose of this book is to show, by exposing the logic and preconceptions of each political ideology, which particular ideas and values, which may appear in isolation in the context of political argument, derive from which particular ideology, so that in political debate the critical listener will see the further implications of each apparently autonomous, non-doctrinaire idea. Since we cannot expel ideological elements from political thought and practice, and since the results would prove disastrous if we tried—all sorts of clandestinely ideological concepts like 'efficiency' and 'consensus' might be sucked in to fill the vacuum—what we should do is acknowledge and try to understand rival ideologies and their component values and then choose between them. In reply to the objection that adherence to any ideal or ideology must be arbitrary, given their unverifiable nature, it can be argued that, different though facts are from values, the latter can assist us to make rational choices between doctrines. For example, the incontrovertible fact that a large part of the world's population suffers poverty and malnourishment might cause me to espouse some form of internationalist socialism, which advocated world-wide redistribution on the basis of material need, rather than an ideology which commended distributions based on merit or legal entitlement. However, facts are not themselves neutral, but are usually selected—or constructed—on the basis of pre-existing, ideological, values. So facts can only give qualified guidance in choosing or justifying political positions, and are not themselves absolute truths. The relation between facts, values, and ideology is complex and much debated. That they are all interconnected is clear: it is less clear whether one causes the others, or vice versa, or whether there may not be a constant process of mutual adaptation going on between them.[16] The arguments which follow assume that ideology conditions values and our selection and presentation of facts—although the 'brute facts' of the world around us may well, in turn, condition our selection of an ideology.

Since this book treats as ideologies some doctrines which would deny having ideological status, some account of the conception of ideology on which the analysis is based is called for. I would argue that an ideology is a doctrine about the right way, or ideal way, of organizing society and conducting politics, based on wider considerations about the nature of human life and knowledge. The 'action-guiding' aspect of such doctrines derives from the fact that they claim to establish what is politically true and right, and so give rise to imperatives which are essentially moral. They inevitably include the recommendation that their ideals should be realized, or should continue to be realized. I do not argue that ideologies are bad, or that politics should be conducted on the basis of 'fact' or 'truth', because such facts and truths, uncontaminated by values, do not exist in most areas of human thought and discourse. It is a necessary consequence of the relativity of knowledge and different political doctrines will conceptualize society differently according to when, where and from what group they emanate. Certainly, ideologies are, in Mannheim's phrase, 'incongruent with reality', but although we are unlikely ever to perceive the nature of reality in a neutral, objective way (this is ruled out by the relativity of his perceptions and analysis to the situation and personality of the knower), we may at least be able to gauge that some doctrines are less incongruent than others, and thus to criticize and choose between ideologies, with the help of facts. The real deception is not ideology, but the idea that there could be a single explanation or one set of truths about something as complex and heterogeneous as society.

The inclusive approach to ideology taken here does not imply that we should abandon the quest for political ideals, or adopt ideologies arbitrarily, unthinkingly. Quite the contrary. The more aware someone is of the ideological nature of his own thought, and the more explicit about his values, the better will he be able to identify and criticize those of others and to promote his own. Most important of all, understanding the pervasive nature of ideology helps us to expose and scrutinise the hidden premises and values which are treated as established facts in a particular society.

Ideology determines the use of political concepts and language, and even the form of logic used to prove political points: the liberal equates formal logic with rational argument, while Marxists use dialectical reason, which they consider scientific, and many right-wing thinkers are prone to argue by analogy (which does not formally constitute proof) or to invoke symbols or myths. The forms of reasoning typical of each ideology are discussed in Part II. Part III is an analysis of political ideas and ideals in the light of the discussion of the main ideologies. There is no pretence at 'objective' conceptual analysis leading to definitive, neutral definitions such as linguistic philosophers recommended to political philosophers in the recent past. But the intention has been to set out as objectively as possible different ideological conceptions of ideas such as liberty, obligation, and the state and to assess them critically — such assessment still being, inevitably, an ideological process.

This approach bears out the argument of those who have argued that the major political ideas are 'essentially contested concepts', meaning that no single, final definition of such terms can be established which will not itself be contested sooner (most probably!) or later.[17] This view is sometimes used to justify intellectual quietism: 'all knowledge is relative, all ideas are ideological, all concepts are contested' may lead to the conclusion that political beliefs should never be challenged — de gustibus non disputandum. Some disciples of logical positivism even recommended an end to political argument about values, since nobody could ever convince anyone else of the rightness of his own values, these being unverifiable. Weldon, a champion of this view, asserted that all rival political arguments should be reduced to statements of fact which could then be compared and found to correspond with reality, or not, resolving the dispute. He suggested a similar factual 'unpacking' process for finding the meaning of political concepts. As has been suggested above, the assumption that such facts are neutral cannot be accepted. The facts do not speak for themselves, we speak for them. Anyone embarking on political theory — or practice — must remember that facts are largely 'constructed' on the basis of ideological commitment, and that argument must therefore take place principally at this level.

We live in an age of relativism which creates painful uncertainties. Studies of the philosophy and method of the social sciences have made us aware of the limitations of our knowledge. 'Pure knowledge' — that elusive ideal — is so vitiated by its relation to place and time, by the subjectivity of the thinker and by his culture, let alone his ideological commitments, that we must wonder whether such an ideal standard is not illusory. All four factors circumscribe and direct the form and content of our social and political knowledge and beliefs. We can make allowances for time, place subjectivity, and culture-specificity when evaluating arguments and theories, in an attempt to come nearer to objective knowledge even though we cannot attain it. The best we can hope for is not objectivity, but the most comprehensive understanding possible of a social phenomenon, which encompasses it in all its heterogeneity. This book, then, is intended to show what sort of allowances must be made for ideological bias in the study of politics, and how we might proceed to a more comprehensive understanding of political life.

Notes

1. K. Marx and F. Engels, *The German ideology*, in *Selected Works*, Vol.1 Progress Publishers, 1969, p.32.
2. K. Marx, *The Grundrisse* (trans. D. McLellan), Harper & Row, New York, 1972, p.72ff.
3. K. Mannheim, *Ideology and Utopia* (trans. E. Shils), Routledge & Kegan Paul, London, 1936, pp.49–53.
4. H. Arendt, *The Origins of Totalitarianism*. revised edn, Allen & Unwin, London, 1967, p.468 and Ch.13 generally.
5. R. D. Putnam, *The Beliefs of Politicians*, Yale University Press, Yale, 1973.
6. See, for example, T. Kuhn, *The Structure of Scientific Revolutions*, 2nd edn, Chicago University Press, Chicago 1970, and P. Feyerabend, 'How to be a good empiricist' in *The Philosophy of Science*, Oxford University Press, Oxford, 1968. (Ed. P. Nidditch)
7. See P. H. Partridge, 'Politics, philosophy and ideology', in *Political Philosophy*, (Ed. A. Quinton), Oxford University Press, Oxford, 1967 and C. Taylor, 'Neutrality in political science' in *The Philosophy of Social Explanation* (Ed. A. Ryan), Oxford University Press, Oxford, 1973.
8. C. Geertz, 'Ideology as a cultural system', in *Ideology and Discontent* (Ed. D. Apter), Free Press, 1964, pp.47–76.
9. D. Apter, 'Ideology and discontent', in *Ideology and Discontent,* (Ed. D. Apter), Free Press, 1964, pp.18–30.
10. H. Marcuse, *Soviet Marxism*, Columbia University Press, Columbia, 1958, pp.88, 159.
11. C. Geertz, 'Ideology as a cultural system', p.58ff.
12. D. Bell, *The End of Ideology*, Free Press, 1960.
13. G. Sartori, 'European political parties: the case of polarised pluralism', in *Political Parties and Political Development*, (Eds J. Lapalombara and M. Wiener), Princeton University Press, 1966, pp.137–176.
14. See especially R. P. Wolff, H. Marcuse and B. Moore, *A Critique of Pure Tolerance*, Beacon Press, 1965 and R. P. Wolff, *The Poverty of Liberalism*, Beacon Press, 1969.
15. M. Weber, *The Methodology of the Social Sciences*, Macmillan, Basingstoke, 1950.
16. A. Montefiore, 'Fact, value and ideology' in *British Analytical Philosophy* (Eds B. Williams and A. Montefiore), Routledge & Kegan Paul, London, 1966.
17. W. B. Gallie, 'Essentially contested concepts', in *Pro. Aristotelian Soc.*, **56**, 167–98. (1955–'6).

Further Reading

J. P. Plamenatz, *Ideology,* Macmillan, Basingstoke, 1970.
M. Seliger, *The Marxist Conception of Ideology*, Cambridge University Press, Cambridge, 1977
H. Drucker, *The Political Uses of Ideology,* Macmillan, Basingstoke, 1974.

Part II

IDEOLOGIES

CHAPTER 3

Liberalism

The description of what Marxists call the 'dominant ideology' is a difficult task. In Britain we imbibe liberal ideas effortlessly from an early age, with the result that liberalism appears as a necessary truth, the basis of reality, rather than as one political ideology among many. One feature of liberal thought which seems to support this view is that it has no ideological bible available for exegesis, revision, and faith. The growth of liberal doctrine is more akin to the growth of the shell of an ancient tortoise, and the slow development and accumulation of its principles promotes the view that there is something natural about liberalism.

The development of liberal thought in England began in the seventeenth century. For many centuries before the Renaissance, political institutions had been subordinated to, or amalgamated with, the religious establishment; kings claimed to rule by divine sanction so that, for their subjects, obedience was a religious duty. The Reformation reversed the balance of power, subjecting the Church to the monarch, but in the seventeenth century divine right was still often cited as the basis of monarchy. The need for a novel, secular theory of monarchy was manifest during the English Civil War and Commonwealth, and Hobbes justified authority on the grounds of a social contract in *Leviathan* (1651), but nevertheless advocated undivided, unlimited sovereignty. But at the time of the Glorious Revolution of 1688 and the establishment of William and Mary on the throne with a parliamentary constitution, Locke encapsulated the current anti-authoritarian, secular idea of politics in his justification of constitutional monarchy, which is often perceived as the beginning of liberal theory. His approach also reflected the effects of a period of rapid social change: as traditional, hierarchical social forms disappeared, so did the strict subordination of some men to others, creating a need for a theory of social order in which all men owed allegiance to a central authority on an equal footing. The hypothesis of the social contract provided such a theory.

A systematic, but controversial, account of the origins of liberal thought has been given by Macpherson, who correlates the theories of Hobbes and Locke with the growth of the commercial middle classes, and with innovatory patterns of wealth accumulation and consumption accompanied by a new, individualistic morality.[1] He sees such writers as the chroniclers and champions of the development of bourgeois society. One problem of Macpherson's reading is that England in the seventeenth century was by no stretch of the imagination a 'bourgeois' society in any accepted sense of the word —as his critics have not failed to point out. Yet his account of liberalism as 'possessive individualism' is a catalyst to understanding the ideology: it reminds us that both Hobbes and Locke start by describing *individuals* in the state of nature, and that both consider the individual and his needs the basic explanatory unit of a systematic analysis of political society. Although individualism as we now understand it is merely embryonic in such theories, the basis for the egoistic economics and utilitarian morality of later liberalism is already present. Whatever dispute there may be about the details of Macpherson's interpretation, he is undoubtedly right in emphasizing the intimate connection of liberalism with capitalism. The similarity of the premises and the structure of liberal political theory and 'classical' economics shows how close-knit are the various strands of the ideology.

The mark of the liberal is a concern with the limits of authority, and opposition to state interference with individual activities. The corollary of this is an emphasis on the importance of the individual and the promotion of human rights and liberties which serve to delimit the area within which the state is entitled to act. Liberal thought evolved at a time when the favoured scientific method was to decompose objects and substances into their smallest parts and to examine how these combined to form the whole, a method which Hobbes claimed to adopt in *Leviathan*. He and other more liberal theorists take the individual as the basic unit of society and view the latter as no more than an aggregate of individuals—an approach which leaves various 'holistic' social phenomena unexplained. There is, of course, perpetual controversy among theorists as to how we should conceptualize society. Just as a jar of pickle could be viewed as a compilation of the listed ingredients, or else as a distinct and different substance, society can be viewed as a combination of individual parts or as a qualitatively different whole. The liberal preference for the former conception, although somewhat modified by thinkers like J. S. Mill and Hobhouse, has important consequences for the liberal view of political and social being.

The Ingredients of Liberalism

Liberalism is better understood through an examination of the elements which go to make up the liberal model of society than through a historical survey of liberal authors, so many and varied were these. This section therefore sets out the main elements of the ideology, proceeding from the basic unit, the individual, to the resulting conception of society and the political ideals which follow from this.

The individual

The preservation of the individual and the attainment of individual happiness are the supreme goals of a liberal political system, at least in theory. The individual person is to be regarded as inviolable, and all human life as sacrosanct; violence is therefore prohibited except in a war to preserve liberal society itself. This individualism is based on a morality which commands equal respect for all persons as moral beings with equal sensitivity. Individualism can take many forms[2], and can rest on a more or a less elevated view of human beings, but its general consequence is to diminish the importance of the social whole, which is viewed as no more than the sum of its parts, and so cannot have a 'public interest' of its own, or any rights against the individual. This outlook can be called *atomistic*. It hindered orthodox liberals from giving a satisfactory account of the ways in which the individual atoms interact, or of the meta-individual structures such as groups and institutions which develop in reality. But then, liberal theory had historically to distinguish its conception of society from the view of society as a hierarchical, incestuously coherent whole which it had displaced: individualism was instrumental in this. From the moral idealization of the individual stems the political necessity of liberty and also various prevalent cultural values which embody the notions of individuality, originality, and self-distinction.

The form which individualistic political theory takes depends on how human nature is conceived. Liberalism assumes the individual to be essentially rational — a necessary premise if the individual is to be the prime source of value, for it would be hard to value highly an irrational creature, who would be no more than a beast. The assumption of rationality also determines the form of political organization chosen, justifying participatory, rather than authoritarian, government. The individual is also attributed with knowledge of his own best interests and the ability to pursue them rationally. Rational economic man, according to classical economists, maximizes profits; political man maximizes his utilities through judicious participation and choice. Liberal thinkers achieved what seemed impossible in the Christian middle ages: they made a virtue of selfishness. From Hobbes and Locke onwards, the pursuit of *self-interest* was accepted as man's proper motivation. Locke said that the 'laws of nature' gave man the right 'to preserve his property — that is, his life, liberty and estate'[3], and that the task of government was to help him in so doing. Bentham's utilitarianism elevated 'enlightened' self-interest to the status of morality and became widely accepted despite protests against this vindication of selfishness such as Dickens' satirization of the self-made man in the objectionable and lying Bounderby in *Hard Times*. Hence Macpherson's recent characterization of the individual of classical liberal theory as possessive and infinitely acquisitive. So much for the materialistic side of human nature.

Man's spiritual side was acknowledged in the assumption that he is a free, rational, self-improving being. Locke considered man's natural state to be that of freedom; the duty of government was to provide the conditions for him to enjoy the maximum possible freedom within a framework of law. The conception of man as a free being led liberals to condemn any social arrangements which put him in a state of dependence, such as slavery or indentured labour. Locke disapproved of the practice of servants of binding themselves to their masters, and thought that they should not have voting rights because they had foregone their freedom. Since man is a free being who knows his own interests best, authoritarian or paternalistic government is against human nature. The problems which liberals encounter in reconciling this premise with the welfare state are discussed later. As for man's capacity for self-improvement, this was largely ignored in early liberal theory. Bentham maintained that 'lower' and 'higher' pleasures were qualitatively the same in any utility calculation: it would be paternalistic of any government to try to elevate people's tastes. Although later liberals did not go as far as the utopians of the Enlightenment and after, who considered man to be *perfectible*, J. S. Mill emphasized 'man's interests as a progressive being' and recommended intellectual pursuits and self-improvement through education and political activity. This — although Mill hesitated to acknowledge it — implied an extension of government activity to make the opportunities for self-development available.

Finally, what of man as a social creature? Hobbes's state of nature, with men engaged in a constant struggle for power and scarce resources, suggested innate anti-social tendencies which only an authoritarian sovereign could hold in check. But liberal theorists (of whom Hobbes was a forerunner in some other respects) rejected this conclusion, but did not, however, assume natural sociability. The assumption is rather that men are 'mutually indifferent' because of their free, independent nature. The pursuit of self-interest can lead to co-operation or to competitive and aggressive behaviour. Strictly speaking, competition only arises when a shortage of resources prevents everyone's being satisfied; likewise, co-operation occurs when it is in men's interests. Locke envisaged the social contract being made co-operatively when it was seen to be for everyone's benefit. It is not true that liberal theory assumes that man is *naturally* competitive, although many adherents of liberalism take that as a necessary truth, and liberal contract theorists such as Locke, and Rawls today, emphasize the voluntary and consensual basis of society. Nevertheless, the counterpart of the strong conception of the individual is a weak conception of the nature and purpose of society and of government, which is seen as a device for performing the residual tasks which individual self-interest leaves undone. This means that liberal theorists are unwilling to invoke concepts such as the common good or the public interest, which are predicated of society as a whole, and would circumscribe their use in justifying state intervention. The only common good which liberals would recognize is the maximization of the aggregate of individual benefits.

Contract and consent

A central political axiom deriving from the idealization of individual freedom and rationality is that government should be based on the consent of the people, which legitimizes it. This forms the basis of the affinity between liberalism and democracy although they are in some respects incompatible. The idea of consent first appeared in the guise of contract theory. Locke imagined a peaceful, sociable state of nature with many of the characteristics of established society; men would own property in such a state. The problem would be that in the case of a dispute no impartial judge existed to arbitrate. The inconvenience of this would cause men voluntarily to contract to form a society 'for their comfortable, safe and peaceable living . . . in secure enjoyment of their properties.' Thus, a community would be formed and a government would be constituted by majority decision. Each individual gives up his natural rights of self-protection and the right to punish transgressors, and the government takes on the duty of protecting its subjects' rights.[4] A consequence of Locke's social contract (though not of Hobbes's) is that governments hold power on trust and in extreme cases the people may resist or overthrow a government which betrays this trust. Locke elaborated the government actions which would be a breach of trust: it may not destroy, enslave or impoverish its subjects, nor rule by arbitrary decress, nor take a man's property without his consent, nor transfer its own powers to others. The third prohibition, popularized in the slogan 'no taxation without representation', was a powerful weapon in the arsenal of the American revolutionaries demanding independence from England and was also proclaimed by taxpaying suffragettes.

Locke's contract was hypothetical device, not a guess at man's pre-history, and was meant to explain the origin of government. Later generations consented 'tacitly' to government, Locke considered, when they inherited property under its laws or enjoyed their protection. Most eighteenth-century liberals rejected the social contract because of its mythical nature, and emphasized the role of consent in legitimizing government, but a modern theorist, Rawls, has used the idea of a hypothetical contract as the basis of his theory of justice and the good (liberal) society. The contract has always played a central role in liberal thinking about politics because it is the paradigm way in which free, rational, knowledgeable individuals would deal with each other. Critics of liberalism point out that many of the real or hypothetical contracts referred to in liberal theory are not made under the paradigmly fair conditions which make contracts just and binding.

As the franchise in Britain was extended and finally made universal, it became increasingly realistic to pin 'the consent of the governed' on the act of voting. This is still the major liberal justification of political obligation and gives rise to the claim that the elected government has a mandate to act—ideas which will be discussed further in Chapters 9 and 10. The usual assumption is that government based on consent must be democratic, so that consent is renewed or refused at regular intervals, but it would not be illogical for a liberal to consent permanently to a different form of government which he trusted to oversee his interests.[5] Liberalism does not entail democracy, but democracy is probably the best guarantee for liberalism.

Constitutionalism and the law

Although democracy is not essential to liberalism, some form of constitution which limits the powers of government is. Locke rejected Hobbes's view that sovereignty must be undivided as potentially tyrannical, and sketched an ideal division and balance of powers to counteract usurpation and tyranny, emphasizing that the legislative power, the power of lawmaking, was supreme, and that this belonged to the people or their representatives.[6] He foreshadowed the limitations placed on the constitutional monarchy established after the 1688 revolution: a century later, his ideas were again made concrete in the checks and balances of the US constitution. When Locke wrote the English parliament was highly unrepresentative, being elected on a narrow property franchise, of which he approved. His contribution to the liberal theory of government was not the idea of representative democracy, but his theory of the separation of powers, which had the same ultimate aim of safeguarding people's rights from tyrannical encroachment. The English constitution which resulted from the 1688 revolution became an object of admiration for the French philosopher Montesquieu, whose *Spirit of the Laws* reasserted the need for legality and constitutionalism and in turn influenced the American revolutionaries.

The constitution and the law play parallel roles in liberal theory: the constitution, a form of higher law, prevents the government from transgressing against individuals while the law prevents individuals from transgressing against each other. From Locke onwards, liberals emphasized the role of law in ensuring individual liberty. He had argued that liberty without law was mere licence, and that

freedom of men under government is to have a standing rule to live by, common to every one of that society and made by the legislative power erected in it.[7]

Law is the paradigm method of solving conflicts: 'force is to be opposed to nothing but to unjust and unlawful force'. Yet, although liberalism is highly legalistic, the closely associated ideas of individual liberty and laissez-faire in economics dictated that only a small nucleus of regulatory laws should be enacted and that interventionist or paternalistic government should be avoided. Nowadays this proviso has to be regarded as precept rather than reality. The idea of 'due process' underlies liberal considerations on government. If proper procedures for making and executing laws can be devised and enforced constitutionally, the risk of arbitrary or tyrannical rule is minimized. The establishment of *procedures* which will best advance the goals of individual freedom and happiness is thus the first aim of a liberal system.

Freedom as choice

Freedom is the primary value in the liberal creed, being the means whereby the rational individual pursues his own interests. Viewed thus, freedom is an instrumental value which helps men get what they want. But liberals have always associated freedom closely with the 'human essence', so that political, economic and social freedom is seen as a human necessity, and a good in itself, rather than merely as a means to an end. The liberal conception of freedom has been widely identified with material choice and the right to spend one's money (if any) as one wishes. In recent years, this has been advanced as the justification for lowering direct taxation and for maintaining public schools and private beds in hospitals. Such a view of freedom is closely connected with the doctrine of laissez-faire which advocated minimum regulation and maximum freedom of action for the entrepreneur. The conception of freedom as choice makes implicit reference to the economic model: socio-political man, the consumer and voter, is viewed as a maximizer in the social 'market place'.

The more ennobling aspects of freedom were emphasized by Mill in the nineteenth century; according to Macpherson, the shortcomings of liberalism based on classical economics were then becoming clear and Mill and others introduced humanitarian elements into the ideology, dwelling on men's *capacities* and *powers*, rather than on their utility-maximizing, consumption role.[8] Mill advocated freedom of speech, thought, and religion as the right of every rational adult, to be curtailed only where their exercise threatens direct material harm to others. Realization of the freedoms of speech and choice in the political sphere requires that citizens should be able to choose between a variety of doctrines: one-party elections are a deprivation of freedom. A pluralist democracy is thus the political outcome of the liberal ideal of freedom. British governments of all persuasions have, in general, zealously upheld the Millean notion of the freedom of the individual against the state and against the tyranny of public opinion, but the contemporary threats to individual freedom come not so much from visible locuses of power such as parliament as from diffuse, irresponsible power structures such as the bureaucracy and the 'military–industrial complex'. These threaten individual freedom by the propagation of their own institutional values (efficiency, security and so on) and momentum (e.g. the arms race), which override any possibility of individual intervention and control: such threats are harder to codify and cope with, theoretically and practically, than the deliberate malice or power-seeking which may threaten freedom overtly in the political sphere. Liberal theory needs updating to comprehend these kinds of dangers. Chapter 11 discusses these problems in greater detail.

Equality of opportunity

Liberalism evolved in conjunction with capitalism, an economic system which operates on the basis of great inequalities of wealth and income. Substantive equality has been conspicuously absent from liberal society, particularly in the nineteenth century. Liberal theorists had to reconcile these 'natural' inequalities of capitalism with their egalitarian view of human beings in the abstract. They therefore attributed various abstract, formal equalities to the citizen and the private individual, such as equal rationality, equal self-interest, equal voting rights, and equal rights before the law. By doing this, liberal theory *formally* equalizes individuals although real individuals have differential levels of wealth, competence, and intelligence. These abstract equalities support the fiction that everybody starts the race of life equal, and this takes the sting out of competition, which liberals assume to be a perennial feature of human life. Competition would, of course, be an invidious basis for social organization if it were admitted that the odds were heavily fixed against some individuals from the start. Therefore, liberals wish to prove that competition takes place in a context of *equality of opportunity* which guarantees a fair outcome, with the most meritorious individuals gaining the rewards. The equality of opportunity which liberals advocate is the contrary of substantive equality, for it denotes the opportunity to differentiate oneself from others by becoming unequal, and better. Even if the education system and other 'equalizing' social services worked perfectly, the natural inequalities of talent and energy would make equality of opportunity a myth. But this myth is important to liberal ideology, which can claim that, unlike conservatism, it is not an inegalitarian doctrine but one based on fundamental human equalities, out of which emerges differentiation based on the just reward of merit.

Social justice based on merit

Gallie characterizes the liberal theory of social justice as *commutative*, based, like capitalism, on exchange.[9] Individuals are said to gain rewards in proportion to their talents and merits and their contribution to society: contribution is assumed to be an approximate measure of talent. The argument asserts that the system is organized so as to reward the most deserving, therefore those who gain most have deserved most. This theory of justice appears as an afterthought attached to liberalism, rather than an analytical theory. It offers justification after the event, allowing the liberal to argue that the rich are rich because they have merited it, and thus preventing him from questioning their deserts or their entitlement to their wealth. Classical economic theory was instrumental in the creation of this notion of social justice, which is reminiscent of the 'just price' for a commodity which results from the interplay of market forces, but in no way necessarily reflects the intrinsic worth of the commodity. But even Hayek, champion of the market system, concedes that the rewards which it delivers do not bear any close relation to subjective merit.[10] Howevei, liberal ideology vindicates the system by arguing that, given equality of opportunity, free enterprise and competition produce a just distribution of income and other goods. This is sometimes referred to as a 'meritocratic' system, but the term 'meritocracy' refers specifically to the distribution of political power to the most talented, a doctrine consonant with the liberal outlook, but one which has been put in the shadow by the general commitment of liberals to democracy. Without the constraint of equality of opportunity (often absent in real life), the liberal theory of social justice would resemble the most puzzling biblical parable, that of the talents.

For unto every one that hath shall be given, and he shall have abundance: but from him that hath not shall be taken away even that which he hath.[11]

Liberals see social justice in terms of specifiable, just procedures, rather than in terms of predictable outcomes. The recent major contribution to liberal thinking on justice, that of Rawls, is discussed in Chapter 12, and his theory too is deliberately 'procedural': it specifies the rules which should govern a just society, but not the social outcomes which should be aimed at. This procedural emphasis is a result of the liberal conviction that each man knows his own interests best: a system of justice must therefore not dictate a specific distribution of goods, but should establish rules by which men can *fairly* pursue their desires. Although all ideologies claim to promulgate justice, in liberalism justice is seen as the result of the pursuit of other ideals rather than as a separately definable principle, and indeed in early utilitarianism justice is explicitly subordinated to considerations of utility, and is only valued for its contribution to utility.

Tolerance

Tolerance originated as an instrumental or secondary ideal, related to freedom, which facilitates the pursuit of individual interest. However, today it is often given the status of a good in itself. Liberal society prides itself on its tolerance and passes unfavourable judgements on societies which suppress dissidence and nonconformist views. The classic argument for religious tolerance was put forward in Locke's *Letter Concerning Toleration* (1689), at the end of a century fraught with religious struggles in England. Locke argued that the government's task is the preservation of peace, while morality is the business of priests, thus delimiting the role of government rather more strictly than is sometimes done today. Civil rights belong to men *qua* human beings and cannot be removed on the grounds of religious nonconformity. Despite Locke, various prohibitions were in force against Catholics and dissenters until the nineteenth century, but his *Letter* initiated the idea that society should should accept a variety of religions, morals and political opinions, and that human and civil rights belong to all by virtue of their humanity.

Another argument for tolerance was advanced by Mill: 'we can never be sure that the opinion we are endeavouring to stifle is a false opinion.'[12] His argument can be summarized as follows: (1) intolerance is an assumption of infallibility by the intolerant; (2) all views contain, or may contain, some grain of truth and only 'the collision of adverse opinions' can lead us to truth; (3) received opinion, even if true, will become mere irrational prejudice or habit if uncontested; and (4) an unchallenged doctrine will gradually lose its power to affect men's conduct.[13] For Mill, tolerance directs us towards the truth. The empiricist epistemology to which he subscribed dictates that we can never know a truth *finally*, and so can never categorically define what is morally or politically right or what is in the interests of an individual: this determines the open-endedness of the liberal approach to political theory and practice. From the ideal of tolerance derives the conviction that a pluralist society which accommodates a multiplicity of beliefs is necessary to the search for human good.

Private and public life

As a result of other liberal ideals, the value and importance of private (economic and social) life is enhanced at the expense of public or political life. The distinction can be traced back to Locke, who separated the formation of *society* from the appointment of *government*. His theory of resistance suggests that he thought that society could still function in the absence of government. This conception departed from Hobbes's view that government and society are co-extensive: if one is overthown, the other disintegrates, since only government can create the order which makes society possible. Locke's view has the clear implication that government should not pervade every area of social life, which is a separate sphere. Mill's conception of individual liberty and the restrictions which he places on government action would, if realized, entail a very large sphere of privacy within which the individual could act without interference. A strict distinction is drawn between the private and the public, the former being seen as the locus of interest and satisfaction for individuals, by contrast with the Greek view of politics as the sphere in which 'homo politicus' realizes himself most fully. Laissez-faire economists like Cobden advanced the view that the state's role was merely that of an arbiter between conflicting interests, a regulatory rather than a constructive role. This view permeated liberal theory, as the inactivity of English governments in the early nineteenth century bears witness: Lord Palmerston, when Prime Minister, said 'We cannot go on legislating for ever.' This limited view of government's functions gave rise to a certain distaste for the business of politics, an outlook which is explicitly opposed to anything approaching compulsion in political participation. A major liberal criticism of totalitarian states concerns the obligatory nature of political activity there, and the extension of politics into spheres which liberals consider private.

The consequence of this outlook, in conjunction with representative democratic practice, is the removal of most political power, except the power of withholding acquiescence, from the people. Most liberal democracies have developed elite systems of government in which politicians pursue what they take to be in the people's interest — or act in their own interests — and are only weakly responsible to their constituents. Justifications of elite governments within liberal democracy are discussed in Chapter 9. The remoteness of government from the people has been perceived as a danger in recent years: the Liberal Party in Britain has become a strong advocate of regionalism, devolution, and other devices to extend popular control over politicians and administrators (although this fits badly with its support for Britain's membership of the European Community!). The problem is that, by enlarging our conception of the private sphere and emphasizing the individual's right to opt out of politics, liberalism has opened the path to an imposition of elite institutions against which people would, *in extremis*, find that they had no protection. Hence the recent development, in self-defence, of theories of participation which are, in effect, applications of the basic democratic theory.[14] Such theorists could draw on Mill's arguments in favour of popular political participation and the extension of the franchise. In contrast to the prevalent laissez-faire view of government (which the excesses of the French Revolution had powerfully reinforced), he argued that participation is educational and improving and that the calibre of a people can be gauged by its level of political activity.[15] Such arguments contrast with his views on liberty, which would tend to support the individual's right to withdraw into his private life, and the tension between these two components of liberal democracy remains unresolved.

The Liberal Model: Perpetual Motion?

When the elements of liberal thought summarized above are combined they constitute a coherent, self-consistent model of society. This is, of course, highly abstract, as the essence of model-making is to extract the fundamental characteristics of a situation and to discard the details which locate it in time and space. However, political theorists can use such a model to expose more clearly the bare bones of an ideology and the basic assumptions which conditioned its development. Many liberal theorists write as if the value of the individual, and of liberty, is neither time-bound nor culture-bound, but a universal necessity, and as if the model will operate for ever. Perhaps every dominant ideology necessarily represents itself as immortal. Because of this, the liberal model tends to be ahistorical, lacking any theory of past history or future development, although endorsing a cautiously optimistic view of human progress, which differentiates it from conservative doctrines. Liberal ideology views society as a voluntarily and rationally constituted aggregate of self-interested individuals. The model is set in motion *spontaneously* by their desires and interests; because human nature is thought to be the same at all times and in all places, this guarantees the possibility of perpetual motion, and the fact that the system operates on the basis of natural desires makes it ideal.

Society, then, is no more than the vehicle whereby men pursue their interests and has no independent existence or value over and above that of individuals. Self-interest is regulated by contracts enforced by law, the ideal means by which free and equal men can deal with each other. Society itself is founded on a contract, or on consent, a weaker form of contract; viewed like this, it resembles a private club whose limited rules the members accepted because they benefit by them, and wish to belong to the club. The most important human activities are deemed to take place in the economic and social spheres, which are self-regulating. Politics is the circumscribed area where interests are furthered by political means, mainly because conflicts have to be mediated there, or because individuals will not agree to co-operate to provide some social necessity, because the costs would be too unevenly divided. Politics is a means, not an end, so it is small wonder that the individual's loyalty to the system is contingent upon its furthering his private interests.

The conception of the individual's duty to society is strictly limited and the idea of the 'common good' is, by and large, discounted except by liberals such as T. H. Green who had a moral conception of individuals' duties to each other as members of that shared enterprise, society.[16] Liberals with a more atomistic view of society hold that the concept of the common good is itself philosophically fallacious.[17] The substance and joy of life is to be found in the private, not in the public sphere, and the virtue of the system is that it allows the individual the chance to satisfy himself as he pleases within the limits of law. In this respect, liberalism represents a utopian ideal although, as Mannheim points out, a realized utopia is no longer utopia. Certainly, liberal practice differs greatly from the model. But the purpose of models is to provide political guidance. Although the model purports to be descriptive, to describe schematically how society works, its main function is a normative and justificatory one. It can be invoked to justify or criticise political practice in liberal society, and elsewhere.

The liberal model of society, as was mentioned, has analogies with the free enterprise system idealized by early economists. The free market was seen as a collection of independent individuals producing, buying, and selling in order to maximize their utilities, without government interference. Adam Smith introduced the notion of the Invisible Hand, which guaranteed that this multiplicity of self-interested transactions would lead to the greatest possible national prosperity, spontaneously, without any individual actually intending this.[18] Earlier, Mandeville's *Fable of the Bees* (1705) had shown allegorically how general prosperity is produced via the pursuit of private interests — unity through diversity, 'private vices, public benefits'. The invisible hand idea has re-emerged recently in Nozick's advocacy of a minimal state within which a multiplicity of free associations can operate, each motivated by self-interest.[19] The virtue of such theories is that they do not seek to change men and make them act altruistically or virtuously. Their shortcomings are manifested in real life, where the universal pursuit of self-interest does not lead to universal fulfilment or happiness: government intervention and some concept of the general good is needed to protect those individuals who fail to prosper. While some orthodox liberal thinkers such as Malthus and Spencer thought that they should be left to perish, to enhance the health of society at large, more humanitarian liberals such as Hobhouse accepted the need for government intervention to ensure some level of wellbeing for all.

Both the economic and political theories of liberalism assume, in different ways, the possibility of a harmony of private interests which ensures the good of all, if not the 'common good', but there is no evidence that this harmony will occur or that conflicting interests will produce overall prosperity. Indeed, the assumption of scarcity which underlies the idea of competition strongly suggests that conflict, rather than harmony, will prevail in the liberal system. Yet, as Macpherson observes, liberal democrats still implicitly hope for harmony or equilibrium, since 'equilibrium is a nice tune for whistling in the dark.'[20] In recent political science, the notion of harmony has reappeared in the guise of *consensus*. This is measured in various ways (a 70% agreement is sometimes taken to constitute consensus on some issue) and its existence is seen as a manifestation of the good health of liberal–democratic society. For Marxists, the concepts of harmony and consensus are mere delusions, ideological defences against a highly inegalitarian and conflictual reality. However, some such concept is evidently vital to an ideology which advocates human diversity and self-interest. In classical economics, harmony reigns thanks to the invisible hand; in liberal political thought, it is achieved through the pluralistic democratic process and via tolerance. And in utilitarianism, the idea of 'the greatest happiness of the greatest number' implies that a harmonious aggregation can be achieved, even though little evidence is offered for this.

Utilitarianism has already been cited as the moral theory with the strongest links with liberalism. The theory was given its first definitive formulation by Bentham in the late eighteenth century, although some of its assumptions were implicit in Hume's writings. As a moral system based on a calculus of pain and pleasure, it justifies morally the self-seeking activities of the individual who made his first appearance in Hobbes's state of nature. Its radicalism lay in its secularization of morality and its vindication of 'enlightened' self-interest. Yet as a social and political philosophy, aggregating individual interests to calculate and achieve the greatest happiness of the greatest number, it could logically offer no protection for individuals or minorities if the wellbeing of the majority required their suppression. By contrast, the liberal formula aims to protect the rights of each individual, which constitute a limitation on the government's power to promote the good of the majority. Liberalism, utilitarianism, and classical economics were all part of a homogeneous intellectual world-view which developed at the time of the Enlightenment. The liberal's political man who knows his own interests and follows them is none other than the utilitarian moralist who calculates the utility of his actions; his alter ego is economic man, who maximizes his profits and miraculously benefits society as a whole. All three theories, because of their individualistic basis, suffer problems of aggregation: they cannot cope with the claim that society has political or moral rights, or with the development of cartels and monopolies. The resulting tension between the individual and the social whole requires that these ideas should be modified in practice, while authors such as Mill and Hobhouse undertook the amendment of the theories—however, amendments could not wholly abolish these internal tensions.

Liberal theory is, then, a political doctrine which exalts the individual at the expense of the state and the social whole, and sees freedom as a condition for human happiness. As the dominant ideology in Britain, the USA, and parts of Europe, it has been assailed from both left and right, and the criticisms which Marxists and others have made of it will be considered in later chapters. But liberalism cannot solve all the internal problems which it harbours, and the following sections will highlight some of these. The permanent problem which liberals face is to find an appropriate division of powers between the individual and society: this changes over time, as social conditions alter. Mill's assertion that 'over himself, over his own body and mind, the individual is sovereign',[21] together with his formula that government interference is only warranted to prevent material harm to others, provides us with a yardstick by which to measure liberty. But it does not offer a ready solution to complex problems such as whether emergency laws against terrorism should be enacted which also threaten the rights of innocent members of the population.

The real problem is that political theorists have to assume that the chain of causality in social life *ends* somewhere—like economists, they must add a *ceteris paribus* clause and ignore some remote possible repercussions of political action—but in reality the effects of government and individual action are too unpredictable and extensive to be comprehended by such simple, formulaic principles as that of Mill. An enabling law, like that which gives the right to picket, may turn out, paradoxically, to curtail the freedom of the whole non-striking population. Some liberals seem to think it possible to reclaim rights from the state and bestow them on all individuals equally—but today the most serious disputes arise over the freedoms allotted to special sections of the population which detract from those of other groups: it is not merely a matter of addition and subtraction. Some of these issues are elaborated in Chapter 11. Here, I shall consider the value of the individual, his interests, and his relationship to the welfare state, as they appear in liberal ideology, along with associated problems.

Why Does the Liberal Value the Individual so Highly?

The ideas of the autonomy, the dignity, and the unique value of the individual are recent acquisitions and have given rise to an ethical system and a political ideology widely different from those of the Greeks and of Christian theology. Plato's organic view of society dealt with the individual only in terms of his social function and measured his virtue and value according to his conduct as a citizen: such a view leaves no room for the cult of individuality. Political theology during the middle ages allocated a similarly insignificant place to the individual, accepting the necessity of a hierarchical society, where the individual was defined by his class. But, curiously, the seeds of modern individualism were also present in Christianity: the tenet that all souls are equally precious in the eyes of God provided grounds for a notion of human equality and dignity, although on an abstract plane. Early liberals built on this, contending that men's intrinsic equality must be reflected in the impartial, equal treatment of individuals by the legal system.

The birth of liberal individualism occurred in the period which saw the final disappearance of feudal remnants from England, as the spread of commerce and then of industrialization created new roles and new fortunes. Rapid social mobility gave rise to the idea of an individual who individuated himself by his achievements and his resulting possessions. Early liberals viewed individuals, theoretically, as bundles of interests which, left to themselves, they would satisfy. During the eighteenth-century revolutionary era, the individual was depicted as the bearer of political rights. Meanwhile, liberal economists assumed individuals to be the free, independent vendors of their own talents and labour power, operating in the free market. The idea of the individual's powers or capacities formed the basis of nineteenth-century accounts of democracy, which assumed political rationality on the part of the individual.[22]

These forms of individualism emphasized the characteristics common to all men. While Mill made similar assumptions in his writings on liberty and government, he also praised *individuality*, which rests on the individual's desire to differentiate himself from others, often through competition — a characteristic essential to the innovatory phase of early capitalism. Mill and Humboldt valued individual originality, creativity, and spontaneity which would, they hoped, motivate progress to a better society.[23] In this century, Ortega y Gasset and other critics of 'mass society' have again praised individuality as a defence against the standardization and mediocrity of modern society.[24] But now, when democracy is acknowledged to be something of a sham, requiring no genuine participation from the individual voter, some liberals once again envisage the individual as a bundle of desires — to be satisfied by the welfare state. Such a view is implicit in Easton's systems theory. This passive individual living in a modern land of Cockayne where all his needs are met may be the logical conclusion of a theory which dwells on individual interests, but he is a far cry from the active self-seeking individual depicted by Locke, Bentham, Mill, and Spencer.

A historical account of the rise of individualism leaves unanswered the philosophical question of how the liberal justifies placing the highest political value on the individual, as he does in his assertion of the sanctity of human life and the right to happiness, viewed as the pursuit of self-interest. The strongest justification for giving human life and happiness a special value is based on the view that egoism and self-love are natural. Human desires are therefore the foremost criterion for deciding human good, according to a naturalistic ethic. Any political value which makes reference to the social whole is suspect as society is itself an artificial aggregate, and because such a value may depart from and contravene individual interests. Hobbes, who is sometimes called a 'psychological hedonist', argued that 'of the voluntary acts of every man, the object is some *Good to himself.*'[25] Locke's account of the state of nature likewise assumed self-preservation and the protection of his interests ('life, liberty and estate') as man's primary motives. Later Hume, entering the current controversy as to whether men are ruled by their passions (that is, their self-interest), came down firmly on the side of passion. 'It is not contrary to reason to prefer the destruction of the whole world to the scratching of my little finger.'[26] His contemporary, Bishop Butler, argued that even altruistic actions are ultimately attributable to self-love. Among the other multifarious apostles of self-interest in the eighteenth century is Sade, who believed that anyone had the right to use any other individual as he or she liked, for sexual pleasure, since it was wrong to break the laws of desire, Nature's laws. The crucial difference between Sade's view and that of liberals is that he denied the existence of inviolable personal rights which would prevent self-interest leading to a riot of mutual destruction.

The egoistic individual received his apotheosis in utilitarianism. For Bentham, the utility principle was a first principle which needed no proof because it was rooted in human psychology. Actions were to be morally judged according to their tendency to augment or diminish an individual's pleasure. Like Butler, he argued that no action was entirely disinterested, for even sympathy rests basically on self-interest: it pleases us to be thought compassionate. However, when Bentham extended the utility principle to society as a whole, he could not resolve the problem of reconciling the individual's right to happiness with the good of the greatest number when these came into conflict. The majority principle threatened the individual rights which liberals considered inviolable.

The focus on the individual as a creature of the senses, rather than a soul, leads directly to liberalism's central value, the pursuit of self-interest, for which the sanctity of human life is a necessary precondition. In secular moral theory, the individual must be the final arbiter of what is good. If he is but a bundle of appetites, the definition of 'good' will centre on what satisfies him. Hence the fallacious equation of 'the desired' with 'the desirable' of which Mill, in particular, is accused. The result of reducing human values to matters of pain and pleasure or approval and disapproval, is what is known as *subjectivist ethics*. But if our definitions of good and evil are rooted in individual desires, and if men desire different objects, there is no appropriate way of judging between their definitions of the good: differences of morals must therefore be tolerated. So the liberal doctrines of freedom and tolerance are closely connected with their moral outlook—an outlook which liberated them from Christian morality, with its disapproval of self-love and self-interest. But if the new morality was liberating for liberals, it also liberated their opponents. If it is my moral conviction that capitalists should be bloodily exterminated, who shall gainsay it? Liberalism relies on a close coincidence of individuals' intuitions on such matters, which allows a consensual ordering of political and moral priorities, but it cannot consistently condemn a situation where diverging moral views and political opinions threaten to disrupt society.

The liberal belief in the absolute sanctity of life needs further examination. Life is clearly a precondition for happiness, but it may not be a good in itself. Should a badly deformed baby be kept alive, when it has no chance of a happy life? The idea of a 'right to life' is itself curious, although the right to a *decent* life, once one is alive, and the right not to be used instrumentally by others, are easier to justify. The American Declaration of Independence held it to be 'self-evident' that men are endowed by their Creator with an inalienable right to 'life, liberty and the pursuit of happiness'. Other liberal professions of faith may not invoke a Creator, but they still assert the value of life as self-evident. Is it? This, surely, depends on the quality of life, and while liberalism guarantees the right to life, it offers fewer sureties about that.

However, self-preservation seems to be an instinctive principle. The isolated individual of the liberal model, seen abstractedly, has no attachment to wider groupings or to society itself and so, logically, no duties or values such as altruism and patriotism: his only duty is to himself. In such a case, since men are mortal and since the individual can only fulfil himself through the subjective experiences he gains through living, he must instinctively value the prolongation of his own life above everything. Yet real men often sacrifice themselves for others, or gladly accept death as the gateway to an afterlife. Perhaps in such cases a doctrine like patriotism has merely outweighed the individual's fundamental prejudice in favour of himself. Or perhaps, alternatively, self-love is merely the product of an individualistic and egoistic ideology —liberalism—and is no more natural than the self-effacing love of family or nation: if so, the sanctity of human life is not necessarily the highest human value. However, in setting up the individual as the supreme source of value, the liberal rejects religious and supra-individual moralities and captures something of the agonizing predicament of the secular individual. Like other metaphysical positions, the liberal view of the status of life cannot be substantiated, but many would adhere to it intuitively. The attempt of liberal political theory to aggregate individual values and choices into a set of social prescriptions, though practically necessary, is theoretically problematic, for social theory tends to impose collective or societal values on the individual against his own good. Herein lies the permanent dilemma of liberalism.

Do I Know my Own Interests?

This question challenges the assumption which provides the dynamic of the liberal political model, that of rational self-interest. At the heart of the theory is an individual with personal interests which he somehow 'knows' and unerringly pursues. His account of his interests, wants, and needs is held to be authoritative. All men are said to be equally deserving of respect, so all should have an equal opportunity to realize these interests. So far so good. But such simple assumptions invite many objections and questions. First, must I know my interests *consciously*? There may be things which would promote my wellbeing of which I am ignorant. But because the individual is assumed to be rational, conversant with his needs and omniscient with regard to the available opportunities, it follows from the unrefined notion of interest just described that if he does not consciously want something it is not in his interests. Also, an impartial observer could tell me that some things which I do not want, or even hate, would be in my interests, such as a daily run. Should I therefore call these my interests? Other things which I *do* want, such as cigarettes and alcohol, are clearly *not* in my interest: these might be called 'perverse wants', but should they be called 'my interests'?

The problems for a political theory based on subjective interest are: (1) whether to take only people's apparent, felt or expressed interests into account; (2) whether to ignore their 'perverse wants'; and (3) whether to modify (1) by imposing a category of 'real' interests, whose realization would benefit people even if they do not consciously want them, or would reject them. Liberalism has always repudiated the idea of 'real' interests, arguing that that way lies totalitarianism. This means that only subjectively felt or expressed interests can count. Liberals also reject the Marxist contention that people *en masse* can be deluded about their interests and suffer widespread false consciousness, since this erodes the concept of rationality.

When it comes to the application of the principle of subjective interests, because it is impossible to ascertain what interests every individual has, it is *expressed interests* that are taken into account. Economics operates with a similar concept, that of *revealed preferences*, stipulating that people's true preferences can be deduced from what they choose. Likewise, the political opinions that people express in voting are assumed to express their interests. This is a wickedly simplifying assumption, since people can only manifest their interests through politics in certain, formalized ways; they are given a pre-selected set of options to choose from, which may exclude their real political preferences. The 1975 referendum on British membership of the European Community is a notorious example. The propaganda was heavily biased in favour of membership and the options were confined to 'Yes' and 'No', when many people would have voted for intermediate proposals. It would be rash to conclude on the basis of such 'revealed preferences' that 66% of the British people felt EC membership to be in their interests. Interests expressed in such ways are only the most approximate guide to what people want. To interpret political or economic choices as free, rational choices made in pursuit of self-interest ignores the large number of constraints which make that untrue. But, for the liberal, expressed preferences are an important part of the practice of freedom as choice.

Another problem which vexes the liberal account of interests is that of the 'free-rider'. This maverick is someone who decides that it is in his interests not to contribute to a collective enterprise because he knows that he will get the benefits irrespective of his contribution. The concept of the free-rider originated in economic theory dealing with the financing of public goods[27], but it can equally be used of joint political activity. The tax-evader who saves his money while enjoying the same amenities as other citizens is a free-rider. It could also be said that those who do not bother to vote are riding on the backs of those who fulfil their citizenly duties and contribute to the stability of democracy. Liberalism has to make special theoretical provision to exclude the interests of free-riders from counting as 'proper'—ironically, for the free-rider is the rational, self-interested individual *par excellence*. Since liberals do not wish to make out a strong case for social duty, they can only argue that a contribution to some collective effort is ultimately more in the free-rider's interests than evasion, which it would be difficult to prove, and which could be seen as a covert assertion of 'real' interests. The case of the free-rider certainly suggests that there is something special about the public sphere and that collective amenities and activities cannot be satisfactorily treated, as they are by liberal theory, as mere aggregates of individual interests. Different forces operate, different rules must apply.

One liberal attempt to escape from the problems of subjectivity surrounding interests takes the form of specifying 'proper' interests for mankind. Mill's reference to 'the permanent interests of man as a progressive being' and his contention that intellectual pleasures are more valuable than those of the senses, lead in this direction. Others, such as Green, substituted ideas of self-realization and self-mastery for the more instinctual idea of pursuing one's interests, and virtually introduced the notion of a higher ethical self, which Berlin maintains is an illiberal idea.[28] This version of interests closely approaches the idea of 'real' interests which liberals have so often branded as totalitarian. But no doubt it is ultimately impossible to cleanse the idea of interests of the paternalistic impulse to make men better, even for the most libertarian of liberals.

A contemporary solution to liberalism's problems is offered by Barry. He enumerates five ways in which 'X is in A's interests' can differ from 'A wants X', and shows how men can mistake their interests in various ways. He then provides a new definition of 'interest' which overcomes such anomalies.

To say, therefore, that an action or policy is in somebody's interests is not actually to say that it satisfies his immediate wants at all; it is rather to say that *it puts him in a better position to satisfy his wants.*[29]

Such a definition could justify handing over the individual's interests in part to the care of politicians who will help people satisfy their wants, perceived and unperceived. Something like Barry's definition is needed to propel liberalism towards progress, for if we equate wants with interests, and interests with expressed interests, given the limitation of choice, little social progress is likely.

The answer to the original question, then, is that I cannot know my interests in the immediate, rational, omniscient way that liberal theory sometimes implies, and that in various circumstances I have to be helped to 'know' them. Government policies in apparent opposition to people's wishes must therefore sometimes be sanctioned, and in all societies some decisions must be taken paternalistically, with reference to people's 'real' interests. The theory of interests therefore needs to be modified to mould it to reality and to justify judicious government intervention. First, individuals are said to know their immediate interests better than their long-term interests, which they tend to ignore. The mature collective wisdom of the community, embodied in the state, brings our long-term interests to our notice, as, for example, in the establishment of a compulsory pension scheme which many young people would opt out of if it were voluntary, despite its being in their long-term interests. The provision of collective defence is a similar case, where people's more remote interests are taken care of by the government. Second, individuals' private interests will inevitably sometimes run counter to those of their fellows, or of society as a whole. Early writers in the tradition soft-pedalled this possibility, optimistically hoping for a harmony of interests. Later, Mill introduced the notion of 'material harm' to demarcate such clashes of interest. Most liberals would concede the need for government intervention to protect the majority's interest where individual or group interests clash. Government intervention when strikers threaten vital supplies falls into this category. Liberals do not abandon their individualism in making such concessions, but in practice they accept the likelihood of conflict and the need for majority rule in such extremities. This constitutes an acknowledgement that not all individual interests can be pursued simultaneously, but this is a fact of life, and the justification for the existence of government.

Can the Liberal Accept a Welfare State?

Freeland was a welfare state. If a citizen wanted anything from a load of bone meal to a sexual partner some department was ready to offer effective aid. The threat implicit in this enveloping benevolence stifled the concept of rebellion.

William Burroughs, *The Naked Lunch*

The liberal case against state interference with individual freedom, and against paternalistic legislation, has already been reviewed. Here I shall examine how it applies to the welfare state, which exemplifies both these sins against individual freedom. The liberal, unlike Burroughs, is not worried that rebellion will be stifled but that the very concept of the free, independent individual will disappear as the state grows. The case against the welfare state can be viewed in several ways: first, it can be seen as straightforward interference with individual freedom. Individuals are forced to contribute to the maintenance of health and social services whether they wish to or not.

Furthermore, before they can benefit from the services for which they have paid, they have to provide the state with private information and submit to various intrusive procedures. Second, welfare measures can be viewed as tantamount to interfering with individuals for their own good. Compulsory education and compulsory medical care at the period of childbirth are two examples of such paternalism in our own welfare state.

These arguments are familiar, but a third line of attack illustrates the harshness with which hard-line individuals might condemn the welfare state. In 1803, Malthus wrote

A man who is born into a world already possessed (i.e. under ownership), if he cannot get subsistence from his parents, on whom he has a just demand, and if society do not want his labour, has no claim or *right* to the smallest portion of food, and, in fact, has no business to be where he is. At nature's mighty feast there is no vacant cover for him. She tells him to begone . . .[30]

We can correlate this with a remark of Spencer's, made eighty years later, when Gladstone's reforming Liberal ministry was introducing considerable reforms, which he regarded as paternalistic.

. . . The command 'if any would not work neither should he eat', is simply a Christian enumeration of that universal law of Nature under which life has reached its present height — the law that a creature not energetic enough to maintain itself must die.[31]

Spencer developed a theory of evolution some years before Darwin, which turned on the vision of a war of all against all: intra-, rather than inter-, species competition. His book *The Man Versus the State* champions laissez-faire, 'survival of the fittest' liberalism against Liberal reformers. He, like Malthus, thought that the 'deserving poor', the concern of so many Victorian philanthropists, were poor because they were *undeserving* and should not receive government aid. He fiercely opposed 'meddling legislation' designed to mitigate the harsh conditions of life for the inadequate. Such views were underpinned by his hypothesis that evolution operated in society, eliminating inferior strains and promoting the eventual physical and moral perfection of the race.

While he held many liberal convictions, such as the belief in laissez-faire and the need to limit the state's functions, Spencer was clearly not a typical liberal, for he callously dismisses the importance of individual life and substitutes a supra-individual value, that of the long-term improvement of society. But his theory suggests what might have become of liberal ideology if, instead of being tempered by humane values, the 'ethical liberalism' attributed to Mill, it had become fused with less humanitarian doctrines such as social Darwinism. Another part of Spencer's argument is that government aid weakens the individual and atrophies his capacity for independent action — a view in which some liberals might concur although today such thinkers are likely to be branded 'conservative.'

Against Malthus we can assert the right of the living to a decent life, a claim made in liberal declarations of rights, while against Spencer the argument is that his analogy is misapplied: evolution does not operate in society as he hypothesized, and the survival of the less adequate members of society does not weaken the structure or health of the 'social whole' (which is, in any case, a concept repudiated by many liberals). It could be added that, when it is a question of life or death, subsistence or starvation, the *deserts* of the pauper should not be taken into account, but only his right to life. But the anti-paternalistic argument is harder to refute: no doubt, to some extent, Freeland-style welfare services sap the independence of the individual and his free, rational status, which he must surrender in part to the state. All that can be said here is that this — hard as it is to measure — should be counted as a cost against the benefits offered by welfare measures, and policies should be evaluated accordingly. One instance where social policy has actually been changed in order to avoid sapping the independence of individuals and to enhance their freedom, is in the treatment of the mentally ill who are now, wherever possible, rehabilitated in the community, to give them more normal lives and to avoid both the ill-effects and the public costs of institutionalization.

Mill conceded the need for some measures to increase welfare, despite his categorical objections to state interference, but the landmark in the adaptation of liberal thought to the inevitable growth of the welfare state was Hobhouse's book *Liberalism*. The welfare measures of Lloyd George's reforming budget of 1909, which created a contributory pension scheme and sickness and unemployment benefits for the lowest-paid workers, had to be reconciled with the liberal creed, since they represented intervention in the market system and, further, interfered paternalistically with individual freedom. Hobhouse argued that modern liberals could justify the extension of public control on humane grounds. The doctrine of liberty should not prevent the general will from acting, where it must, for the common good. He emphasized the contribution which welfare measures make to the realization of that essential liberal assumption, equality of opportunity. This argument could be interpreted as a claim that such intervention is not made paternalistically but, rather, in the interests of maintaining the preconditions of liberal society. Hobhouse also criticized the extreme laissez-faire view of the state as umpire and argued the necessity for intervention where appropriate. Hobhouse's argument about equality of opportunity had been foreshadowed by many socialists, who pointed out that the conditions for a liberal society did not really exist. Thus, paradoxically, what seemed at first to be a concession on a matter of principle ultimately strengthened liberal theory.

In summary, governments and states are bound to intervene to some extent to promote their subjects' welfare, and while this is *prima facie* irreconcilable with particular liberal beliefs, it can be shown to operate in the spirit of the liberal model and, by guaranteeing minimum subsistence to the worst-off members of society, to enhance equality of opportunity and so make com-petition fairer. Welfare policies will always present a problem for liberals because the harm they do to individual freedom is incommensurable with the material benefits which they bring, so that it is never easy to decide whether, on the whole, they are warranted; also, liberals may differ over the priority to be observed between freedom and other goods.

Where do we Draw the Line?

Few contemporary liberal writers have been cited so far, but some of them will now be considered in the discussion of how we should delimit government intervention in the context of the modern state and the complexities of advanced capitalism. Defying the obvious divergences of modern society from the classical liberal model, Hayek has set out a political and economic model similar to that of early liberalism: his ideas have had considerable influence, monetarism being one of their offshoots. Hayek claims that liberalism 'derives from the discovery of a self-generating or spontaneous order in social affairs'. The ideal model for the economy and the polity is what he calls the 'catallaxy', a spontaneous organization resembling the free market, which generates a plurality of values. Social and interpersonal transactions would be modelled on market exchanges, while the government's role would be strictly limited to keeping order and providing some public services which do not spontaneously appear because of the huge capital outlays required.[32] Objections to Hayek are similar to those raised to early, laissez-faire liberalism. The market system which, if perfect, should supply all human needs, did not and cannot adequately supply them, because of its many imperfections; hence the need for state intervention and, if necessary, a welfare state to help those whom the market system neglects because their demands are not backed by cash.

In order to criticize Hayek's attempts at ideological regression further, we can look to the Western economists who have applied themselves to the problem of the provision of public goods, that is, shared amenities such as roads, hospitals, the legal system, and education. Arrow showed that individual preferences cannot be aggregated to provide the best possible social welfare provision: here, in the important field of the provision of major amenities and large-scale investment, there is no way in which individual choices can sanction such provision. Arrow concludes '. . . the only methods of passing from individual tastes to social preferences which will be satisfactory . . . are either imposed or dictatorial.'[33] In other words, the provision of public goods will be necessarily 'undemocratic', that is, not based on expressed preferences, and often 'illiberal', in that such provision may override many individuals' interests. The majority of taxpayers, for example, would probably not choose to finance a new major motorway which they may never use, and such a decision has to be imposed by government.

Arrow's theory should be taken in conjunction with Olson's account of 'the logic of collective action', where the problem of the free-rider is elaborated. Olson's conclusion is that coercion is needed to make everyone contribute fairly to the cost of public or collective goods.[34] These theories together can be construed as an account of the impasse to which individualism leads, when taken as the fundamental principle of liberal theory and social policy. Where market forces and enlightened self-interest will not serve to obtain what many individuals want (but what many others would refuse to contribute to voluntarily), government must intervene. This suggests that a new line should be drawn, which permits government intervention to promote the provision of such 'public goods'. However, there is no self-evident limitation to the concept of public goods: many things that we now consider a matter for individual provision could come within the compass of an interventionist government, as in Burroughs's Freeland. So the question must still be asked by liberals of each new measure concerned with public goods provision, 'Is this public good really necessary?', and assessments will doubtless differ. Arrow and Olson do not solve the problems of liberalism, then, by demarcating the area of public goods, but they suggest that some of liberalism's assumptions about the virtues of the free market and individual choice are untenable, and their scepticism about the ability of self-interest and rationality to produce what society needs has influenced liberal thought to move in new directions.

Liberal democracy, as the dominant ideology in the West, provides the paradigms within which much academic work on politics is conceived. Most of the recent major revisions of liberalism appear not as political polemics but as contributions to academic debate. Rawls's liberal theory of justice, which blossoms out into a full account of the Good Life, is one such text, as is Nozick's Hayekian utopia, mentioned above. Another influential development of liberalism is the theory of pluralism: pluralist society is composed of many different interest and opinion groups who are obliged to co-operate and compromise in order to promote their own interests. In a sense, this is liberalism writ large. The self-interested individual has been replaced by the self-interest group. It is a descriptive theory of how American politics works, rather than an ideal, but many theorists, notably Dahl, now propose pluralism as a normative theory which resolves various problems of liberalism such as its over-individualistic basis and its inability to cope with group phenomena or to analyse institutions properly. Pluralist theory retains the methodological individualist approach, but can explain these features of society more satisfactorily. More will be said about this in Chapter 9. Many other books of political science written in this century have aimed at reconciling liberal theory with political fact. While still professing methodological individualism, theorists have concentrated on larger units of analysis, submerging the individual in the interest group or party or even in 'the system'. The fact-gathering of modern political scientists has also produced results which are discrepant with liberal assumptions about individual rationality and capability and these, too, have been instrumental in producing modifications of the theory of liberal democracy.

New theories are now advanced to vindicate the elite nature of politics in representative liberal democracy[35], while others seek to explain how the system can survive and flourish when so many people are the exact opposite of the ideally free and rational individual who stars in liberal and democratic theory. Exchange and transactions analyses of politics have also been developed, both suggesting that all human interaction is conducted on the basis of profitable exchange.[36] Such theories illustrate the continuing intimacy between liberal political thought and the economic theory which upholds capitalism. Whether such analyses will survive as amendments to liberal theory or will pass away as academic ephemera, time will tell. They exemplify an interesting fact: each major ideology needs a large body of academics to service and maintain it, smoothing out anomalies and explaining new developments in terms of the doctrine: as Marx said, each ideology needs its apologists. Zinoviev's acclaimed novel, *The Radiant Future*, suggests that this is equally true of Marxism in the USSR. Ideologies may derive from a few basic texts, but there will always be a role for ideologues.

In Western society, the association of liberalism with democracy is usually taken for granted, and one term is understood to embrace the other. For this reason, perhaps this chapter on liberalism should be immediately followed by one on democracy. However, there are other varieties of democracy than that practised in liberal societies, and it seems preferable to treat these all together, after the other main ideologies have been discussed. Logically, liberalism is separable from democracy, as has been intimated, for the liberal ideal entails no particular form of government, as long as that government does not encroach upon individual rights. There are risks of liberal and democratic ideals conflicting in liberal democracy which hinge on the potential conflict between individual and majority interests: these flashpoints will be discussed in Chapter 9.

Liberalism in practice is less clear-cut, more diffuse, than the ideology as it has been described here. The schematic presentation has been intended to expose the internal logic and the consistency, or otherwise, of the ideology which underpins our own form of society, and to suggest the reasons for its continuing force and appeal. The 'pure' theory is modified by the details of each major text—Mill's chapter on 'Applications' almost entirely annuls the principles which he advances in the first part of *On Liberty*:—and even more by practice. What must be said, before going on to consider the major rival and critic of liberalism, Marxism, is that this ideology presided over what were arguably three of the most progressive and liberating centuries of human history. It should therefore be credited with many of the advances of this era, even if it is rightly blamed for many of our endemic social problems.

Notes

1. C. B. Macpherson, *The Political Theory of Possessive Individualism*, Oxford University Press, Oxford, 1962.
2. The varieties of individualism are discussed in S. Lukes, *Individualism,* Blackwell, Oxford, 1974.
3. J. Locke, *An Essay Concerning the True Original, Extent and End of Civil Government*, Dent, London, 1924, p. 159. Referred to hereafter as *Essay*.
4. Locke, *Essay*, Chaps VIII–IX.

5. I. Berlin, 'Two concepts of liberty' in *Political Philosophy* (Ed. A. Quinton), Oxford University Press, Oxford, 1967, p. 148.
6. Locke, *Essay*, Chap. XIII.
7. Locke, *Essay*, p. 127.
8. C. B. Macpherson, *Democratic Theory*, Oxford University Press, Oxford, 1973, pp. 3-23.
9. W. B. Gallie, 'Liberal morality and socialist morality' in *Philosophy, Politics and Society*, Ed. P. Laslett, Blackwell, Oxford, 1956.
10. F. Hayek, 'The principles of a liberal social order' in *Ideologies of Politics*, (Eds A. Crespigny and J. Cronin), Oxford University Press, Oxford, 1975, pp. 67-9.
11. *St Matthew* 25:29.
12. J. S. Mill, *On Liberty*, Collins, Glasgow, 1962, p. 143.
13. Mill, *On Liberty*, Chap. 2.
14. See, e.g. C. Pateman, *Participation and Democratic Theory*, Cambridge University Press, Cambridge, 1970.
15. J. S. Mill, *Considerations on Representative Government*, Oxford University Press, Oxford, 1912, Chap. II.
16. T. H. Green, *Lectures on the Principles of Political Obligation*, Longmans, London, 1901, pp. 123-6.
17. J. P. Plamenatz, *Consent, Freedom and Political Obligation*, 2nd edn, Oxford University Press, Oxford, 1968, Chap. 3.
18. A. Smith, *The Wealth of Nations*, London, 1776, Bk IV, Chap. 2.
19. R. Nozick, *Anarchy, State and Utopia*, Blackwell, Oxford, 1974.
20. Macpherson, *Democratic Theory*, p. 192.
21. Mill, *On Liberty*, p. 135.
22. See again Lukes, *Individualism*.
23. Mill, *On Liberty,* Chap. 3, and W. Humboldt, *The Sphere and Duties of Government* (trans. J. Courtland), London, 1854.
24. J. Ortega y Gasset, *The Revolt of the Masses*, Unwin, London, 1961.
25. T. Hobbes, *Leviathan* (Ed. C. B. Macpherson), Penguin, Harmondsworth, 1968, p. 192.
26. J. Hume, *Treatise of Human Nature*, Fontana, London, 1972, Bk II, p. 157.
27. M. Olson, *The Logic of Collective Action*, Schocken, 1971.
28. Berlin, 'Two concepts of liberty' in *Political Philosophy*.
29. B. Barry, *Political Argument*, Routledge & Kegan Paul, London, 1965, p. 183.
30. T. Malthus, *Essay on the Principles of Population*, 2nd edn, London, 1803. This passage was removed from subsequent editions.
31. H. Spencer, *The Man Versus the State*, Penguin, Harmondsworth, 1969, p. 83.
32. Hayek, 'The principles of a liberal social order', pp. 58-61 especially.
33. K. Arrow, *Social Choice and Individual Values*, 2nd edn, Yale University Press, Yale, 1963, pp. 59-60.
34. Olson, *The Logic of Collective Action*.
35. A survey of such theories is offered in P. Bachrach, *The Theory of Democratic Elitism*, London University Press, London, 1968.
36. These are discussed in S. Waldman, *The Foundations of Political Action*, Little, Brown & Co., 1972.

Further Reading

J. S. Mill, *On Liberty*, Collins, Glasgow, 1962.

T. Hobhouse, *Liberalism*, Home University Library, 1911.

D. J. Manning, *Liberalism*, Dent, London, 1976.

J. P. Plamenatz, *Readings from Liberal Writers,* George Allen & Unwin, London, 1965. Extracts.

G. Himmelfarb, *Liberty and Liberalism*, Alfred Knopf, 1974.

CHAPTER 4

Marxism

To give an account of the whole of Marxism in one chapter is an impossible undertaking. Changing circumstances have produced many different theoretical currents within the ideology during the last hundred years, with many subtle divergences from Marx's own text. Since subsequent Marxist thinkers explicitly locate themselves in relation to Marx, however, the most important thing is to understand the principles of his own theory. These will be examined in this chapter, which will also give a brief account of later developments of his theory by Marxists such as Lenin and Trotsky.

Problems in Reading Marx

A number of obstacles face anyone who tries to learn about Marxism from reading Marx's own works. The first is the remarkable breadth of topics and disciplines which they span. In 1840 the death of the Prussian king Frederick William III resulted in the lifting of strict censorship, which had limited freedom of expression in Prussia for a long time. Karl Marx, previously a doctoral student, was able to start his career as a political journalist—but two years later censorship was re-imposed and he moved to Paris, where he met Engels. His activities in France and Prussia during the 1848 revolutions caused him to be expelled and he went to live in England, ending his days in Highgate Cemetery. During this exile, he was involved in the International Working Men's Association (the 'International') from 1864 until 1872, when he quarrelled with Bakunin and the movement split. Marx was therefore exposed to a wide variety of European cultures, historical dramas, and political activities, so that much of his theory appears in the guise of commentary on recent events, such as the coup of Louis Bonaparte, the 1870 Paris Commune and the formation of the German SDP. This makes it less accessible to the student searching for a compact and definitive account of Marx's views.

Another difficulty is that much of Marx's theory grew out of polemics against contemporary thinkers, some of whose views have long been forgotten. At first, he engaged battle with the 'Young Hegelians', who were obsessed with the semi-mystical idea of 'absolute negation' and whom Marx condemned as 'idealist'. In particular, he rejected Bauer's simplistic view of revolution: 'once the kingdom of ideas is revolutionised, reality cannot hold out'. The early Paris manuscripts of 1844 contained Marx's critiques of Hegel and of the economists Smith, Say, and Ricardo, who nevertheless influenced his own economic ideas. Politically, Marx counterposed his own 'scientific' socialism to the 'utopian' socialism which was then prevalent, another idealist doctrine which he feared would produce political quietism and forestall revolutionary activity. To understand Marx properly, then, one needs an acquaintance with all the authors with whom he takes issue — or at least some idea of their theories.

A further complication is the contemporary controversy about the 'two Marxes'. One recent, influential Western interpretation of Marx hypothesizes a split between the work of the young and the older Marx, following the belated publication in translation of some of his early writings, which seem to soften the impersonal economic theory of *Capital*. His writings are said to fall into two periods, the crucial transitional link being his *Introduction to the Critique of Political Economy* (The *Grundrisse*), written 1857–8 but unpublished until 1953, which is heralded as a bridging work which combines ethics and humanism with economic theory. Western commentators such as McLellan acclaim the young, 'humanist' Marx who discusses alienation, human nature, and morality and is less distant from liberal individualism than his later self.[1] But orthodox communists such as Althusser discount the early works as juvenilia, deny the presence of humanism in Marx's works, and maintain that only the later economic texts such as *Capital* are important for Marxist science. In part this controversy rests on the spurious assumption that great thinkers should manifest consistency — or at least a linear progression — throughout their thinking life. But anyone approaching Marxism should know of the existence of this controversy, for otherwise these diametrically opposed interpretations of Marx are confusing. One further complication is the collaboration of Marx with Engels. In the exposition which follows, Engels's views are subsumed under those of Marx, although in his later writings after Marx's death, he departed in some respects from Marx's views.

The Vocabulary of the Dialectic

Despite his many disagreements with Hegel, Marx employed a version of Hegel's dialectic. This form of argument often mystifies readers who are accustomed to the empiricist way of thinking based on inductive and formal, deductive logic, and this section is intended as a guide for those wishing to read Marx's own writings. The dialectic is claimed to be a form of argument which can explain developmental processes and the oppositions which exist in the phenomenal world. Formal logic, which is based on the laws of identity and non-contradiction, is said by Marxists to be static, unable to explain change or contradiction, whereas the dialectic can encompass historical developments, and shows contradictions to be progressive.[2] Hegel viewed history as a dialectical progression, where unstable, seemingly contradiction-ridden stages of society resolved themselves into higher socio-political forms, which still preserved elements of the earlier stages. Any historical process is said by Hegel to consist of 'moments', or temporary states, which contain contradictory elements. Each moment is succeeded by a new moment which *negates* it, *transcends* it (that is, progresses beyond it) and yet *conserves* its particular characteristics. Thus there is a constant historical progression towards a more sophisticated reality. Hegel used the verb *aufheben* to connote this complex process of transcendance, and the familiar example given is that of the process of a bud, which becomes a flower, which becomes the fruit, each stage of its life going beyond the previous stage, yet in a sense conserving it.

Marx used the dialectic less technically and insistently than Hegel, but it forms the basis of his conception of capitalism as 'contradictory' and ridden with class conflict. If we focus on the composition of a particular state of affairs, it will consist of two opposed elements, and the situation can be examined from the point of view of each element. You can examine the process of capitalist production from the viewpoint of *labour*, one factor of production, or from that of *capital*, the other factor in a simplified model. Labour (the worker) sees itself as a subject, and sees capital as an object, something set outside itself and apart from itself, despite the fact that capital is created by labour. Likewise, capital sees labour as an opposing, separate force, although it could not function without labour. As each is essential to the other in the economic process, the polarity which both perceive is false, and appears as a result of looking at the process from only one side. Because labour and capital have a symbiotic relationship, Marx said that the bourgeoisie, by creating a class of wage labourers to work with their capital, called into existence their own gravediggers. All the social and political divisions of capitalist society result from this labour–capital polarity but the socialist revolution, Marx predicted, would abolish this opposition and transcend it, bringing about a classless society, which would conserve the previous elements, since industrial production would continue under socialism.

A warning should be added against any attempt to anglicize the dialectic by paraphrasing it in terms of thesis, antithesis, and synthesis, as does Berlin[3]: this formulation fails to capture the subtlety of the dialectical process of *Aufhebung* or the co-existence of contradictory elements in a state of affairs, and suggests that the whole can be seen as analogous to an argument in formal logic, which Marx would have denied strenuously. The consequence of Marx's utilization of the dialectic in conjunction with economic determinism is his conclusion that there is a causal, predictable process at work in human history, of a dialectical kind.

Some of the other terms and definitions which Marx used need clarification. *Capital*, which he also referred to as *private property*, was wealth used productively, to produce more wealth, which is then reinvested in more capital goods. In pre-capitalist societies, wealth was generally used for immediate consumption purposes, or merely hoarded, and so did not become capital. *Labour* can be productive, in the sense that it produces capital, or unproductive. Marx gives the example of the piano-maker, who is productive, and the pianist, who creates no new wealth, but merely exchanges his services for money. The terms *subjective* and *objective* are also often contrasted by Marx. The working class is objectively the revolutionary class, although subjectively it is not so. That is, seen from the viewpoint of history, the proletariat is the class which has the potential for making the revolution, although it may not *feel* itself to be revolutionary, or have any self-awareness, alias class-consciousness. A class's subjective viewpoint can differ from its objective reality because, being within a contradictory situation, it has only a partial view of the totality, whereas a scientific theory, as Marx believed his was, which takes account of the whole, can explain that class's objective position. Western commentators who accuse Marx of forgetting the psychological aspects of human life should perhaps see his acknowledgement of subjective viewpoints as a gesture in this direction. Two other key terms in Marx's analysis are *appropriation* and *expropriation*. From the viewpoint of the capitalist, who is engaged in accumulating profits, he is appropriating this private property, setting it aside for himself. But from the labourer's point of view, the capitalist is expropriating him, seizing the goods which he has produced and depriving him of a proper reward for his labour.

Marx borrowed the term *objectification* (which some translators render as 'reification') from Hegel, for whom it was part of the dialectical movement of individual consciousness. The dialectic begins with a thinking subject, and objectification means that something which is really part of the subject itself is placed outside itself in its mind, and regarded as an object, which results in a distortion of the subject's view of the situation. For Marx, one of the prime causes of the worker's alienation under capitalism is that he is forced to objectify his own creations, the products which he makes, and he then sees them as no longer part of himself, or as not belonging to him, so that his products appear as alien, hostile objects, appropriated by the capitalist. Here, Marx may mistake what seems to be the aftermath of all creative activity, as any author would vouch, for a peculiar property of capitalist production. But the account of alienation is important for his general criticism of the capitalist way of life.

Marx's way of thinking is often referred to as *dialectical materialism*, a term which needs some explanation. Materialism is a philosophical position based on the axiom that all events in the phenomenal world can be explained adequately in terms of other events, or causes, in the world. A major influence in the development of materialism was Locke's view that all our ideas are caused by the perceptions of the external world which reach us via our five senses, and by our reflections on these. In asserting this, he was rebutting Descartes's claim that men were born with innate ideas of God and other absolute truths, such as those of geometry, on which our knowledge was constructed. For Marx, as for Locke, ideas can have no existence without prior causes in the external world, but while Locke was asserting this doctrine against those who wished to maintain that man's knowledge was ultimately produced by divine intervention or other metaphysical (literally, 'beyond the physical') influences, Marx used it against the eighteenth-century philosophers who had used such fictions as 'human nature' and 'pure reason' in their explanations of society. Most of all, he disputed the German idealists' claim that ideas can arise independently of social context and act as causes within society. He held that all social phenomena and human consciousness itself are produced by material causes, and that these causes lie finally in the economic arrangements of society, which he called *the mode of production*. 'Man', his thoughts and his activities are therefore determined by society—an axiom which deliberately strikes at the liberal assumption of individual autonomy and free will. 'My own existence is a social activity', Marx said, and 'Activity and mind are social in their content as well as in their origin; they are *social* activity and *social* mind'.[4]

Relating this general insight to his economic theory, he also asserted that 'what (individuals) are coincides with their production, both with *what* they produce, and with *how* they produce.'[5] It is, of course, possible to espouse materialism without agreeing with Marx that the ultimate causes of social events are economic, and many Enlightenment philosophers accepted that man is determined by the social environment without this additional hypothesis. Marx was not so much original in adopting the materialist epistemology as in postulating that economic activity was at its basis (which, however, some early socialists also posited) and systematically building on it a coherent theory of social and political relations and ideology. But his materialism and his claim that man is a being formed by society does not, emphatically, imply that man is a passively determined creature and can never bring about social change. However, Marx asserted that such changes will not come about through the force of ideas conceived *in vacuo*, as the utopians had hoped, or through sheer will-power, but via ideas and circumstances arising in the material, social world.

Marx's Economics

The early manuscripts which Marx wrote in 1844, which were only published in this century, explain the distinctive nature of human life and its basis in economic activity. Man differs from other animals which merely produce to satisfy their immediate needs, even when, like beavers, they appear to work in a systematic, quasi-human fashion. Man produces things according to preconceived plans: the architect's construction is planned, whereas that of the bee merely follows an instinctive pattern—we would now say that it was genetically programmed. Furthermore, man 'produces free from physical need and only truly produces when he is thus free.'[6] Liberated from the stark physical necessities which motivate other animals, man can work creatively and make things according to canons of beauty. In fashioning the natural world consciously, man 'affirms himself as species-being'. That is, the essential characteristic which differentiates the human species and gives it a generic identity is man's productive activity. In making these claims, Marx comes near to idealism, in that he seems to be describing a universal human essence despite his scorn for other thinkers who posit such an abstraction, but he would no doubt have argued that there was nothing mysterious or non-material about this 'essence' since it emanates from man's biological and intellectual constitution, and has no teleological connotations.

From the centrality of economic activity to mankind, Marx infers that the way in which that activity is organized determines all other aspects of social life. The mode of production, together with the form of distribution, constitutes the economic structure, and determines the superstructure. The 'relations of production' determine the social relations on which the political system and all other features of social organization base themselves. As is well known, Marx had an elaborate theory of history, which is discussed below, and he applied his analysis to earlier modes of production, but the focus of all his work was the capitalist mode, and this was crucial to his political theory, so only his account of capitalism will be detailed here. The capitalist economy rests on a fundamental dichotomy between capital and labour, the two sides of the 'contradiction' of capitalism, and this is transmuted at the level of social relations into the antagonistic and potentially conflictual relations between the bourgeoisie and the proletariat. First, Marx defines productive labour as having the unique quality of being able to create new values. Labour is the ultimate source of all value (this statement entails a simplifying assumption about natural resources, which most people would call valuable in themselves, and which Marx discusses further in *Capital*), and capital is merely accumulated, or 'objectified' labour—the result of the exploitation of past generations —in the form of machinery, factories, and other apparatus which contributes to the productive process. Capitalist manufacture is based on private property, accumulated capital, which, concentrated in the hands of the capitalist, enable him to hire 'living labour'—the wage labourer, whose position in the economic process is defined as someone who does not own the means of production. It is in the productive process that the contradiction between capital and labour becomes manifest. Marx assumes, like other economists of the time, that labourers are paid subsistence wages. The commodities which they produce have a certain *exchange value*, measurable in money terms, which is determined by the amount of labour which they embody, and can also vary with the state of the market. For example, the labourer works, say, ten hours per day. In six hours he produces goods whose *exchange value* (price) is equal to the wages that he earns in a day. Marx calls this six hours 'necessary labour', the labour necessary for the labourer and his family, the next generation of labourers, to survive. But he is not paid for the remaining four hours that he works, and their value is expropriated by the capitalist. This Marx calls *surplus value*, and this is the yardstick of the exploitation of the worker. The residue of surplus value, after rent, dividends, and other costs have been paid, becomes the capitalist's profits, which Marx's model assumes to be reinvested in further production. Each new injection of capital increases the capitalist's power to hire ('appropriate') more labour, and so to expand his business.

The past appropriation of alien labour is thus the simple condition for fresh appropriation of alien labour.[7]

The process is thus a dynamic, continuing one for each individual capitalist and is sure to continue because of its own momentum unless the capitalist's incentive, the *rate of profit*, is reduced. (A simplified definition of this is that the rate of profit is the ratio of wages paid to surplus value produced.) And what is true of individual firms is true of capitalism as a whole: it must expand to survive. But, as capitalism thrives on competition, Marx thought that the less successful capitalists would be driven out of business, and he predicted the rise of monopolies and the cartelization which has led to today's giant corporations.

Marx shows that capitalism is endangered by various processes which threaten to reduce the rate of profit. First, there is an internal contradiction in the productive process. As expansion and reinvestment continue, the proportion of machines ('constant capital') to workers ('variable capital') will increase, assuming that machinery becomes more sophisticated. In other words, Marx predicts that industries will become more capital-intensive. But since it is only the labour component that creates surplus value, the more machines and the fewer men used, the lower the surplus value and the lower the rate of profit. Marx assumes that the capitalist's motivation is to maintain his rate of profit at all costs, although modern economists suggest that as long as the business expands fast enough for turnover and the *amount* of profit to remain constant, or grow, the actual *rate* of profit is not crucial. But in terms of Marx's analysis, if the rate of profit falls, the capitalist's reaction will be to cut wages to restore surplus value, and his profits. This will impoverish the working class, especially as the presence of a 'pool of unemployment' will ensure that workers have to take what is offered, and wages will therefore never rise above subsistence level. We should note that Marx's preliminary analysis omits factors like unionization, which might prevent wage-cutting. But he is deliberately analysing the free market situation of the classical economists, in which individual employers and workers negotiate in a state of 'perfect competition'.

Other, external factors may cause the rate of profit to fall. Unionization has the effect of forcing up wages and lowering profits. If prices in the market fall because of a glut or a drop in demand, the worker takes longer to earn his wages (in terms of the price of the goods he produces) and so, again, surplus value is squeezed. There was also the possibility that markets would be permanently satiated, with similar results. When employers *en masse* cut wages, a depression ensues. Marx expected the trade cycle of booms and slumps to oscillate ever more violently until the severity of a depression brought about a revolution. The causal mechanism was the pauperization of the proletariat; workers would become aware of their expressed and exploited condition and their common predicament as a class and begin to engage in political activity to remedy it. The major contradiction of capitalism is that as it expands its tendency to collapse increases: the workers erupt into action in the political sphere, which has hitherto safeguarded the interests of the capitalists. Hence the importance of knowing Marx's economics in order to understand his theory of revolution.

This, then, is Marx's economic model, much simplified. But *Capital* and his other works are rich in insights as to how the economic organization affects the whole of social life. Two apparent paradoxes result from the nature of capitalism. First, that capitalism can only flourish through the creation of extremes of wealth and poverty. The capitalist grows richer while 'only the growing impoverishment of living labour is its own'. The early socialists observed this too, and remarked on the anomaly that labourers could not afford to buy the luxuries that they produced for others. Second, and more dialectically, the capitalist and the workers, antagonistic though their interests might be, cannot survive without each other. 'Proletariat and wealth are opposites; as such they form a single whole.'[8] This bears out the intuition of classical economists that the pursuit of individual interests leads to the benefit of all, although Marx gave the doctrine a pessimistic twist because he was convinced that capitalism's contradictions would lead to its demise.

The market system which endows manufactured objects with exchange value perverts our perception of them, which ought to be based on their *use value*, that is, on their usefulness to mankind. 'I speak of this as the *fetishistic character* which attaches to the products of labour, so soon as they are produced in the form of commodities.'[9] Since social relations reflect the relations prevailing in the economic sphere, other things begin to be regarded as mere commodities, in particular the labourer himself. What we now refer to as 'instrumental relationships' pervade society: the bourgeoisie regards his wife and family as forms of private property, a fact on which Marx and Engels based their critique of the nuclear family. In the free market, *money* assumes a dominant role as the chief means of exchange.

The more production is shaped in such a way that every producer depends on the exchange value of his commodities, the more must *money relationships* develop.[10]

Money becomes omnipotent and has the power to distort all human relationships.

What I have thanks to money . . . is what I, the possessor of the money, am myself . . . I am ugly, but I can buy myself the most beautiful women. Consequently I am not ugly . . . (Money) changes fidelity into infidelity, love into hate, hate into love, virtue into vice.[11]

Individuals and relationships are thus perverted by the 'almighty being', money, and this contributes to the alienation of those living under capitalism.

Apart from these subsidiary distortions, Marx condemns the capitalist system for being fundamentally exploitative, first of all because of the extraction of surplus value from the labourer who is not justly rewarded for the values which he creates, and also because of the manipulation of men's needs by the capitalist (who has to ensure his market) which has the paradoxical result that 'the growth of needs and of the means to satisfy them results in a lack of needs and of means.'[12] Marx's economic analysis was, of course, based on his observations of the English system where capitalism was relatively advanced, but he considered it applicable to all capitalist countries.

The Social Consequences

Marx's political writings employ a different terminology from his economic works. The *bourgeoisie* is the class embodiment of capital, the owners of private property, the proletariat, the propertyless class, that of labour. Class is, for Marx, fundamentally an economic category, determined by an individual's relation to the means of production. His class position determines his ideas and his possibility of action. The *Communist Manifesto* gives a historical account of the emergence of the two classes out of the dying feudal system. The 'elements' of the bourgeoisie were to be found in the burgesses of mediaeval towns, and the modern bourgeoisie 'is itself the product of a long course of development'. As technology advanced and the mode of production changed through the industrial revolution, the bourgeoisie 'called into existence' the proletariat, whose members can only live as long as they sell their labour. As industrialization spread, social relations were brought into harmony with the new state of economic relations. Such changes are not sudden: the bourgeoisie was 'involved in a constant battle', at first with the aristocracy, then with sections of itself and with the bourgeoisie of foreign countries. The fact that the motive force of capitalism is competition actually divides the bourgeoisie internally. 'The separate individuals form a class only insofar as they have to carry on a common battle against another class.'[13] In relation to the proletariat, the bourgeoisie became the dominant class by virtue of its dominant position in the economic process. Like all dominant classes, it gradually creates society in its image, establishing a political and legal system which supports its hegemony. Laws for the maintenance of private property are established, which treat all social relationships as if they were money relationships. Politically, the bourgeoisie becomes the ruling class: 'the executive of the modern State is but a committee for managing the common affairs of the whole bourgeoisie.'[14] Because of the class antagonisms which are implicit in capitalist society, even when they are not expressed, the state develops as an apparatus for the oppression of the proletariat, with its panoply of weapons — the police, the army, and a judicial system devoted to upholding property laws. Again, Marx based his social analysis on the empirical evidence which he gathered in England. But how did he square the fact that England had a democratic form of government with his description of the repressive functions of the state? His view was that democracy purports to reconcile class interests, to create the illusory impression that a parliamentary assembly embodies the will of the people, as if such a unity could exist among irreconcilably opposed interests. The rights which the liberal state bestows on its citizens were all dismissed by Marx as a thinly disguised assertion of bourgeois individualism, egoism, and property rights, and his criticisms will be discussed later in the chapter on liberty and rights.

Not only does the bourgeoisie control all social relationships, it also dominates society at the level of thought. Bourgeois ideology reflects the ascendancy of the bourgeoisie and vindicates capitalism. Marx gave as examples classical economic theory, with its justification of laissez-faire and competition, and the utilitarian ethic which exonerates self-interest as the basis of all action and reflects the profit-maximizing activity of the capitalist. He also considered that Christianity, with its doctrines of humility, earthly poverty, and its assertion of the necessity of social hierarchy, served the interests of the bourgeoisie — although religion had always been 'the opium of the people'. Marx's view of how ideology arises has already been discussed at some length, and need not be recapitulated here. But it must be emphasized that in describing the creation of bourgeois ideology and the bourgeois state, Marx was not putting forward a conspiracy theory, as some critics suggest. Ideas and institutions are produced by the fundamental economic arrangements in society, without anyone necessarily *willing* their appearance. Marx drew a sharp distinction between writers such as Adam Smith, who he thought had attempted to give a theoretical account of the bourgeois economy and those like Bentham, whom he regarded as a mere propagandist and apologist for capitalism. Nor did Marx morally condemn the bourgeoisie or the individual members of that class. His is intended as a non-moral, scientific analysis, and even the *Communist Manifesto*, where his indignation at the capitalist system is most forcefully expressed, admits that the bourgeoisie had made important innovations, and a valuable contribution in dispelling the remnants of feudalism. 'The bourgeoisie, historically, has played a most revolutionary part'. It was simply that its course was run. This is not to say that Marx did not deplore the cruelties and social injustice which resulted from the capitalist system, but he did not blame particular individuals for this, because it would have been in contradiction to his materialist account of the formation of individuals by social conditions to hold them responsible for being born into a certain class or for acting according to the dictates of its position and ideology.

Since the individual's wellbeing is the ultimate materialist standard for judging a society, however, Marx's condemnation of capitalism rested on the bad effects that it had on people — not only on members of the proletariat but also on the bourgeoisie. The impoverishment of workers and the atrocious conditions under which many of them laboured was the cardinal indictment of the system. So also was the perversion of social relations through the prevalence of money relationships and commodity fetishism. In some respects, Marx thought that mankind was worse off under capitalism than it had been under feudalism, despite technological advances. This is made clear in his early writings on alienation, in which he comes closest to Hegel. In ideal circumstances, creative man, the worker, 'appropriates' the external world by his labour, making raw materials into artefacts which are his own. But under capitalism his product, the commodity, is instead appropriated by the capitalist.

The worker relates to the product of his labour as to an alien object . . . The worker puts his life into the object and this means that it no longer belongs to him but to the object.[15]

As a result, the worker is alienated—from himself, from his product, from his fellow men, and from his 'species-being'.[16] The worker objectifies himself in his product, and alienation is the resulting state of mind. But the capitalist suffers as well, for he too has a less than ideal relation to the material world and to his fellows. This echoes the famous 'master and slave' dialectic in Hegel's *Phenomenology of Spirit*, which demonstrates that the master, despite his advantage over the slave, can gain no true satisfaction from his dominance and has an imperfect relationship with other men and with nature.[16] In this sense, capitalism benefits nobody. Alienation is thus a major reason for a moral condemnation of capitalism. Marx's writings on alienation are far closer to those of the German idealists than to the work of psychologists and sociologists who have since developed the notion, and his remarks on alienation should, I think, be interpreted as philosophical or ontological, rather than as an attempt to psychologize.

History and Revolution

Every change in the social order, every revolution in property relations is the essential result of the creation of new productive forces which no longer correspond to the old property relations.[17]

Marx's conviction that revolution would occur in capitalist countries, and that a socialist society would result, is bound up with his theory of history. The *Manifesto* states that 'the history of all hitherto existing society is the history of class struggles' and supports this generalization by delineating the triumph of capitalism over feudalism as the most recent example of full-scale change. The origin of all historical change is economic and technical innovation which changes the mode of production and creates new economic relations: social relations have to adapt to these, more slowly, and this entails a complete change of the socio-political superstructure. Thus, the hierarchical feudal system was dismantled and gradually replaced by the nation-state. History is a dialectical process, in that it proceeds through contradictions: the contradiction between economic and social relations, and the antagonisms between the two major classes which develop in each new historical period. The new form of society which emerges negates and transcends the previous one, while conserving many of its elements.

This is the skeleton of Marx's doctrine, which is often referred to as 'historical materialism' or 'historical determinism'. Marx was not alone in propounding a theory of history: in the eighteenth and nineteenth centuries such theories abounded and most had the tendentious aim of showing that mankind was progressing to ever higher levels. Many of these theories were teleological and conjectured about the final, perfect state of society; for Hegel, this was marked by the self-realization of 'Absolute Spirit' through society. Fourier and Saint-Simon also used theories of history to prove that their versions of socialism constituted higher stages of social development, and the latter influenced Marx considerably despite his repudiation of utopian socialism. But Marx differed from other philosophers of history in several ways. First, he rejected the idea of progress as being an idealist notion. As we have seen, he thought that society could progress materially while it regressed spiritually, so there was no inevitability about humanity's advance towards perfection or happiness. He also abstained from teleology in his account of history, refusing to postulate a final goal: this was in keeping with his dialectical view of society. If every society develops contradictions which must be transcended, there is no end to the process, and to hypothesize that history will one day come to an end and that change will cease is another idealist notion, belied by man's creative nature, which constantly transforms his surroundings. Although Marx did not speculate on what kind of society would supersede socialism, he would not have denied that it, too, would eventually be transcended. Marx regarded his own theory of history as scientific in a way which rival theories were not, because it was founded on the postulate that real, economic changes produced advancement in all other spheres of life in a determinate, predictable way. He accused other philosophers of failing to offer any material causes which would explain the movement from one stage of society to the next. But while abjuring any idealist content, he profited from locating his political ideal, communism, at the next, higher stage in what was undeniably a progressive theory of history. It is, after all, good propaganda to assert that the form of society which you advocate will inevitably develop, and this is the rallying cry of his *Manifesto*.

Revolution is the dynamo of history in Marx's account, and his doctrine of the socialist revolution gave rise to more hopes and fears, perhaps, than any other political theory. We have already seen the economic determinants of revolution: internal and external contradictions in capitalism lead to ever greater pauperization of the workers, which necessitates increasingly severe oppression to stifle their discontent. At the social level, Marx thought that these crises would polarize the two major classes, displacing other, subsidiary classes and forcing them into the proletariat, which will absorb the petit bourgeoisie (small businessmen) and failed capitalists who have been squeezed out by competition. The intelligentsia would, he hoped, side with the proletariat as polarization occurred. These new recruits would increase the degree of self-awareness and solidarity among the proletariat. Thus, the subjective feelings of workers would at last catch up with their objective situation and they would become, subjectively as well as objectively, 'the most revolutionary class'.

Marx did not commit himself to predicting the precise nature of the proletarian revolution or the exact means which would be used to overthrow the bourgeoisie. He countenanced violence, but not in the form of bloodbaths and purges: rather, violence might be a necessary instrument because the bourgeoisie would never relinquish its privileges without a struggle—but revenge is not part of his theory. On the other hand, he speculated that the transition to socialism might come about peacefully in England, the country most ripe for revolution, given that the workers already had representation in parliament. What Marx did predict was the necessary steps which the victorious proletariat would take. The first would be to establish a democracy which will automatically raise the workers, who form the majority, to the status of the ruling class.

The proletariat will use its political supremacy to wrest, by degrees, all capital from the bourgeoisie, to centralise all instruments of production in the hands of the State, *i.e.* of the proletariat organised as the ruling class.[18]

The immediate measures which Marx thought would be 'generally applicable' after any such revolution are worth quoting at length[19]:

(1) Abolition of property in land and application of all rents of land to public purposes.
(2) A heavy progressive or graduated income tax.
(3) Abolition of all right of inheritance.
(4) Confiscation of the property of all emigrants and rebels.
(5) Centralization of credit in the hands of the state, by means of a national bank with state capital and an exclusive monopoly.
(6) Centralization of the means of communication and transport in the hands of the state.
(7) Extension of factories and instruments of production owned by the state . . . .
(8) Equal liability of all to labour. Establishment of industrial armies, especially for agriculture.
(9) Combination of agriculture with manufacturing industries . . . .
(10) Free education for all children in public schools . . . .

What is noticeable is that, although Marx stated the abolition of private property (capital) as the aim and precondition of socialism, this programme does not recommend *instant* expropriation of all capitalists, but suggests a progression towards collective ownership of the means of production which would extend over time and be achieved by heavy income tax and the extension of state ownership. Such a programme could conceivably be implemented by democratic means in a country with universal suffrage, without violent revolution. The gradualist intention is emphasized when Marx continues:

When, *in the course of development,* class distinctions have disappeared . . . the public power will lose its political character. Political power . . . is merely the organised power of one class for oppressing another.[20]

This is another formulation of Marx's belief that the state would 'wither away'.

What would happen to the state after the revolution was made clearer in Marx's criticisms of the programme put forward in 1875 by German socialists. Because they planned to take over the state without radically transforming it, he accused them of treating it 'as an independent entity that possesses its own intellectual, ethical and libertarian bases' (an excusable mistake for those brought up on a diet of Hegel!) and he re-emphasized the oppressive, class nature of the state. A successful revolution would entail 'a political transition period in which the state can be nothing but the revolutionary dictatorship of the proletariat'.[21] The dangers of merely capturing and using the repressive state apparatus were indeed made manifest in the Russian revolution. So Marx was sceptical of the hopes of social-democratic parties of a gradual assumption of power within the existing system.

It is now possible to consider some of the problems of Marx's historical and revolutionary theory, and various criticisms. The major question is how the deterministic and voluntaristic elements of the theory are to be reconciled. The political consequences of maintaining that the revolution would be fully conditioned by economic factors would be quietism, and in fact a section of the Second International maintained that socialists had only to wait for capitalism to collapse of its own accord. Engels outlived Marx and was drawn into the debate after his death. He strove to rebut the charge that Marx was an economic determinist who thought that revolution would arrive automatically, while upholding the doctrine that certain objective economic and political conditions must be realized before the proletariat could create a revolution.

Revolutions are not made deliberately and arbitrarily, but everywhere and at all times they were the essential outcome of circumstances quite independent of the will and the leadership of particular parties and entire classes.

When the conditions are appropriate, revolution is a product of voluntary activity, of men's wills, but these themselves are formed by the context. 'Men make their history themselves, only they do so in a given environment' and often 'what emerges is something that no-one willed'.[22] Engels, elaborating

Marx preserved an important place for individual will and action in the revolution without allowing that revolutions and their outcomes could be attributed to the independent initiatives of individual heroes. Seen thus, Marx's theory is not so deterministic as to enable us to predict when revolution will arrive, although it provides strong pointers as to when it is likely, and enables us to recognize when the conditions for revolution do not exist.

Marx and Engels were often accused of subordinating all aspects of society to the economic in a way which falsified the real workings of society. Engels denied this, maintaining that they held that economic elements were the *ultimate*, but not the *sole*, determinants of history.

The economic situation is the basis, but the various elements of the superstructure (constitutions, legal forms, philosophical theories, etc.) also exercise their influence upon the course of the historical struggles and in many cases preponderate in determining their *form* . . . We make our history ourselves, but, in the first place, under very definite assumptions and conditions. Among these the economic ones are decisive.[23]

So, although primary causes are economic, elements of the superstructure can and do interact and set up other causal networks and can even, Engels admitted, react on the economic base and produce changes there. Those who called Marx an economic determinist were not altogether mistaken, because he emphasized the economic at the expense of the social so as to make his theory more rigorously scientific — political economy being the first major social science. But 'economic determinism' should be viewed as an emphasis rather than a dogma, for Marx did not ignore the complex interactions of the other parts of society.

Various other criticisms can be offered of this part of Marx's theory. The socialist revolution is not strictly analogous to the bourgeois revolution which routed feudalism, because it is caused not by technological progress, but by the exhaustion of an existing economic system. And a socialist revolution will not in one sense transform the *mode* of production, since Marx envisaged that industrialism would continue, but will merely change the ownership of the means of production. So the socialist revolution does not exemplify the paradigm which Marx set up, but he evades this objection by saying that distribution is a 'feature' of the mode of production: so capitalist industrialism is a different mode from socialist production. Some commentators have found it curious that Marx thought that the proletariat, the most fragmented and alienated class, could be the bearers of revolution.[24]

This is a practical rather than a theoretical objection, and pessimism about the workers' capacity and inclination to make the revolution led to Lenin's theory of the vanguard party. Marx's justification of his theory was that, as the major oppressed class under capitalism, and half of the contradictory whole, the proletariat was objectively the revolutionary class, however far it might be, subjectively, from realizing this. Also, Marx did not endorse the idea of a glorious revolution and heroic violence, or the role of charismatic individuals, so the lack of political acumen or personal courage in the worker was irrelevant: the precondition of the revolution was his desperation, not his daring. Of course, Marx expected strong and charismatic leaders to arise, despite the downtrodden state of the majority of workers. His description of the general condition of the class does not entail that each of its members is equally ignorant and oppressed—as those who level this criticism imply. The other major objection to Marx, that his theory has been disproved by the constant failure of his predictions, is discussed in a later section.

Communist Society

Since Marx criticized the utopian socialists for providing blueprints for the future society, an endeavour which he considered idealist in the worst sense, he was reluctant to offer any detailed picture of the communist utopia. But the formal characteristics of communist society are made clear in his works, as are the particular principles on which it would rest. Essentially, communism connotes the abolition of private property, capitalist modes of production and alienated labour. It establishes the appropriation of nature *for man* by contrast with the appropriation of human life by the capitalist. After the exacerbation of class conflict had produced a proletarian revolution, and the revolutionary dictatorship of the proletariat had been established, Marx predicted that communism would develop in two stages. In the first stage, under the revolutionary dictatorship, when the state retains its oppressive nature but is turned against bourgeois counter-revolutionaries, there are still classes and there are still wage labour and a division of labour. But capital will be collectively owned, which changes the mode of production, and a new principle of distribution operates, 'to each according to his contribution'. But, 'in spite of this advance this *equal right* is still constantly stigmatised by a bourgeois limitation' because workers have different skills and talents, so that even when they are paid proportionally to the value of their labour, without exploitation, inequalities occur.[25] Payment will reflect labour time, with small deductions for public facilities and welfare programmes. No surplus value will be extracted.

The second stage, 'higher communism', also referred to by Marx as 'true socialism', is the classless society. Here, the division between mental and physical labour has vanished and nobody has one exclusive sphere of activity, but can become skilled at whatever work he wishes.

Labour has become not only a means of life but life's prime want . . . the springs of co-operative wealth flow more abundantly—only then can the narrow horizon of bourgeois right be crossed in its entirety and society inscribe on its banners: 'From each according to his ability, to each according to his needs'.[26]

Marx's suggestion that after the division of labour had ended man could be a hunter, fisherman, shepherd, and critic all in the same day,[27] although it may represent a dig at the elaborate work schedules of Fourier's utopia, is of interest because here he idealizes non-industrial types of work while elsewhere he suggests that industrial labour will be the basis of communism. In *Grundrisse* he argues that capitalism has provided the conditions for widespread leisure in socialist society because it maximizes surplus value which could then be restored to the labourer.

What is new in capital is that it also increases the surplus labour time of the masses by all artistic and scientific means possible . . . Thus, despite itself, it is instrumental in creating the means of social disposable time, and so in reducing working time for the whole of society to a minimum and thus making everyone's time free for their own development.[28]

So, while communism transcends capitalism, it still preserves valuable capitalist innovations.

Under higher communism the state, representing oppressive (political) power, would wither away, although government would presumably continue to be necessary. What form Marx envisaged this would take may perhaps be deduced from his essay on the Paris Commune of 1870, where he praises the organization set up by the communards. The governing commune was formed of municipal councillors, mainly from the working class, chosen by universal suffrage, responsible to their electors and subject to rapid recall if they displeased them. The commune was both executive and legislative: the protective liberal separation of powers is unnecessary in a truly representative and responsive democracy. Like the councillors, police and other officials were responsible and revocable delegates of the commune, and all received workers' wages, which prevented the development of any hierarchy with vested interests. Marx called the commune an 'expansive' rather than a repressive form of government and he doubtless expected some similar embodiment of popular sovereignty to emerge in a communist society.

Its true secret was this. It was essentially a working-class government, the produce of the struggle of the producing against the appropriating class, the political form at last discovered under which to work out the economic emancipation of labour.[29]

The Marxist ideal of popular sovereignty is often likened to Rousseau's vision of direct democracy, and liberals see both as potentially totalitarian because of the absence of limitations on the government's powers. Marx's reply would be that the 'checks and balances' of representative democracy are unnecessary where accountability is strong and representatives have no special privileges or status. Furthermore, in the classless society of higher communism there would be no conflicting wills which needed to be reconciled by a division of sovereignty: the people would have a unified will.

How ideal would a communist society be for its inhabitants? Marx talks of fulfilment rather than of happiness or utility. Man under communism is a fully developed individual, enjoying many forms of activity, rather than being 'the mere bearer of a particular social function', that is, a specialized worker. He experiences the true freedom only available in a co-operative, communist society. Using Hegelian terms, Marx said that communism accomplishes the appropriation of the human essence by man for man, that it emancipates all man's qualities and senses, and that it achieves the union of man with nature. Man reassumes his species-being as a creative worker in co-operation with his fellows. Alienation, the disease of capitalism, disappears as the proper relationship is restored between the worker and what he produces: although his products are still for the use of others, as they must be with any division of labour, he feels his labour to be socially necessary and valuable in satisfying the needs of others. Like all other socialists who believed in co-operation, Marx assumes (tacitly) that it will fuse the egoistic and altruistic impulses. Since he did not believe in any human nature other than that determined by a particular form of society, he expected—logically enough—that the communist form of organization would eventually produce co-operative man, hardly recognizable as the descendant of competitive, utility-maximizing capitalist man. The dispute between Marxists and those who believe human nature to be irreducibly competitive and greedy cannot be resolved scientifically, perhaps, but the widespread acceptance that environment plays the major part in determining character is at least *prima facie* evidence for Marx's optimism.

Criticizing Marx

This section discusses problems in the theory itself, rather than the 'Marx was wrong' and 'Marx was a totalitarian' lines of argument which are the common responses of many people in the West to his ideas. Arguments between liberals and Marxists are ultimately sterile because their world-views are antagonistic at every point. This is no accident, since Marx saw capitalism as a unified whole, in terms of the intimate relations between all the elements of the structure and superstructure: his doctrine therefore necessarily denied the validity of capitalist economics *and* of capitalist morality, ideology, and politics. The antagonisms, briefly, are as follows: liberal ideology presupposes ultimately harmonizing individual interests, independent and mutually indifferent individuals, the supremacy of the individual, government based on consent, and it advocates maximum privacy, minimal government and the impartial rule of law. Marx would retort that capitalist society rests on irreconcilably antagonistic interests, that men are, even if unwillingly, interdependent and exploiting or exploited, that class is more important politically than the individual and that government is based on force and domination, while all aspects of life are in fact pervaded by politics and ideology. Thus Marx gives a conflictual account of bourgeois society while liberals had a consent or consensus model. Marx's materialism, and in particular the doctrine that man is determined by society and his class position, threatened the fundamental liberal tenet that man is free and rational, able to choose his goals and activities in private isolation. Marx's views on ideology, discussed in Chapter 2, challenge both this and the bourgeois belief that capitalism is a natural, rational, and permanent system. His theory of ideology brands the whole theory of liberal democracy as an ideology, and anticipatorily refutes any reply by claiming to be scientific itself.

Liberalism is based on the empirical method, which claims to attain knowledge through an accumulation of data and the generation of general hypotheses via induction. The empiricist demands visible proof and immediacy in any hypothesis, and rejects Marxism as being 'theoretical', based on *a priori* assumptions about such matters as surplus value, which cannot be empirically verified. Marxists would in turn accuse empiricists of working on the basis of a covert theoretical framework which validates and supports capitalism—of having a surrogate metaphysic.[30] There seems to be no satisfactory way of choosing between these rival theories of knowledge according to their view of what makes a doctrine scientific, for each invalidates the other, just as the Marxist view of politics invalidates the liberal view, and vice versa. Empiricists consider their own system to be open to refutation and say that Marxism is a self-enclosed, self-validating system like some theologies. Certainly, Marxism represents itself as a privileged philosophy, since it can both account for the existence of rival philosophies and refute them. Without a 'higher' theory of knowledge which can comprehend both Marxism and empiricism and measure them against a yardstick of validity outside them both, there seems to be no philosophical way of justifying adherence to one rather than the other: personal preference must operate. But it might be argued that whichever theory can explain most and has the more universal scope should be preferred. These remarks are meant to alert the reader to the insoluble contradictions between opposed ideologies, rather than attempt to resolve them.

However, we may ask why Marx considered his own theory to be scientific, and whether it succeeds according to his own criteria for science. Marx defined his doctrine as scientific socialism by contrast with utopian socialism, which he thought was a rationalist attempt to impose the utopians' brainchildren on the world. Fourier, Owen, and Saint-Simon, he said, had rashly *invented* 'social laws' to explain the necessity of socialism before the 'material conditions for the emancipation of the proletariat had arisen'.[31] They were before their time, and had therefore misunderstood the true nature of class: they dreamt of class unity rather than of the abolition of classes. Marx criticized the utopians for being idealists, belated Enlightenment rationalists who thought that their blueprints could simply be imposed on the world. He also condemned them politically for hampering working-class action by their illusory theories, but at the same time he and Engels admired their critiques of early capitalism and agreed with many of the ideals which they invoked, such as co-operation and distribution according to need.

It was not Marx's view of socialism that differed widely from that of the utopians so much as his conception of how it would come about. He gave a materialist, and therefore 'scientific', account of the transition, while the utopians imagined that socialism could be suddenly inscribed on society, as if on a blank sheet. This is why theory and practice must be seen in relation to each other, in order to check such utopian idealism. In his acknowledgement of the need for a transitional period, the first stage, Marx anticipated Popper's criticism that he, like Plato and other enemies of the 'open society', requires a clean canvas which would entail the purging, banishment or murder of those adhering to the old way of life.[32] The transitional period would be one of gradual habituation to the new way of life: the ideal society was not to be achieved at one, violent, stroke. In relation to liberalism, Marx would maintain that his own theory was more scientific since it gave an accurate account of the economic and social relations of which liberal theory gave a distorted, one-sided picture. It was also more scientific because he provided a theory of history which liberals could not give, since they regarded capitalism as a realized utopia, the culmination of historical progress, a self-perpetuating system. So it is on the basis of his theory's scientific nature and its comprehension of the whole dialectical movement of society and history that Marx asserted its truth against its rival.

The validity of scientific theories is generally held to lie in the success of their predictions. Marx's theory, and his claims for it, are vulnerable in this respect, because many of his predictions failed—which leads his critics to rename them 'prophecies'—and many of his hypotheses now appear not to be applicable. Responses to this vary: liberals are relieved that history has 'disproved' Marx. Popper argues that Marx's theory is not scientific because it has been reinterpreted to explain falsified predictions: a theory which can be stretched to explain *anything* has no explanatory power, the criterion of good science. He said that since Marxism is not falsifiable in principle it could not be scientific. By contrast, Marxists have constantly revised Marx's theory to take account of the changing circumstances which have defeated his predictions, and would still consider it scientific. Some of their revisions are examined in the final part of this chapter. What, then, were the predictions which have failed, and should such failures count as refutations of Marx's theory?

The fact is that capitalism has not yet collapsed even in the countries of Europe which Marx thought most likely to succumb to a proletarian revolution. Paradoxically, most communist revolutions have occurred in countries which were not industrialized and where the peasantry, which Marx did not see as a revolutionary class, preponderated: Russia, China, Cuba, and Indochina. Furthermore, capitalism, in moving towards monopoly capitalism as he predicted, has raised the standard of living of the workers in a way which he did not envisage. Despite the current world depression, the degree of affluence achieved in the West in the postwar period is unprecedented. Does this constitute a refutation of Marx's predictions, and hence of his whole theory? First, it must be remembered that Marx set no time limit to his predictions, even though he worked for their fulfilment in his own lifetime. It can reasonably be argued that a prediction not yet fulfilled is different from a prediction refuted, and Marxists would argue that the preconditions for revolution do not yet obtain in the capitalist world, although there are increasingly indicators of a general crisis. Marx himself refined his basic theory in many ways, enumerating the exogenous factors which might postpone the final crisis. The danger of saturated markets, for example, could be staved off as capitalism created new needs and hence new markets. The bourgeoisie was renowned for its inventiveness, and would create new industries with higher rates of profit as old industries declined. The growth of the computer and micro-chip industries, simultaneously with the decline of heavy industries like steel and coal, provide one current example. On the other hand, the ability of highly automated industries to produce high rates of profit calls into question his stipulation that surplus value is only created by labour, which entails that capital-intensive industries would have low rates of profit.

The demise of the individual capitalist entrepreneur and the wide dispersal of capital also seem to threaten Marx's basic assumptions. If workers own shares, or participate in profit-sharing schemes, can the class distinction between capitalist and worker be maintained? From a purist viewpoint it can, since the profit-sharing worker still does not *own* the means of production: his bonus could be regarded as a hostage given to fortune by the capitalist, as can other features of modern society which mitigate the exploitation of the proletariat, such as the welfare state. What Marxists have to admit, however, is that the new, paternalistic capitalism, together with ideological and super-structural elements, have prevented impoverishment and the sharp polarization of classes which Marx predicted. But the non-fulfilment of his prediction is explicable in Marxist terms and is not an outright indictment of his theory. There is also the possibility that Marxism is a self-defeating theory, since capitalists have recognized their enemy in it and taken steps to protect themselves: many social theories run this risk. Undoubtedly, had Marx lived for another hundred years, he would have refined his own theory in many respects to explain modern developments. It may even be that the ruling class's ideological strength and capitalism's capacity for innovation will enable it to postpone a socialist revolution indefinitely, so that social change will eventually take an entirely different form. And those who pin their hopes for the demise of capitalism on the exhaustion of natural resources may well be misled, since that would probably cause a universal calamity, eliminating class differences and leading to a quite different kind of revolution.

The judgement that Marx's theory is scientific, then, is best seen as a claim made at a time when most social theories were not scientific, and made partly with the tactical aim of gaining more credence for it. While much of his theory of history is as idealist as the rival theories which Marx rejected, his material-ism and the sophistication of his economic theory give him a claim to be as scientific a political economist as any, given that social science can never attain to the certainty and universality of the natural sciences. His theory of politics and revolution is more of an optimistic codicil, tacked on to the theory of history which makes many valid points about conflict and change in society, but which must be taken as less scientific than his economics. As a political theorist, Marx deserves respect for the precision of his analysis, which makes his theory systematic if not *per se* scientific. Many English readers find Marx indigestible in translation, but this is partly because he used terms in a precise, technical way and coined new words which have a strange ring to us. An example is his use of the word 'class' to describe categories of people according to their role in the productive process. Our uses of the word today are many and diverse: it can signify status, prestige, income group or occupation group, and sociologists use the term in a way which cuts across economic categories. Someone who is in Marx's sense a worker, might still have a high status and income and identify entirely with bourgeois values, and vote Conservative, as do approximately one-third of the working population here. Marx would say that such a person was still exploited however much this was alleviated by superstructural elements. His idea of class must not therefore be assimilated to our own.

Ultimately, the force of Marx's theory rests on the precision of his theoretical terms, which is why one must adopt his language and use an abundance of quotations to represent his theory adequately. Attempts to paraphrase Marx usually end in disaster. If we summarized his theory as 'Marx said that history was a series of struggles between the oppressors and the oppressed', we lose the sense of a *class* struggle which relates social conflict to the economic basis, and end up with something like Bakunin's theory which was based on sentiment, on his identification with the oppressed, rather than on analysis. Marx's claim to be objective, to describe the dialectics of society from a position outside the two major classes, also bolsters his claim to be scientific, although this claim is the easiest point of attack for his critics. But if Marx's ideas, like everyone else's, were determined by his class position, how could he be objective? This apparent inconsistency had probably not escaped Marx himself. As was said earlier, his hypothesis that men are determined by their class position does not state that they are *fully* determined. Their different experiences and, in the case of intellectuals like Marx, their relative social mobility and freedom to criticize, as well as natural differences of intelligence, allow individuals to produce transcendent theories which are not mere re-assertions of ideology but are what Mannheim calls *utopias*. And this fact does not prevent Marx's hypotheses holding good for a class as a whole, even where individuals, like Marx himself, elude them.

Marx's scientificity or otherwise is part of a wider controversy about the nature of social science: even the certainty and objectivity of the natural sciences is widely questioned today, by writers such as Kuhn and Feyerabend. Therefore no conclusive answer as to whether he was scientific is likely to be forthcoming, although dogmatic Marxists still make 'Marxism' and 'science' synonymous. It is more rational to adhere to Marxism because it coincides with one's convictions, or because of its potential for bringing about social change, than because of its scientific standing.

The Evolution of Marxism

This section deals with the major modifications of Marx's theory which aim to adapt it to changes in the capitalist system and developments in the third world. There is unfortunately no space to deal here with the large corpus of academic literature on Marxism which has appeared in the last few decades, but some references are included in the bibliography. Lenin's major contributions to Marxist theory were made in the context of the quarrels of the Second International and the objective unreadiness of Russia for a socialist revolution. In reply to socialists who advocated an evolutionary or gradualist approach towards socialism, such as Bernstein and Kautsky, Lenin emphasized the need for an act of will to create the revolution, for voluntarism rather than determinism. He argued that a revolutionary vanguard party was needed, with a proper understanding of theory, to initiate a revolution in the absence of a politically aware proletariat — or, in Russia's case, to lead what was only an embryonic working class. He advocated a small, secret party of professional revolutionaries: secrecy was essential in the Russian police state. Lukacs characterized Leninism as a 'double break' with the mechanistic theory of revolution espoused by some Marxists. Revolution was no longer seen as an automatic outcome of economic events, and workers' consciousness was not expected to arise spontaneously: the party would engineer this. This was, of course, Lenin's own achievement as leader of the Bolshevik party. This enhancement of the role of the vanguard party was strongly condemned by Rosa Luxemburg. She believed that direct, independent action by the mass was a necessary part of the class struggle: she anticipated and criticized the centralism and elitism which Leninism did in fact bring about in the USSR.

Lenin also allocated a revolutionary role to the peasantry, which Marx had believed to be an essentially conservative class, a remnant of feudalism irrelevant to the socialist struggle, despite its exploitation by landlords. Lenin's espousal of the Russian peasants appears to be opportunistic rather than the result of a theoretical revelation about their importance; in the event, the peasants rapidly defected from the Bolshevik cause when their demands for land had been met. Lenin restated the importance of the state, transformed into a revolutionary dictatorship, in the first stage of communism, when it would become an instrument for the oppression of the ex-bourgeoisie, but he also issued prophetic warnings about the need for some form of state. Dreams of abolishing management are utopian, and 'serve to put off the socialist revolution . . . until human nature is different', whereas, 'human nature itself cannot do without subordination, without managers and clerks.' Lenin did not believe that the state, or some similar apparatus, could wither away entirely.

Most of Lenin's additions to Marxism were the result of adapting the theory to circumstances, and his theoretical account of imperialism was no exception. Imperialism, 'the highest form of capitalism', was a new form of monopoly capitalism in which the advanced countries plundered the less developed by exporting capital and setting up industries, usually for the extraction of natural resources, which yielded superprofits.

Out of such *superprofits* . . . it is possible to bribe the labour leaders (at home) and the upper stratum of the labour aristocracy.[33]

The capitalist countries had developed unevenly, some industrializing faster than others, and these variations were intensified by colonization. Lenin was clearly thinking of the 'race for Africa'. Hence, he argued that imperialist wars for the redistribution of the spoils would occur, rendering the system highly unstable, and eventually destroying it. Since he wrote *Imperialism* in the middle of the First World War, these observations could be regarded as political commentary rather than theory, but it adds an important international dimension to Marxist thought.

Other leading Bolsheviks shared Lenin's view on the interdependence of capitalist countries, which led to the cheering conclusion that when the system began to collapse, revolution would be universal. Even in 1906, Trotsky was arguing that the Russian proletariat would carry revolution into Europe, first to Germany and Poland. But in 1924, in the face of the failure of the German workers' uprising of 1917 and the retrenchment and opposition of capitalist countries to the USSR, Stalin propounded the doctrine of 'socialism in one country', to explain and justify Russia's position as a communist enclave in a hostile world. This in effect denied the necessity of world revolution and asserted that a self-sufficient communist country could still develop satisfactorily. Trotsky refuted Stalin's argument in *Permanent Revolution*, which reasserted the inevitability of world revolution. He said that there were three senses in which the revolution must be 'permanent'. First, the proletariat, once in power, could not stop after a bourgeois democratic revolution had given workers a majority voice — here, he referred to the liberal regime set up in Russia after the first revolution of 1917 — but must in turn destroy this illusion of democracy.

It (the proletariat) must adopt the tactics of *permanent revolution*, i.e., must destroy the barriers between the minimum and maximum programme of Social Democracy, go over to more and more radical reforms and seek direct and immediate support in revolution in Western Europe.[34]

Backward countries, Trotsky added, would achieve socialism via dictatorship, circumventing the bourgeois democratic revolution. Second, revolution must become world-wide. For an isolated country such as Russia

The way out lies only in the victory of the proletariat of the advanced countries . . . a national revolution is not a self-contained whole, only a link in the international chain.[35]

This *ad hominem* contention did not endear Trotsky to Stalin. Finally, socialist society must be self-revolutionizing, and initiate technical and social innovations:

it was not to be regarded as the terminus of history. Society constantly changes its skin, 'therein lies the permanent character of the socialist revolution as such'.

This latter part of Trotsky's doctrine, directed against the ossification of the Bolshevik regime under Stalin, could well be cited as a justification of Mao Tse Tung's 'cultural revolution' which was aimed against the entrenchment of the party bureaucracy. Trotsky claimed to have been aware of the dangers of bureaucracy from the very start of the Bolshevik revolution, and in *The Revolution Betrayed* (1937), he criticized the hierarchical structure of the party and the 'caste system' established by Stalin which was antithetical to egalitarian socialism. He characterized the Soviet system as 'state capitalism', a label now widely accepted. State capitalism signifies an exploitative mode of production in which surplus value is still taken from workers by the state, which becomes increasingly unlikely to wither away because of its dominant role in the economy. Marx had acknowledged that collective ownership of the means of production would entail some centralization, but had not conceived of the state as becoming the new exploiter.

What Trotsky himself referred to as the 'sin of Trotskyism' has become a major focus of attention in England today. The main reason for the revival of Trotskyism is that many European Marxists who felt that the established communist parties were discredited by their implication in Russia's invasion of Hungary in 1956, turned to Trotskyist groups, as did those who eschewed the sin of Stalinism. It is not altogether clear what Trotskyism represents to its diverse supporters, beyond a rejection of Soviet state capitalism and bureaucracy, and a commitment to international revolution. Among the various groups, some are intellectual and elitist, others are 'workerist', dedicated to involving workers in the economic and political struggle, while others are reputed to be engaged in 'entryism', the infiltration of social-democratic parties, such as the Labour Party in Britain. What is clear is that contemporary Trotskyism has a strong appeal for left-wingers critical of the USSR, but no single identifiable theoretical position, except its critique of that system as state capitalism, and as a deviation from Marx's ideal.

The problem for Marxists in the West has been to modify his theory to explain the continued strength of capitalism and the lack of revolutionary enthusiasm among the working class. Symptomatic of this is the predominance of social-democratic parties which generally uphold the capitalist system. Many influential theories about this have been developed, of which only a few can be mentioned here. The theoretician of the French Communist Party, Althusser, has offered an account of 'ideological state apparatuses' which develop their own independent momentum and support the system, including trade unions.[36] This helps to explain the persistence of the system even in bad times. The Frankfurt School, which developed in the thirties in Germany, a dangerous climate for Marxists, has offered a subtle analysis of advanced monopoly capitalism. Habermas gives an important account of how knowledge is 'manufactured' to support the system.[37] Among the Frankfurt School, the best-known philosopher is probably Marcuse. As a response to 'embourgeoisement', the assimilation of workers to the bourgeois system and their adoption of bourgeois values in a time of relative affluence, he discarded the working class as a revolutionary force and looked to the 'New Opposition', the oppressed everywhere. These include students, intellectuals, oppressed ethnic groups, and the inhabitants of the third world. The puzzle is how such diverse groups could develop sufficient sense of solidarity to become a revolutionary force. But it is certainly true that the interests of the Western proletariat are opposed to those of workers in the third world, since their affluence depends on the latters' poverty, a view which has led some Marxists to see exploitation as a global phenomenon, existing between countries as well as between classes. Marcuse has analysed the new superstructural mechanisms whereby advanced capitalism defends itself, including repressive tolerance and perversion of language to prevent the development of criticism. He advocates the 'Great Refusal', the destruction of all the institutions of repressive society.[38] Marcuse's use of Hegelian and Freudian ideas make him a highly unorthodox Marxist, but one who achieved widespread credence after the events of 1968 in France, especially among students. For such Marxists as Marcuse, the problem is that the objective conditions for revolution have failed to materialize and so therefore has the subjective condition, the development of class consciousness. The proposed solution is a return to theory and a drive to win intellectual converts from all classes. Finally, we must note that even established communist parties in the West have tacitly acknowledged the need to modify Marxism–Leninism by their recent decisions to abandon the doctrine of the dictatorship of the proletariat, and to declare their acceptance of the parliamentary road to socialism. As with so many other developments in Marxism, it is debatable whether 'Eurocommunism' is a tactical decision or a genuine theoretical innovation.

The problems facing Marxists in the third world are, needless to say, altogether different. Marxist parties have everywhere been associated with nationalism and the struggle against colonialism and revolutionary theories have been developed to direct these endeavours. In most such countries the proletariat is small or non-existent and the peasants constitute the main oppressed class, which has two enemies to fight, the capitalist countries and the 'national bourgeoisie', the indigenous ally of the imperialists which advances its own interests by fostering neo-colonialism, a form of capitalism which rests on the export of capital, often disguised as 'aid' to developing countries. With reference to Algeria, Fanon developed a theory of revolution resting on the peasants and the *lumpenproletariat* (the 'dregs of society' and the criminal classes); he also, unlike Marx, emphasized the need for violence, which would enable the colonized peoples to purge themselves of the humiliation of their experience.[39] Drawing on the guerilla war waged by Che Guevara in Bolivia, Debray adapted Marxism to the situation in Latin America where there is no direct colonization and the oppressors are the military and, indirectly, the USA. Again, the peasants are seen by Debray as the potentially revolutionary class, and the tactics recommended are those of guerilla warfare. The revolutionary vanguard consists of guerillas operating from the countryside, winning over the peasants to their cause and acting independently of political parties, although such parties may arise as a result of their success. Debray indicts the established, urban communist parties which hindered rather than aided the efforts of Guevara.[40] Again, this seems like a guerilla's manual rather than a political theory. The way that communism is viewed in third-world countries varies considerably. Sometimes, when independence has been achieved, the revolutionary party is revealed to be more nationalist than Marxist. As Chapter 5 suggests, leading African socialists have disputed the relevance of Marxism and the European experience to the creation of socialism on the African continent. However, many of them turn to China for aid and advice, feeling the Chinese version of socialism to be nearer to their own than that of the Soviets.

Mao Tse Tung is inseparably associated with the Chinese revolution, even if his achievements are at present being undone and his memory effaced. His voluminous writings, like those of Lenin, offer both tactical advice and theoretical innovations. To chart the various divagations of Chinese policy with respect to Moscow and the West would be a lengthy task: here we need only note the main points of Mao's revolutionary theory. His own revolution was anti-colonial and nationalistic; he viewed it as a class struggle with the peasants as the revolutionary class. In the absence of an industrial proletariat and of the economic conditions which Marx saw as essential to revolution, Mao expounded a doctrine of revolution which was emphatically voluntaristic, writing that 'the people of China are poor and blank', but have the will to make a revolution. It is the man who *wills*, rather than the man who *knows*, who is the true revolutionary. Mao's party therefore always differed greatly from Lenin's group of informed theoreticians and he strove to prevent an entrenchment of the Chinese Communist Party like that in the USSR. At the time of the cultural revolution (1965 onwards), he divorced himself from the party apparatus and appealed over the head of the party directly to the people. The cultural revolution was intended to remove possible sources of stratification in society by destroying respect for the standing of party members, or for experts, for Mao maintained that political authority lay in the mass.[41] Evidently, this is a very different form of socialism from that practised in the USSR, despite their common theoretical origins.

In general the nationalist emphasis of third-world communism and the non-capitalist conditions in which it is created differentiate all these varieties of communism from that proposed by Marx. Their nationalism need not conflict with the theoretically internationalist aspect of Marxism, but it does entail a view of the revolution analogous to that of Stalin: 'socialism in one country'. Likewise, the achievement of communism in a predominantly peasant country entails a different socialist mode of production from that which industrialized socialist countries would establish, such as the system of agricultural communes in China. The opportunities for leisure and self-development which capitalism establishes, according to Marx, do not exist in such countries. One possible response to this is to industrialize rapidly, so as to 'overtake' capitalism — a mistake made by many emergent third-world states.

Revisionism or Recantation?

The Marxists whose amendations of Marx's theory have just been discussed were essentially commenting on the conditions which they faced at particular times —so was Marx. This in itself suggests that his theory, however self-sufficient, scientific, and universal he claimed it to be, should not be treated as an authoritative text any revision of which constitutes heresy. This in turn suggests that a would-be Marxist is not obliged to adopt Marx's theory in its entirety, but may adapt or omit aspects of it without rendering what he does accept false because of its incompleteness. No doubt this suggestion that we can accept Marxism partially would be anathema to theorists in the USSR, the self-appointed guardians of 'pure' Marxism, or to communist party members elsewhere. But it is sheer dogmatism to claim that a theory which boasts of its basis in material circumstances should not be adapted to changing material conditions. What may be suspected to underlie disputes about the purity of Marxism is a feeling that 'mine are revisions, yours are heresies'—an authoritarian attitude to be avoided at all costs if Marxism is to remain a living political force. Perhaps Marx himself should have the last word on this: 'All I know is that I am not a Marxist.'[42]

If it is accepted that revision does not constitute an abandonment or a diminution of the central truths of Marx's theory, Marxists are spared a lot of agonizing about what is the proper course of action in certain cases. For example, there is a continuing controversy as to whether all countries must undergo a bourgeois-democratic revolution before a communist revolution is possible, since this was the historical sequence which Marx described—with the particular examples of England, France, and Germany in mind. If his theory is regarded as a persuasive set of extrapolations from recent history rather than as a set of necessary truths, such controversies can be avoided and anomalous events need not be reinterpreted to fit Marx's categories. If it were accepted by Marxists themselves that Marxism does not constitute a watertight, self-sufficient doctrine, eternally opposed to every point of liberal ideology, their chance of convincing others that it is in many respects true would be enhanced.

Notes

1. See McLellan's introduction to his translation of Marx's *Grundrisse*, Harper & Row, 1971, pp. 1–15 and his introduction to Marx's *Early Texts*, Blackwell, 1972, pp. ix–xliii.
2. G. Novack, *The Logic of Marxism*, Pathfinder Press, 1971.
3. I. Berlin, *Karl Marx*, Home University Library, 1939.
4. The major discussion of the material causes of consciousness appears in K. Marx and F. Engels, *The German Ideology* in *Selected Works*, Progress Publishers, 1969, Vol. I.
5. Marx and Engels, *The German Ideology*, p. 20.
6. Marx, *Early Texts*, p. 140.
7. Marx, *Grundrisse*, p. 104.
8. Marx and Engels, *The Holy Family,* Progress Publishers, 1956, p. 51.

9. Marx, *Capital* (trans. G. D. H. Cole), Dent, London, 1972, pp. 45–6.
10. Marx, *Grundrisse*, p. 60.
11. Marx, *Early Texts*, p. 180.
12. The paradoxes of capitalism are set out in the *Early Texts*, pp. 134–7. Needs are discussed in the *German Ideology*, pp. 30–1.
13. Marx and Engels, *German Ideology*, p. 65.
14. Marx and Engels, *The Manifesto of the Communist Party* in *Selected Works*, Vol. I, pp. 110–11. To be referred to hereafter as *Communist Manifesto*.
15. Marx, *Early Texts*, p. 135.
16. Marx, *Early Texts*, pp. 137–41.
17. The materialist view of history is discussed in Marx's *Contribution to the Critique of Political Economy* and in *The German Ideology*.
18. Marx and Engels, *Communist Manifesto*, p. 126.
19. Marx and Engels, *Communist Manifesto*, pp. 126–7.
20. Marx and Engels, *Communist Manifesto,* p. 127. Emphasis added.
21. Marx, *Critique of the Gotha Programme* in *Marx and Engels: Basic Writings* (ed. L. Feuer), Doubleday-Anchor, 1959, p. 127.
22. Engels, *Letters* in Feuer (Ed.), pp. 399, 411.
23. Engels, *Letters* in Feuer (Ed.), p. 398.
24. J. P. Plamenatz, *Karl Marx's Philosophy of Man*, Clarendon Press, Oxford, 1975, p. 13.
25. Marx, *Critique of the Gotha Programme,* pp. 118–9.
26. Marx, *Critique of the Gotha Programme*, p. 119.
27. Marx and Engels, *The German Ideology*, p. 36.
28. Marx, *Grundrisse*, p. 144.
29. Marx, *The Civil War in France* in *Selected Works,* Vol. II, p. 223.
30. See, e.g., R. Blackburn (Ed.), *Ideology in Social Science*, Fontana/Collins, 1972.
31. Marx and Engels, *Communist Manifesto*, pp. 134–6.
32. K. Popper, *The Open Society and Its Enemies*, Routledge & Kegan Paul, London, 1962, Vol. 1, pp. 157–68.
33. V. I. Lenin, *Imperialism, The Highest Stage of Capitalism* in *Collected Works*, Progress Publishers, 1960–70, Vol. 22, p. 281.
34. L. Trotsky, *Results and Prospects* and *Permanent Revolution,* Pathfinder Press, 1969. Introduction to first Russian edn.
35. Trotsky, *Results and Prospects* and *Permanent Revolution.* See Engels' earlier statement of the need for world revolution in *Principles of Communism* in *Selected Works*, Vol. I, pp. 92–3.
36. L. Althusser, *Lenin and Philosophy* (trans. B. Brewster), New Left Books, 1977, pp. 122–73.
37. J. Habermas, *Knowledge and Human Interests* (trans. J. Shapiro), Heinemann, London, 1972. See too M. Jay, *The Dialectical Imagination*, Heinemann, London, 1973.
38. H. Marcuse, *An Essay on Liberation*, Penguin, 1969.
39. F. Fanon, *The Wretched of the Earth* (trans. C. Farrington), Penguin, 1967, p. 74.
40. R. Debray, *Revolution in the Revolution?* (trans. B. Ortiz), Monthly Review Press, 1967.
41. S. Schram, *The Political Thought of Mao Tse Tung*, Penguin, 1969.
42. Engels, *Letters*, in Feuer (Ed.), p. 396.

Further reading

It is important to read Marx's own texts: in particular, *Early Writings, The German Ideology, The Communist Manifesto, The Critique of the Gotha Programme,* and

Contribution to the Critique of Political Economy. There is no shortage of secondary works. For introductory purposes, the following are recommended:

D. McLellan, *The Thought of Karl Marx,* 2nd edn, Macmillan, Basingstoke, 1980.

G. Lichtheim, *Marxism*, Routledge & Kegan Paul, London, 1961.

D. McLellan, *Marxism After Marx*, Macmillan, Basingstoke, 1979.

S. Avineri, *The Social and Political Thought of Karl Marx,* Cambridge University Press, Cambridge, 1970.

P. Anderson, *Considerations on Western Marxism,* New Left Books, 1976.

CHAPTER 5

Socialism

For many people in the West, socialism, Marxism, and communism are synonymous. But to classify them together ignores the many theoretical differences between the three doctrines, and the constant disputes about political practice which take place within 'the left'. To expose these important differences more clearly, I shall treat socialism as the genus of which Marxism is a major species, and anarchism another. As the title of Engels' book, *Socialism: Utopian and Scientific*, implies, he and Marx were aware that they formed only part of a wider movement whose origins could be traced back to the French Revolution and the utopianism which ensued, although the term 'socialist' was probably first used in 1830 by a Saint-Simonian journalist, Pierre Leroux. And English socialists are apt to trace their lineage even further back, to the Diggers and Levellers of the Civil War period.[1] Ethically, some forms of socialism spring from a Christian impulse, others from atheistic humanism. So, even more than liberalism, socialism is an amalgam of philosophies springing from diverse social movements, which consequently presents certain difficulties of definition.

Despite this, attempts have been made to define the 'essence' of socialism so as to give the ideology a unity and uniformity which it otherwise seems to lack. The penalty of such attempts is to reduce its many contours to a single dimension. For example, Caute in *The Left in Europe* argues that popular sovereignty (rule by all the people) is the doctrine which most typifies the left, distinguishing it from both liberals and conservatives. He regards it as both a means and an end. 'The notion of self-government is a single manifestation, albeit a primary one, of a wider, egalitarian impulse'.[2] But surely Caute undermines his own argument here, by taking equality as the more comprehensive principle and, by implication, viewing self-government as a *means* to that. And although the French revolutionaries gave the notion a special nuance, allying it to Rousseau's idea of the General Will, the idea of government by and for the people had been advocated already by Locke and instantiated in the American Constitution, without any other trace of socialist principles. Durkheim offered what became a classic definition of socialism as all doctrines which 'demand the connection of all economic functions . . . to the directing and conscious centres of society'.[3] Clearly, this definition again takes just a *means* of achieving socialism to be its major goal and suggests no other reason for the choice of that goal, which might merely be chosen for the sake of efficiency. Durkheim relies too heavily on Saint-Simon's technocratic theory and takes no account of the rival demands for non-centralized and even non-industrialized socialist systems. His definition does not convey the values of socialism, only one of its possible forms.

These reductive definitions rely too heavily on the obsession of particular luminaries of the early socialist movement, and fail to indicate the breadth of the socialist ideal, because they search for a single essence. By contrast, a deliberately pluralist approach is offered by Berki, who finds four basic 'tendencies' in socialist ideology: egalitarianism, moralism, rationalism, and libertarianism.[4] According to which tendency is uppermost, socialist doctrine will vary in its choice of methods. Berki goes on to identify each tendency with a major strand of modern socialism. Social democracy in the West rests heavily on moralism, communism in the Eastern bloc emphasizes rationalism; the third-world socialists pin their hopes on egalitarianism, while the contemporary New Left is fundamentally libertarian. While Berki's approach is helpful in accounting for the differing developments of socialist movements, it does not adequately convey the fundamental philosophical coherence of the ideology. In trying to demonstrate and explain this unity, it is best to follow Cole's modest but eclectic approach to the subject: 'the most that can be attempted . . . is the discovery of a central core of meaning.'[5] The next section illustrates the idealism and coherence of this central core.

The Nucleus of Socialism

It really is impossible to understand either the French revolution or the early socialists unless one possesses some awareness of the challenge which the new liberal individualism represented to older ways of life.[6]

Socialism began as a revolt against capitalism and its conception of man and society was initially developed as an alternative to the one which in the socialist view under-lay and reinforced capitalist society.[7]

As these quotations suggest, socialism cannot be analysed apart from the liberal ideas which it sought to combat, and which have already been reviewed. Many conservative thinkers likewise opposed the social and political developments of early capitalism, but they did so by trying to reinstate feudal or paternalistic values, as did Disraeli in his novel, *Sybil*.[8] By contrast, socialists wished to transcend, not to reverse, the tendencies of the new order, even if their ideas sometimes appear as outright negations of liberal values. Socialist doctrine in the West must always be examined with liberalism and capitalism in mind although, as we shall see, African socialism took a different path, having no such tradition with which to contend. In the account which follows of the major elements of socialist doctrine, it is evident that one socialist ideal rests on another, and all flow from the original perception of the evils of capitalism. Taken together, they form a complete social philosophy, which will now be examined point by point.

(1) The concern with poverty

Poverty is seen by socialists as the root cause of oppression, and as a form of direct oppression itself. The utopian socialist, Fourier, in an analysis much admired by Engels[9], proclaimed 'Poverty is the principal cause of social disorders'. For him, the paradox of capitalism was that workers could not afford to buy what they produced, and that 'an excess of work brings them to poverty as does excessive idleness'.[10] Others shared this perception who, like Fourier, blamed the system as a whole for manufacturing poverty and demanded its total abolition. In the nineteenth century, *absolute* deprivation was the worst evil, forcing people into crime, prostitution, and the workhouse. With the recent precarious affluence in the West, socialists have changed the object of their concern to *relative* deprivation[11]: the million or so people in Britain below the 'absolute' poverty line remain a matter of concern, but it is the great differentials or relativities of wealth and income that most clearly indicate the injustices of our society. Five per cent of the population owns 95 per cent of the wealth, and so on—these are familiar statistics that have changed remarkably little since Marx wrote. However, when we turn to the third world, it is still absolute deprivation that is the focus of socialist demands. The socialist's indignation about poverty may originate as an emotion but is soon converted into the political ideal of egalitarianism. Other ideologies cope with the phenomenon of poverty quite differently. The almost fatalistic Christian approach (similar to that of some other religions such as Hinduism) which appears to influence the conservative view, considers that poverty provides the 'deserving poor' with the opportunity for spiritual development in adversity and the rich with the chance of doing good works. Socialism is closer to so called 'primitive Christianity', with its communistic outlook. Extreme liberals take another view: Spencer's social Darwinist approach led him to argue that 'the undeserving poor' should be winnowed out in obedience to the universal law of nature 'that a creature not energetic enough to maintain itself must die'.[12] While liberal humanists would deplore such a savage sentiment, it nevertheless reflects a philosophical tenet of liberalism, that wealth is the reward for merit or desert. And although no politician today would dare to voice such ideas as Spencer's about the treatment of individuals, those who believe in monetarism apparently hope to see the winnowing-out process at work in the economy, with inevitable ill-effects for particular individuals. The evils of property are not, then, self-evident, because certain ideologies view it as a useful mechanism.

Therefore the socialist attack constitutes a distinctive starting point for social analysis.

(2) A class analysis of society

This follows from the perception of poverty, although not in the case of all socialists. Marx's major objection to the utopian socialists Fourier, Owen, and Saint-Simon was that they had failed to understand the class basis of society[13], and his own theory of class has been discussed in Chapter 4. Class analysis adds a new dimension to socialist egalitarianism, which demands the abolition of classes as well as the equalizing of incomes: it also suggests that the transition to socialism may entail violence. But not all socialists acknowledge the need for class analysis or for the class struggle which Marxists predict. Today, some blame the system as a whole—the system of international finance capitalism of which individual capitalists are just as much the victims as workers. The sociologists' sliding scale of classes (which merely labels people by their income group in most cases) has helped to dilute the Marxist analysis of class according to economic and productive categories, and to reduce its political importance. Typically, social-democratic parties have shown reluctance to rock the boat by provoking class tensions. The decision to omit the class struggle from one's political analysis may thus be dictated by philosophical or by policy considerations. Certainly, not all class-aware socialists follow Marx's account of the class division between bourgeoisie and proletariat: Bakunin, an anarchist who shared many socialist ideals, perceived a broader division stretching back across history between the oppressors and the oppressed and later Marxists have re-defined class categories to suit the context—a recent effort being Marcuse's vision of students, blacks, and third-world workers as the new revolutionary class.[14]

(3) Egalitarianism

This is the central ideal of socialists, inseparable from their view of social justice. The socialist achievement is to have extended the notion of justice from the legal and political into the economic and social sphere. The socialist idea of what constitutes equality moved from Babeuf's proclamation of the complete, literal equality of human beings which entailed uniform treatment to the Saint-Simonian notion of a differential equality of treatment, 'from each according to his capacity, to each according to his works', then to the Marxist ideal, 'from each according to his ability, to each according to his needs'. Equality need not entail levelling down and uniformity, as critics suggest; even the early socialists such as Fourier and Saint-Simon depicted ideal societies which accommodated natural differences of talent and temperament within an egalitarian framework. Utopian socialists also hoped for a situation of abundance in which all genuine needs could be satisfied non-competitively, although this provoked disbelief. The British social security system is (or was) an example, however imperfect, of the socialist idea of the satisfaction of basic needs in a non-competitive context.

The vision of equality contrasts with the liberal doctrine of *equality of opportunity*, which implies the opportunity to compete for scarce resources in a zero-sum game where one man's gain is necessarily another's loss, although liberals argue that the system taken as a whole increases *everyone's* prosperity. The conservative vision of a natural hierarchy of status and ability also militates against the egalitarian ethic. The demand for equality follows from the socialist perception of poverty as a remediable problem rather than as the divinely decreed or well deserved state of some unfortunate or inadequate individuals: the call for the abolition of classes is a further important dimension of the ideal for some socialists, and is the most controversial political consequence of egalitarianism. As a result of this ideal of equality, social justice is seen as primarily a matter of distribution, although, as the 'from each' clause of Marx's famous maxim suggests, it also embraces contribution and the productive process and requires a fair allocation of work.

(4) Communal ownership of the means of production

Although previous thinkers — Plato, More, Owen, and Babeuf, for example — attacked the evils of 'private property', Marx analysed the term most precisely. For him, it meant the means of production, productive assets, the ownership of which placed an individual in the bourgeois class and enabled him to employ workers and extract profits from the process of production. Equality could not come about without the abolition of private property, which was synonymous with the abolition of the bourgeoisie. Even without so precise an economic definition of class and property, socialists everywhere demanded the abolition of private wealth, but the virtue of the Marxist account is that it makes it clear that socialism only entails the expropriation of productive assets, not of everybody's favourite personal possessions — a misinterpretation which has cost socialism dear in political terms.

The positive corollary of the elimination of private property is the collective or communal ownership of the means of production — factories, land, machinery, and so on. There are exceptions: Fourier believed that private property would survive, but in such a way that its tendency to accumulate and its harmful social side-effects no longer operated, while for Proudhon the ownership of land and tools by each peasant was the goal. The meaning of 'communal ownership' was the subject of fierce disagreement between Marxists and anarchists in the Second International (1869). The latter feared that local and national institutions would have to be set up to administer it, and that the state which they detested would thus be reinstated. Anarcho-communists like Kropotkin advocated the ownership by each local village producer group of its machinery, factories, and land. Durkheim's description of Saint-Simonian socialism, 'the connection of all economic functions to the directing and conscious centres of society', foreshadowed state capitalism such as now exists in the USSR — a spectre which more than justifies the anarchists' detestation of national 'collective' ownership.

The famous Clause 4, Part 4 of the Labour Party's Constitution, subject of so many internecine disputes, reads as follows:

To secure for the workers by hand or by brain the full fruits of their industry and the most equitable distribution thereof that may be possible upon the basis of the common ownership of the means of production, distribution and exchange, and the best obtainable system of popular administration and control of each industry or service.

This does not indicate whether state or local ownership is to be preferred. Modern social-democratic parties have advocated the nationalization of strategic industries as a half-measure, but the British experience shows that the mixed economy goes little way towards producing the equality of wealth and income, or the unalienated, unexploited labour, which socialism idealises.

What socialists and their critics should both remember is that common ownership is a means rather than an end in itself, and that opinions can therefore legitimately differ about this and other programmatic elements of an ideology as the circumstances of its implementation differ. In largely agricultural countries like Tanzania or Portugal collective farms have been established relatively free from the dreaded statist overtones. But in the industrialized world it is hard to see how any socialist government could communalise the elaborate cartels and conglomerates of capitalism without resorting to state capitalism, with all its attendant dangers.

(5) Popular sovereignty

As the quotation from Caute given above suggests, this ideal derives from a belief in the equal ability of men to govern themselves and to express their interests, a premise shared in principle by liberals, although the institutions of representative democracy belie it. There is a divide between the social democrats who find representative democracy acceptable in principle and those more radical socialists, including most Marxists, who espouse the sort of direct democracy proposed by Rousseau, at least in principle. To complicate matters, there are two readings (at least!) of Rousseau's *Social Contract:* his idea of the General Will[15], which a group or even one man might express, has been invoked to justify the dictatorship of the proletariat, Lenin's 'revolutionary vanguard', and a departure from the one-man-one-vote ideal.[16] But the basis for Rousseau's reputation as a forerunner of democratic socialism is found in the same text, in the social conditions which he sets out for direct democracy: as Lichtheim explains, 'the general will operates only in a society with equal distribution of property (or with socialized property)',[17] a safeguard lacking, for example, in post-revolutionary Russia. The Workers' Soviets in the early days after 1917 were perhaps a genuine attempt to implement popular sovereignty on Rousseau's lines, albeit a short-lived one.

Within the liberal-democratic tradition, socialists are often accused of seeking to undermine democracy, like their colleagues in communist states—an accusation forcefully rebutted in Benn's *Arguments for Socialism*, where he argues the case for open government and greater parliamentary control.

There are both theoretical and practical reasons why democracy under socialism might be different from liberal democracy: the expression of class interests would no longer be necessary, nor would the wide variety of competing economic pressure groups exist, so that parties as they are now might cease to operate. If the possibility of a classless society is accepted a one-party state can be viewed theoretically as still democratic.[18] In principle, the socialist ideal of popular sovereignty, which makes the people as a whole supreme, deliberately transcends the liberal ideal of representative democracy, which exalts the role of the individual but has in practice sought to select soundly middle-class representatives or to institute indirect elections (as the early USA Constitution did for the Senate), in order to withhold power from the majority of individuals and from the people as a 'whole'. These differences will be discussed further in Chapter 9.

(6) 'Subordination' of the individual to society

This hostile description is used by critics to emphasize that socialism does not acknowledge the free, rational, independent individual of liberal theory and swamps the individual interest in the general interest of society. But, as Parekh states, men *are* 'necessarily interdependent not only in the obvious material sense but also in the cultural and spiritual sense . . . (man) is totally unintelligible outside of society'.[19] This conception of man in society derives from the definition of man as a creature formed by the environment, rather than as an autonomous individual endowed with innate or hereditary characteristics. Within society, our fellow-men constitute the greater part of our environment; the individual's behaviour can only be fully explained, and his interests can only be properly consulted, with reference to them and to the social ensemble. This seems uncontroversial, but when socialist thinkers insist on dealing thus with man, many critics weigh in, since this verges on giving the impersonal, suspect 'general interest' priority over individual interests. Fourier denied that this approach entailed the subordination of individuals, showing that self-interest could promote the general interest *spontaneously* in a rightly organized society.[20]

Many socialists would conceptualize this supposed subordination as Rousseau does: in making the social contract, the individual gives up most of his power over himself, but gains a fraction of power over every other citizen. If *all* are equally subordinate, tyranny is not a danger.[21] Rousseau was worried by the economic and political dependency of man upon man, which he thought degrading.[22] The utopians followed him in arguing that if *each* depended on *all*, the degrading individual dependency would be averted: modern socialists would agree. This nice conceptual solution is clouded by the fact of the growth of the welfare state, which makes the realization of Rousseau's ideal impossible: for each to be dependent not on his fellows collectively, but on the state (an elite organization with its own interests) is a very different proposition. Some socialists today are trying to combat this new form of dependency by schemes for participation.[23]

The conceptual reduction of the individual to a mere fraction of the whole may be a logical consequence of other elements of socialist doctrine, such as the commitment to popular sovereignty and the premise that human nature is eminently sociable and is formed by society. But this 'subordination' need not entail the loss of human rights or the 'standardization' of individuals which critics fear.

(7) Homo faber—creative man

The basis of every ideology is its concept of man or of human nature. Socialists typically assume that man is naturally creative and can find pleasure and fulfilment in unalienated labour. Marx was influenced by Hegel's account of how man, in transforming nature, transforms himself, a process which makes the 'slave' superior in some ways to the 'master'.[24] Saint-Simon too speaks of the need to gain control over nature and to be creative: 'for man, being happy is to act, then to enjoy'. Not for socialists the utopias of the middle ages, which were one long round of lazy gourmandise: for them, the pleasures of consumption and acquisition are inferior to those of creation, which explains the importance of *work* in a socialist society, although technological advances have forced us to envisage the possibility of socialism in a super-automated leisure society.[25] The importance accorded to work by socialists must not be confused with the puritanical, capitalist 'work ethic', which applauded the moral virtue of hard work: socialism emphasizes the *joy*. And the distributive principle, 'from each . . . to each', separates contribution from reward, which will be according to need, and is quite distinct from the bourgeois idea of 'paying your way'. This vision of creative man has consequences for the socialist view of freedom, as we shall see.

The socialist conception of man has other parts: man's natural sociability is widely assumed. Not all socialists would go so far as to postulate innate goodwill to others, but their accounts still differ greatly from the Hobbesian picture of greedy and aggressive man, or the liberal view of autonomous, splendidly isolated man, and produces a different social theory in which co-operation and collectivism, rather than individualism, are uppermost. The French revolutionaries' term, 'fraternity', in part expresses the socialist conviction of men's natural sociability and solidarity.

(8) The virtues of co-operation

If men are naturally sociable, then co-operation is the natural and necessary form of social organization.[26] It provides both the moral and the practical dynamic of society and guarantees equality of benefits for all the co-operators. Early socialism grew up in conjunction with co-operative movements for the production and distribution of goods, rather than through political parties. For those socialists who accepted that industrialization and the division of labour were irreversible, the problem was to find a form of voluntary co-operation which differed from the enforced co-operation experienced in factory production. Owen — who set up a producers' co-operative in London in 1832 — saw co-operation as the moral basis of social life, as well as the only successful mode of production. For modern socialists, co-operation is still both an ideal and an operational idea, and constitutes the absolute antithesis of the ethic of competition and individualism which vindicates capitalist production. Although the 'Co-op' today may be indistinguishable from other department stores, the principle remains fundamental to small-scale left-wing movements: experimental producers' co-operatives and communes are constantly being set up *within* capitalist societies. The practical problem of socialists is whether the scale of co-operation can be magnified beyond the local group with a common interest, where it flourishes naturally, and become the basis of the whole of social organization, without losing its voluntary and ethical qualities.

(9) Idealization of work as unalienated labour

This ideal results from the socialist account of man's natural creativity. The pleasures of work can exceed even those of consumption, as the utopian Fourier amply illustrates: in his ideal community men would pursue eight different occupations during a long working day, in two-hour shifts. His principle of 'attractive labour' requires that each works at what he enjoys most: the rose-lover grows roses, and so on. Marx gently satirized Fourier's vision in his proclamation that under communism man could be a fisherman, hunter, philosopher, and critic all in one day[27]: but for him it was less the content than the form of work which mattered. Working for a capitalist could never be enjoyable because of the exploitative situation, whereas any work under socialism should be fulfilling because of its 'social' nature. For nineteenth-century socialists, work appeared to be man's perpetual burden, while today we can speculate about the possibility of a leisure-based society, which requires readjustment of the vision of *homo faber*. Marcuse points out the need to transform work into *play*, an interesting instance of the adaptation of a central philosophical idea to changing material circumstances.[28] But the contrast remains between the socialist idealization of the place of work in society, and both the Biblical stigmatization of labour as Adam's curse, appealing to some conservatives, and the Calvinist identification of work with virtue.

(10) Freedom as fulfilment

The corollary of the widely-shared socialist conviction that man is formed by the environment is a redefinition of freedom which comprehends this deterministic element, and the premise of man's creativity. Socialist freedom is the freedom to unfold and develop one's potential, especially through the medium of unalienated labour. Freedom is separated from its liberal synonym, choice: if, for example, someone has great mathematical talent, all that is necessary is that a mathematical career should be open to him, rather than a whole range of baffling and inappropriate choices. The superfluity of consumer products which capitalism offers is also irrelevant to the socialist analysis of freedom—they offer the illusion of choice, yet cannot enhance the development of the individual. Another aspect of the socialist account of liberty is the Marxist critique of liberal political rights, which is discussed in Chapter 11.

(11) Change—revolution or persuasion?

Some would consider this a tactical rather than a philosophical question, but the various positions adopted follow from certain philosophical assumptions. The perception of misery and oppression demands social change, as does the egalitarian ideal, but does not dictate the *means* of change. Since men are formed by the social environment, this must first be altered, and the utopian socialists tried to do this experimentally by setting up co-operative communities. They also believed that men are governed by reason, so that the success of such exemplary experiments would convert the rest of society. On the other hand, Marx's class analysis led him to conclude that the ruling class would never part with its privileges without a struggle: hence, within the logic of his analysis, revolution was essential. As is well known, the social-democratic branch of the movement has elected to act through parliamentary means, partly in the hope that reason will prevail within the electorate, partly following the Fabian axiom concerning 'the inevitability of gradualness'. These two assumptions appear to be fallacious, both philosophically and practically. One elaboration of the Marxist view, adapted to third-world problems, is Fanon's argument that colonized peoples must perpetrate violent revolutions with bloodshed against the colonizers, to purge symbolically their past oppression and assert their virility.[29] This introduces a dubious element of mass psychology to justify the project of historical revenge, which was absent from Marx's theory, even if omnipresent in communist practice. The selection of a strategy for change is clearly a matter of circumstance rather than philosophy: for example, the predominance of the gradualist, social-democratic approach in Britain cannot be dissociated from its emergence in a political climate where conservatives praised the strength of tradition while liberals treated the system, theoretically at least, as a timeless, self-perpetuating machine.

(12) Internationalism

The international dimension common to most versions of socialist doctrine needs no further justification than the argument that, for the humanist, all humanity is one race. National boundaries cannot circumscribe political truths. The utopian socialists, writing after a long period of warmongering in Europe, were instinctively internationalist. Fourier planned a world confederation of phalansteries. Saint-Simon wanted a federation of industrial countries — for which both have been accused or totalitarian ambitions! But these utopians, who believed that they had hit upon *the* truth about social organization, were quite consistent in trying to extend it universally. Marx and Engels promoted the International on the basis of their analysis of the economic interdependence of capitalist countries — a fact which no-one could deny today — and the socialist movement was self-proclaimedly, deliberately internationalist until the end of the nineteenth century. The First World War forced existing social-democratic parties into patriotic, even chauvinistic attitudes, although not without considerable internal rupture.[30] The Russian revolution posed, and the Soviet bloc continues to pose, problems for communist and social-democratic parties who wish to manifest internationalist sentiments, yet to avoid accusations of being under Moscow's thumb. Meanwhile, Trotskyist parties continue to proclaim their unalloyed loyalty to the 'Fourth International'. But the third-world dimension presents further problems: how can solidarity subsist between the proletariat of industrial and that of developing countries, when their standard of living is inversely related? In some ways, internationalism is the highest ideal of the socialist movement, with its demand for equality throughout the world, yet the strength of nationalism and international capitalism and the myopia of individuals concerning distant countries make it the hardest to pursue practically.

These twelve ideas, then, constitute the 'common core' of socialism. Caute has denied that many of them are exclusively characteristics of the left[31], but this needs qualifying. Of course, there are sometimes egalitarian conservatives or revolutionary liberals, but this does not mean that a unique configuration of characteristics cannot be said to constitute socialism. Yet, as has been shown, not all socialists coincide on all twelve points, and this raises the problem of the identity of the ideology. How many key concepts can you jettison, and still remain a socialist? For the British Labour Party in 1959, Clause IV was the sticking point and was retained, despite the desire of some centrists to abandon it. Clearly, some parts of the doctrine are more central than others: it would be impossible to call an advocate of social inequality a socialist. Other parts are more dispensable, and Chapters 4 and 6 show the extent to which various Marxists and anarchists have modified or disputed some concepts. But if anyone is searching for an essentialist definition of socialism, he had best take the notion of equality, or egalitarian social justice, which seems to be a fundamental, moral, and some would say intuitive, attitude on which other substantial parts of the ideology rest.

The presentation of the twelve ideas was intended to illustrate the logical connections between them and the way in which political policies are derived from philosophical assumptions, so as to demonstrate the coherence of

98

socialist ideology and the inseparability of its components. To conclude this section, these interconnections are set out diagrammatically.

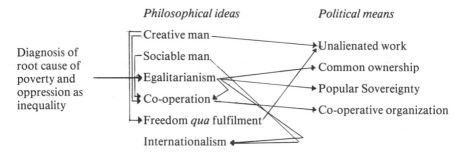

Practical and Conceptual Problems

Since there is no space here to embark on an intellectual history of the world labour movement which would highlight the practical problems of socialism, I shall discuss some representative and significant developments in modern, non-Marxist socialist thought, taking as examples the British Labour Party and some African theories of socialism. These illustrate the problems involved in trying to implement what is in fact a strongly idealistic doctrine.

Britain's first major experience of socialist government was the postwar Attlee government of 1946–51, whose measures included nationalization of the mines, the steel industry, and the health service. The later Labour governments of 1964–70 and 1974–9 were markedly less doctrinaire in their measures although the renationalization of steel, previously denationalized by the Conservatives, and the comprehensivization of schools, for egalitarian reasons, took place. Both governments could claim in mitigation that they were facing intolerable economic pressures and, during the 1970s, a world recession. But already, during the affluent 1950s when the party out of power was trying to obliterate the memory of postwar austerity over which it had presided, and to appear less dogmatically socialist, Crosland had written in *The Future of Socialism:*

In my view Marx has little or nothing to offer the contemporary socialist, either in respect of practical policy, or of the correct analysis of our society, or even of the right conceptual tools or framework.[32]

This signifies the apogee of social democracy's attempt to detach itself from the revolutionary and workerist currents in a society rapidly becoming middle-class and acquisitive, at least in aspiration. Twenty-five years later, the party's problem is not to 'respectabilize' itself and get back into government, since several elections have gone in its favour, but to analyse why socialism seems no nearer after several Labour administrations. Two prominent Labour politicians, Benn and Luard, have analysed the problems, albeit from opposite ends of the socialist spectrum, and their conclusions merit some attention.

Both agree that the mixed economy does not work: that we are no closer to securing the workers 'the full fruits of their industry and the most equitable distribution thereof', nor to ending work alienation and dissatisfaction. Public ownership and government attempts to induce private investment in needy areas have not worked and, in Benn's words, 'we have come to the end of that road'.[33] His prescription is for a further extension of state ownership, increased industrial democracy, and greater public accountability of nationalized industries. But this is precisely what Luard fears, as the title of his book, *Socialism Without the State*, indicates. He deplores the size and scale of organization in modern society and the ubiquitous presence of the state, and proposes 'grassroots socialism' with experiments in local production and neighbourhood ownership.[34] In fact, Luard opposes the state in communist *or* capitalist countries because he has individualistic ideals and a dislike of standardization shared by liberals such as Mill and Ortega y Gasset, and not because he takes a Marxist view of the state as oppressor. This debate between left and right Labour Party members echoes the anarchists' quarrel with Marx, but the exponential increase in the state's size makes the problem more urgent today. The recurrence of this debate indicates that not merely contextual, but conceptual, issues are involved.

For Marxists, the issue is clear: the state continues to be the bourgeoisie's instrument of oppression even when it takes on the guise of the welfare state or of state socialism—a Western form often said to be convergent with the so called state capitalism of the USSR. Social democrats regard the state more ingenuously—a fault for which Marx criticized the German SPD even in 1875[35]—and believe that it can be democratically captured and diverted to socialist uses. The unpromising results of such attempts have caused many who think like Luard to seek alternatives which at the periphery merge into the commune and alternative technology movements. Communists observing the progress of the USSR have come to parallel conclusions. The French Communist, Garaudy, argues

The concept of State ownership is highly contradictory: State ownership connotes . . . the abolition of capitalist private ownership . . . but it is also a form of ownership which perpetuates the alienation of the means of production with respect to the worker by excluding him not only from decisions affecting production and the allocation of surplus-value but also from the general administration of the economy.[36]

He recommends an alternative resembling the workers' management schemes of Yugoslavia.

Experience suggests that the technologically advanced, bureaucraticized state is bigger than the bourgeoisie, the Politburo, and any Labour government, let alone the individual! Marxists can recollect that Marx's rubric always rejected the preservation of the state, but social democrats, committed to working through the existing apparatus, have both a conceptual and a practical problem with the state, the latter being exacerbated for many European social-democratic parties by membership of the European Community superstate. If flirtations with decentralization and regionalism fail, even social democrats might be reluctantly led to accept the logic of Marx, that leviathan must be destroyed by revolution. The question of the state is overwhelmingly important for modern socialists since, if communist countries are afflicted with it no less than capitalist ones, the implication is that a new theory must be developed to analyse and combat a state which is not just the tool of the bourgeoisie but an independent, self-aggrandizing and self-perpetuating force. Analysis on these lines is now common among socialist thinkers, but their effect on practice is negligible so far. The new approach crosses the socialist/non-socialist divide, since almost everyone fears the escaped monster, and it may indeed be true that the technological developments which make the totalitarian state feasible render socialist ideology irrelevant just as the rise of capitalism superseded mercantilist doctrines.

But the ideal of socialism is not confined to the parochial problems of the West and advanced capitalism, and by contrast I shall now look briefly at some classic exponents of African socialism. Such thinkers frequently dismiss social democracy, Marxism, and Soviet communism as foreign ideologies inappropriate to Africa's material conditions and predicament. President Nyerere of Tanzania wrote

These two revolutions (agrarian and industrial) planted the seeds of conflict within society, and not only was European socialism born of that conflict, but its apostles sanctified the conflict itself into a philosophy . . . The European socialist cannot think of his socialism without its father — capitalism!

Brought up in tribal socialism, I must say I find this contradiction quite intolerable. it gives capitalism a philosophical status which capitalism neither claims nor deserves. For it virtually says 'Without capitalism . . . there can be no socialism'.[37]

So Nyerere emphasizes the contingency of historical events out of which socialist ideology grew, in defiance of Marx, and rejects the 'necessary' dialectical connection between capitalism and socialism via the class conflict, arguing that 'tribal socialism', a qualitatively different social form from the European variety, already existed in Africa, without the capitalist preconditions.

We, in Africa, have no more need of being 'converted' to socialism than we have of being 'taught' democracy. Both are rooted in our own past — in the traditional society which produced us. Modern African Socialism can draw from its traditional heritage the recognition of 'society' as an extension of the basic family unit.[38]

Nyerere's socialism centres on the concept of Ujamaa — 'family' or 'brotherhood' — and is practised in Tanzania at village, not state, level. Despite various problems caused by the initiation of the project from above, by 1973 there were 4484 Ujamaa communities, villages run on the basis of the people's ownership of the means of production, communal co-operative production, participatory decision-taking and total self-organization. Such villages offer various social services: they tend to reinvest surpluses to increase production. 'Self-reliance' is the watchword of Tanzanian co-operativism.

Although some observers see Ujamaa merely as the rehabilitation of traditional co-operative forms, the emphasis on participation and socialist ideas is new, and we can deduce from it the principles of an alternative, African socialism. The stress — naturally enough, in an agricultural continent — is on production on the land and co-operative labour. The social obligation to work is proclaimed by Nyerere, who points out that in traditional society nobody was idle. African socialism concerns the joint *creation* of wealth rather than its redistribution (which is the common theme of European manifestoes). The traditional extended family is to be further extended, in theory at least, to embrace the whole village, for greater social cohesion: this is an interesting alternative formulation of Fourier's belief that systematic permissive and polygamous behaviour would eventually unite all members of the utopian community by ties of blood or love, an ideally unified situation. Although Nyerere uses the phrase 'tribal socialism', perhaps to explain himself to Westerners who are obsessed by African tribalism, the basic socialist unit is the village, which is viewed as an organic, familial entity.

Most of the proponents of indigenous African socialism assert that it is a classless phenomenon. Ex-president Nkrumah of Ghana — whose views became increasingly Marxist over time — asserted in 1964 that Africa was by tradition a classless society and that the imperialists were the chief enemy (even though in 1970 he wrote *The Class Struggle in Africa*, an attempt to fit the Marxist matrix on the African situation and to explain how the revolution could occur in predominantly peasant countries). The reputed classlessness of African society also offers a theoretical justification on Marxist lines for the one-party democracies widely adopted throughout the continent, although the practical reason for such developments is undoubtedly the need to modernize rapidly. President Senghor of Senegal also characterized African society as classless because community-based, with a hierarchy founded on spiritual and democratic — not economic — values. The hope, then, in the 1950s and 1960s during decolonization was that traditionally homogeneous African society would undergo a socialist metamorphosis painlessly and without revolution. But the emergence of the 'national bourgeoisie' in most countries after independence and the accelerating absorption of African economies into the world capitalist economy make this appear over-optimistic and outdated.

African socialists attack the alienation and spiritual poverty of Western life and emphasize spiritual values and freedom. Senghor wrote

Our socialism is not that of Europe . . . we are forced to seek our own original mode, a Negro-African mode, of attaining (maximum satisfaction of spiritual and material needs), paying special attention to the two elements I have just stressed: *economic democracy and spiritual freedom.*[39]

His emphasis on the spiritual elements relates also to his concept of 'negritude', the assertion of the racial and intellectual uniqueness of the Africans. The freedom which such socialists demand is clearly not that of liberals, but something closer to Rousseau's ideal: freedom through one's development as a full member of society. Typically, African socialism declares itself *evolutionary* (when it is not declaring that Africa was socialist all along), although pressures such as the struggle against colonialism and the growth of economic-based neo-colonialism have produced theories of revolution such as Nkrumah's.[40] Nkrumah is also associated with the doctrine of pan-Africanism: he argued that socialism should be organized on an all-Africa scale, and worked for African unity, though with little success. This doctrine differs from socialist internationalism significantly, being still a sectional doctrine—the organization of the third-world oppressed in a way which would necessarily set them at odds with the proletariat of the capitalist world. This divide is yet another proof that socialist doctrines which evolved when the world was regarded as consisting of Europe, America, and a mass of subject races, urgently need revising to take account of conflicts which cut right across the old categories.

The consideration of African socialist writings also proves how relative to time and circumstance the substance of ideas is. Even when the same concepts are used—co-operation, for example—their interpretation and implementation differ greatly between the European and African contexts. Most African socialists firmly reject the European experience, and the logic and categories of Western socialism, while retaining the name of the ideology for their own sets of values. The African doctrine may be applicable to other third-world, agricultural countries, or may not if it is true that tribal socialism is the precondition for the emergence of a unique form of socialism in Africa. So, ideologies are inseparable from their social, political, and economic context even when they share a name.

The problems which socialist ideology faces today are not easy to classify as conceptual or practical, as was clear in the debate over the modern state. Does the rise of the benevolent welfare state suggest that Marx's analysis of the nature of the state was true only in his own time, and that the very nature of the state has changed? Or should we, like Marcuse, try to circumvent this benign facade and, by revealing the covert violence on which the state rests, prove that Marx's theoretical analysis was essentially right? Each approach has its champions and terms like 'revisionist' and 'opportunist' punctuate the debate. However, I would suggest that *all* revision has a theoretical and an empirical aspect and that the two are not analytically separable.

One practical problem in the dissemination of socialism, especially in Britain, is that it is not the dominant ideology—voting Labour is different from having socialist convictions—and that socialism is not the prevailing form of organization, despite our mixed economy, so that socialist values are always challenged from the stronghold of the liberal ideas which they contradict. The dominant ideology, even if its own intellectual status is dubious, has the inestimable advantage of being transmitted explicitly or covertly in schools, through the media, and throughout the culture. A rival ideology therefore appears to threaten all that we have been taught to hold dear. The dominant ideology also has the privilege of setting the conditions for knowledge: that is, of excluding all doctrines which fail the tests set by its own epistemology. The liberal epistemology, based on an empirical and inductive method can thus dismiss Marxism because there is no 'conclusive' evidence of class conflict or because its predictions do not come true. Similarly, in many ways the non-Marxist socialist is ruled offside before he even starts to play because his premises do not coincide with the prevalent political preconceptions.

Finally, I would like to discuss some theoretical objections to the general principles of socialism. The socialist conception of man has often been challenged by liberals and conservatives. Why assume him to be naturally sociable, co-operative, and creative rather than aggressive, competitive or idle? Casual observation, and modern socio-biology support the latter view, it is said.[41] The socialist is then constrained to point out that men compete only because they are born into a society whose institutions are competitive — nurture not nature, conditioning not heredity. The perpetual controversy about the extent to which behaviour is genetically determined, to what extent learned or conditioned, shows no imminent signs of being resolved and, failing a solution, the political thinker may make any assumption he likes about human nature. The socialist suffers from positing a human essence which everyday behaviour belies. But he in turn can cite accounts of non-competitive and co-operative societies (among them, Nyerere's depiction of tribal socialism) to justify his premises and to demonstrate that man's naturally sociable inclinations are perverted by capitalist institutions. Ultimately, any conception of man is an act of faith, not a scientific fact, which means that no conception can conclusively be ruled out. All conceptions which diminish the role of self-interest are suspect in the West, but socialists do not have to claim that all men are altruists to prove their point. They only need to show that co-operation creates greater abundance and prosperity than competition, to show that self-interest is served by 'sociable' behaviour.[42]

The challenge most frequently issued by liberals to socialists is that equality cannot be reconciled with liberty: a socialist society is necessarily unfree. In part, this is an inductive argument based on the suppression of civil liberties in communist states, but it is backed by several conceptual arguments, which run as follows: given the natural inequality of talents and abilities, any system offering equal treatment will thwart some individuals and hamper the free development of their potential — a point often made about comprehensive schools. Likewise, a system of equal reward for work unfairly discourages the more able in their attempts to succeed (this of course has no bearing on freedom unless we define it to include the liberty to get ahead of others). It is also said that an egalitarian society prevents individuals from getting their just rewards. These arguments focus attention on the problems which an authentic socialist society would face in operation; they can, I believe, all be circumvented by the concept of *equal treatment.*

Hardest to answer is the accusation that the transition to socialism would destroy present liberties. Given existing financial and social inequalities, any move towards equality through redistribution would, it is said, necessarily make some people worse off, thus limiting their freedom. Liberty, choice, and money are closely associated in the liberal mind, hence this criticism. 'Levelling down' is a common accusation made against socialists, but the logic of it is only correct if the situation is static, like a game of Monopoly in which a limited quantity of money circulates, a typical zero-sum game where gains must equal losses. Since in a world recession a fixed supply of prosperity is the most we can hope for, the introduction of socialism today might indeed entail levelling down. Some socialist governments even find themselves having to redistribute 'negative income', like the Labour government of 1974–9, which administered cuts in the real standard of living. But such circumstances are only contingent. Utopian socialists answered the challenge by hypothesizing that their systems would produce ever-increasing abundance so that *everyone* could have more, yet inequalities would be reduced or eliminated. Whether redistribution deprives men of income and freedom therefore depends on what accompanying assumptions are made about the quantity of wealth available. It also depends partly on the degree of existing inequality: the greater that is, the more impossible 'levelling up' and the more likely it is that some rich people will be compulsorily deprived of their wealth. Critics of socialism assume that the rich would not voluntarily give up this wealth, which also constitutes their liberty, and that, in being coerced to do so, they would undergo a double encroachment on their freedom. A further refinement of the criticism is that levelling up, if it were ever possible (as it has been to some extent in suddenly oil-rich countries with small populations like Kuwait and Libya), would still deprive the better-off of their relative privileges over others, entailing a loss of social status, so that it would still be unfair.

The breathtaking assumption behind all such arguments is that there is some inherent *fairness* in the existing accidental distribution of goods. No convincing evidence is offered for this assumption: even a conservative liberal like Hayek admits that market mechanisms are not *just*.[43] Furthermore, there is a degree of self-contradiction involved. If freedom equals choice, signified by money, and money is redistributed to worse-off people, they thereby receive greater freedom, simultaneously with the better-off losing some freedom. We thus move towards an equality of individual freedom, to which the liberal is also committed by all his other ideals. As Hart argues, if there is any natural right, it is the equal right to be free.[44] So how can those who maintain that money is an important component of freedom begrudge it to those who have less, or hold that existing income and wealth differentials promote maximum freedom?

There is a certain inconsistency in liberal thinking about freedom in terms of civil liberties, which are allocated to all men equally, and liberalism's practical equation of freedom with the choice which cash provides: as is well known, the latter form of freedom, alias economic power, can negate the value of the formal political liberties. This is one important socialist response to liberal criticism. Another part of the liberal's case rests on the prohibition made in utilitarianism of interpersonal comparisons of utility. We are not allowed to hypothesize that one unit of freedom redistributed from a free to an unfree man will cause him less pain than it gives the other pleasure. Yet this is clearly true at the margin and such comparisons must be made in politics. Carritt uses an extreme example of this to show that equality is not only compatible with, but supportive of, liberty: he imagines an island where one man has the monopoly of the water supply, greatly incommoding the freedom of other inhabitants. If water ownership is then equalized, only the monopolist loses his liberty, while the others gain dramatically. Hence Carritt's conclusion, which vindicates socialist thinking:

To be forcibly deprived of superabundance or even of conveniences impairs liberty less than to be forcibly prevented from appropriating necessities.[45]

Greater equality should therefore conduce to a greater total sum of liberty and happiness except where the original inequalities were very slight. Here we must distinguish between particular liberties and general personal liberty to which income and other factors contribute. It would be wrong to redistribute someone's voting rights, since everyone has an equal, invariable amount of vote, but other freedoms are more accidental, divisible, and available for redistribution. The exaggerated nature of Carritt's example does not nullify the force of the general argument which he is advancing, but in less clear-cut cases the benefits of redistribution are harder to assess.

What about the fear of coercion during the transition to socialist equality? Only by assuming that the rich would defend their wealth and have to be coerced can this transition be seen as a greater threat to liberty than any other government policy: but this assumption is hypothetical, and certainly not true in every case. Britain, for example, has had progressive income tax backed by sanctions since 1842 and taxpayers accept, or even forget, this infringement of their liberty. The present government's policy of reducing income tax along with public expenditure and welfare benefits is an interesting example of a redistribution of income and, hence, liberty towards the better-off, and is justified by the government precisely as a measure which increases liberty.

Socialists are concerned with the negative aspect of the cash–freedom nexus: poverty equals *unfreedom*. They resent not the fact that some have more, but the fact that some have less. But where relativities are concerned you cannot give someone more without giving someone *relatively* less (even if their total amount remains the same) — a problem which has haunted governments trying to help low-paid workers during periods of income restraint, when the better-off workers object to the erosion of pay differentials. But, as Carritt shows analytically, this process actually increases the total amount of liberty, viewed in cash terms. Another reason why the socialist denies the dichotomy between liberty and equality is that, as was said, he defines freedom differently from the liberal, as the opportunity to fulfil one's potential. To arrange this would not require great discrepancies of wealth; it certainly would require an equality of differential treatment which rests on the 'to each according to his needs' principle, and an adequate definition of liberty for the socialist might be 'freedom from unsatisfied needs', which could be interpreted to include self-realization. This raises tricky questions about true, false, real, and acquired needs, and which needs are allowed to count in social justice calculations, but these could surely be worked out programmatically, even if the distinctions between them cannot be made philosophically. Thus, for the socialist, the principles of freedom and equality are interlocking and complementary, equal articles of the socialist catechism.

The Contradictions of Social Democracy

The failure of social–democratic parties in power to achieve socialism can be explained historically by their involvement with trade unions, which tend to be conservative and concerned with economic demands, and by the strength of world capitalism, which makes 'socialism in one country' hard to achieve except in total isolation. Such explanations are based on historical contingencies, and the experience of social–democratic parties has been widely different in the various European countries. More satisfying as an explanation of this failure is the theoretical approach which shows the incompatibility of the social–democratic strategy with socialist ends. Social democrats repudiate the class analysis of society in order to advocate parliamentary reconciliation of interests—which Marx considered impossible. But when they attempt redistributive measures, those with vested economic interests block or modify them, so that only minor reforms can be achieved. By taking a democratic and parliamentary approach to socialist goals, the social–democratic movement has tried to make use of the bourgeois state, bourgeois techniques, and values. Because these very instruments and techniques developed or were devised to protect the system and the rule of the bourgeoisie, they cannot be used against capitalism. Social democrats, like liberals, pretend that the state and the political system is neutral—mistakenly. In fact, the task which they have undertaken, of achieving socialism through the liberal-democratic state, is structurally and theoretically impossible.

The history of social-democratic politics in Britain demonstrates how those social democrats who entered parliament were swiftly beguiled into believing liberal doctrines about the supremacy of parliament and the virtues of the existing system[46]: Ramsey MacDonald's apostasy is the classic example of such delusion. Those who, like the Fabians, hoped to 'permeate' the system were themselves permeated and assimilated. Experience suggests, then, that Marx was right in thinking that the state, an epiphenomenon of capitalism, cannot be diverted to achieve socialism, and that some form of 'revolutionary socialism' is necessary for this goal—which does not, however, *entail* violence, although it may occur. The most that social democrats can hope to achieve, given their assumptions and chosen strategy, is to socialize and humanize the existing state—which may itself be a worthy aim—but their collaboration with that state necessarily precludes the achievement of most of the central ideals of socialism.

Notes

1. A. Benn, in *Arguments for Socialism* (Ed. C. Mullins), Cape, London, 1979, pp. 29–32.
2. D. Caute, *The Left in Europe*, Weidenfeld & Nicholson, London, 1966, p. 33.
3. E. Durkheim, *Socialism and Saint-Simon* (Trans. C. Sattler), Antioch Press, 1958, p. 19.
4. R. N. Berki, *Socialism*, Dent, London, 1975.
5. G. D. H. Cole, *Socialist Thought: The Forerunners,* Macmillan, Basingstoke, 1958, p. 1.
6. G. Lichtheim, *The Origins of Socialism*, Weidenfeld & Nicholson, London, 1969, p. 11.
7. B. Parekh (Ed.), *The Concept of Socialism*, Croom Helm, London, 1975, p. 3.
8. B. Disraeli, *Sybil: or, The Two Nations*, London, 1845.
9. F. Engels, *Socialism: Utopian and Scientific* in *Selected Works*, Vol. III, p. 122.
10. J. Beecher and R. Bienvenu (Eds), *The Utopian Vision of Charles Fourier,* Cape, London, 1972, pp. 87, 124.
11. W. G. Runciman, *Relative Deprivation and Social Justice,* Penguin, Harmondsworth, 1972.
12. H. Spencer, *The Man Versus the State*, Penguin, Harmondsworth, 1968, pp. 82–3.
13. Marx & Engels, *Communist Manifesto, Selected Works,* Vol. I, pp. 134–5.
14. H. Marcuse, *One Dimensional Man*, Sphere, London, 1968.
15. J.-J. Rousseau, *The Social Contract* (Trans G. D. H. Cole), Dent, London, 1913, pp. 22–4, 85–7.
16. B. Holden, *The Nature of Democracy*, Nelson, London, 1974, pp. 41–51, shows the similarities between the Rousseauist and the Marxist theories of democracy.
17. Lichtheim, *The Origins of Socialism*, p. 13.
18. The case is put for the developing countries by C. B. Macpherson in *The Real World of Democracy*, Clarendon Press, Oxford, 1966, Chap. 3.
19. Parekh, *The Concept of Socialism*, pp. 4–5.
20. Beecher and Bienvenu, *The Utopian Vision of Charles Fourier*, pp. 252–5.
21. Rousseau, *The Social Contract*, p. 12.
22. Rousseau, '*A Discourse on the Origin and Foundations of the Inequality of Mankind',* in *The Social Contract*, pp. 189, 202.
23. See, e.g., E. Luard, *Socialism Without the State*, Macmillan, Basingstoke, 1970, Part II.
24. G. Hegel, *The Phenomenology of Spirit* (Trans A. V. Miller), Oxford University Press, Oxford, 1977, Section B.IV.B.
25. This is discussed in H. Marcuse, *Eros and Civilisation*, Sphere, London, 1969.
26. P. Kropotkin, *Mutual Aid*, reprinted, New York University Press, New York, 1972.
27. Marx & Engels, *The German Ideology*, p. 36.
28. Marcuse, *Eros and Civilisation*, p. 151ff.

29. F. Fanon, *The Wretched of the Earth* (Trans. C. Farrington), Penguin, Harmondsworth, 1967, Chap. 1.
30. Caute, *The Left in Europe,* pp. 219–20. For a British case study see M. Winter, *Socialism and the Challenge of War,* Routledge & Kegan Paul, London, 1974.
31. Caute, *The Left in Europe,* Chap. 1.
32. A. Crosland, *The Future of Socialism,* Cape, London, 1956, p. 2.
33. Benn, *Arguments for Socialism,* p. 52.
34. Luard, *Socialism Without the State,* Chap. 9.
35. Marx, *Critique of the Gotha Programme,* 1875.
36. R. Garaudy, *The Turning Point of Socialism* (Trans. P. Ross and B. Ross), Fontana-Collins, 1970, pp. 180–1.
37. J. Nyerere, 'Ujamaa: the basis of African socialism', in *African Socialism* (Eds W. H. Friedland and C. G. Rosberg), Stanford University Press, 1964, pp. 245–6.
38. Nyerere, *Ujamaa,* p. 246. See also Nyerere's *Freedom and Socialism,* Oxford University Press, 1968, pp. 1–32.
39. L. Senghor, 'African-style socialism', in *African Socialism,* p. 264.
40. K. Nkrumah, *Neo-Colonialism, The Last Stage of Imperialism,* Panaf, 1971.
41. From K. Lorenz's *On Aggression* (Trans. M. Latzke), Methuen, London, 1966 to R. Dawkins's *The Selfish Gene,* Oxford University Press, 1976, the innate selfishness and aggressiveness of man has been a focus of sociobiology.
42. This proof would depend on what level of production one considered: clearly, at a macro-level, capitalism expanded because of competition between firms, while resting on co-operation at the micro-level.
43. F. Hayek, 'The principles of a liberal social order' in (Eds A. Crespigny and J. Cronin) *Ideologies of Politics* Oxford University Press, 1975, p. 69.
44. H. A. L. Hart, 'Are there any natural rights?' in *Political Philosophy* (Ed. A. Quinton), Oxford University Press, Oxford, 1967.
45. E. F. Carritt, 'Liberty and equality', in *political Philosophy* (Ed. A. Quinton), pp. 138–9.
46. R. Miliband, *Parliamentary Socialism,* Allen & Unwin, London, 1961.

Further Reading

R. N. Berki, *Socialism,* Dent, London, 1975.
A. Gray, *The Socialist Tradition,* Longman's, Green & Co., London, 1946.
G. Lichtheim, *The Origins of Socialism,* Weidenfeld & Nicholson, London, 1969.
B. Parekh, ed., *The Concept of Socialism,* Croom Helm, London, 1975.

CHAPTER 6

Anarchism

Although I am a strong supporter of order, I am in the fullest sense of the term, an anarchist.   (*Bakunin*)

He who says 'No' says 'Yes' by affirming values beyond the boundary.   (*Camus*)

Anarchist doctrine has always been dogged by the vulgar interpretation of the word 'anarchism', which equates it with disorder and chaos, the fear of which plays a central role in Western political thought.[1] The literal meaning of the word, the absence of authority, seems less menacing, and expresses the central anarchist conviction that government is an absolute evil. It is no coincidence that anarchist theories originated after the triumph of secular and scientific thought in the Enlightenment, and were concurrent with the development of the sophisticated apparatus of the modern state. Although some, like Woodcock, have traced the ancestors of anarchism back to Müntzer and the anabaptists[2], modern anarchism is transparently a political consequence of the *rejection* of Christianity. Both Proudhon and Bakunin equated the idea of God and that of authority[3]: from the notion of divine authority derived justifications of the oppressive domination of man over man, which is inimical to individual freedom and happiness. They concluded that once authority in all its forms had been abolished, in particular the contemporary form of the legal–bureaucratic state, together with all the varieties of domination parasitic on economic inequalities, society could be re-fashioned on a new moral basis and human nature, no longer degraded by subjection or corrupted by authority, would come to fruition. It must be understood that anarchists consider the state and society completely separable: the former is an artificial, manipulative device, the latter a natural formation, so that the destruction of the state will not jeopardise society itself, nor civilization.

It is hard to generalize about anarchist thought because of the variety of doctrines to which the label has been attached, and the anarchists' congenital individualism, which makes them even less likely to agree than doctors. Broadly speaking, the nineteenth century produced a few anarchists who were emphatically individualistic, and a far greater number whose analysis of capitalism and the ideal society resembled that of socialism in many respects. The former group includes Godwin, Stirner, and Thoreau, while the latter encompasses Proudhon, Bakunin, Kropotkin, and Malatesta. While some twentieth-century thinkers have adapted the anarchist analysis to advanced industrial society, a lot of what passes for anarchism today is a crusade for escape from the society of total alienation, and for the salvation of the individual psyche. This chapter discusses the anarchist critique of capitalism, and then examines the form which an anarchist society might take; finally, it considers the ethics of violence, which some anarchists espoused as a means of political change. During the course of the argument, I hope to dispel three prevalent misconceptions about anarchism by showing that: (a) the anarchist is not just a nihilist who has no constructive ideas; (b) he is not merely a socialist who happens to dislike the state; and (c) he is not inevitably committed to terroristic violence, even though he may espouse it as the only way to social salvation.

Anarchist thinkers, like many socialists, feel revulsion and moral indignation at the state of society; this is coupled with a perception of the individual as naturally 'good' — or at least, as not naturally *bad*. They then have to explain the paradox that, while man is good, society is bad. This leads to an analysis of the social evils which have turned some men into authoritarian monsters, others into mere subjects or slaves. Three major evils are identified: government, the law, and private property. The source of all these is seen to be the institution of authority.

The Critique of Authority

Whether it is embodied in the Church, the state or even in the schoolteacher, authority is seen as oppressive by anarchists since it brings about the suppression of the individual's beliefs or actions in deference to another and violates his freedom and equality. There is no good reason why one adult individual should exercise authority over another, even in his best interests, and power is generally used in the interests of whoever wields it. Wherever there is power, it is likely to be abused and result in coercion and oppression. This is a practical observation *and* a theoretical axiom of anarchism. Unlike liberals, anarchists cannot accept the validity of constitutional limits on the abuse of power, since constitutions and rights are established by the very institution against which they supposedly provide protection, and are therefore likely to prove illusory. Godwin called government 'regulated force', a definition curiously close to the sociologist Weber's 'neutral' definition of the state as having a monopoly of force. Bakunin perceived a categorical division between self-interested rulers and their oppressed subjects, and claimed that government is a permanent conspiracy against 'the drudge people'. The whole of world history could be analysed in terms of oppressors and oppressed. Bakunin's loose class analysis was disapproved of by his rival, Marx, but had considerable emotional appeal. Bakunin asserted, in effect, that authority is inimical to the very nature of man: even the ruling class does not *like* government, but needs the state for the purpose of exploiting, and thereby oppressing, the mass.

It follows that anarchists reject the conservative view that authority is sanctified, and its wisdom increased, by tradition. Likewise, they refute the liberal view of government as based on contract, and see the origins of society as a deception perpetrated by the rich or the strong against the poor or the weak: this makes government exploitative by definition. 'Conquest,' wrote Bakunin 'is also the basis of every state, . . . the organization guaranteeing the existence of this complex of historical iniquities (property, the Church, misery and ignorance)'.[4] Early anarchists attacked 'government' where modern anarchists might speak of the state, but their butt is essentially the same: the panoply of the modern state is a relatively recent outgrowth of government. Parallel with the attack on government is the attack on nationalism which is seen as a drive to territorial self-aggrandisement made inevitable by the predatory nature of governments. The nation is not a natural social unit and should be dismantled in favour of self-sufficient communities which, by definition, would have no territorial ambitions.[5]

The consequence of this condemnation of government is a repudiation of all political systems and political methods, a stance which differentiates anarchists from socialists and fosters the cliché that the anarchist is politically impotent, a man without a party. The anarchist's theoretical reasoning here is impeccably consistent: apart from the fact that politics is itself corrupting for individuals, if someone successfully campaigns for change by political menas, the result is that he himself ends up in power, and so the 'oppressors and oppressed' cycle recommences—a point often made about Lenin's revolution. Government and the state can only be abolished by non-political means, from the outside. (Of course, in the wider sense of 'political' current today, all actions with political intent are political, even though they may not be institutionally so.) This dictate of conscience led some anarchists into strategic backwaters, as they felt unable to join any form of organization and ended up in a state of apolitical paralysis. Proudhon, for example, refused leadership and support to the delegates of the International who called themselves Proudhonists. By contrast, Bakunin spent his life indefatigably organizing associations and meetings, with propagandistic and educative aims.

The corollary of the attack on government is the rejection of *law* as the instrument of government *par excellence.* If government consists of a self-interested ruling class, its laws are inevitably biased in its favour: anarchists from Godwin onwards accepted that the ultimate purpose of law was the protection of private property. The *form* of law, a class weapon, and its *content*, the protection of various class interests, are thus inseparable, and the whole legal system must therefore be abolished. Godwin refuted the theoretical basis of law and punishment, arguing that the law neither deters nor informs, as it purports to do, and that it inevitably distorts by forcing particular acts into general categories of crime, inhumanely ignoring individual circumstances. The philosophical justifications of punishment are also fallacious because they are predicated on free will and responsibility. Since crime is socially determined, like all other actions, punishment is arbitrary and unjust: nor can it lead to individual or social improvement.[6] Although Godwin advanced his argument in the spirit of Enlightenment humanism, his logic reflects the new, 'scientific' social determinism too. A third reason for abolishing the legal system as an instrument of control, as both Godwin and Bakunin perceived, is that it abrogates the individual's rational moral judgement and so impairs his freedom: Bakunin defined freedom as following one's own reason and understanding justice.[7] Law is thus rejected by anarchists because it is a class weapon, is based on a false conception of freewill, and usurps individual reason and morality.

The anarchists perceived as clearly as the socialists the paradoxes of early capitalism: the co-existence of luxury and indigence, the fact that a diligent worker might nevertheless starve, and that he could not afford to buy what he produced. They too traced these evils to the institution of *private property*, alias capital accumulation, which enables the capitalist to exploit the worker. Proudhon's analysis of exploitation preceded that of Marx: he argued that the employer pays for individual workers' efforts, but pays nothing for the value of the collective effort of his workforce: it is this collective addition, created by the division of labour, that constitutes his surplus.[8] Accumulated capital should therefore be shared by all, Proudhon concluded, as nobody could claim exclusive ownership. Bakunin argued that conquest was the basis of the 'rights' of property and inheritance which permitted and legitimized the exploitation of the masses for the benefit of the few, and kept them in misery and ignorance.[9] For Kropotkin, the state, surplus value and wage labour constituted an invidious nexus which had to be totally destroyed. The adherence of most anarchists to a system of payment based on labour shows that their analysis of labour as the source of all value was close to that of Marx if less sophisticated. Their conclusion was the same: expropriate the owners of capital.

The relation of the anarchists to Marx and other socialists in the International was complex and turbulent.[10] Bakunin's theoretical and tactical disagreements with Marx ended by splitting the movement. The struggle for the International was fundamentally one of libertarian versus authoritarian socialism. The anarchists, with their plurality of views, opposed the dogmatism of the Marxists; they were also against the capture and use of the state as advocated by the German SPD. The anarchists had a less rigid notion of class than Marx or Lenin and did not all believe in the inevitability of class war—an idea which Proudhon considered merely wasteful! Bakunin's inclusion of the peasantry and lumpenproletariat in the revolutionary class antagonized Marx. The dictatorship of the proletariat, seen by Leninists as a necessary antidote to counter-revolution, merely signified the substitution of a new class of oppressors to the anarchists. As Sorel said, proletarian dictatorship merely meant a change of masters.[11] Furthermore, anarchists rightly doubted the state's capacity to 'wither away'.

So, while agreeing on the necessity for the revolution and the destruction of all capitalist institutions, anarchists disagreed with Marxists over the tactics by which this should be achieved, condemning the use of unions and political parties, and over what form the revolution would take. With regard to the organization of socialist society, the anarchists were deeply suspicious of Marx's proposed large-scale collectivism, fearing (again correctly) the emergence of what we now brand as state capitalism, and nationalism. In their turn, the Marxists considered the anarchists romantic, anti-scientific and impractical, and condemned their dream of federations of small communities as obsolete. Evidently, the Marxists had the best of the argument, although anarchists might draw consolation from having been right.

While defining itself as distinct from socialism and opposed to liberalism, anarchism shares characteristics with both. The dislike of the state and love of individual liberty is also found in the works of liberals such as Mill. But there is a crucial difference: liberals accept the necessity of a state to act as arbiter between individuals, though they prefer it to be minimal, and deny the class nature of the state; they also believe that the state can protect the people against itself, by means of civil rights. The liberal gives an account of freedom in terms of unlimited choice (usually expressed in money terms) and analyses freedom abstractly, as if the individual acted in a vacuum. The anarchist defines freedom through an account of the individual's place in society; likewise, his individualism is modified by the social context and in no way resembles the bourgeois 'egoism' which Marx decried, except in the doctrine of Stirner, who was in some ways a liberal extremist, rather than an anarchist. The resemblance of the two ideologies is therefore superficial at most. The tension between individual freedom and social needs is the focus of both theories, but in anarchism it is solved via a whole-hearted acknowledgement of the centrality of society to the being of each individual. While the liberal safeguards individual freedom with laws and rights, the anarchist solution rests on a faith in the natural unity of the individual's interests with those of his fellows, in the ideal society.

The Anarchist Order

Contrary to the popular opinion that the anarchist's ideas go no further than destruction, and that he is committed to 'the permanence of a revolutionary state of flux and to the impermanence of all social order'[12], a clear account can be given of the principles on which anarchist society would be based, although the details remain hazy. Anarchist society would be a 'natural', stateless entity based on morality, reason, and unmediated relationships between men, free from poison or distortion by the state, exploitation, and commerce. Despite the abolition of government and law, anarchist society is not a state of disorder or licence; order is produced by the internalization of moral values and norms, brought about by the development of the individual's moral faculty, and his reason. Self-control replaces control from above. Some anarchists even hoped that social good behaviour could become completely instinctive and spontaneous.

Anarchism would be organized on the basis of small communities bound together in a loose federation, a social form which avoids the centralization and nationalism so hated by anarchists, and removes the necessity for any vestige of state authority. The proposed nature of the communities varies: Godwin's craft-based 'parishes' and Proudhon's peasant villages might well be self-sufficient, whereas the Russian 'anarcho-communists' envisaged the federated communities as productive units in an economy built on the special-isation of functions, so that interdependence would be inevitable. The federal power (if any) would in all cases be kept to a minimum, strictly under the control of the community delegates. Some anarchists wish to eliminate industrial and urban life entirely: from Tolstoy to the advocates of alternative technology, they constitute the 'back to nature' strain of anarchism. But Kropotkin and others who accepted the irreversibility of industrialization also dreamed of re-integrating rural and urban life: Kropotkin's model was the communities of the Jura watchmakers—who actually claimed to be followers of the utopian socialist, Fourier!

The Moral Basis of Anarchist Society

The real interest of anarchism lies not in the precise details of communal organization, but in the universal principles on which such communities would rest. The claim that society could be governed by morality alone rests on an optimistic view of man's capacity for sociable behaviour which contrasts vividly with the orthodox view of man as a creature whose sinfulness or rampant egoism necessitates authoritative government. We cannot understand the moral optimism of anarchism without some appreciation of certain Enlightenment ideas which also influenced the development of socialist thought. Both ideologies held it to be axiomatic that man's nature and behaviour are determined by society.

Man is a social animal . . . he does not create society by means of a free agreement . . . society shapes and determines his human essence, man is dependent upon it as com-pletely as upon physical nature . . . social solidarity is the first human law; freedom is the second law.[13]

It follows that by changing the circumstances you can change the individual for the better: here is the rationale for radical social and political reform. Several consequences for the conception of human nature follow from such determinism. First, egalitarianism becomes a factual premise, rather than a moral claim. Equally blank or malleable men are necessarily equal, and so have equal rights and duties.

Second, environmentalism opens the way for an optimistic account of man. Godwin deduced the possibility of human perfectibility from his environmentalist premise, and hoped for limitless progress. However, social determinism led most anarchists to adopt Rousseau's more modest supposition that natural man is essentially innocent, knowing neither virtue nor vice. Bakunin wrote that

From his birth not a single human being is either bad or good . . . 'good', that is, the love of freedom, the consciousness of justice and solidarity, the cult of or rather the respect for truth, reason and labour can be developed in men only through upbringing and education.[14]

Hence, for the anarchist man starts out as a blank sheet, innocent and morally neutral. In the context of other doctrines which take a Hobbesian view of man's evil nature, this innocence has a positive moral quality about it, being in effect an assertion of man's *potential goodness*, and contradicting the dogma of original sin. In addition to innocence, the anarchists imputed various other qualities to man which were tantamount to the assertion that human goodness would be attainable in the right social context. The anarchist's second major ethical premise is that man is naturally sociable—a parallel to Rousseau's assumption that he has natural compassion.

Such sweeping premises about man's good nature inevitably raise the question 'How did society reach such a deplorable state?', which cannot be satisfactorily answered on the basis of the anarchist's methodological individualism, which emphasizes the actions of individuals. If all men are potentially sociable and compassionate, how do we explain the eternal division into oppressors and oppressed?[15] If men are only corrupted by institutions, how do we explain the origin of such evil institutions? Bakunin's suggestion that human misery is caused by a lack of hygiene and rational upbringing, by inequalities and ignorance, fails to explain how *these* arise. In fact, the premise of man's natural sociability and goodness mainly functions in anarchist ideology to exclude Hobbesian accounts of man, and most anarchists prefer to overlook the contradiction implicit in maintaining that man is good while society is bad.

Like most post-Enlightenment atheists, the early anarchists looked to 'Nature' as the source of moral values and other norms. Proudhon argued that social science has laws as natural and inexorable as those of physics: that societies are based on natural groups: that property (in the sense of collective ownership) and the division of labour are both natural, although capitalist property is 'impossible', against nature. Society is created by the spontaneous development of man's nature. He also saw *rightness* as lying in an 'organic equilibrium' of which truth, beauty, and justice are manifestations. While Proudhon blandly asserts such analogies between nature and society without further justification, Kropotkin's *Mutual Aid* details the parallels between society and the animal world, which he had studied scientifically. He used this evidence to prove that small communities were the natural form for human society, thus damning national boundaries and the centralized state as being *against Nature*. Bakunin maintained that whereas obedience to human authority was unacceptable, 'obedience' to natural social and economic laws constitutes freedom. Tolstoy displayed an instinctive 'naturalism' similar to Rousseau's when he extolled country life and decried the unnatural corruption of town and city. Even in the present century, Goodman uses 'natural society' as a measuring stick, while Read claims that only anarchist society is 'natural'. The anarchists' advocacy of spontaneous anti-state action is also symptomatic of their naturalistic convictions.

The appeal to Nature for the validation of political beliefs is open to many objections. Anarchists hold that there is a 'natural' form of society distinct from actual society which is 'unnatural': to prove the point, they cite primitive communities or animal groups as essentially natural. But in this realm of hypothesis, pre-history or natural history, it is anyone's guess what is the most natural form of society. Nature's book is open to too many readings. And the distinction which is drawn between the natural and the artificial will not stand up to scrutiny. (Man's most 'natural' state might be that of the pre-linguistic, cave-dwelling hunter, but no anarchists propose reversion to that condition; they are no more primitivist than Rousseau. They wish to discard only the aspects of civilization which they choose to regard as unnatural.) A parallel problem of defining 'the natural' arises when freedom is equated with obedience to natural laws. Who identifies these — the High Priest of Nature? Who decides whether marriage is more natural than polygamy, or vice versa? Natural laws are not self-evident, contrary to Bakunin's belief, nor is the form which a 'natural society' should take. At most, so-called natural laws reflect their discoverer's perception of human nature. Then again, it is not certain that if such natural principles could be unearthed they would necessarily be good, or promote happy and harmonious living among irreversibly *civilized* men. Similar objections can be made against the concept of 'authenticity' invoked by Goodman and other modern anarchists, which rests on an untenable distinction between man's 'authentic' essence and subsequent artifice, between Nature and nurture. Certainly, some of the anarchists' judgements based on the appeal to Nature seem intuitively right: small communities *are* preferable to conurbations, but surely this is because of their manifest advantages, not their 'naturalness'. Evidently, the vindication of anarchist principles by the appeal to nature is challengeable in many respects. However, this does not necessarily impugn other anarchist values, or contradict the idea of a society based on morality, for these ideas can be justified without any such appeal.

Freedom Within Society

Anarchism's supreme political ideal is individual freedom: supporting ideals are equality, co-operation, and solidarity. Freedom is specified in contrast to authority. For Bakunin, the term denotes both freedom from oppression by the external world, attained via knowledge, and freedom to act in conformity with one's own judgements. Furthermore, individual freedom has a social dimension.

Thus, too, the freedom of all is essential to my freedom. And it follows that it would be fallacious to maintain that the freedom of all constitutes a limitation upon my freedom for that would be tantamount to the denial of such freedom. On the contrary, universal freedom represents the necessary affirmation and the boundless expansion of individual freedom.[16]

For this reason, Bakunin says, even the master is in fact a slave in an oppressive society. The arch-egoist Stirner likewise maintained that to rule others destroys one's own independence. Such views reflect Kantian morality and Hegel's insight that only recognition by equals affords the individual satisfaction. Anarchists are thus able to argue that the abolition of authority will be as beneficial for the oppressors as for the oppressed!

But is individual freedom really connected analytically with the freedom of all? Given a certain conceptualization of the causal links operative in society, this can be shown to be true theoretically, but in reality many societies based on inequality and oppression seem to accord a remarkable degree of freedom to the elite. To equate personal freedom with freedom for all, therefore, either we must make it part of the definition that one cannot feel or be truly free while others are oppressed — and this is the upshot of the arguments of Hegel, Bakunin and others — or else we could use an analytic argument like Hart's, that the very idea of freedom contains the notion of equality of freedom. He shows that a natural right to be free would entail a right to *equal* freedom.[17]

But the liberal's analytic argument for equal freedom contrasts with that of the anarchist because it rests on the premise of free will (Hart asserts that 'the right is one which all men have if they are capable of choice'), which conflicts with the supposition of most anarchists that man is socially determined. Partial determinism is compatible with partial free will, of course, and this is the position that many thinkers today would accept, but Bakunin goes much further, demanding:

The negation of freewill . . . since every human individual is but an involuntary product of natural and social environment . . . The negation of freewill does not connote the negation of freedom. On the contrary, freedom represents the corollary, the direct result of natural and social necessity.[18]

Godwin undermined free will with philosophical arguments, showing that any action not fully determined by motives would not be free, but merely capricious. The freedom he most valued, private judgement, would in fact be freedom to operate in accordance with the dictates of reason.[19] By attacking free will in various ways, anarchists demarcated their idea of freedom from that of liberals, for whom free, abstract man performed his acts of choice in a vacuum created by theory. They advocate freedom, then, without subscribing to the philosophical and religious notion of free will: it is freedom *from* the coercion and oppression typical of the modern state, and from inequalities and scarcity. In other words, it aims at the rectification of our present state. And in freeing one individual by abolishing oppressive institutions, the anarchist would necessarily free *all*.

Freedom for one in the negative sense can thus be equated with freedom for all, but would the realization of more positive forms of individual freedom be limited in reality by the strongly collective nature of anarchist society? There seems to be a paradox here, and we must turn for a solution to the anarchist conception of the nature of society. Rousseau—who influenced many early anarchists—stipulated that in the formation of society, viewed ideally, man surrenders his natural being and freedom in exchange for a new moral being, capable of far greater satisfaction and enrichment. Proudhon echoes this in arguing that the free individual is also an integral part of the collective existence and carries in himself a 'social' morality which serves the collectivity. Two hypotheses about social morality are possible. Either we could suppose that morality is the creation of society and hence necessarily social, or else that an instinctive altruism is to be found even in pre-social man, which comes to fruition in the ideal society. These views are not, of course, incompatible and either would support the anarchist view of society as a collective moral entity greater than its individual parts.

From asserting the social nature of man and of morality, which is both created by society and binds it together, it is a short step to deducing the necessarily integrated and coherent nature of society and the importance of solidarity. However, the anarchists' appeal to social solidarity often seems mystificatory. We can perhaps understand how solidarity might be manifested in the workplace, a limited context—not so, solidarity in the community at large, where its scope and application would be unspecifiable and unlimited. Is there really any substantive content in Read's dictum, that 'subjective harmony would be reflected in personal integrity and social unity'? Or are the ideas of solidarity, integration, and unity vague hopes which turn out to be analytically vacuous?

Whatever the answer, the anarchist still has to explain how the strong social integration that he wants, which would presumably require conformity and sacrifices of individual self-interest on behalf of the whole, can be made compatible with extensive individual freedom. Various solutions are offered. Godwin and Bakunin both define freedom primarily in terms of reason or opinion, rather than as the pursuit of interests.

> To be personally free means for every man living in a social milieu not to surrender his thought or will to any authority but his own reason and his own understanding of justice . . . not to submit to any other law but the one arrived at by his own conscience.[20]

For Godwin, 'private judgement' (reason) is the essence of freedom, but reason entails giving justifications for one's actions which will be publicly assessed and accepted as valid. Hence, there is already a social element built into private judgement. Ultimately since society forms man as a free and rational being, the exercise of the individual's rational judgement should not run counter to society's interests — in the anarchist utopia, where pure reason rules. Thus, when freedom is severed from self-interest and transformed into a quality of mind, the collective nature of freedom and the necessary connection between individual freedom and social unity, can be asserted. Another possibility is to define freedom, as Bakunin sometimes does, as obedience to natural laws, which would favour society as a whole — but this sounds suspiciously like being free to do what we ought to want to do, and to the liberal way of thinking at least, freedom should include the chance to be bad, and to make mistakes. This is where the anarchists make an act of faith: they believe that a society could be created which was so harmonious and benign that everyone would freely wish to do what was good for society as a whole, and thereby for themselves.

Order Without Dependence

For a further understanding of the individual's relationship with his fellows in anarchist society, we must examine the concept of *dependence*. 'Dependence' may denote a loving, caring relationship, such as that of child to mother, but in anarchist argument it signifies dependence upon another's arbitrary whims or commands, a relation of inequality. The anarchists were strongly influenced in their condemnation of dependence by Rousseau. Analysing the origins of inequality, he asked 'What ties of dependence would there be among men without possession?' As property develops, so do inequalities and dependence, whose origins lie in both need and in power-seeking greed. Man becomes an extended being in the worse sense — 'social man . . . only knows how to live in the opinion of others' — and so is corrupted, although, paradoxically, dependence is the only road to self-fulfilment since moral being presupposes society and society presupposes interdependence. For Rousseau, dependence comes about because civilized man, unlike the savage, is not self-sufficient: the power of man over man is always degrading, because it detracts from his human essence, his free choice, and his natural independence. Rousseau therefore proposed in the *Social Contract* to substitute the law for the personal domination of powerful individuals, and proposed the General Will as a means whereby each should depend on all. However, some critics interpret this as requiring the complete subjugation of the individual to the whole.[21]

The anarchists concurred with Rousseau on the corrupting influence of man's authority over man and its corollary, dependence, being witnesses to archaic feudal relationships in Russia, the domination of employer over employee in Europe, and the domination of oppressive governments everywhere. Dependence in social life and economic production they accepted as *natural*, but the dependence created by authority was not so, and ran counter to the proper equality of mankind. The dependence of one man on another because of his power was a degradation of his nature. Godwin's dislike of it led him to reject all forms of co-operation, even playing in orchestras! Bakunin deplored the 'incessant mutual dependence' of individuals and the mass, and demanded independence from the despotic acts of men. Such strictures are quite compatible with many anarchists' acceptance of men's natural interdependence as social animals, which would form the basis of anarchist society. It was the elements of personal, irresponsible power, inequality, and coercion which made the prevalent forms of dependence so obnoxious. Like the utopian socialists, the anarchists proposed that *each* should depend on *all*. Such reciprocal dependence would not degrade man's nature. How, then, would such a society, which eschewed political dependence and authority, function?

Rousseau's solution of the organizational problem by the impartial, truth-embodying General Will was not satisfactory for anarchists, since it would entail the perpetuation of the state. But since they accepted that order must somehow be maintained, other solutions had to be sought. Bakunin recommended obedience to natural laws, and independence from the commands of men, whether individual or collective. This typifies the anarchist idea of a self-regulating society in which individuals 'spontaneously' obey unwritten, unenforced laws through instinct, reason, morality or a combination of all three. Self-control is the watchword. Proudhon defined anarchy as the government of each by himself; order would be enforced by public and private consciousness. Godwin too proposes that order be maintained by self-control and mutual moral surveillance—he even argues that each man should appoint himself the moral inquisitor of his neighbour![22]

At this point, it becomes clear that *absolute* freedom is as much a chimera for the anarchist as for the liberal, even when the worst forms of dependence are abolished. Whether I am controlled by my neighbour's disapproval or my internalized moral precepts and conscience, I am not paradigmly free: self-government by guilt and conscience may be more oppressive than government by law. My neighbour's interventions may not always be rational and benign, and even if I govern myself entirely, according to morality, someone else still has to inculcate the moral code, which suggests a relationship of domination. In any case, such self-control would only leave me free to do what I should do. These difficulties explain why anarchists tried to fuse the moral and rational with the *instinctual* and to prove that obedience to natural laws would be spontaneous, free of *any* control or restraint since morality itself is *natural*. But this idea of a spontaneous morality constitutes another dubious appeal to nature.

An alternative way of creating order without dependence and domination is advocated by Proudhon—contractualism, or 'mutualism'. *Free* association is not oppressive, he argued, and can be achieved by a multiplicity of contracts governing all social action. The idea of a fair contract, also the lynch-pin of liberal thought and practice, presupposes equality and good faith between the parties, a paradigm which capitalism belies; capitalist contracts, therefore, produce dependence and injustice rather than mutual benefit for equal contractors. The contracts which Proudhon envisaged would be made after the abolition or equalization of property, and so would be fair. Economic organization would be based on contractual exchange operating through a voucher system which would reflect the value of labour in each product; Proudhon's People's Bank, which never came to fruition, was meant to establish just such a system. As to political organization, he condemned all 'existing' social contracts as unfair, taking more freedom from the citizen than he kept, and he proposed to substitute contracts between citizen, commune, and federal authority which would reserve the majority of powers to the individual: his rights would only be restricted so as to avoid encroaching on the rights of others in the commune. What Proudhon had in mind was, clearly, a series of explicit contracts, not the hypothetical social contract by which liberals justified state authority.[23]

Two major criticisms can be made of contractualism. First, it is doubtful that such contracts would be observed in the absence of law or authority: such reasoning led Hobbes to deduce the necessity of a sovereign. Proudhon might reply that in a situation of freedom and equality contracts will be made only when they are so beneficial that the parties are motivated to keep them. But circumstances, and people's wants and needs, change: a beneficial contract today may be deleterious in a year's time. This leads on to the second criticism, which Godwin made long before Proudhon was writing: permanent contracts infringe our liberty.[24] Godwin attacked marriage and similar institutions for this reason. If an anarchist holds that being bound to keep a promise he has voluntarily made infringes his liberty then, logically, he should never make promises: yet contractualism is an important element in some anarchist theory. Can the anarchist who wants to maximize individual freedom consistently hold that men are bound by contracts and promises? According to some accounts of self-identity—for example, Godwin's, where the individual is viewed as an ever-changing entity—a promise freely made by Self I at Time I would intolerably restrict the freedom of Self II at Time II. But if the Self is instead regarded as a persisting, rational entity, it would be irrational and immoral for him to repudiate promises and contracts unless external conditions had changed dramatically. The first, extreme, position, which Godwin advocates, if followed to the letter would destroy the possibility of society or self-fulfilment since most of the activities which make life worth living rest on explicit or implicit contracts or promises—making friends, joining a club, marrying, and so on. Without such promises, or if they were made but constantly repudiated, life would be chaotic and pointless. The anarchist who rejects all contractual notions is bereft of a constructive basis for society.

Anarchist Individualism

The goal of anarchism is to eliminate dependence and oppression. The abolition of authority will bring about freedom which in turn will promote individual happiness. Anarchism, like liberalism, focuses on the individual: how, then, do their concepts differ? First, most anarchists accept the essentially social nature of man and would dismiss as unrealistic the abstract individuals who populate orthodox liberal thought — for example, rational economic man, whose maximized profits are attributed entirely to his own efforts, rather than to the social network which facilitates his enterprise. Their criticism of liberal individualism parallels Marx's attack on bourgeois rights. Proudhon and Kropotkin both divined that, since capitalism depended on co-operative labour, the liberals' declaration of extreme individualism was false. Kropotkin also condemned the 'narrow-minded' individualism which results from the absorption of so many functions by the state, a condition exacerbated by the modern welfare state. Nevertheless, capitalism was a necessary precondition for the development of anarchist ideas of individualism. Read argued that individualism is only possible in a complex society with an elaborate division of labour.[25] Anarchists conceive of individualism as self-fulfilment within society, not as the withdrawal and self-differentiation which liberals emphasize and which ultimately rests on wealth. While anarchists, like liberals, locate the ultimate value in the individual, they re-define satisfaction in non-economic, non-utilitarian terms and their conception of freedom highlights the inseparability of the individual-society amalgam. Society is analogous to a multiple equation in which each interconnecting variable (each individual) is to be maximized at a level consistent with equal maximization of all the other variables.

Individual fulfilment is achieved through *creative work*. Godwin's ideal of leisurely craftsmanship is echoed in many other anarchist accounts of work. Proudhon said that 'social communion and human solidarity' are the products of ideal labour. Properly organized work would surpass leisure pursuits in the pleasure it provided. He considered the division of labour a natural, permanent phenomenon which makes each individual equally useful to society. For Kropotkin it was axiomatic that 'everyone should be pleased with his work' and he, like William Morris, cited mediaeval cathedrals as symbols of co-operative, spiritually uplifting labour. Bakunin was less idealistic: work was, simply, the source of all value and utility, and men must work to live. He also suggested that those unwilling to work should be deprived of political rights for shirking their duties to the community, and left to starve.[26] A severe pronouncement (possibly addressed to future ex-capitalists), but one not altogether antithetical to anarchist ethics: love for the individual does not entail sympathy for the 'free-rider'. For the more socialistic anarchists, work was the all-important source of social value, individual satisfaction, and moral virtue. They probably underestimated the alienating nature of industrial work: whether satisfying work is possible in the industrial context is a question which neither Bakunin nor Marx debated at sufficient length, since they predicated work satisfaction upon the ending of exploitation.

Godwin and Thoreau sought to reduce labour to a minimum, so as to maximize the time available for intellectual pursuits. Despite his admiration for craftsmanship, Godwin prophesied that machinery would reduce necessary labour time to half-an-hour a day, while Thoreau praised 'fruitful idleness', a concept which seems to presuppose the backdrop of an industrious society which nurtures the fruitfully idle.[27] Admittedly, both were prepared to settle for a more ascetic form of life in exchange for greater leisure, but neither had much understanding of the irreversibility of industrialization. However, many contemporary anarchists would find themselves more in accord with these two than with the anarchists who imagined that industrial work would continue, in an idealized form.

Co-operation, of which capitalist production offers a sad travesty, was to be the basis of anarchist society. This could take various forms. 'Natural' co-operation, seen in the lives of animals, was instanced in the family, an institution which many anarchists upheld, unlike the early socialists, perhaps for the reason invoked by modern pluralists, that it constitutes a defence against the potentially authoritarian state. 'Social' or 'artificial' co-operation is exemplified in the division of labour. Proudhon's contractualism formalizes co-operation between individuals and groups, while other anarchists hoped for spontaneous co-operation based on the moral sense which would pervade all social activity. Obviously, all forms of human life rest on some degree of co-operation, whether conscious, unwilling or unwitting. But the anarchists were not merely stating this truism, for they asserted the principle of co-operation against the prevalent ideology of competition which social Darwinism had reinforced.

Can the co-operative organization of society be reconciled with the anarchist preoccupation with independence and freedom? Not for Godwin, who considered it a violation of individuality. But if the individual is viewed as a being-in-society, and the essentially co-operative nature of society acknowledged, the two can be reconciled, at least in theory. Co-operation is a quasi-moral concept which reconciles altruism and egoism by asserting that the individual enhances his own good by promoting the good of all.

Anarchist Values

Social justice necessarily results from organizing society on anarchist principles. All anarchists advocate the abolition of property and inheritance, and egalitarian policies, but there is no general agreement among them on the form which the new distribution should take. Proudhon favoured the ownership of land and tools by peasants to safeguard their independence. The Russians, influenced by socialist doctrines, advocated collective ownership of the means of production by each 'productive unit': Kropotkin envisaged these as communities, Bakunin as industrial associations. But by contrast, the maverick Stirner asserts 'What man can obtain belongs to him: the world belongs to *me*. Neither God nor Man ('human society') is proprietor, but the individual'.[28] Few anarchists would have agreed with this solipsistic view of social justice.

The idealization of equality is a necessary consequence of the anarchist view of man. Equality is implicit in all propositions about the abolition of authority and property: it is also a precondition of co-operation, which cannot succeed among unequals. Various definitions of equality were proposed to serve as the basis of social justice. For Godwin, justice is the distribution of goods to those who can best benefit from them (equality of satisfaction). Proudhon advocates equality of conditions (equality of opportunity) but not of wellbeing, which is the worker's own responsibility. He also says that anarchy is 'an order where all *relationships* are of equality'. Bakunin espouses distributive justice according to 'deeds', or work, measured in labour time (equality of treatment), whereas Kropotkin, true to the principles of mutual aid, and doubting that anyone would shirk the joys of creative work, proposes distribution according to need (equality of satisfaction). Anarchists tend to ignore the haunting problem of scarce 'positional' goods, which cannot be distributed on an egalitarian basis, and also that of natural inequalities. But it could be argued that most positional goods would disappear altogether—for example, power and prestige—as would the desire for such things. Godwin predicted that the desire for distinction would disappear along with property. If such hopes fail, maybe an authoritative allocation would still be needed, and this could undermine the basis of anarchist society. Or perhaps a non-authoritarian principle of distribution could be agreed, such as a lottery or a rotation system, to preserve the essentially egalitarian nature of anarchist justice.

An important instrumental value in anarchist society is *education*. Enlightenment philosophers such as Condorcet had remarked that the ignorance of the masses made them prey to exploiters and charlatans, a theme taken up by the anarchists, some of whom, like Godwin, advocated education for its spiritually elevating effect while others, like Proudhon and Bakunin, saw it as an instrument of liberation, since the strength of authority decreases as the level of education increases. The ideal was a 'polytechnical' education: a balanced training in science, the arts, and professional studies. The need for education follows from the view that man is a *tabula rasa*: education can transform him. In the anarchist scheme of things, it has three distinct functions: first, to increase the understanding of workers so that they are able to throw off the yoke of authority and, second, to re-educate those brought up under the old system. The third, continuing, function would be as a device for maintaining order: the process of reasoning would be taught in school, as would the moral principles which formed the basis of the anarchist order. Education is a recurrent theme in radical and anarchist thought today, with writers such as Illich and Frire rejecting the structures of authority built into education systems and recommending forms of education which emphasize *learning* rather than *teaching*.[29] The belief in education as a pure tool of enlightenment is redolent of the anarchist's basic optimism about human nature.

This account of the principles of anarchist society has drawn mainly on nineteenth-century anarchism and has said little about the innovations of the libertarian anarchists of the last two decades, mainly because they offer no coherent theoretical account of anarchist society. Those brought up on a countercultural diet of Marcuse's Freud, Timothy Leary *et al.* perceive the anarchist ideal largely in terms of personal spiritual liberation or escape, which can hardly form the basis of a *social* theory. The vaguely defined psychological focus of such theories is alienation, and there is a resigned acceptance that authority is an insidious Hydra whose heads appear everywhere: individual release is the best hope. But today's anarchists preserve some of the old doctrines—a resistance to Marxist-Leninist authoritarianism and a refusal to organize politically, which means that they prefer spontaneous action and 'situationism' to concerted activity. In many cases the anarchist impulse has been transformed into self-centred spiritual preoccupations, like Zen and other forms of meditation. The tactics vary between violent, hopeless conflict with police and troops, and the peaceful symbolism of putting flowers in the barrels of soldiers' guns. The plurality of approaches and aims among modern 'liberationists' makes it hard to codify their thought as a political ideology: nevertheless, they offer important critiques of contemporary society.[30]

Objections to Anarchist Theory

The most frequent objection to anarchism is that, nice though it would be, we could never entirely eliminate anti-social acts and crimes by the use of morality. Undoubtedly, some small communities have successfully eliminated deviance on the basis of shared moral or religious codes: the mechanism of self-enforcement and mutual surveillance has been proved very effective—while the supposedly deterrent effect of punishment is still a subject of controversy. A combination of morality and incentives to good behaviour could perhaps maintain social order. As for criminals or disruptive elements, Godwin suggested expulsion, while Bakunin suggested starvation for the anti-social individuals who refused to contribute. But later, 'having become exceedingly rare exceptions, those cases of idleness shall be regarded as special maladies to be subjected to clinical treatment'.[31] To be consistent, anarchist society should tolerate 'deviance' (the concept itself is an authoritarian one, according to radical sociologists) but this might threaten social unity. The objection about deviance is a practical one, but is based on a theoretical disagreement over the nature of man: if you accept the anarchists' optimistic view, the possibility of a society without deviance follows. A related question is whether the moral principles which anarchist individuals followed would coincide sufficiently to produce social unity without some authoritarian imposition of a moral code. Some anarchists emphasized private judgement in moral matters, but would the result not be a wild diversity of moralities? This seems a risk in the days of moral subjectivism, but the early anarchists believed that there were discoverable moral *truths*, existing in nature or in human reason, which could be universally known and followed—and this was the basis of their optimism, although it appears as their weakness to the modern moral philosopher.

Another frequent criticism of anarchism is that *leadership* is a 'natural' phenomenon which cannot be abolished. Leadership is not identical to what the anarchists meant by authority which was, for them, an essentially coercive phenomenon, and leadership might therefore exist in the absence of authority. In a society of equals, people could accept the leadership of, say, a scientist on some decision in his field of expertise, without following him on other matters: he would be *an* authority, not *in* authority. The fact that many people today think of leadership as natural and necessary is partly the product of their education and of the structure of society, both of which are tailored to produce two classes, the leaders and the led. But the idea of a leaderless society is not self-contradictory, or inconceivable, and in the last two decades there have been experiments in decision-taking without leadership: for example, consensus management in the British National Health Service, and collective decision-making in the women's movement. The major disadvantage is the slowness of decisions taken collectively rather than by executive: the great advantage is that those involved afterwards feel that their views were taken into account, and will adhere to the decisions. It is this sense of control over one's own destiny, which can never be achieved under authority, which anarchist society would promote. And the anarchist analysis is valuable in illuminating the conceptual separation of leadership and authority.

The Ethics of Violence

The strongest criticism of anarchism concerns its exponents' willingness to use violent methods. In fact, the pervasive caricature of the bomb-throwing anarchist is belied by most anarchist theory. A variety of non-violent means have been proposed for the realization of the anarchist ideal. Godwin believed in the force of moral persuasion, while Proudhon advocated propaganda plus passive resistance to government, both of which he practised himself. Similarly, Thoreau engaged in civil disobedience and personal withdrawal from the society which he found so corrupt. The most commonly canvassed tactics were those of propaganda, education, and self-help. In the 1880s the 'narodniki' set out to live with and educate the Russian peasants as the first step towards revolution. Bakunin's preference for violence and conspiracy is usually attributed to his collaboration with the anarchist Nechayev, who was obsessed with assassination and terror; at other times Bakunin also favoured education. Tolstoy was famous for his pacifism and Kropotkin too was essentially pacific, although he argued that violence was justifiable as retaliation against governments using force. This argument is reiterated by modern anarcho-socialists such as Marcuse, who maintains that the covert violence of the modern state justifies a violent response; other modern 'liberationist' thinkers advocate withdrawal from the oppressive society and the establishment of communes which have a propagandistic intent as well as offering the free life on a microcosmic scale. In this sense Nozick's recent recommendation of a plurality of small communities as the anarchist utopia constitutes a kind of anarchist theory based on the commune movement, although the egoistic terms in which he describes the dynamics of the system make him undeniably a liberal or conservative thinker.[32] Ridicule has also been used as an anarchist tactic, as it was by the American students who nominated a pig for president. It could be more widely used as a powerful, non-violent weapon but its main disadvantage is that it offers no *positive* message to the unconverted. This brief survey suggests that anarchists cannot and should not be universally identified as advocates of violence and terrorism.

Militant and violent anarchists fall into two main groups: the anarcho-syndicalists, and the many individual anarchists who espoused assassination and 'propaganda by deed', methods which are branded as 'terrorism' by the modern state. Any account of their activities falls into the area of history rather than theory, but the arguments justifying such tactics must be considered. Anarcho-sydicalism flourished in France and Russia (1890–1910) and in Spain in the 1930s. The anarchist syndicates, or unions, used the economic strike weapon for political purposes. Strikes were spontaneous, often violent, and were prolonged even when employers made concessions, for political effect. The movement declined in France and Russia for various reasons — partly because many improvements were gained and employment increased, partly because moderate workers preferred to join different unions as the militant unions antagonized government and public opinion.

The writer Sorel attached himself to the cause of anarcho-syndicalism, and his book, *Reflections on Violence*, justifies violent means. He maintained that middle-class violence is pervasive but disguised, and justified by reference to God and the state, whereas proletarian violence is 'purely and simply an act of war', and one thoroughly justified by the brutal nature of state violence. Sorel glorified the general strike as a myth by which workers could act, and terrorize politicians. Although agreeing with some tenets and aims of Marxism, he emphasized the mythical nature of the strike and the 'catastrophic' nature of the transition to socialism to show that the revolution would be a practical, spontaneous, emotional act not capturable in 'scientific' theory. This anti-intellectual, apocalyptic vision was combined with tactical advice to syndicates: bourgeois attempts at conciliation of the strikers must be repulsed by increased violence and higher demands, to intensify the struggle. Violence itself had an expressive and educative function. Sorel presents his advice as a tract on the ethics of violence, distinguishing it from 'brutality' (the middle-class epithet for proletarian violence) and finding in it something pure, a virtue of its own.

In the total ruin of institutions and morals there remains something which is powerful, new and intact . . . the soul of the revolutionary.[33]

Although today Sorel is associated as much with fascism as with anarchism, owing to the espousal of his views by some Nazis, his arguments widely influenced the anarchists of his time.

What Sorel, the syndicalists and the individual anarchists who committed acts of terror, had in common was a belief in the exemplary nature of action. Propaganda by deed would intensify people's feelings of oppression and initiate the struggle. The individuals who planted bombs, often suicidally, or attempted assassinations were partisans of heroic violence — the logical choice for the anti-political anarchist — whereas the syndicalists had to concede the necessity of organization, since individuals cannot make a strike. However, all forms of violence, including those like political strikes, which do not necessarily involve physical coercion, meet with the same objections from the modern democratic state. They are categorized and condemned as criminal, as anti-democratic, as violating the sanctity of human life, and as treating human beings as means to an end — a moral crime in itself, which is exacerbated when the end is only desired by a minority.

It seems that the state, which claims to speak for the people, whatever its political complexion, holds all the moral trumps. So can any defence be offered of violence by anarchists who choose it as a method? Three defences suggest themselves, which may be used in combination, but which sometimes get misleadingly confused. The first is that *violence merits violence*. This principle can be justified in two different ways. First, it could be argued that whoever uses violence deserves, in some absolute moral sense, retaliation — the *lex talionis*. Advocates of violence in a secular era hesitate to use this justification since it invites many challenges: in what sense does the attacker 'deserve' the retaliation? Who shall judge precisely what degree of violence he deserves, and ensure that it will not be excessive? Although the assassination of a despotic ruler sometimes appears as rightful revenge, it is hard to decide when such revenge is proper, and against whom. In democratic societies, the power-holders are our own representatives, and if they are held to be guilty of oppression and to merit revenge, then so do we all: their victimization then appears merely arbitrary and, equally, the assassination of any individual elector would logically be justified by his complicity in their actions. (The violence of the IRA against private individuals is sometimes justified on such grounds, and because 'he who is not with us is against us'.) The consequence of using revenge as a justification is that in a democratic society with the diffusion of responsibility all are equally implicated!

In fact, the crude be-done-by-as-you-would-do morality which revenge implies would be eschewed by most anarchists, although the principle of revenge is sometimes cited as a rhetorical justification of violence. But as anarchists believe in the social determination of individuals, and often condemn punishment for this reason, they should, consistently, reject the idea of revenge.

The other version of the 'violence merits violence' argument more often invoked today, does not maintain that two wrongs make a right, as the first version seems to, but that violence in self-defence against violent attack, duress or coercion, is permissible. This view condones and limits, rather than justifies, violence. The principle of self-defence is established in law and was accepted by Hobbes and Locke as a consequence of the first 'law of nature', which commands self-preservation. Perhaps the right to self-defence *is* axiomatic and requires no further justification, but the situations in which it is usually invoked are not analogous to the paradigm case of the directly threatened individual. The revolutionary or terrorist often claims to be acting *on behalf of others* (not always with their consent), whose lives are *not directly threatened* (even if they are made miserable), by attacking those who are *functionaries* of the state and are not themselves the oppressors. Imagine that an anarchist discovers the whereabouts of a state computer which secretly amasses data with potentially coercive uses; he plants a bomb in the building which destroys the computer but kills several clerks and programmers. The dead individuals scarcely merited this violence (unless one accepts the dangerous principle of guilt by association), which was really aimed at the originators of the system and the state in general, both of which are well out of reach of the bomb. Nor was this a paradigm case of self-defence, unless the term is extended so far as to become meaningless. Similarly, when bombs are planted in expensive metropolitan restaurants, a practice common to past and present anarchists and other revolutionaries, those killed are not usually members of 'the establishment', but are said to be symbolic representatives of state power because of their wealth and status. Again, their 'violence' (as members of the ruling class, even if passive ones) can only be said to justify the violence done to them by a roundabout chain of reasoning, whether self-defence or retaliation is cited as the grounds. The assassination of a repressive monarch or an authoritarian politician seems, *prima facie*, more justifiable, and it should be remembered that most anarchist theory was developed at a time when such individuals were numerous: but the attempted adaptation of the justifications by revenge and self-defence to the modern democratic state causes grave difficulties.

The anarchist's predicament is that he wishes to destroy an abstraction — authority, or the state — but can only kill individuals. The state's structure is impregnable and somewhat intangible, and so the tactics of erosion are used: but these destroy innocent individuals. The 'reciprocal violence in self-defence' arguments seems morally valid as a general justification of violent opposition to a state which is provenly coercive, but it fails to vindicate particular cases of violence against individuals who are in no sense guilty of violence themselves, or whose complicity in an oppressive system does not justify making them suffer for the guilt of all the rest. It is also hard to establish when the case really is one of self-defence: that there is a real threat to individuals' lives or wellbeing. And how many people must be under threat before self-defence can be invoked? In the modern state most social control is now so unobtrusive that it does not manifest itself as coercion or repression — but rather as indoctrination, or the manipulation of the rate of employment — and so does not seem to merit a violence response, which would appear excessive.

The second justification of violence offered by some anarchists is that *the ends justify the means*, a necessary precept of revolutionary thought. This implies that violence, even against a symbolic victim, is justified by its consequences, and the ideality of the revolutionary's goal. But both the Christian and humanist moralities prevalent in Western society hold that the preservation of human life is an end in itself—the highest end—and that taking life cannot be justified as a means to an end, except possibly in the controversial cases where this preserves many other lives, as in a war, or the shooting of a terrorist holding several hostages. This stance is reinforced philosophically by Kant's injunction that men should be treated as ends in themselves, never as the means to other men's ends. But the anarchist who advocates violence may provisionally accept the sanctity of life, while arguing that in an oppressive society this has in some instances to be subordinated to the struggle for a better life for all: it cannot therefore be regarded as inviolable. Unfortunately, the terrorist does not pause to consult his victims on this fine moral point. (If his victims are power-holders, he might also argue that the 'right' to reciprocal violence overrides the sanctity of life argument. The implication of this would be that there are two classes of individuals, one whose right to life is forfeit because of their oppression of their fellows.) Ultimately, an anarchist employing this argument has to contend—and believe —that the goal of an anarchist society, with benefits for the many, justifies violence against the few. Violence is thus vindicated by a calculation of the social good. But this argument is nullified by those who maintain the absolute sanctity of life, and in advancing it the anarchist or revolutionary finds himself with strange bedfellows, the utilitarians!

A third defence, which avoids directly sanctioning violence, runs as follows: the state creates a self-justifying moral ideology, which includes the doctrine of the sanctity of life (often extended to cover property), not through a genuine respect for life, but so that the state can condemn *a priori* any move towards revolutionary change. This morality is hypocritical and deceptive. The revolutionary should therefore disregard its precepts and create his own revolutionary ethic. Marx, Lenin, and Sorel would all have agreed with this reasoning, even if they sometimes appealed to the false morality's concept of responsibility in arguing that the ruling class deserved violent destruction. This approach, then, justifies violence indirectly by refusing to debate it in terms of the orthodoxy which condemns it.

There is evidently an unbridgeable gap between the individual's desire for self-preservation and respect (which the precept of the sanctity of life expresses as a moral right), and the moral calculus which justifies violent means by good ends, which benefit society. No advocate of revolutionary violence, including the anarchist, is likely to produce a justification which would satisfy his victim, because of this lacuna. Subjective morality, which puts self-preservation at a premium, is on a different level from the 'objective' social morality to which revolutionaries make appeal. And because the state, including the Church, is the source of moral authority, the revolutionary is unlikely to be able to justify his actions to the majority of the population which has been inculcated with such ideas, even if his victims are carefully selected politicians, not randomly chosen civilians. He must simply accept being treated as a criminal and a moral outlaw, according to their legality and morality, and hope for the triumph of his idea through the enlightenment of the population by his propagandistic deeds. The process is a long one.

Curiously, anarchists have been attacked more fiercely for their sporadic, spontaneous use of violence than have Marxists for their explicitly revolutionary violence—perhaps this is because its random, terroristic aspect makes it so menacing to the mass of the population. The early association of anarchism with the pure destructiveness of nihilism also discredited it. But such associations have distorted the public image of a political ideology which has never ceased to advocate a pacific, moral form of society based on *good will* free from all violence and oppression. While the virtues of the anarchist ideal can and should be evaluated separately from the question of methods, the anarchists' reflections on the ethics of violence also deserve consideration in a world where political violence is increasingly common. However, anarchism's strength lies not in its occasional advocacy of violent means, but in the model which it offers of a free society which differs from the liberal model, of which it constitutes a criticism. Although some forms of anarchism, such as those of Nozick and Stirner, manifest themselves as extreme forms of right-wing individualism, anarchism in general is a political ideology which realizes the best socialist ideals without the intervention of the potentially authoritarian state.

Notes

1. D. Hall, 'Irony and anarchy', in *Alternative Futures*, Vol. 2. No. 2., pp. 3–24.
2. G. Woodcock, *Anarchism*, Penguin, Harmondsworth, 1963, pp. 36–9.
3. M. Bakunin, 'Social and economic bases of anarchism. in *The Anarchists* (Ed. I. Horowitz), Dell, 1964, p. 133.
4. Bakunin, 'Social and economic bases of anarchism', p. 142–4.
5. W. Godwin, *Enquiry Concerning Political Justice* (Ed. K. C. Carter), Oxford University Press, 1971, pp. 210–14. To be referred to as *Enquiry* hereafter.
6. Godwin, *Enquiry*, pp. 244–77. See also B. Goodwin, *Social Science and Utopia*, Harvester, 1978, pp. 93–100.
7. Bakunin, 'Social and economic bases of anarchism', p. 137.
8. P.-J. Proudhon, *Selected Writings* (Trans. E. Fraser), Macmillan, 1970, pp. 42–7.
9. Bakunin, 'Social and economic bases of anarchism', p. 143.
10. These disputes are charted in Woodcock, *Anarchism*, Chap. 9.
11. G. Sorel, *Reflections on Violence* (Trans. T. E. Hulme and J. Roth), Collier, 1961.
12. Horowitz, 'Postscript' in *The Anarchists*, p. 590.
13. Bakunin, 'Social and economic bases of anarchism', p. 135.
14. Bakunin, 'Social and economic bases of anarchism', p. 141.
15. This point is made in connection with the modern anarchist, Paul Goodman, in T. Roszak, *The Makings of a Counter Culture*, Faber, 1971, p. 195.
16. Bakunin, 'Social and economic bases of anarchism', pp. 136–7.
17. H. A. L. Hart, 'Are there any natural rights?' in *Political Philosophy* (Ed. A. Quinton), p. 53.
18. Bakunin, 'Social and economic bases of anarchism', p. 134.
19. Godwin, *Enquiry*, Bk IV, Chap. 7.

20. Bakunin, 'Social and economic bases of anarchism', p. 136.
21. For Rousseau's comments on dependence see his *Discourse . . . On Inequality*, Dent, 1913, pp. 189, 208.
22. Godwin, *Enquiry* Vol. I, 1st edn, Dublin, 1973, pp. 106–7.
23. Proudhon, *Selected Writings*, pp. 56–70.
24. Godwin, *Enquiry,* pp. 102–11.
25. H. Read, 'The philosophy of anarchism', in *Anarchy and Order*, Faber & Faber, 1954.
26. Bakunin, 'Social and economic bases of anarchism', pp. 137. 141–2.
27. H. D. Thoreau, *Walden* (Ed. J. Krutch), Bantam, 1962.
28. M. Stirner, 'The ego and his own' in Horowitz, *The Anarchists*, p. 311.
29. See I. Illich, *Deschooling Society*, Penguin, 1973 and N. Postman and C. Weingartner, *Teaching as a Subversive Activity*, Penguin, 1971.
30. For accounts of modern anarchist theory and practice see Roszak, *The Makings of a Counter Culture* and D. Apter and J. Joll (Eds), *Anarchism Today*, Macmillan, 1971.
31. Bakunin, 'Social and economic bases of anarchism', p. 142.
32. R. Nozick, *Anarchy, State and Utopia*, Blackwell, 1974.
33. Sorel, *Reflections on Violence,* p. 49.

Further reading

R. P. Wolff, *In Defence of Anarchism,* Harper & Row, 1970.
I. Horowitz, *The Anarchists*, Dell, 1964, Extracts.
J. R. Pennock and J. W. Chapman, (Eds), *Anarchism*, New York University Press, 1978.
J. Joll, *The Anarchists*, Eyre & Spottiswoode, 1964.

CHAPTER 7

Conservatism

Conservative mentality as such has no predisposition towards theorising. This is in accord with the fact that human beings do not theorise about the actual situations in which they live as long as they are well adjusted to them . . . Conservative mentality as such has no utopia.
(Mannheim)

It is with infinite caution that any man ought to venture upon pulling down an edifice which has answered in any tolerable degree for ages the common purposes of society.
(Burke)

As Mannheim suggests, conservatism is not an explicit or self-proclaimed ideology. There are no essential conservative texts, although many texts are conservative. The literal meaning of the term comes from the idea of *conservation*, and conservative ideology is formulated anew in response to each attack made on the existing social order, which conservatives wish to conserve. Thus, conservatives in the last two centuries have taken issue in turn with radicalism, liberalism, and socialism. The conservative ideology discussed here is not to be confused with the doctrines of the British Conservative Party, which are presented to the electorate in the form of concrete policies. It should also be remembered that we conceive of conservatism differently from other Europeans, as a result of our political history. In the nineteenth century, reforming conservative ministries were not uncommon — those of Peel and Disraeli are famous — while after 1922 the Conservative Party displaced the Liberals and became the chief opponent of socialism, absorbing in the process many liberal beliefs. The acceptance of constitutional government and individual rights distinguishes our tradition of liberal conservatism from that elsewhere in Europe, where conservatism was, and often still is, associated with royalism, catholicism, and other reactionary or authoritarian tendencies. This should be borne in mind, since the conservative outlook described here may seem more illiberal to British readers than the Conservative politics with which they are familiar. In so far as conservatism can be presented as an ideology, it is because it derives from a small number of beliefs and intuitions which form a coherent world-view: the connection between these beliefs and conservative political doctrine will be traced.

Against Change

First, it is a commonplace that conservatives dislike change. The classic critique of change is that of Plato, who wrote in the fourth century BC, when the democratic city-states in Greece were past their heyday and Athens, where Plato lived, had undergone a series of turbulent political changes in a short time, experiencing tyranny, demagogic democracy and reactionary oligarchy. Plato's political theory developed in reaction to such political uncertainties and abuses. His philosophy was in part a rejoinder to the runaway relativism implied in Heraclitus's doctrine, 'all is flux', which suggested that no definite, permanent truths could be established. Plato believed that there existed, in some transcendental or metaphysical dimension, absolute Ideas, political and moral truths which constituted the models that men should aspire to imitate in their behaviour and social organization. His ideal republic was to be ruled by Philosopher Kings, whose wisdom and goodness came from their contemplation and understanding of the Ideas of truth, beauty, justice, and the supreme Idea, the Good. This perfect society would instantiate the Ideas — perfect Justice, absolute Good. A consequence of his absolutist notion of the Good and the derivative ideal of the state was that Plato regarded any departure from the model republic as being tantamount to imperfection and decay.

Having described the republic, Plato sketched the inferior political reforms which would result if various aspects of it were changed.[1] Although some interpret this as a prophecy of the course which decadence would follow with democracy, then tyranny, marking the final, furthest departures from the ideal, it can also be read as a non-historical, purely theoretical argument: we can infer from his system of thought that any change in the perfect system leads away from the Ideas, towards imperfection. The greater the changes, the greater the evil. Since Plato it has been a common conservative conviction that change equals decay or presages dissolution into chaos. A similar belief is manifested in *Leviathan* when Hobbes enjoins men to obey the sovereign in all circumstances, lest the overthrow of his authority should lead to a dissolution of society and a return to the savage anarchy of the state of nature. Stability is therefore the dominant conservative ideal, arising from this aversion to change: *peace* and *order* are instrumental ideals which help promote social stability, although they are also valued for their own sake.

Plato's argument, that if a perfect society could be achieved, any alteration to it would lead to imperfection and evil, is logically impeccable. However, problems arise when this 'no change' doctrine is applied to societies which are patently less than perfect, that is, to all real societies. Here, the conservative might argue the undesirability of change on three different grounds. First, it can be said that any existing, functioning political form is preferable to the new system which change might bring about. Better the devil you know . . . . All man-made change is risky since the outcome of reform — and, *a fortiori*, of revolution — cannot be accurately predicted and so cannot be proved desirable in advance. This is necessarily true, for just as the problem of induction in the empirical sciences is that future events cannot be predicted with absolute certainty, the problem in social and political science is that we cannot foretell the results of social innovation, especially as, given the unique and historical nature of each political society, we have fewer similar instances on which to base our generalizations and predictions than the natural scientist. Conservatives rightly hold that the results of a revolution cannot be known in advance to be an improvement. By contrast, their own theory draws safely on the knowable past and present and is immune from such uncertainties. However, the would-be reformer might retort that society is so unjust that it is strongly probable, if not certain, that his proposed changes will constitute an improvement. He could also contend that, since unplanned changes will occur in any case, which might be more harmful than planned change, rationally planned reforms should be inaugurated. But many conservatives would reject this point too, having, like Hayek, a dislike of artificial or contrived change and a predilection for unplanned change or 'evolution'.

It is important to note that the conservative case against change often rests on a distorted account of the alternatives. A false dichotomy is posed, suggesting that the choice is between: (a) what exists at present; and (b) one particular, undesirable, alternative. 'The House of Lords may be an anachronism, but single-chamber government would give a dangerous monopoly of power to the House of Commons, hence the House of Lords must remain as it is.' Imputing one, unacceptable, alternative to your political opponent is a well-known sleight of hand.

A second, archetypal argument in favour of 'no change' is that advanced by Burke, that existing social and political forms have a special virtue because they are refined and sanctified by *tradition*, and so should be preserved unchanged. The problems involved in the notion of tradition will be considered further below, but as an argument against change it does not have the compelling force which Burke attributed to it. Tradition is itself built up out of a series of historical changes, reforms, and evolutions and there is no reason why each new innovation, or even a revolution, should not later be seen as part of a tradition. Historians speak of France's revolutionary tradition without self-contradiction. The argument from tradition can be seen as a more sophisticated version of the third argument against change, that *whatever is, is good*, however imperfect it may be. Few conservatives would like to be caught out expressing such an overtly reactionary sentiment, but it underlies many conservative arguments. This dictum, 'whatever is, is good', violates the philosophical convention that values cannot be derived from facts: that is, the mere fact that society is as it is cannot entail or prove that it is *good*. Such evaluations are merely the product of our minds. The absurd consequences of this philosophical error were satirized in Voltaire's novel *Candide* where the philosopher Pangloss, says, every time that a grotesque disaster smites him and the hero, Candide, 'All is for the best in the best of all possible worlds'.

In fact, the argument that no changes should be made because what exists is good is not always the result of spurious optimism of the kind which Voltaire satirized. It could be theoretically vindicated by a thinker with the religious conviction that the world is as God made it, and is therefore good, because willed by God. (This is not the place to embark on theological arguments as to whether God could will suffering and imperfections.) Alternatively, someone might believe that there was a natural evolutionary process at work in society which meant that the existing form of society, whatever it might be, represented the best achievable at this stage of development — so, whatever is (now) is good (now). Hegel's idea of Absolute Spirit actualizing itself through the historical process, becoming concrete in various societies, led him to a similar optimism and the view that 'the real is the rational', which validated existing social forms. Each stage of historical development is good, therefore, in that it forms a necessary part of the whole, dialectical process. The thinkers who consider that a form of society gains a special moral value by virtue, simply, of existing, are those who see society as reflecting a fixed order, divine or natural, or as instantiating some metaphysical ideal, such as Plato's. Such convictions are unlikely to be held by those who consider society as a human artefact which can be changed and perfected by man himself, at will — these are the reformers.

The idea of degeneration through change on which many conservative arguments implicitly rest is based on what could be called an 'essentialist' view of the existent, which holds that it is not merely constituted by a series of accidents and contingencies, but has some immutable, and valuable, essence. Conservatives will define certain elements as constituting the essence of a particular political system, then will strive to preserve them. But with an entity as complex as society, there are many differences of opinion as to where the 'essence' lies. In any case, the belief in such essences is philosophically dubious.

In resisting change, the conservative resists the theories of human progress which flourished in the Enlightenment and have dominated liberal and, to some extent, socialist thinking ever since. For Enlightenment philosophers, each new historical period marked a higher stage of civilization and human achievement. But the literal meaning of progress is neutral — a moving forward (in time or space) — and many conservatives equate progress in time with decadence in morals. Indeed, there are a number of conservative theories of history as *regression*, from the myths of classical times which located a Golden Age in the distant past and charted the decline of mores through the Silver to the Iron Age, and the revelations of Christian eschatology, which predict the decline of men into bestiality and the reign of anti-Christ before the end of the world, to those eighteenth-century philosophers who considered the culture of the 'moderns' greatly inferior to that of the 'ancients' of classical times. So, if history is the record of change, and change is synonymous with decline, it follows that the best we can do is to resist change, halt man's decline and so — by implication — end history!

Nevertheless, Burke's doctrine of tradition seems implicitly to rest on a conception of human and social progress, for if the present is good, in that it incorporates the accumulated wisdom of the past, civilization is, presumably, progressing cumulatively. But Burke would have denied this interpretation. His famous attack on the revolution in France, wherein he extolled the virtues of the English political tradition, was equally a rejection of the liberal theory of progress as innovation. For Burke, what is preserved of the past is good, what is new is — often — bad. The present is good because of the residue of the past which it contains. Conservatism is not progress, but the avoidance of regression. The inconsistency of Burke's position is that, while he vilified the French Revolution, he also, as a Whig, justified the English Revolution of 1688 (which had in effect established a constitutional monarchy) as the vital source of England's proudest constitutional traditions, and as a defence of traditional rights. For Burke, adherence to tradition was essential because it created social continuity and continuity furthered social tranquillity, the ultimate political goal.

Tradition signified building on the wisdom of past generations. As Burke said, 'We procure reverence to our civil institutions on the principle which Nature teaches us to revere individual men: on account of their age, and on account of those from whom they are descended'.[2] Society is conceived of by Burke as a partnership between living, dead and future generations. A more recent definition by G. K. Chesterton, which reflects the same conviction, runs as follows:

Tradition means giving votes to the most obscure of all classes: our ancestors. It is a democracy of the dead. Tradition refuses to submit to the arrogant oligarchy of those who merely happen to be walking about.

Oakeshott too has praised the role of tradition as the accumulation of experience and it is often cited as a justification of policy by the British Conservative Party, particularly when defending established institutions against attack — for example, the House of Lords.[3]

The debate is often depicted as one between the common-sensical conservative, who realizes that wisdom is inherited across generations and that we cannot extirpate the past, and the naive and fanatical utopian (probably a Marxist revolutionary) who wishes, in Popper's words, to make a blank canvas of society, on which to scrawl his own prejudices.[4] Needless to say, those who want reform or even revolution accept that some traditions are ineradicable. A revolution may leave traditional ways of life and many institutions untouched It is often said that the Russian Revolution substituted one authoritarian regime for another, thus preserving the traditional political culture of deference to an omnipotent leader. The quarrel is really between those who want more tradition and less change, and those who want the reverse, not between total preservers and all-out destroyers. So the conservatives are, in a sense, right in emphasizing the strength of tradition, but not in using it to mean something necessarily good.

Three further criticisms can be made of the notion of tradition espoused by Burke and some modern conservatives: first, it assumes that what is preserved over time is what is *best*. Burke believed that time 'refines', but there is no conclusive evidence to support such optimism. Some things are preserved because they are socially useful, but others survive by accident and others, though socially undesirable, survive because they satisfy certain needs — for example, the use of alcohol, and prostitution. Any argument that the preserving and/or weeding out of political institutions, social mores and other behaviour systematically conserves what is best must ultimately make appeal to a hypothesis of social evolution, or some concept of divine purpose, neither of which is verifiable. Second, there is no good reason why past traditions should be binding on the present. Written constitutions are often justified on the grounds that they may prevent rash future generations from committing political follies — but the suspicion that future generations will need such protection already presupposes that history is a process of decline rather than progress, for otherwise it would be reasonable to suppose that they would be wiser (more advanced) than ourselves, and so to avoid binding them. A belief in progress therefore annuls the principle that tradition should be binding. In fact, political institutions do not function on the assumption that we are bound by the decisions of our forefathers. In Britain, no parliament can bind a future parliament, and even in countries where there are written constitutions or higher laws, these can only delay popular changes for a certain time. (It would, of course, be purely sentimental to justify the maintenance of traditions on the grounds that we owe it to our ancestors.) Third, once the concept of tradition is invoked, as was suggested earlier, any existing institution can claim its protection. Burke's idea of refinement by time is too indefinite to serve as a criterion to demarcate true traditions. How long does it take for a tradition to be constituted? Is the French Fifth Republic a political tradition yet, or should it be seen as the usurper of the Fourth Republic? Are all traditions worth preserving? No doubt some Russian communists are still striving to preserve the 'Stalinist tradition': what would Burke have said to that? In short, there are no criteria for what counts as a tradition, and so conservatives may find themselves defending the upholding of tradition *per se*, whatever it might be. (Hobbes finds himself in the parallel position of advocating obedience to the sovereign, whoever he may be, for fear of impending chaos.) 'Preserving tradition' is not a substantive doctrine and cannot help the conservative to discriminate between good and bad institutions or to escape from the dangerous conclusion that whatever is is good.

Imperfect Man

The pessimistic view of human nature held by many conservatives is another cornerstone of their doctrine. Typically, their assumptions about man emphasize his weakness, selfishness, and irrationality. The Judaeo–Christian account of the fall of man and original sin was the foundation of such views which were later presented in secular guise — for example, in Machiavelli's account of man's depravity,[5] and in Hobbes's depiction of the aggressive and selfish behaviour of man in the state of nature which justified the creation of an absolute sovereign.[6] These and similar premises suggest that man is incapable of self-government, or even of moral and sociable behaviour, in the absence of coercion, and so entail the need for authoritarian forms of government. Government is seen primarily as a device for keeping order, and only secondarily as an instrument for satisfying men's needs. If such human inadequacy were genuinely universal (as the hypothesis of innate badness deriving from original sin suggests), mankind would certainly be in difficulties, with nobody capable of governing himself or others, but conservatives —inconsistently? — combine this premise with a hypothesis of *natural inequality*, which resolves the problem as follows: since some men are innately 'superior' to others, it is both reasonable and natural that they should govern. This conclusion is not illogical in the absence of a belief that men can and should be made equal. Elite government and hierarchical, class-stratified society are therefore the necessary consequences of the conservative view of human nature. Plato's ideal republic consisted of three classes (plus the slaves, fourth-class noncitizens), class membership being determined partly by birth, partly by the individual's abilities. If, as Plato expected, every individual is ideally suited to his appointed role in society, as the Philosopher Kings are to ruling and the artisans are to labouring, there could be no discontent at the class system since all would experience equal, though differentiated, satisfaction. But the basis for such rigid classification of individuals is very dubious, theoretically and practically.

However, Plato's justification of inequality (each class in the *Republic* has a different, specialized function) and his insistence on the parallel between the composition of the state and of the individual inaugurated a metaphor which became of great importance for conservative political theory.[7] Whereas convinced egalitarians may liken society to a complex machine, with interchangeable and equally important parts, those who believe in deep-rooted inequality find it more condign to envisage society as a living organism in which each specialized organ plays a different but crucial part in the wellbeing of the whole, with all the organs acting in harmony and receiving their reward, good health and nourishment. While Plato likened society to a living human being, Aristotle drew an analogy between the polity and vegetable organisms, and speculated on the natural limits to growth and development which society, like plants, would experience.[8]

The organic analogy, whether animal or vegetable, reinforces the case for specialization of function within society and elite government, which is justified on the grounds that some are naturally best equipped to rule. Burke talked of the 'natural aristocracy' as the repository of virtues.[9] Carlyle asserted that 'the few Wise will have . . . to take command of the innumerable Foolish'.[10] Even in the semi-egalitarian present, the British Conservative Party represents itself as 'the party of government', trading on the same connection. This is not to say that conservatives do not accept democracy as a means of validating the rule of the elite, but they reject it as a device for popular government. In terms of social organization, the premise of inequality and that of natural class distinctions militate against the social mobility which liberals advocate. Burke talked of society as operating according to a '*fixed compact* sanctioned by the inviolable oath which holds all physical and all moral natures each in their *appointed place*'.[11]

Knowing your place, and sticking to it, is a virtue prized by orthodox conservatism. There was in Burke's thought an incipient conflict between this virtue and the 'getting ahead' on which capitalism rests. In retrospect, Burke appears to be trying to accommodate the rising, mobile middle classes in his theory — without much enthusiasm — by demonstrating that they too belong to the natural aristocracy of talent. Knowing your place is the basis of life in the traditional societies which conservatives often admire and this doctrine rests not only on the premise of inequality but also on the hypothesis that there is a divinely ordained order in society. A notorious example is the caste system in India, where moral duty, *dharma*, consists of living as well as possible according to the conventions of the caste into which one is born, and not seeking to rise above it. (Hence the acute hostility from the higher classes to attempts of the *harijans*, the outcasts, to better their situation.) Orthodox Christianity likewise reminds us that 'the rich man in his castle, the poor man at his gate, God made them high and lowly, and ordered their estate'. Conservatives often believe that inequality exists not only between classes but between other categories of people, such as men and women: the strongly conservative 'fundamentalists' in the USA oppose women's rights on the basis of biblical texts which declare women to be inferior to men.

Conservative thinkers, being convinced of the superiority of some men over others, at least in terms of their abilities, if not of their immortal souls, accept the permanent necessity for hierarchical and inegalitarian social and political institutions, justifying them on the grounds that class differences will not create social conflict or disorder because all will belong to the classes to which they are naturally suited (how?) and organic harmony will reign between the classes (why?). As a model of socity, this may be feasible, but it must surely be relinquished as the paradigm as soon as individuals start to manifest discontent at class distinctions or exhibit the desire and the capacity for upward social mobility. Ironically, despite this presupposition in favour of class society, many modern conservatives declare themselves 'against class' and against class politics, and plead for social unity. This plea may be partly tactical, given that socialists take their stand on an assumption of class antagonism: the conservative response is to assert that classes are unimportant and that what is vital to social good health is the unity of the whole. The organic analogy 'proves' that class harmony is natural. There is an unresolved paradox in this conjunction of ideas, class society and social unity, which conservatives overcome either by an act of faith or by the organic analogy — but analogies are fallacious grounds for proof. Disraeli proposed an alliance between the upper and lower classes against the encroaching middle class, calling for 'one nation'. But the more usual approach is to deny the problem altogether. In quotidian politics, the denial of the class problem is probably self-defeating: 'if you shut your eyes it will go away' is a political maxim which stores up trouble.

The political consequence of the pessimistic and inegalitarian view of human nature is an acceptance of the need for either *authoritarian government* or, at least, *authoritative leadership*, carried on by an elite, often without the participation or control of the mass. Conservatives have typically been associated with royalist movements in Europe and have advocated monarchy mainly on the ground that the hereditary monarch symbolizes tradition and continuity, rather than on the grounds of his inherent superiority! In countries where the monarchy has been superseded, they transfer their loyalty to a strong president or some other form of elite government: in Britain, this often takes the form of upholding the supremacy of parliament and, in particular, of the executive, against interference by other groups.

Many conservatives, now and in the past, express the desire to eschew adversary and conflictual politics (which they often associate with democracy) and promote *consensus*, as if institutionalized disagreement were disruptive and distasteful. Social and political stability is the underlying goal, but there is also a hint of the mediaeval theological view of politics as being occasioned by the fallen nature of man, which entails that political activity could never be a good in itself, only a necessary evil. This view contrasts sharply with the Greek theorists' idealization of political life and citizenship. The chief task of politics, seen in the light of conservative presuppositions, is the maintenance of law and order, the restraining of the unruly. To this end, many conservatives before the democratic era would not even have conceded the propriety of constitutional restraints on government and would have agreed with Hobbes that the scope and powers of government, or of the sovereign, were necessarily unlimited. As Hobbes said of his absolute sovereign, he who wills the end (order) must will the means. But Burke later indicated how conservative and constitutional politics can blend, advocating a 'mixed government' on the English lines, with a monarch constrained by parliament and parliament restrained by the electorate. While the sovereign, the Monarch-in-Parliament, is not subject to supreme laws, he is obliged to obey higher ethical principles, one being that he may not break the law. Burke also disapproved of conflict in elections which were in his day often violent, not to say corrupt, but thought that parties need not be 'outlawed' if they promoted 'healing coalitions' — that is, social unity. His famous definition of a political party was:

A body of men united for promoting their joint endeavours the national interest upon some particular principle in which they are all agreed.[12]

Burke's well known theory of representation by the wise and his rejection of delegation and advocacy of the independence of representatives follow directly from his belief in a natural aristocracy. The political arrangements which Burke proposes reflect his suspicion of men's baser motives, his desire for moderation and, above all, his hopes for social unity.

The fear of disorder and impending anarchy, and the yearning for stability, are fundamental to conservative psychology and the ideology is, largely, the translation of these fears and desires into political proposals. Social disruption is to be avoided at all costs, and an authoritarian form of government can best ensure this. By 'authoritarian' in this context I mean not necessarily a dictatorship, but a government where the people have little or no control. With regard to the individual's position in relation to government, conservatives reject 'inner freedom' as an ideal (as Mannheim notes) since this could lead to unorthodoxy or anarchism, and they wish to subordinate individual free will to 'objective freedom'—usually in the guise of duty—that is, freedom to do what you ought to do. Except when conservatism is fused with liberal ideas, as in the English tradition, individualism is seen as dangerous and undesirable: conservatism is holistic in its approach to politics. Burke anathematized the abstract 'rights of man' as revolutionary nonsense and defended individual freedoms only as far as they were 'prescriptive' or traditional, like the rights established in the tradition of common law and equity. He viewed political liberties 'as an entailed inheritance derived to us from our forefathers, and to be transmitted to our posterity'.[13] Rights cannot be created in a rationalist vacuum.

In political practice conservatives cannot ban change for ever, nor is that a necessary consequence of their ideology in every case. For Plato, it was a consequence of his philosophical system that change in the ideal republic would be evil, and religious believers who claim to perceive a divine order in society might take a similar stance. But for most conservatives what matters is how change comes about, and its scope. Burke argued that 'a state without the means of some change is without the means of its conservation' and justified moderate change when this was necessary for the survival of the system. Conservatives often resort to the organic metaphor in defending their society against sudden or radical change—which would be as drastic as amputation or shock treatment to the body—and also employ the metaphor to explain how acceptable degrees of change might come about, likening it to 'pruning' or 'healing'. Even before Darwin, a concept of evolution was implicit in conservative thinking: political society was said to evolve gradually, conserving the best in its traditions, which guaranteed its survival and prosperity. Revolution is the precise opposite of evolution and threatens the whole organism with sudden death. An evolutionary theory of change demands little or no political action for it is seen as a spontaneous process. Spencer, for example, believed that society and mankind would be improved by evolution and thus reach the highest ethical state.[14] A similarly fatalistic view is found in Hegel, for whom change occurred through the dialectical movement in society, by means of which the World Spirit, acting through individuals and nations, moved nearer to its final self-realization.

Discussions of change and conservation raise philosophical problems which constitute potential challenges to conservatism. This is demonstrated in the modern 'systems theory of politics' pioneered by Easton, which takes a model of society based on a simple organism or cell. The goal of the political system is said to be 'survival' (like that of the cell), and it tries to preserve itself by processing the people's demands ('inputs') via various policies ('outputs') to win their approval. The problem with Easton's model is that it offers no satisfactory criteria for measuring how much change a system can absorb before it becomes a different system, or 'dies'. To apply his analysis, Easton, like other conservatives, must define the 'essence' of the system, which must be preserved for it to survive—and such definitions will always be controversial and insubstantiable. The upshot of Easton's analysis could be summarized as 'A system is a system is a system'—an uncritical conclusion which tends to support the status quo.

One other political ideal common to all conservatives is that of nationalism, which entails the duty of patriotism. For the Greeks, city-states were sacred places and likewise, for many conservatives, the nation is sacrosanct—by contrast with the internationalist doctrines of socialism and, to some extent, of liberalism. The conception of the nation is based either on the organic analogy, again, which suggests that the nation is a natural unit (despite the constant gerrymandering of boundaries throughout world history), or on the supposition that the national entity is the product of evolving tradition, a slow but indestructible accretion of land, mores, and institutions. Some conservatives, like fascists, base their nationalism on the idea of race, arguing that the 'natural' national unit is one which embraces the whole of a racial group. More will be said of this contention in the section below on fascism.

The Conservative Mentality

The conservative philosophical tradition is diverse. Some thinkers, in their search for *absolute authority*, accept the existence of absolute ideas— unchanging truths which can act as political and moral standards for all time. But modern theorists with conservative leanings such as Oakeshott, Hayek, and Popper (the latter two are best described as liberal-conservative) stand squarely in the tradition of empiricism and advocate a search for political truth through trial and error, accumulated wisdom and modest change. All three are *anti-rationalist*, and object to reformers who try to impose rationalist schemes dreamt up in their heads on society, an aspiration which they attribute to utopians and totalitarians. By contrast with such rationalists, the conservative approach to politics seems haphazard, untheoretical and largely pragmatic.

Indeed, it has usually been the boast of the British Conservative Party that it is pragmatic, not dogmatic, in the sense of not being entangled in rationalist schemes, and non-ideological, ideology being condemned as an inflexible, distorted, partial, and non-pragmatic approach to politics. The rejection of ideology in principle (although conservatism cannot fail to be ideological in essence) contrasts sharply with the general conservative predilection for certainty and for authoritative sources of knowledge. But conservatives see ideology as the creation of self-interested men, and a powerful poison. In the search for absolutes, they have preferred to look to religion and to nature.

Many parallels exist between the Christian and the conservative ways of thinking and perceiving the world. This is not to say that all conservatives are necessarily Christians, although Lord Hailsham, in *The Case For Conservatism*, makes religious belief a central tenet.[15] The connection is one of analogy, and lies in the coincidence of assumptions. Both Christians and conservatives see man as fundamentally marred and weak, in need of redemption or of a political saviour ('strong leadership'). Both have an eschatological outlook, being obsessed with the fear of chaos, the breakdown of order, and both predict moral decline and decadence. They are willing to defer to absolute values and absolute authority as a refuge from social and moral dissolution. Non-religious conservative thinkers often replace God with Nature and regard inequality, leadership, and evolution as a social phenomena justified by nature's own processes. Burke argued that conservation was nature's own pattern:

By preserving the method of Nature in the conduct of the state, in what we improve we are never wholly new, in what we retain we are never wholly obsolete.[16]

The fallacy of reading natural laws into the artifices of society is self-evident. But many conservative thinkers who would disagree with Rousseau on everything else, agree with him that society corrupts men, and so look to nature as a moral indicator of how we should behave.

It is clear from these observations that conservatives usually have a strong moral sense. Their political theory and social policy revolves round the enforcement of law and order and the maintenance of moral standards in sexual and other matters, so as to control the 'beast within'. Naturally or religiously sanctioned institutions such as the family are to be preserved and politics must operate on the natural basis of the leaders and the led. Political obligation is seen as a moral, not merely a contractual, duty. In the past, this was justified on religious grounds, by the 'divine right' of monarchs, but today conservatives are more likely to refer to the organic view of society which views the individual as a small but essential part, owing a duty to society because he benefits from the wellbeing of the whole. Evidently, such doctrines are far removed from the 'amoral' attitude of liberalism, with its emphasis on rational utilitarian calculation and on contractual and prudential obligation.

As to government's responsibility for social welfare, conservatives would prefer individuals to look after their own needs, being suitably rewarded for fulfilling the duties of their stations in society—a reasonable hope in unchanging, traditional societies but one unlikely to be realized in periods of rapid social and economic change. The doctrine of *self-help*, taken together with social Darwinism ('the survival of the fittest'), appealed to the liberal conservatives of nineteenth-century England, with its corollary of the weeding out of the inadequate, but the more customary approach to inequality and poverty has been the idea that the rich should help and protect the poor, this being one of their natural duties—an attitude reminiscent of feudal practice. Hence, the tradition of philanthropic aristocrats in Victorial England. From the conservative viewpoint, a welfare state based on individual contribution is an artificial, impersonal creation which destroys the natural relationships of men in society and precludes the ancient duty of *charity*. Although mutual dependence and charity may not sound like the present policies of the conservative parties in Britain and the USA, it must be remembered that they have both taken on themselves the mantle of classical liberalism, which emphasized self-help and independence.

In terms of the *practice* of politics, the conservative's rejection of ideology, rationalism, and radical reform stems from his perception of society as a natural entity, which cannot be artificially manipulated. Nor can the rich and complex 'tapestry of life' be governed by simplistic theoretical principles: pragmatism is the only valid political method. Conservatives may therefore advocate diverse or even contradictory policies at different times, but the aim of their intervention in politics is always the conservation of what is good in society and the promotion of social cohesion and harmony. These are the highest political ideals of conservatism, ideals which, it should be noted, allocate a minor place to the individual and the foremost place to the social whole. In practice such politics almost invariably uphold the status quo. Conservatism therefore tends to support what Lukâcs called 'the sterile tyranny of the existent'.

Because of conservatives' refusal to construct or adhere to an explicit ideology, various accounts of the meaning of conservatism can be pieced together through the excavation of particular beliefs and convictions. In *The Psychology of Conservatism*, Wilson unearths nine aspects of the 'conservative character' which include a belief in strict rules and punishment, conventionalism, anti-hedonism, militarism, opposition to scientific progress, and intolerance of minorities.[17] Despite the absence of a bible of conservatism and the piecemeal nature of many conservatives' understanding of their own ideology, when the fundamental assumptions are examined, they show the essential coherence of the specific beliefs, and suggest that conservatism is indeed a unified doctrine. But, given its pragmatic approach to politics, conservatism is perhaps better classified as a world-view than treated as an explicit ideology. Mannheim's exploration of the 'conservative mentality' takes this approach. He notes the conservative's unthinking inclination 'to accept the total environment in the accidental concreteness in which it occurs, as if it were the proper order of the world'. Conservative philosophy is only developed as a result of challenges from other ideologies, in particular, from liberalism, and takes the form of a counter-utopia, an instrument of self-defence. 'Intellectual conservatism' is created to defend a social order which is already determined and fixed: Hegel's achievement as a conservative was to raise 'an already present mode of experience to an intellectual level'.[18]

For the conservative, 'the fact of the mere existence of a thing endows it with higher value'. Mannheim also remarks on the conservative propensity to accept or exaggerate the irrational elements of the mind. Mannheim's contention is that conservatism only becomes an ideology *after the event*, justifying a way of life which has already been established. This fits with what has already been suggested, that conservatism is a formal, not a substantive, doctrine, which recommends the preservation of what exists, whatever that may be. The particular doctrines to which conservatives adhere at any time are therefore dependent on the social context. For these reasons, conservatism can be neither progressive, nor determinate in the content of its beliefs. Nevertheless, some right-wing movements have pronounced themselves progressive including, in this century, fascism. It is therefore instructive to consider fascism as an example of how conservative preoccupations can be combined with radical, even revolutionary, political practice.

Radical Conservatism

To avoid misunderstanding, I must emphasize that fascism is not being equated with conservatism by its inclusion in this analysis. It is appropriate to examine it here because some of its basic assumptions coincide with those of conservatism and because, in presenting itself as the 'third way', fascism seems to fall on the same segment of the political spectrum as conservatism does, being opposed to both socialism and liberalism. Fascists, like conservatives, are instinctively anti-intellectual and emphasize the irrational components of behaviour. Fascism presented itself as a myth, a set of beliefs above rational explanation. The resulting paucity of fascist theory, and its poverty, means that the commentator has to aggregate its various beliefs in order to analyse it as an ideology. The best known aspect of fascism is its racialist basis. The premise is that of natural inequality, shared by conservatives, but fascists hold that this exists between races as well as between individuals. The 'myth of race', and that of Aryan supremacy, was founded on various pseudo-scientific doctrines of the nineteenth century, particularly on those of Chamberlain, who developed the idea of a 'folk nation' destined to triumph.[19] A confused blend of these doctrines was used to justify first imperialism, then the colonization of 'inferior races', then anti-semitism. Volk/Nation and Blood/Race, with its corollary of racial and sexual purity, were key components of the Nazi myth.

Social Darwinism plays an important part in fascism, both in justifying the natural selection and triumph of some races at the expense of others

(Bernhardi said 'War gives a biologically just decision'), and also in vindicating the elite political leadership which characterized fascist states, the strong ruling the weak. Needless to say, the doctrine of the survival of the fittest is directly opposed to humanitarian ethics and to welfare politics. Fascists advocated elite and authoritarian government while invoking the masses to validate their dictatorships by popular acclaim, as in the Nuremberg rallies. This ambivalent attitude towards the mass — contempt and invocation — caused Talmon to refer to such states as 'totalitarian democracies'.[20] Mussolini's dictum 'Believe, obey and fight' illustrates the authoritarian aspect of fascism and its reliance on the deference of the masses.

It would be too facile to say that fascists are totalitarian and conservatives are not, especially as the concept of totalitarianism is itself called into question in Chapter 8. But conservatives in fact share with fascists the vision of society as a totality, an organic unity, and this, conjoined with a belief in elitism, is liable to produce authoritarian politics. Where the two part company is at the fascist insistence that the state is above morality and can do no wrong — a view in support of which Nietzsche's Superman, above all moral constraints, was invoked. Neither individual rights nor tradition nor law are allowed to hamper fascist leaders or the actions of a fascist state on the world stage. Conservatives by contrast have strong moral inhibitions which they import into politics, and a high respect for the law and ancient rights and traditions. But fascism might still be viewed as conservative pragmatism taken to extremes — the no-holds-barred approach to politics. This explains why, historically, fascist parties were able both to distinguish themselves doctrinally from socialism (and to savagely persecute communists) while simultaneously introducing quasi-socialist welfare measures to alleviate social problems and win support. It is no accident, although it *is* a paradox, that Hitler called his party the National Socialist Party. Given the fascists' elevated notion of the 'Volk' or race, it is quite consistent for fascist governments to improve the wellbeing of the chosen race as far as possible, while treating other races as sub-human.

While a point-by-point comparison of conservative and fascist beliefs shows a number of shared convictions and assumptions — nationalism, inegalitarianism, appeal to traditional virtues, hatred of socialism, and pragmatism — these do not constitute a good reason for equating them: rather, fascism should be viewed as the concrete form which conservatism might take under particular historical circumstances. The fascist idea is one of a revolutionary start — which conservatives would, naturally, reject, followed by conservative stability. It could be argued that the initial impulse to change and restructure society distinguishes fascism completely from conservatism — but the opposing case for considering fascism a manifestation of the 'radical right' is discussed in Chapter 8. Fascists share the 'conservative mentality' to some extent, but lack the moral inhibitions with respect to political behaviour and the fear of tampering with existing social forms, hence the radical and inhumanitarian face of fascism. To take an example near home, conservative politicians, although they wish to halt immigration, accept the existence of an immigrant population in Britain as a *fait accompli*: it must now be regarded as part of the social whole, and treated accordingly. Perhaps in a few decades, conservatives will even boast of our 'multiracial tradition'. By contrast, the various fascist or neo-Nazi parties do not accept the accomplished fact, and wish to undo it by compulsory repatriation or by harassment leading to voluntary self-repatriation of immigrants. While the conservative tries to make the best of social developments which he may deplore, the fascist will seek to reverse them.

The vast majority of conservatives would repudiate fascist theory and practice. But the twentieth-century experience of fascism could be read as a solemn warning to conservatives: inegalitarian and authoritarian political premises potentially constitute the basis of inhumane, elitist, and dictatorial political ideology unless they are circumscribed by a strong religious or humanitarian ethic which asserts the individual's right to equality of respect.

Conservatism Today

An analysis of conservative ideas in contemporary political debate cannot ignore the resurgence of right-wing ideals and policies which coincides — not merely by chance — with the world recession which has put an end to the postwar decades of affluence. As political psychologists contend, voters become more right-wing when their standard of living is threatened. In Britain, the result has been the election of a more 'radical' and doctrinaire government than the country has known for many years. Mrs Thatcher's approach to policy is clearly ideological although, since the term jars with the conservative tradition of pragmatism, she might prefer the epithet 'government by principle'. The major plank of the government's programme is the monetarist principle expounded by the economist Friedman, which entails minimum government intervention in the economy, except for a strict control of the money supply to curb inflation. (Could we have stumbled on another conviction shared by conservatism and Christianity, that money is the root of all evil?) This is, essentially, a neo-liberal policy, founded on the belief that free enterprise, unhindered by state interference, will produce a healthy, efficient economy via the market mechanism. This constitutes a deliberate rejection of the Keynesian policies favoured by socialist governments, which require intimate state involvement with the economy and an expanding public sector to stimulate growth and employment. Thus, the choice of an economic policy is not politically neutral: both monetarism and the government's policy of raising indirect taxes and lowering income tax (a move towards 'regressive' taxation which redistributes money towards the better-off sections of society) reflect ideological choices. The justification of such moves is the orthodox liberal one, that low direct taxes encourage individual responsibility, enterprise, and productivity. The large cuts made in public expenditure are also intended to shift the balance of the economy back towards private enterprise and laissez-faire.

A seemingly paradoxical aspect of present Conservative policy is the diminution of the state's role as an economic agent and as distributor of welfare (as social services are curtailed) simultaneously with an *extension* of its role in terms of social control and its control over local government. The maintenance of law and order is an important aspect of government policy, and the state's powers of control are slowly being enlarged — over unions and over 'rebel' local councillors who defy government policy and try to assert their autonomy. It seems that, while the benevolent face of the state is being erased its disciplinary role is deliberately being reinforced — from paternalism to patriarchy? This development reflects the incongruous mixture of conservative and liberal beliefs which animates the British Conservative Party: state control in the social sphere, free enterprise in the economic sphere. But the extension of centralization and of the state's coercive functions is in turn hard to reconcile with the Conservative government's declared dislike of the state itself and its attendant bureaucracy. One other, less tangible, goal of government policy seems to be a 'remoralization' of society, a revival of non-permissive morality and the restoration of conservative values such as discipline, thrift, hard work, and the family.

What is remarkable about the new British Conservatism is its ideological approach to policy-making — a radical innovation for a habitually pragmatic party — and the fact that what the government actually chooses to conserve is the free enterprise society beloved of classical liberalism. The resulting blend of statist and individualistic, inegalitarian, and formally egalitarian, policies illustrates the idiosyncratic nature of Conservatism here, which has eschewed the reactionary attitude of many European conservatives. Britain is not alone in undergoing a resurgence of conservative neo-liberalism: the economic policies initiated by President Reagan are similar, and 'Thatcherism' has found admirers and emulators in France and Germany. Conservatism has in fact been spurred on to a new ideological self-definition by the failure of social-democratic governments to maintain prosperity (although the factors involved in the failure were probably structural, not ideological) — thus bearing out Mannheim's observation that conservatism manifests itself in a coherent, ideological form as a result of antagonism to other ideologies. Adamant anti-communism is also a feature common to all the new Conservatives.

Ideology or Intuition?

The pragmatic nature of political conservatism has been emphasized. It is, in the literal sense of the term, a reactionary ideology, evoked as a reaction against other doctrines. It therefore manifests itself in different political stances according to circumstance. Nevertheless, it is rooted in widely shared intuitions and emotions. Many people who do not vote Conservative are instinctively conservative. Some say that biologically we are *all* conservative — the human organism tries to preserve itself and to avoid violent effort, disruption and change — and Freudian analysis holds the same to be true of the individual psyche, with 'Thanatos', the conservative principle, symbolizing the drive to inertia, or the 'death wish' and striving to prevail over 'Eros', the active life instinct.[21] Our conservative instincts are pre-intellectual, but may come into play when rationalist ideologies fail us. The conservative must hope for such contingencies to arise if he wants political success. But, typically, conservatism dictates a passive approach to politics, and even a certain fatalism, since conservation and the prevention of change can often best be brought about by *inaction*. Conservatives usually object to planning and major reforms. This is partly because the success of reforms can never be guaranteed, whereas the virtues of existing systems are tried and tested, and partly because of the conservative's pessimism about human nature. Being sceptical of man's capacities and intelligence, he is unlikely to trust the reformer or utopian in preference to nature and custom. Reform and social revolution also rest on ideologies or abstract theories of which the conservative is congenitally suspicious, being anti-intellectual at heart, and knowing the ability of the mind to deceive itself, and others.

Because conservatism appears so often as the opponent of change, and as a reaction against more constructive ideologies, it must finally be asked whether it truly merits the title of 'ideology'. No doubt conservatism is the chameleon among ideologies, since its guise depends on the context and the nature of its enemy, but certain fundamental convictions have been identified which constitute a distinct political standpoint. The premises on which these convictions rest, that human nature is imperfect and inequality is natural and desirable, are certainly credible, and can perhaps claim more supporting empirical evidence than, say, the premise of human goodness or perfectibility. But conservatism seems an essentially incomplete and unsatisfying ideology because it offers no constructive goals for the future and can hardly inspire political commitment and activism: the conservative would, however, make no apology for this, seeing activist or utopian movements as dangerous and doomed to fail. Burke's defence of conservatism amounts to the claim that it tempers change with caution and respect for tradition. If we already lived in utopia, this might be the right path to follow, to prevent a fall from grace, a diminution of social perfection. But in real societies, the justification of existing imperfections by conservative arguments can delay or altogether prevent much needed social improvement.

Notes

1. Plato, *The Republic* (Trans. H. D. P. Lee), Penguin, 1955, Part 9.
2. E. Burke, *Reflections on the Revolution in France* in *How Conservatives Think* (Ed. P. Buck), Penguin, 1975, p. 49.
3. M. Oakeshott, *Rationalism in Politics*, Methuen, 1962, Chaps 1, 7.
4. K. Popper, *The Open Society and its Enemies,* Routledge & Kegan Paul, 1962, Vol. 1, pp. 157-68.
5. N. Machiavelli, *The Prince* (Trans. G. Bull), Penguin, 1961, p. 96.
6. T. Hobbes, *Leviathan*, Penguin, 1968, Chap. XIII.

7. Plato, *The Republic*, ss. 344, 368–75, 429, 520.
8. Aristotle, *Politics* (Trans. T. A. Sinclair), Penguin, 1962, pp. 27–8.
9. Burke in *How Conservatives Think*, p. 52.
10. T. Carlyle, 'The present time' in *How Conservatives Think*, p. 59.
11. Burke in *How Conservatives Think*, p. 51. Emphasis added.
12. Burke in *How Conservatives Think*, p. 51.
13. Burke in *How Conservatives Think*, p. 49.
14. H. Spencer, *The Principles of Ethics*, London, 1893, 2 vols.
15. Q. Hogg, *The Case for Conservatism*, Penguin, 1947, Chap. 2.
16. Burke in *How Conservatives Think*, p. 49.
17. G. Wilson (Ed.) *The Psychology of Conservatism*, Academic Press, 1973.
18. For Mannheim's view of conservative thought, see *Ideology and Utopia* (Trans. E. Shils), Routledge & Kegan Paul, 1936, pp. 132, 206–15.
19. See, e.g., H. S. Chamberlain, *Ideal und Macht*, Munich, 1916.
20. J. L. Talmon, *The Origins of Totalitarian Democracy*, Praeger, 1960.
21. H. Marcuse, *Eros and Civilisation*, Sphere, 1969.

Further Reading

P. Buck, *How Conservatives Think*, Penguin, 1975, Extracts.
M. Oakeshott, *Rationalism in Politics*, Methuen, 1962.
A. Quinton, *The Politics of Imperfection*, Faber & Faber, 1978.

CHAPTER 8

Totalitarianism

A system where *technologically advanced instruments* of political power are wielded *without restraint* by *centralised leaderships* of an *elite movement*, to effect *total social revolution*, including the conditioning of man, based on an *arbitrary ideology* proclaimed by the leadership in an atmosphere of *coerced unanimity* of the entire population.

This description of totalitarianism[1] suggests that it is a clearly definable phenomenon. However, the concept of totalitarianism presents many problems to the political theorist, by contrast with such definitive usages by political scientists and the simplistic use of the term in political argument. Although the term 'totalitarian' was used by Mussolini to denote his own fascist corporate state, it was later popularized by the detractors of fascist and communist dictatorships, such as Neumann[2], and is now invariably used in the pejorative sense, often very loosely. It is therefore difficult for any analysis to distinguish a purely objective meaning of the term. Totalitarianism, although included in the section of this book concerned with ideologies, is not an ideology like the others discussed here: nobody advocates totalitarianism for its own sake, or proclaims himself 'proud to be totalitarian'. And yet the term is used by its critics as if it represented a distinct political anti-ideal, despite the fact that they concoct their definition of the concept on the self-contradictory basis of two mutually opposed ideologies and political systems, fascism and communism. Totalitarianism is included here partly to expose the fallacy of treating it as a distinct, if deplorable, political ideology, and partly because it is methodologically instructive to see how the self-appointed critics of totalitarianism have constructed the idea on shaky theoretical foundations.

The most influential views on the subject have been propounded by political scientists, historians, and psychologists, rather than by political philosophers, hence the diversity of approaches. Taken together, their works offer much useful information about the activities of absolutist states in this century, but whether they have succeeded in isolating a *sui generis* political form and ideology must be doubted. These various approaches will be summarized and discussed, and then a theoretical critique will be offered.

The Phenomenological Approach

This approach identifies the phenomena characteristic of totalitarian societies and consists largely of an account of their political methods and institutions. The 'six-point syndrome' of Friedrich and Brzezinski is the best known characterization.[3] They say that the totalitarian state is constituted by:

(1) An official ideology incorporating a vision of the ideal state, belief in which is compulsory. Unorthodoxy is punishable.
(2) A single party which is bureaucratic and hierarchical, usually led by one man.
(3) A terroristic police.
(4) A monopoly of communications.
(5) A monopoly of weapons.
(6) A centrally directed economy.

These are characteristics which the authors found to be common to Nazi Germany, Russia under Stalin, communist countries in Eastern Europe and Mussolini's Italy. As they point out, conditions (3)–(6) are strongly dependent on advanced technology, so that totalitarianism can only emerge in societies at a certain stage of their development. We should note that this definition deliberately discounts the 'illusion' of democracy found in some totalitarian societies and centres on the essential elitism of such systems.

Each of the six points can be elaborated further to convey the repressive nature of totalitarian society. The single party brooks no institutional rivals: despite the official dualism which may exist between state and party (as in the USSR where institutions are duplicated), the state is subjugated by the party and remains an empty form. The independence and impartiality of that traditional watchdog, the judiciary, is subverted, as are other potentially autonomous sources of authority, such as the Church and the family. All popular opposition to the party is eliminated, being branded as anti-social and immoral. In this respect, as in many others, totalitarianism is the antithesis of pluralism, which tolerates heterodoxy, and accepts that there is a multitude of competing political truths; for this reason, Finer calls totalitarianism 'monistic'[4], while others describe it as 'monolithic'.

Later elaborations of the totalitarian syndrome give special prominence to the role of the self-proclaimedly infallible and invincible leader, the symbolic figurehead parodied in Orwell's *1984* as 'Big Brother'. It is immaterial whether the leader is dead or alive, Orwell implies, or even who he is—he is primarily the emblem of the state, the embodiment of the will of the people. The totalitarian state rests on unlimited, unconstitutional power (official constitutions are disregarded by the critics, as they are so often abrogated) and effects an enlargement of the public or political sphere so as to include even private life and morality within the reach of political action. This averts the unorthodoxy and opposition fostered within the extensive sphere of individual privacy found in liberal democracies. To this end, the people are controlled coercively by the laws, the police and the use of terror, and by the direction of labour in the planned economy. The most powerful means of control is ideology, the instrument of persuasion and indoctrination. All the critics of totalitarianism remark on the 'irrational' nature of totalitarian ideologies, which is apparent even when they purport to be scientific, like Marxism. Cassirer analyses the ritual and mythical aspects of fascist ideology while Marcuse has commented on the 'magical' quality which Marxist doctrine has assumed in the USSR.[5]

Clearly, the various parts of the totalitarian syndrome are not accidentally combined but are intimately and necessarily connected, each being essential to the reinforcement of the others and to the maintenance of the totalistic nature of such systems. The elements taken together form a coherent, self-perpetuating political system. A further impression of life in such a system can be gained from the celebrated dystopian novels which depict totalitarian societies. Orwell's *1984* and Zamyatin's *We* emphasize the elitist and terroristic aspects of such societies, while Huxley's *Brave New World* and Karp's *One* suggest how the physical and mental conformity which destroys the identity of the individual can be achieved by ideology, conditioning and even by genetic engineering. These fictions embellish tendencies observable in real totalitarian societies and all focus chiefly on the annihilation of individuality, which seems to Westerners the most abhorrent aspect of such societies. These novels therefore constitute useful appendices to the academic expositions of the phenomenological approach.

However, from a theoretical viewpoint, the chief objection to the approach exemplified by Friedrich and Brzezinski, although it may be factually accurate, is that it assumes what it seeks to prove. First, certain societies are branded as totalitarian — presumably on the basis of some intuition or adverse judgement — then, the characteristics which they share are listed, while their dissimilarities are conveniently forgotten. The fact that left-wing and right-wing totalitarian states rest on antithetical ideologies is glossed over. (This method is similar to that used by some political scientists to 'analyse' democracy. The USA is declared to be democratic, then the characteristics of democracy are enumerated by abstracting from its political institutions.) The descriptive approach precludes deeper analysis of the idea, and its critical application. Another danger of the phenomenological approach is that non-totalitarian states may exhibit some of the six features: indeed, recent works have pointed out a convergence between totalitarian and advanced industrial states which makes it hard to maintain that totalitarianism is a distinct species of political society, the contrary of liberal democracy. The question of how many of the six features a state must exhibit before it becomes totalitarian is essentially unanswerable. Ultimately it is unsatisfactory to define a political concept purely in terms of appearances and characteristics which may be accidental, as do Friedrich and Brzezinski, since this gives rise to the problems already mentioned and provides no understanding of the nature or motivation of the totalitarian state. Nor does this approach substantiate the view that totalitarianism is a *sui generis* ideology, for a collection of political methods does not constitute an ideology. In essence, the phenomenological approach mistakes a set of political *methods* for a homogeneous political *goal*.

The Socio-Historical Approach

The political theorist and historian Arendt attempted to explain the emergence and the nature of totalitarianism by searching for its roots in historical events and in political culture. She called totalitarianism 'total terror'. She also *assumed* that Nazi Germany and communist Russia were totalitarian and that the concept had a distinct, definable meaning. Using Germany after the first world war as an example, she identified the four conditions essential to the formation of a totalitarian state[6]:

(1) Class and community breakdown has occurred during and after war, and because of rapid industrialization and the spread of individualistic liberal doctrines.
(2) The unpoliticized mass is suddenly enfranchised, but its lack of political culture and ignorance of democratic procedure makes it an easy prey to demagogic leaders.
(3) A 'negative solidarity' is artificially generated within the mass of individuals who were sundered by conditions (1) and (2); this has, however, none of the positive connotations of 'class solidarity'. Individuals flee from their isolation and search for personal identity through mass activities, such as vast political rallies. Displaced intellectuals espouse the movement in a similar search for identity, and legitimize it.
(4) The precondition for a totalitarian society is a large population, since such states habitually generate internal cohesion by the creation and persecution of scapegoats on a large scale.

It can be seen that the six characteristics of the totalitarian 'syndrome' are necessary consequences of these objective historical conditions. A powerful, if irrational, ideology is needed to explain the world to the politically naive masses, while the breakdown of classes and other social groupings and the isolation of individuals makes terror and mutual spying a convenient way of keeping order at low cost, with little risk of mass retaliation. An omnipotent symbolic leader supplies—albeit illusorily—the solidarity which individuals lost when the traditional community vanished.

Arendt gives a powerful insight into the working of Nazi Germany, from which she was a refugee, and her hypothesis that terror in the absence of opposition does not disappear but becomes *total* may prove to be an important and sinister political truth. Nevertheless, her 'theory' of totalitarianism rests largely on the special case of Germany, and the induction of general laws from single instances is a risky procedure, however inspired the theorist. One consequence of Arendt's account is that totalitarianism could only emerge at a certain historical point in a country's development. Therefore, if the problems posed by (1) and (2) could be resolved in other ways the risk might be avoided altogether. The socio-historical approach also offers no evidence that totalitarianism is a homogeneous political phenomenon or a distinct political ideology.

Another historical analysis of right-wing totalitarianism, again based on the German experience, is that of Weiss, who considers fascism a resurgence of an older political phenomenon, the 'radical right', which is often reactivated during periods of rapid social change and modernization when 'upstart' liberals and radicals become the dominant class and other groups suffer anomie.[7] Weiss argues that in the unstable postwar period in Germany an alliance was formed between threatened landowners and the fearful lower-middle class, whose sentiments were vocalized and vulgarized by Hitler. These rightist elements disliked urbanization and the resulting crime and decadence and were attracted by solutions such as the creation of an 'organic' state, and the revival of peasant virtues. In an era when reactionary conservative politics seemed outmoded, fascism provided an answer to the right's deep hatred of both liberalism and communism. Thus, Nazism called itself 'the third way' — a cry echoed by fascist parties in Britain today. Weiss's account of fascism again provides no theoretical analysis of totalitarianism and suggests that fascism itself is not an original ideology, but a negative and pragmatic reaction to prevailing ideologies, which provides a new outlet for those who would otherwise be conservatives. The analyses of Arendt and Weiss show clearly that any attempt to understand fascism or communism as historical movements has the inevitable effect of dissolving the notion of totalitarianism as a general, unified phenomenon.

The Essentialist Analysis

An attempt has been made to incorporate the concept of totalitarianism into political theory by various writers who seek to show the special and unique nature of the political form through an examination of the assumptions and implicit premises of totalitarianism. Foremost among these are Talmon, who finds the origins of 'totalitarian democracy' in eighteenth- and nineteenth-century thought dating from Rousseau[8], and Popper, who traces the advocates of the 'closed society' back to Plato, and also finds theoretical antecedents of totalitarianism in Hegel, Marx and utopian thinkers.[9] The following characteristics are singled out as conditions for totalitarian thinking:

(1) A utopian vision

The dominant ideology offers an explicit vision of the ideal society, a goal to which everything must be subordinated, even if it is never achieved. On the basis of this unique political truth, all rival ideologies are outlawed: there is no acceptance of a plurality of truths, and no tolerance. Talmon finds the origin of this in Rousseau's General Will—though he might equally have blamed exclusive religions such as Christianity for this mode of thinking—while Popper detects them in Plato's absolute Ideas, and condemns this way of thinking as antithetical to the 'open society'. In institutional terms, the 'utopian' way of thinking leads to one-party states and one-candidate elections —to the 'monolith'.

(2) Despondency about man's nature

Like other ideologies, totalitarianism rests on a view of human nature: this is Hobbesian in its pessimism and conservative in its condescension and also harks back to the views of mediaeval political theologians about original sin. Man is seen as innately wicked, weak, selfish, and hence anti-social. He is childlike, incapable of leading an autonomous life or of taking decisions for himself, is in need of security, and can only exist as part of the social entity. Because men are irrational and irresponsible, their salvation lies in their leaders: in the Middle Ages, in the King-cum-Shepherd, in modern times, in the state. These premises are diametrically opposed to the liberal view of man as rational and independent, and equally opposed to Marxist assumptions about sociability, but they reflect and elaborate the standard 'pessimistic conservative' view of man's fallen state. Cassirer contends that the rituals and myths of Nazism were devised expressly to make men resemble this archetype in reality, reducing them to irrational, primitive beings. Since all totalitarian theories and other theories resting on similar premises recommend elite rule, the obvious objection is that if this is man's universal nature, the leaders themselves must be equally blemished and incapable of leadership. But, needless to say, such theorists also—paradoxically?—posit ineradicable inequality and would retort that there are two natural classes, the leaders and the led, a doctrine found in Plato, in Nietzsche's idea of the Superman and elsewhere, and one which critics read into Lenin's account of the role of the Party. This view of human nature, and of the necessity of elitism, is self-evidently opposed to democratic aspirations and gives the lie to the false pretensions of some totalitarian states to democratic institutions.

(3) Real needs

Totalitarian ideologies make a distinction between men's felt and real needs, arguing that men's defects make them incapable of knowing their own good. Talmon analyses Rousseau's dictum that man can be 'forced to be free' in being made to conform to the General Will (which is but his own *real* will) in these terms. A benevolent despot, or the Party acting as the 'vanguard of the people', enacts the 'real' needs of the people, often against their will and even coercively. The result is paternalism backed by force. According to liberal-democratic theory, the only possible guide to people's 'real' needs is their democratically expressed preferences. People may not think deeply enough, or in the long term, but if we disregard their 'felt' needs or preferences, there is no guarantee that the rulers will not substitute their own selfish interests for those of the people, which is exactly what totalitarian leaders are reputed to do. The liberal argument that each man knows his own interests best contradicts the idea that he can have 'real' needs unknown to him, although most liberals would readily admit that people can be mistaken about their interests and must on occasion be guided by governments.[10]

The liberal critique of the idea of 'real needs' or 'real interests' arises partly from the 'openness' of liberal thinking, the conviction that there is no single political truth but a multiplicity of individual interests and value-judgements, and partly from the more cynical conviction, reinforced by studies of elitism and Michel's 'iron law of oligarchy'[11], that power-holders will invariably pursue their private interests when unrestrained by a free, democratic system, although they may try to disguise these as the 'real' interests of the people or as the state's interest, falsely equating the state and the people. The exclusive vision of the ideal society mentioned above explains and exonerates references to 'real' needs and even, in some cases, the adoption of coercive means to achieve the ideal. Thus, the exclusive vision of truth, plus the notion of 'real' needs explicates and justifies the arbitrary and repressive nature of totalitarian rule. If the leaders or the party, their eyes fixed on a utopian vision, are acting to realize that vision, why should they be impeded by the superficial preferences of the uneducated, by legality or by other conventional rules of procedure which might delay the attainment of the goal? The Good sweeps all before it.

(4) The sacrifice of freedom

In order to attain the ideal, totalitarian states reduce the degree of personal and political freedom, sometimes offering greater material security instead, but not always. This is not an accident, but the result of the view of man outlined above. If men are basically incapable of freedom, freedom cannot realistically have priority among political ideals. As is well known, the citizens of communist countries have little political freedom, but a fair degree of economic security, which reflects the relative values allocated to these two ideals.

(5) The hypertrophy of politics

In Talmon's words, totalitarianism in operation 'politicizes' the whole of life, extending the public sphere unduly and invading individual privacy in ways injurious to the wellbeing of the individual. This point may seem to be merely a generalization about what we most dislike in totalitarian societies, but Talmon interprets it as being symptomatic of a reconceptualization of the role of the public and private spheres, the effect of which is greatly to reduce the latter, by comparison with the prominent place that it occupies in liberal theory. It should be pointed out that this criticism is based on the remarkably attenuated view of the scope and importance of politics and public life held in Britain and the USA, and the resulting conviction that it is possible to be politically neutral and objective about major social issues. This view is certainly not shared by other cultures, past or present. For Plato and Aristotle, man was *homo politicus* and his self-fulfilment was to be found, precisely, in the public sphere and through political participation rather than in economic and private life.

In Britain, we tend to see politics as something which people have the right *not* to participate in. As a consequence, we deplore the political education, 'indoctrination', which occurs in communist schools as a forcible politicization of children and, by contrast, we eschew political subjects in school. (But there is much to be said for not allowing children to grow up ignorant of political matters, believing that politics is 'out there' beyond their control and irrelevant to their personal lives.) Making voting compulsory would be regarded here as a gross violation of privacy. Similarly, liberals look with disfavour on totalitarian states' interventions in matters such as birth control, seeing this as an intrusion into the private lives of individuals, although the effects of population explosions are indisputably political. Examples of our deliberately myopic view of politics and the 'public interest' could be multiplied indefinitely: they reflect our individualistic political culture. But, if totalitarian states extend the scope of political action to include aspects of life which *we* consider private, this is not a perversion of a universal norm, because there is no 'natural' limit to political activity or to the scope of legal regulation, even though we may wish to set such a limit, as liberals do. In South Africa, the law extends into the bedroom: in totalitarian states it may try to regulate men's minds, but this is not *per se* illegitimate. But for the liberal critic, totalitarianism characteristically acknowledges no boundary between the public and the private, and sees social life as a homogeneous phenomenon, subject to political regulation in all its parts.

(6) State supremacy

Closely associated with the expansion of the political sphere is the exaltation of the state in totalitarian thinking. The individual is perceived as a subordinate part of the greater whole and not, as by liberals, as the locus of the supreme political value. Individuals are, as a consequence, treated as if they were uniform ciphers, with identical needs and wants — 'enforced homogeneity'. The survival of the state at all costs and by all means becomes the dominant political goal. In fascist Germany, the state was viewed as a mystical entity, whose existence was bound up with the purity of the race and the territorial integrity of the nation. By contrast, Marxism is, officially, anti-state, but communist practice has strengthened and exalted the state apparatus and also, contrary to the internationalist aspirations of socialism, although under-standably in the context of the emergence of the USSR, adopted a highly nationalistic outlook. So the two archetypal ideologies which support totali-tarian systems have very different theoretical analyses of the state, even if their practice looks similar. As Barber points out, 'statism' is what most people would identify as the defining characteristic of totalitarianism. As can be seen, this is merely an inevitable consequence of the assumptions made about human nature and human needs.

The essentialist definition of totalitarianism can therefore be summarized as 'total methods in pursuit of a total goal', which Popper claimed to find origin-ating in Plato, and Talmon in Rousseau. Evidently, the assumptions and ideals imputed to totalitarianism by their critics deny and negate the values cherished by liberal democrats at every point. Four liberal convictions are particularly menaced by totalitarianism:

(1) That social good cannot be precisely defined, so that an open-ended approach should be taken towards the ideal society, and no dogmatic political ideology should be officially adopted.
(2) That men know their own real needs and their best interests, and it is mere presumption for rulers to gainsay these, which should be expressed through the democratic process. Totalitarian forms of democracy on the Rousseauist or Marxist model are discounted, being defined as not demo-cratic in the liberal way.
(3) That if state power is minimized, under a system of democracy and consent-based laws, men can make the choices which maximize their personal utility.
(4) That the plurality of needs, desires and tastes in political and private matters can only be catered for in a system based on tolerance which allows legitimate opposition.

The underlying value which gives rise to these convictions is the uniqueness and importance of the individual and his rights. It is a commonplace that 'individuality' is suppressed or extinguished in totalitarian societies: enforced equality and uniformity takes over. Yet it may be said that we in the West have a questionable notion of individuality, resting heavily, as it does, on the individual's ability to distinguish himself from others by means of expenditure and possessions. It is said that totalitarian states suppress individuality by conditioning the minds of their inhabitants — but nowhere, even in the free world, do individuals resemble the rational, autonomous beings of Enlighten-ment philosophy. All individuals are conditioned one way or another, but we happen to prefer the covert conditioning which takes place in the West. It cannot, of course, be true that totalitarianism eliminates individuality — the existence of individuals is a biological fact, and no society can entirely succeed in curbing self-assertion, although attempts may be made to control its manifestations, via norms and conventions as in liberal society, or coercively.

What is true, on the other hand, is that the ideologies dominant in totalitarian societies tend to allocate a less prominent place than liberals do to the individual in their conception of the social whole. This may justify a more holistic approach to policy, but it cannot abolish real individuals, although it can curb their freedom.

A further point in mitigation of liberal criticism of totalitarianism is that it, like liberal democracy, claims to realize the good of the people, and both may be right in their own sense. Western democracies are slaves to the short-term preferences of electors and realize the people's good in that respect, whereas a one-party democracy could claim to realize the long-term good of the community taken as a whole. Likewise, both forms of democracy might assert that they follow the will of the people: in the case of liberal democracy, this is the immediate subjective will, and in totalitarian democracy it is the real, objective will, similar to Rousseau's General Will. If we accept that both sides make such claims seriously, totalitarianism cannot be summarily dismissed as a cynical contravention of the will, and the good, of the people.

The problem in considering the essentialist definition is that the 'ideology' of totalitarianism has been compiled by its detractors in such a way as to show it to be the antithesis of liberal individualism. Whether such a doctrine exists is therefore highly questionable. The inhabitant of a communist society will call himself a communist, not a totalitarian. And communism and fascism, which are habitually equated with totalitarianism in Western parlance, do not share every one of the assumptions and values said to constitute the essence of the ideology. Popper *et al.* have in effect deduced these unstated assumptions and values from the practices which they consider totalitarian, then pieced them together into a coherent political outlook which, nevertheless, differs fundamentally from the two archetypal ideologies of totalitarianism. Popper and Taimon proceeded to reinterpret the works of earlier theorists in terms of this constructive ideology — retrospectively and anachronistically.[12] This is not the place to enter into the details of such debates as 'Was Rousseau a totalitarian?' which are, in any case, self-evidently futile, but it should be said that the theories of Rousseau and Plato coincide only at some points with what are held to be the main tenets of totalitarian ideology, and that Popper notoriously distorted Plato's views at many points in order to brand him as the first enemy of the open society.[13]

What can reasonably be inferred from the essentialist analysis is that there is a recurrent tendency towards absolutism and elitism in political thought. But these writers wish to establish a stronger thesis, namely, that totalitarianism itself has been implicit in certain works of political theory since classical times. As the six-point syndrome suggests, what we recognize as totalitarian systems could not have existed before advanced industrial society, since so many of their features depend on high technology and efficient communications, so that to suggest that totalitarianism is one of the perpetual themes of political thought must be nonsense. Certainly, we can concede that autocracy and so-called totalitarianism rest on some shared beliefs, particularly that of the need of the populus for strong, even dictatorial, leadership. In that respect, both are the polar opposites of the 'optimistic' views of liberals and socialists about the possibility of self-government and popular sovereignty. Autocracy and totalitarianism may also put the nation or state above the individuals who compose it, but not always for the same reasons. Modern autocrats often display transparent self-interest, whereas totalitarian states at least purport to further the good of the people.

The essentialist approach, then, goes further towards descrying a theoretical element in totalitarianism than the other two, but unfortunately the totalitarian ideology which they concoct has no self-styled adherents and has to be imputed to individuals who would themselves claim to be Marxists or fascists. To avoid this incongruity, totalitarianism might be said to be a meta-ideology, belonging to the system itself: a curious and untenable idea, for what can an ideology be which has no individual adherents? These difficulties suggest that the advocates of the essentialist analysis have not discovered a distinct totalitarian political theory, nor a totalitarian ideology, although their approach has been fertile in generating spirited witchhunts for the progenitors of the totalitarian bastard.

A significant by-product of the essentialist approach is that *utopianism* has been categorized as a species of totalitarianism, or as being potentially totalitarian. Schapiro lists the reasons for this, arguing that the utopian[14]:

(a) is preoccupied with ends and indifferent to means;
(b) views man and society as a totality;
(c) makes firm and dogmatic assumptions;
(d) is preoccupied with management (as opposed to democratic politics); and
(e) neglects human variety, and seeks to impose uniformity.

Since the diversity of utopian texts far exceeds the diversity of those states called totalitarian, generalizations about utopianism are even more ill-founded. What utopians have in common with totalitarian states is a single-minded commitment to a definite social ideal, although their ideal societies differ vastly. This is thought by Popper to entail that they will attempt to realize that ideal in the face of all opposition, by force if necessary[15], an invalid inference, as most utopians proposed to use rational persuasion to realize thier goals and relatively few gained, or even tried to gain, the political influence necessary to pursue their ideals. Totalitarianism and utopianism are both seen by liberals as forms of thought which justify ignoring people's legitimate wishes in order to impose some higher aim, but there is scant evidence for this in the case of the utopian, who pursues his ideal precisely because he believes that it will make people happy and that, when they understand it, they will also pursue it.

Needless to say, few utopias exhibit more than one or two points of the six-point syndrome, nor do they share all the assumptions and values specified in the essentialist view of totalitarianism, except, of course, the first. It is this commitment which seems to make utopianism antithetical to the liberal-democratic ideal which declares that the good society is whatever the democratic will of the people makes it (in theory at least), so that the 'good society' is a fluid and flexible concept: democracy is an ideal *procedure* rather than a substantive ideal. The rationalist approach to changing society favoured by utopians is opposed to the pragmatic, piecemeal method of social change which Popper sees as appropriate to the open society and is compared with that sinister feature of totalitarian societies, planning, by Popper, Talmon, and Oakeshott. Utopianism is a particular method of political *theorizing*, while totalitarianism has been defined by its critics on the basis of political *practice*: these two 'isms' are therefore qualitatively and conceptually different and it is hard to accept that they have anything in common except their arousal of suspicion among liberal democrats.[16]

The Psychological Roots of Totalitarianism

While Arendt specified the social and historical conditions for totalitarianism, others searched for its roots in the psychology of individuals. Adorno and others produced an influential book on these lines in the aftermath of the Second World War, *The Authoritarian Personality*. During the research individuals were asked to agree or disagree with long lists of statements, some very crudely expressed, designed to elicit anti-semitic and other fascist prejudices. The totality of their answers gave them a ranking on the 'F-scale', said to measure fascist tendencies, and on a scale of ethnocentricity which showed their inclination to adhere to their own in-groups and to be hostile to, or make scapegoats of, outsiders and members of other ethnic groups. What was revealed was that a worryingly high percentage of individuals had deep-rooted fascistic, ethnocentric or anti-semitic prejudices which, along with other attitudes, added up to the 'authoritarian personality'. Also, potentially fascist individuals were found to combine a high degree of aggression towards the groups they hated with a high degree of deference to those in authority, from which Adorno concluded the permanent danger of fascist or other authoritarian forms of government arising.[17]

The phenomenon of deference was also studied experimentally by the psychologist Milgram, who induced his subjects to give electric shocks of increasingly high voltage to 'victims' (who were in fact actors, placed behind glass screens, simulating pain and anguish as the 'shocks' were given) in the belief that they were participating in an experiment to show the connection between pain and short-term memory. His aim was to study the reaction of those giving shocks, and to see what percentages refused at the outset on humanitarian grounds, or stopped during the experiment, or went on to the end, giving what they knew to be painful or lethally high-voltage shocks. An important feature was the presence of white-coated 'psychologists' who assured the subjects that no lasting pain or damage would be caused to their victims (contrary to common sense!) and encouraged them to go on if they wanted to stop. In many cases the psychologists' orders outweighed the agonized pleas of the victims and the main experiment showed a 65% rate of obedience. In *Obedience to Authority* Milgram draws out the political implications of his findings, arguing that people low down in a legitimized chain of command will commit atrocities because they are merely obeying the orders of those above, which absolves them of personal responsibility: this, he considers, explains the inhumane behaviour of guards in Nazi death camps and some of the atrocities committed by US troops in Vietnam.[18] The level of pure deference to authority, especially when clad in a white coat and speaking with the voice of Science is, he concludes, disquieting and threatening to our democratic political culture.

Both Adorno's and Milgram's work met with highly critical receptions, not merely because their conclusions were unpalatable, but also because their research techniques were dubious and, in Milgram's case, highly unethical, since he had deceived his subjects. But if there is some truth in their results and conclusions, they imply that there is always the possibility for a totalitarian state to establish itself with the ready acquiescence of the large percentage of 'deferentials', and to use them to coerce or victimize their less acquiescent fellows. This may be so, but what these experiments could not reveal was whether such deference and other authoritarian attitudes are innate or acquired, which is crucially relevant to any political inferences to be drawn. It is unlikely that they are innate: Germans were not born hating Jews, but socially conditioned to do so. Deference to authority is also as likely to be conditioned response as to be a genetic trait of the 'weaker' members of society. So such experiments do not finally establish definite unchanging facts about personality and political attitudes. We can hypothesize that appropriate kinds of education and socialization could do much to lower future generations' rating on the fascist and deference scales.

The Freudian psychologists Reich and Fromm also attempted to explain the origins of fascism by 'the fear of freedom'. Reich located the cause of individual acquiescence in the rise of fascism in the strict patriarchal family traditional in Germany at the time. This produced, in the children who suffered an illiberal upbringing, sexual inhibitions, strong deference to authority, and a psychic structure full of contradictions which made conversion to the irrational doctrine of fascism easy, and led to a fear of, and flight from, freedom, into the arms of Hitler. Fromm too argues that alienated modern man sought to escape from freedom through authoritarian political structures.[19] Such theories represent a more speculative approach to psychology than, say, Milgram's, and do not offer empirical evidence, but only hypotheses — which may, nevertheless, be valid. But all the psychological theories cited here offer support for the major assumption pinpointed by the essentialist theory of totalitarianism, namely, the irremediable weakness of men, which entails the need for authoritarian governments. Whatever the validity of such theories, it is salutary to be reminded that the potential for totalitarianism is located in men's minds rather than, or as well as, in historical circumstance or in the wickedness of would-be despots. The reaction to such revelations as Milgram's should be a concerted search for techniques of child-rearing and socialization which produce independent, anti-authoritarian adults.[20] (But those who believe that personality is genetically determined are likely to draw more pessimistic conclusions, and to recommend authoritarian institutions.) The psychological approach to totalitarianism does not, of course, constitute a political theory in itself, but provides circumstantial evidence for those analysing it theoretically.

Totalitarianism Dissolved

In the 1960s and 1970s, as the spectre of fascism receded and détente quelled some Western fears about communism, political theorists reassessed the work on totalitarianism in a calmer and more sceptical mood and acknowledged the deficiencies of the accounts of totalitarianism described above. Barber contrasts the essentialist or 'traditionalist' approach, which sees totalitarian-ism as a political condition found potentially in all places at all times, with the phenomenological or 'modernist' view which depicts it as a uniquely twentieth-century phenomenon, particular to high-technology societies. He criticizes both approaches for their lack of objectivity and in their place offers a theoretical analysis of a more limited concept, that of 'totalism', the total integration of all parts of society and the fusion of individuals with the whole. Most people think of totalitarianism as necessarily being 'statist totalism', where the state coercively obliterates the boundaries between the public and private spheres and subjugates individuals, but other forms are equally possible. Indeed, Barber suggests that the USA may be becoming totalist 'by seepage' (by gradually adopting totalitarian methods), despite the pluralists' constant assertion of the distinction between the public and private spheres. A third possibility is 'communitarian totalism', where individuals realize that they can gain the greatest fulfilment by activity in the public sphere, and voluntarily surrender their private selves. Ideally, this is what socialism would achieve. Barber asserts that the standpoint from which totalitarianism is defined and condemned is that of an outmoded liberal individualism, and criticizes the current use of the term as 'conceptually archaic', suggesting that we should replace it with the more precise concept of 'totalism'.[21]

Even if Western political scientists still consider totalitarianism a unique political form, many theorists would accept the import of Barber's argument, that the concept itself is meaningless because of the contradictions inherent in every approach which seeks to elucidate it. But certainly there are still important distinctions to be drawn between individualist and totalist political systems and between authoritarian and democratic forms of government. A society can be authoritarian with or without the devices and methods found in the states which are called totalitarian, whenever an elite dictates to the majority of the population, in whatever guise—whether as experts, pro-fessional politicians or as 'the voice of the people'. Totalitarianism cannot be treated as a political ideology because it is not itself based on a political ideal: rather, it represents a set of methods which some political ideologies have assimilated as a means of realizing their chosen ideals, while other ideologies, like liberalism, repudiate them utterly.

However, another factor which caused political theorists to call into question the established view of totalitarianism is the detectable convergence between the 'free world' and those societies stigmatized as totalitarian, with respect to various aspects of social and political organization. As left-wing critics have argued, many of the six points of the syndrome are also instantiated in the West. Marcuse argues that capitalism is based on covert violence and that the tolerance which we vaunt is essentially repressive since it outlaws political views outside the liberal consensus and makes life unpleasant for the advocates of such views — vide McCarthyism and the 'Berufsverbot' which excludes political 'extremists' from public office in West Germany. Ideology in the West is every bit as strong as in the Eastern Bloc, but is presented as a common-sense, consensual view about the right and proper nature of society, rather than as a quasi-scientific dogma embedded in obscure texts. The media may be free but, by and large, they reinforce this consensus. Cynics would argue that Britain and the USA have now virtually got one-party systems, disguised as two-party adversary politics. The American President may not be Big Brother, but he has more power of life and death than any other world leader. And from the point of view of the individual, what difference is there between living in a state-planned economy and living in a private enterprise economy directed by uncontrollable, giant corporations hand-in-glove with the military and the politicians? Anyone who thinks that Western countries operate on the free-market, individualistic, and pluralistic basis which liberal-democratic theory extols, should read Mills's The Power Elite and the anonymous satire, Report From Iron Mountain, which expose the power of the military–industrial complex.[22] In terms of its byzantine structure, the Western elite, viewed objectively, may look much like that of the USSR, except that the titles of the power-holders are different.

Such analogies between the 'free' and the 'totalitarian' world can be extended endlessly. Because those who operate with an idea of totalitarianism based on the six-point syndrome do so largely in order to distinguish political systems which they dislike from liberal democracy, the appearance of such convergences is sufficient reason to abandon the phenomenological approach, which can no longer serve this tendentious purpose. The essentialist approach is defective because it specifies a loose set of political attitudes, assumptions, and ideals, some of which have been shared by a disparate variety of political theorists, thus giving rise to the absurd claim that all sorts of past thinkers were totalitarian. By concentrating on ideas rather than methods it, too, fails to prove that the political forms which are its target are uniquely totalitarian: rather, it suggests a continuum of political ideas and forms stretching from the absolutist to the democratic, with various so-called totalitarian states located at different points on the continuum. This approach would at least distinguish left- and right-wing totalitarianism, since the communist states would presumably appear nearer to the democratic pole than the fascist states. The historical approach offers a conception of totalitarianism as a political form specific to certain social conditions and does not provide any account of it as a political ideology.

Barber's analysis of the core idea of totalism, an emphasis on the social whole, which can be realized in different ways, is nearer the mark, and suggests that totalism is not itself an ideology, but a value which might be adopted by different ideologies and might even be realized, unwittingly, by seepage, or accidental, incremental growth of the state. If his account is accepted, it can be used to distinguish between fascist and communist states, both totalist in different ways—an important consequence, since analyses which conflate two such different and opposed systems must be erroneous. Of course, from a limited viewpoint, fascism and communism can be made to seem the same. Both threaten and oppose liberal democracy, and from the perspective of the repressed individual there may be nothing to choose between them. But from the wider, theoretical perspective, they differ significantly, and any adequate analysis must acknowledge this.

The conclusion of this assessment of the various accounts of totalitarianism is that political theory should eschew the concept on the grounds that it contains contradictions, is too wide (in the essentialist account) or too narrow (in the phenomenological and historical accounts) to operate satisfactorily in political analysis, and conflates widely differing political systems. We might in its place profitably adopt Barber's idea of totalism, or a notion of authoritarianism. The function of such ideas in political ideologies could then be analysed. Jettisoning the concept has a further merit: the term 'totalitarian' has been hopelessly debased by its regular use as a term of abuse. When the USSR, China, Cuba, Haiti, the Philippines, El Salvador, Argentina and Greece, Spain, and Portugal (until the mid-1970s) are all described by the same epithet, there is no possibility of analysing the differences between their political systems, or passing discriminating judgements on their varying ideologies and goals. All are condemned as equally bad, because 'totalitarian'. The revulsion induced by the adjective 'totalitarian' in too many cases prevents us from trying to understand and assess the aims of the ideology prevailing in a so-called totalitarian country.

To deny that the concept of totalitarianism has a useful role to play in political theory is not to condone the practices of reputedly totalitarian states. In the modern world, where most people are educated (at least rudimentarily) and where lip service is almost universally paid to humanitarian values, there is no justification for authoritarian governments or for coercion and brutality. But dissolving the concept of totalitarianism should have the constructive result of widening awareness of and sensitivity to the potentially totalistic or authoritarian aspects of all societies. If totalitarianism remains a pejorative term, confined by a narrow definition to Hitler's Germany, the USSR, and a few other unfortunate cuntries, it will not be conceived of as an immediate

168

threat to liberal-democratic societies. If, instead of thinking of totalitarianism like this, we consider the nexus of authoritarian and totalistic features found in the so-called totalitarian countries, we can inquire to what extent they also manifest themselves in capitalist society. As Friedrich and Brzezinski admit, the methods which they characterize as totalitarian are simply the methods available to any government in advanced industrial society. With the increasing degree of state activity in Western countries, the state might well choose to adopt any or all of the methods which constitute points (3) to (6) of the syndrome. Some have already been adopted in part — the inhabitants of many Western countries go in terror of armed and aggressive police forces. Democratic control appears to be ineffective against the momentum of state self-aggrandisement. So liberal democracies, instead of defining their preferred political system as the total antithesis of totalitarianism, should contemplate the shared risks. This suggests that, although the classical works on totalitarianism have grave shortcomings *qua* theoretical analyses of the idea, they should still be read, but read askance, with an eye on our own predicament.

Notes

1. This passage is a compilation of the totalitarian characteristics listed in Z. Brzezinski, 'Totalitarianism and rationality', *American Political Science Review* L, 3, 751–63 (1956).
2. See, e.g., S. Neumann, *Permanent Revolution*, Pall Mall, 1965.
3. C. J. Friedrich and Z. Brzezinski, *Totalitarian Dictatorship and Autocracy*, 2nd edn, Harvard University Press, 1965, pp. 21–2 especially.
4. S. Finer, *Comparative Government*, Allen Lane, 1970, p. 77.
5. E. Cassirer, *The Myth of the State*, Oxford University Press, 1946, Chaps II, XVIII.
6. H. Arendt, *The Origins of Totalitarianism*, revised edn, Allen & Unwin, 1967.
7. H. J. Weiss, *The Fascist Tradition*, Harper & Row, 1967.
8. J. L. Talmon, *The Origins of Totalitarian Democracy*, Praeger, 1960.
9. K. Popper, *The Open Society and its Enemies*, Routledge & Kegan Paul, 1962. Vols 1 and 2,
10. B. Barry, 'The public interest', in *Political Philosophy* (Ed. A. Quinton), p. 116.
11. R. Michels, *Political Parties* (Trans. E. Paul and C. Paul), Free Press, 1962, pp. 342–56.
12. See Popper and Talmon as cited, and also R. Crossman, *Plato Today*, Allen & Unwin, 1937, A. Cobban, *Rousseau and the Modern State*, Allen & Unwin, 1964, and E. Cassirer, *The Question of Jean-Jacques Rousseau*, Columbia University Press, 1954.
13. Popper's misrepresentations and misquotations are catalogued in R. Levinson, *In Defence of Plato*, Harvard University Press, 1953, Chap. 9.
14. L. Schapiro, *Totalitarianism*, Macmillan, 1972, pp. 85–90.
15. K. Popper, *The Open Society and its Enemies*, Vol. 1, pp. 157–68.
16. For further references to the attack on utopianism, see G. Kateb, *Utopia and its Enemies*, Collier-Macmillan, 1963.
17. T. Adorno *et al., The Authoritarian Personality,* Harper & Bros, 1950.
18. S. Milgram, *Obedience to Authority,* Tavistock, 1974.

19. W. Reich, *The Mass Psychology of Fascism* (Trans. V. R. Carfagno), Farrar, Strauss, and Giroux, 1970.
20. See D. Wright, *The Psychology of Moral Behaviour*, Penguin, 1971, who recommends techniques for producing the 'autonomous-altruistic' personality.
21. B. Barber, 'Conceptual foundations of totalitarianism' in *Totalitarianism in Perspective* (Eds C. J. Friedrich, M. Curtis and B. Barber), Pall Mall, 1969.
22. C. Wright Mills, *The Power Elite*, Oxford University Press, 1956; *Report From Iron Mountain* (Ed. L. Lewin), Penguin, 1968.

Further reading

L. Schapiro, *Totalitarianism,* Macmillan, 1972.

B. Chapman, *Police State,* Macmillan, 1970.

C. J. Friedrich, M. Curtis, and B. Barber, *Totalitarianism in Perspective*, Pall Mall, 1969.

C. J. Friedrich, *Totalitarianism*, Harvard University Press, 1954.

Part III

IDEAS

CHAPTER 9

Democracy

The fundamental task of political theory is to offer justifications for certain dispositions of power in a political system. Such justifications are usually moral as, if people can be induced to adopt and internalize moral principles, it is more conducive to social order than if they have to be coerced into obeying the political authority. As Chapter 2 suggested, these justifications are invariably and inescapably ideological and reflect the 'total ideology', the wider culture within which they are formulated. In the past, many different philosophies of power were advanced: Plato argued that political power was the province of the wise, the Philosopher Kings, who were in intimate contact with the world of Ideas from which they could infer correct political decisions. In the Christian mediaeval period, many thinkers held that the king was the vice-regent of God on earth, so that obedience to him was the first duty of the good, Christian citizen. Other theorists, including Nietzsche, have argued, in effect, that 'might is right' although many would condemn this as immoral. What these justifications have in common is that they make no appeal to law, laying stress instead on Absolute Truth, the divine will, or tradition, custom or force.

By contrast, the democratic justification of political power is essentially *legalistic*, being based on the legal idea of a contract. Modern democrats have discarded the fallible idea of the social contract and argue instead that democracy is based on the consent of the people which, once given through the voting process, obliges them to obey the chosen government.[1] The conceptual problems which arise here are discussed further in Chapter 10. Behind the democratic viewpoint lies the hypothesis that power and the right to hold power inheres in the people: in some theories, 'the people' refers to an aggregate of individuals, in some, to a collective entity. Democratic theory not only specifies that the people should govern themselves, but also that the purpose of government is the good of the people. The following ideas are central to what may be called 'classical' democratic theory:

(1) Supremacy of the people.

(2) The consent of the governed as the basis of legitimacy.
(3) The rule of law: peaceful methods of conflict resolution.
(4) The existence of a common good or public interest.
(5) The value of the individual as a rational, moral active citizen.
(6) Equal civil rights for all individuals.

The conjunction of these ideas in a political doctrine is somewhat accidental as they are not all logically connected. But as the theory developed historically they were moulded into a unified theory. Before discussing the problems of democratic theory and practice, some account of the theory is needed. This is not intended as a history of the idea, but it shows the movement from elitist conceptions of democracy with a limited franchise to the egalitarian ideals of the nineteenth century, and the swing back in the present century to restrictive, elitist views which cast doubt on the capacity of the people to participate in politics.

The Classical Ideal

The Greek notion of democracy influenced modern views, but differed from them substantially. Contrary to popular mythology, Greek democracy was far from ideal. Etymologically, the word means 'the rule of the *demos*, the mass of people', and it denoted a form of government distinct from aristocracy and from oligarchy, the rule of the few. Nevertheless, democracy was still a *partial* form of government, since the 'mass' would naturally pursue its own interests at the expense of other sections of the population, penalizing the wealthy by taxation. In modern times, fear of the 'populist' aspect of democracy—mob rule and vendettas—was reawakened by the French revolution. Plato considered democracy a decadent form of government, an 'imperfect society', three removes from the perfect republic and only one notch better than tyranny. He called it 'an agreeable, anarchic form of society, with plenty of variety, which treats all men as equal, whether they are equal or not'.[2] Plato emphasized the degree of individual freedom under democracy, of which he disapproved, because it weakened society as a whole. Aristotle was also disenchanted with this form of government, but he offered an analysis of the ethical principles of democracy.[3] Liberty is its aim, which means 'ruling and being ruled in turn', and implies a 'live as you like' principle from which spring various problems because, in conjunction with equality, it entails being ruled as little as possible, ideally by nobody.[4] Justice in such a democracy is based on numerical equality, and the rich and poor exercise exactly the same influence, but the danger here is that justice will be decided by the numerical majority and will be unjust towards minorities, such as the rich.[5] Aristotle's analysis acutely exposes the social dangers entailed by realizing the concepts of liberty and equality.

In the middle ages, doctrines of the mystical unity of all believers in the Church (above and below) and their equal subordination to God's will as expressed by kings, made democratic ideas irrelevant. The rise of the secular monarch called forth new, embryonically democratic ideas which at first aimed at curtailing the king's power over the people—or rather, over their elected representatives. Social contract theory, discussed in Chapter 3 above, was crucial in establishing a foundation for democracy, since the idea of a contract made when all men could be assumed to be equal led to the conclusion that the present power-holders only hold power on trust for the people.[6] Locke's second *Essay* sets out the principles for the composition and overthrow of governments. Government is set up to protect 'life, liberty, and estate' and emerges from a quasi-civilized state of nature via the social contract. From the original postulate that men are naturally rational, capable, and self-interested, he deduces that government must be by the people and aimed solely at their own good. They may elect representatives, delegate powers, and agree to abide by majority decisions, but ultimately the representatives and officials hold their powers on trust and are responsible to the people.[7]

The other details of Locke's version of democracy follow naturally from his original assumptions. Given that consent is the only legitimate basis for authority, we can only be subjected to laws by our own consent. Those who do not explicitly consent to a government are said to consent tacitly by living under its laws and accepting its protection.[8] The principle of consent is the theoretical basis and justification of democratic rule, and the important characteristic of government is the rule of law, which Locke describes as 'not so much the limitation as the direction of a free and intelligent agent to his proper interest'.[9] Law does not infringe, but supports, individual liberty—an important liberal tenet.

For liberty is to be free from restraint and violence from others, which cannot be where there is not law; and is not . . . 'a liberty for every man to do what he lists'.[10]

Locke envisaged the law as mainly being concerned with the protection of property: indeed, his democracy was an association of property-owners. Despite this slant, Locke also propagated an idea of equality among citizens. All preserved their equal natural rights, which the government was bound to protect, and all were equal in their subordination to government. At the same time, citizens are independent, equal members of the sovereign people.

At the heart of Locke's idea of democracy is the conviction that individuals know their own interests best, so that paternalistic government is inappropriate and oppressive. The government's only duty is the protection of those interests. The fiduciary nature of government leads to the radical conclusion that the people are entitled to overthrow a government which breaches their trust, for example, by taking away their property or enslaving them. This invitation to popular revolution is less open than it seems, for Locke was wary of specifying the conditions under which it would be justified.[11] The ultimate sovereignty of the people constitutes an important safeguard in the democratic tradition, at least in theory. Much of Locke's *Essay* is devoted to the checks and balances which would prevent the organs of government from exceeding their powers, although these are of interest to the constitutionalist rather than to the theorist.

Almost a century after Locke, Paine wrote vindications of both the American and French revolutions—*Common Sense* (1776) and *The Rights of Man* (1791-2). Although he was not a systematic philosopher, the now familiar ideas of Locke appeared in his writings with new additions. 'Every citizen is a member of the sovereignty, and, as such, can acknowledge no personal subjection: his obedience can only be to the laws'. Government is properly based on a social compact, but the English government of the time had arisen out of conquest, '*over* the people'.[12] Having thrown off the yoke of absolute monarchy, the individual's only duty is to laws which, in effect, he has himself made. Paine quoted the French *Declaration*:

The law is an expression of the will of the community. All citizens have a right to concur, either personally or through their representatives, in its formation.[13]

The concrete corollary of such a requirement was elected, representative government with universal suffrage. Paine emphasizes the equality of all men in respect of their rights and, above all, their extensive right to liberty, which 'consists in the power of doing whatever does not injure another'. The emphasis of democratic theory was thus already shifting from the assertion of the people's collective rights against the king to the individual's rights, which would protect his independence against the government or state. Indicative of this shift was the addition of a Bill of Rights to the American constitution, which had originally weighted the odds heavily against the individual.

The drawing up of the American constitution provided the first chance for the pragmatic development of democratic theory, by trial and error. *The Federalist*,[14] a paper produced by the Constitution's 'founding fathers', debated the theoretical issues. Hamilton's fear of mob rule, a democratic bogey since the time of Plato, was reflected in provisions for indirect elections to the Senate and Presidency, and for allowing state legislatures to set restrictive qualifications for the franchise. Nevertheless, logically democratic theory should not acknowledge the danger of mob rule, because the basis of the theory is the ideal of the active, intelligent citizen. Madison feared the creation of a permanent, tyrannical majority in a homogeneous democracy such as Rousseau had described, but hoped that the size of the USA and the people's diversity of origins and interests would itself be a safeguard. He wished to forestall the formation of political parties which might lead to factionalism and majority tyranny, but in fact American political parties rarely espoused dogmatic policies or threatened to become permanent majorities, except briefly during the Civil War, because of the wide interests which they represented. It was once said that 'the two great parties were like two bottles. Each bore a label denoting the kind of liquor it contained, but each was empty'. And as Dahl has argued, 'the majority never rules, consequently it can never tyrannise'.[15] The constantly changing composition of the political majority in the USA thus fortuitously prevents a permanent majority developing—a fact which underlines the importance of social conditions for the achievement of democracy.

The writers of the *Federalist* favoured co-operation, deliberation, and bargaining as methods of decision-making, by contrast with the straight majority voting practised in the English parliament. The American approach is reminiscent of Rousseau's idea that members of the community should know and understand each others' points of view and interests. Implicit in the arguments of the *Federalist* is the justification for what Americans now idealize as consensus politics and bipartisan policies—although it could be said that these are only another manifestation of the power of the now permanent centrist majority, and that factions, disputes, and decisions by voting might be preferable. From the inception of the US Constitution, British and American versions of the democratic ideal began to diverge, despite the common influence of Locke, so that the differences today between revised Madisonian democracy or 'pluralism' and the populist democracy of Britain are considerable. The latter accepts that permanent, opposed interests should be represented through adversary politics, and that policies should be imposed by a majority vote without attempts at co-operation and conciliation. The federal nature of the USA necessitates a pluralist system, while the British conception of democracy favours strong, majority government without mediation.

The classical democratic theory of the eighteenth century was revamped by J. S. Mill to emphasize its idealistic and individualistic nature. *Representative Government* (1859) discusses the practical organization of government which would achieve democratic ideals yet avoid evils such as the dominance of the working classes, while *On Liberty* (1861) sets out the background of individual rights required for a proper democracy. Democracy itself no longer needed justifying, for democratic republics and constitutional monarchies were common by the time Mill wrote, so that he abandoned any preamble about contract and consent and merely asserted that the ideal form of government 'is that in which the sovereignty . . . is vested in the entire aggregate of the community'.[16] This is conducive to order, progress, and permanence. Mill's account of representative democracy is strongly individualistic: the most important feature of a democracy is the calibre of the individuals who compose it, who should be rational, educated, and active. Taking part in political debate and voting would, Mill supposed, educate people, and the prime aim of government is their mental advancement. Underlying such claims is a vision of man as an independent creative and moral agent, capable of development. Hence, Mill's emphasis on freedom and the right to self-determination.

No intention, however sincere, of protecting the interests of others can make it safe or salutary to tie up their hands.[17]

Clearly, Mill views political activity as a good in itself, and this proposition is central to the defence of democracy, which is a less than ideal form of government in some respects — for instance, with regard to efficiency.

Writing in support of universal suffrage before it was attained in Britain, Mill put forward a theory of representation to justify his demand. He argued that the representative system produced government by intelligent men, whose wisdom outreaches that of their constituents and safeguards the government from 'popular clamour', since elected representatives must act on their own judgement and not be mere delegates. This 'theory', an idealized account of the workings of the British parliament, recalls the claim of James Mill (Mill's father) that the middle-classes were the repository of wisdom and should supply moral leadership.[18] J. S. Mill's stress on representation and his proposal for a plural vote for the educated or, failing that, the wealthy, reintroduces an elitist element into democratic theory which, by its own logic, should be strictly egalitarian. In Tocqueville there is a parallel admission of the moral rightness of democracy, coupled with a revulsion from its implications; Tocqueville described the majority principle as absurd because it extended the theory of equality to men's intellects.

The problem of minorities greatly exercised Mill, who foresaw his own class, the intelligentsia, being swamped when the franchise was enlarged. For such an individualist, the question of minorities is really the question of oppressed individuals writ large. He advocated proportional voting as an institutional safeguard for permanent minorities, but also argued that their best defence was to consolidate themselves as interest groups and to remain informed and active.[19] *On Liberty* states the need for the individual to protect himself from public opinion, and Mill's support of minorities reiterates this at the political level. Both Mill and Tocqueville, who made a study of American democracy in the early nineteenth century, acclaimed the theoretical virtues of democracy in producing active, public-spirited citizens, but both issued practical warnings about its social consequences, fearing pressures to conformity and the tyranny of majority opinion.[20] Mill's advocacy of democracy must be seen in this light, and also in the light of his argument that the scope and activities of the state should be limited as narrowly as possible, to prevent oppression and preserve the independent initiative of the citizens.[21] Even 'the ideally best polity' has its limitations.

Elitists and Pluralists

The twentieth century has seen an explosion of writing about the nature of democracy. The approach taken has often been critical, deploring the fact that the democratic ideal, now widespread, has not created world peace and prosperity. Bryce bemoaned the absence of goodwill, public spirit, and co-operation among democratic citizens, and he and Schumpeter both consider that democracy has been degraded to a *means* for procuring material benefits for the people and is no longer an end in itself. Schumpeter proposed a realistic, procedural account of democracy as competition among leaders for the people's votes. But these critiques, which are discussed later, did not really impinge on the individualistic ideals of democracy, citizenship, and participation, although they showed them to be inadequately realized in reality. However, recent American political science has produced political data which have given rise to two rival theories of modern democracy, the *elitist* and the *pluralist*.

The term 'elite' connotes exclusiveness in combination with special skills or resources; not every minority or interest group is correctly described as an elite.[22] The sociologist Pareto distinguished governing from non-governing elites and contrasted both with 'the mass'. There has been extensive investigation of the role of elites in politics since Pareto's study, and the parallel analysis by Michels of the 'iron law of oligarchy' at work in every political organization, but these discoveries were viewed as ominous for democracy, except by those like Ortega y Gasset who deplored the mass mediocrity of democratic society and praised elitism.[23] To test the truth of these hypotheses, empirical studies were devised to identify the supposed political elites by looking at the stratificiation of power and the positions and the reputations of 'notables' of local communities. Such studies flourished in the 1950s and 1960s. Much criticism was directed at the methods used, but this did not prevent general political conclusions being drawn. A particularly influential work was Mills's *The Power Elite*, which exposed the workings of an industrial–military–political complex in American politics. Miliband produced a similar, but more critical exposure of the British elite in *The State in Capitalist Society* (1969). A combination of aesthetic distaste for 'mass society' and disillusion with the 'ideal' democratic voter, whose extensive apathy was revealed in Berelson's study, *Voting* (1954), conduced to the development of an empirically-based theory about the compatibility of elite rule with democracy, now known as 'democratic elitism'.

The politically active elites in a modern democracy are, of course, an iceberg, only the tip of which appears in national parliaments, although the political leadership itself constitutes an elite which develops special interests which are not typical of the people it represents. The Burkean theory of representation is often invoked to prove that the political elite is necessarily wise and chooses what is best for the electorate, but this justification contradicts the current definition of an elite as a group pursuing its own interests. Another defence of elites states that their power is not a threat to democratic procedure because, with a multitude of elites which can freely 'circulate' in and out of power, each is kept within bounds. Indeed, to achieve anything, they must negotiate and co-operate so that no one elite is wholly autonomous or in control of the others. The average voter is assumed to have little or no control over these elites, but Key, Truman, and others take the view that the elites share a consensus on the rules of the democratic game, which they observe. This is small comfort to the democratic citizen since it is conceivable that one or several elites will one day find themselves in consensual agreement to break the rules and destroy the democratic system. Mills considered that other elite groups were powerful enough to withstand the combined 'power elite' — hence the promotion of the armaments industry and arms race. He argued that the power elite should be submitted to the control of intellectuals, while Schumpeter thought that it could be made periodically responsible to the people through elections. But in all democratic theory, responsibility is a poor second to control since the leadership presents *faits accomplis* to the electorate: responsibility as a concept has a built-in time-lag, which may be fatal.

Advocates of elite democracy enumerate the various political virtues of elites in the political arena. It is argued that elites are the educated, active, and dynamic force in modern democracy, a necessary replacement for the mythical ideal citizen. Keller believes that the elite's set of articulated beliefs, or its ideology, gives it moral and social leadership, a disturbing suggestion from the viewpoint of tolerance and freedom of opinion. Truman argues that the consensus of elites precludes a demagogic rising of the masses, referring to Hitler's meteoric rise to power in a country which lacked a leadership elite. Mills praises the ability of elites to centralize power and so to make history in an unprecedented way. But many of the arguments for accepting elites as part of the democratic system are mere apologies resting on the weakest form of functionalist argument. The political system works, and we think it good; elites form part of this system, therefore elites perform a function in the system and hence are good.[24]

From the viewpoint of individualistic, liberal-democratic theory, many objections must be raised to accepting democratic elitism as the revised version, and to idealizing it. The elite outlook treats the majority of men as passive consumers, incapable of exercising power or judgement, and totally apathetic. But, as Bachrach points out, the 20% of apathetic voters in the USA of the 1950s and 1960s significantly coincided with the poorest stratum of the population.[25] Perhaps we should reform social conditions rather than revise the democratic ideal. Elite theory treats democracy as a mere means, not as an end in itself and an ethical process, participation in which will educate and develop men. It completely negates the ideal of political equality, readily accepting the fact that some have more power than others and making no attempt to redress the balance. The typical elitist version of political equality is 'equal eligibility to power status' which, like 'equality of opportunity', leaves much to be desired. Elite theory also falls foul of Madison's and Rousseau's interdiction of factions, but capitalizes on studies of voter ignorance and apathy and the modern tendency to analyse groups rather than individuals, to vindicate itself. And, as Bachrach points out, the definitions of this theory are tailored to show that the existing system meets the requirements of democratic elitism.[26] These conclusions support the existing system as being a comfortable equilibrium, not far from ideal. Of course, many people believe elite leadership to be a natural and necessary phenomenon, and a number of utopias have featured elite ruling groups — Plato's Guardians, Saint-Simon's technocrats

—and many societies have prospered under elite government, but this is hardly the point. Democracy is on principle antithetical to all elite or oligarchic forms of government, and puts its faith in the political capability of the common man. A theory which tries to join elite rule and democracy seeks to reconcile the theoretically irreconcilable.

In the heyday of elite studies, Dahl published *Who Governs?* (1961), a study of New Haven politics, which found no identifiable, dominant elite among a whole galaxy of 'notables'. Dahl concluded that New Haven was a *pluralist democracy* and went on to develop his theory of pluralism, or 'polyarchy', the rule of the many, which he claims to be the form that modern US democracy takes, deriving from the original Madisonian ideal.[27] Polyarchy is rule by a series of minorities, some self-interested, some public-spirited, all of whom accept the established form of politics; their policy proposals lie within boundaries prescribed by consensus. Anyone in an interest group is, as it were, represented in this political process, although Dahl's theory has been criticized for ignoring 'political marginals' such as the very poor who have no resources and belong to no groups. The pluralist system is decentralized; advances in policy depend heavily on bargaining.

It could be said of such a political system that it aims to reach compromises, rather than to discover political truth or the 'right' policy. This interpretation is borne out by Dahl's emphasis on the 'instrumental goals' of the pluralist system, which are the conditions for the sort of government which will maximize the 'primary goods'—of which he says little. The theory of polyarchy is, it appears, about the *process* of government rather than about the ideal political system. But this limitation has not prevented it from being presented as if it described an ideal which is instantiated by American democracy today. Dahl's account of polyarchy answers Madison's fear of the permanent majority: the multiplication of minorities and the endless negotiations between them forestall any possibilities of tyranny.

The advantage of pluralist over elitist theory is that it suggests that the political system is all-inclusive, and operates on the basis of consensus, which ensures that everyone's interests are taken into account, and everyone attains satisfaction, while elite theory entails the possibility of a dangerous divergence of interests between rulers and ruled. However, the two theories are not far apart: it is perfectly feasible that in a pluralist system some elites would become dominant, and indeed Dahl has often been branded an elite theorist, although he denies it and asserts the polarity between the theories. There has been much controversy about method among the adherents of the two theories, and each group accuses the other of choosing methods which suit their prejudices; these disputes need not concern us here, except to suggest that political theorists should be wary of the claims of political science to establish factual truth.

The debate must be seen in the light of increasing scepticism about the validity of orthodox democratic theory. Berelson's voting study concluded with the paradox that incompetent citizens produced competent government;

political scientists then began to speculate that apathy and passivity were actually 'functional' to democracy and that the system was best maintained by active elites making choices for the passive masses.[28] Thus the political scientists produced an account of democracy in operation and endowed it with normative value, claiming both that it factually refuted the classical democratic ideal and that it evaluatively replaced that ideal. One criticism of this claim is that elite and pluralist theories of democracy merely idealise what exists and disguise the imperfections of the system; another is that classical democratic theory never pretended to be factually true, but was intended as a yardstick by which real democracies could assess themselves and strive for improvement.[29] But one might also defend the new theories against the accusation that they are descriptions of the present disguised as ideals; although theories such as Locke's now appear to have a timeless ideality, they emerged from the existing political situation just as elite theories do. The main objection, though, to elite and pluralist theories is that they have no critical purchase on the present system, since they are devised to justify it. This must arouse our suspicions.

One other modern theory of democracy deserves mention. Downs analyses the democratic process in terms of economic concepts. He hypothesizes that citizens behave rationally, aiming to maximize their personal utilities through political participation, while parties act to maximize their votes. Self-interest is the dynamic of the system, which also has affinities with utilitarianism. Voting is seen as a short-term sacrifice which will only be undertaken if the potential rewards are adequate and if the voter's 'party differential' is high. The parties are therefore induced to distinguish themselves sharply from each other, and to offer high rewards for the voter's vote.[30] This 'descriptive definition' of democracy omits most of the ethical ideals found in classical theory, but it has a normative component, for it implies that the system will spontaneously maximize everyone's utilities. Here are echoes of Adam Smith's hope that an invisible hand would aggregate the self-interested acts of economic individuals into a general prosperity. Similar to Down's theory are the exchange and transactionist theories of politics which view each political act as a profitable exchange between individuals or groups.[31] As with the elitist theories, Down's theory has a descriptive basis: its normative element lies especially in its validation of the existing form of politics and its implication that all is for the best in this world.

The group of democratic theories developed this century share certain traits which distinguish them from classical theory. They deliberately omit the idealistic aspects and describe political activity in realistic, factual terms, reducing political motivation to self-interest. Consequently, democracy is seen purely as procedure, a procedure justified as being the most efficient or the best utility-maximizing method. This justification has the disadvantage that, once ethical reasons for choosing democracy have been abandoned, if it can be shown to be less than efficient (as it is), any *more* efficient form of government should, logically, be chosen to replace it. The new theories often emphasize as goals the maintenance and stability of the system, rather than its instrumental role in satisfying or developing the individuals who compose it; as Davis says, such theory 'vindicates the main features of the status quo and provides a model for tying up loose ends'.[32] By restricting the scope of theorizing to the narrowly political sphere of action, the new theories ignore imminent threats to democracy from outside the political system: large corporations and the bureaucracy tend to promote non-democratic ideals and exercise a good deal of control over the political process, without having any accountability to the electorate. Nearly all these theories commit what Holden calls 'the definitional fallacy':[33] because the American political system is *called* a democracy, they deduce the characteristics of democracy from what they observe there. This is particularly true of Lipset's account of democracy in terms of the material and social conditions he observes in Western societies.[34] A theory constructed like this has no critical force and is inherently conservative.

This is why the comparison of modern and classical democratic theory is not merely an academic issue, an artificial confrontation between the living Dahl and the long-dead J. S. Mill. Arguments which 'prove' that the USA (or Britain) is a democratic country give important support to the prevalent liberal ideology, and stultify the radical critique of political institutions. Hence, an understanding of modern democratic theory and its methodological and idealistic failings is important. The table which follows makes a schematic comparison of the classical and modern theories of liberal democracy.

'Radical' Democracy

In the period of the Enlightenment, while Locke's idea of democracy was becoming more and more closely associated with the liberal ideal, another version of democracy was developed by Rousseau which, in the present century, has become closely associated with Marxism. Rousseau was born in Geneva, then a small, independent city ruled by the Calvinist Fathers and small enough to be a direct democracy. Although he spent most of his life in France, this greatly influenced his ideas. Rousseau has been called 'timidity personified' but his theory constituted an indirect attack on the corrupt despotisms of continental Europe. Also, unlike other French philosophers who admired the English system, Rousseau argued that its representative nature made the citizens no better than slaves.

The people of England regards itself as free; but it is grossly mistaken; it is free only during the election of members of parliament. As soon as they are elected, slavery over-takes it, and it is nothing.[35]

The solution was a direct democracy in which everyone could represent himself and Rousseau looked admiringly to the democracies of classical antiquity for this ideal. Such a democracy solves the problem of political obligation and other paradoxes, for when the individual confronts the law, he is confronting laws which he himself freely made. To obey oneself is to be free. Hence,

Classical and modern democratic theory compared

Classical democratic theory	Modern democratic theory
(1) From Locke onwards, enshrines supremacy of people.	(1) Tends to emphasize supremacy of *the system*; one goal is maintenance of the system.
(2) Makes consent of governed a pre-requisite for legitimate government, which makes periods of defeat acceptable to minorities.	(2) Dismisses idea of consent (with good reason) but replaces it with weaker notion of consensus, giving citizens at most a retrospective control of government.
(3) Often postulates a common good (cf the 'right answer').	(3) Argues there can never be *one* good; the conflict-consensus balance will produce tolerable selection of policies, a variety of goods.
(4) Emphasizes individual freedom; individual to pursue his own best interests with minimum interference; commitment to minimum law.	(4) Emphasis on system detracts from notion of minimum law—a discarded ideal. National security, welfare legislation require the law to be more extensive.
(5) Takes individual as basic unit of democratic model; assumes he is rational, ethical, active, and self-interested. His political actions have importance since the majority is composed of individuals.	(5) Sees interest group as fundamental, politically active unit. Disregards all individual characteristics except self-interest. Makes mass-apathy functional and necessary. Political man plays many roles, has multiple loyalties—classical democrat considered him single minded and one dimensional.
(6) Stipulates that political equality is a fundamental ideal—although this can lead to injustice in a simple majoritarian democracy, when permanent minorities are submerged. Solutions to 'the intensity problem' would undermine political equality.	(6) Transforms idea of political equality from one-man-one-vote into equal access to interest groups etc. Would argue that pluralist theory gives minority bargaining power and therefore greater equality. Can cope with 'intensity problem' in this way.
(7) Early democratic theory emphasized the possibility of radical, though controlled, change.	(7) Modern democratic theory, idealizing stability, equilibrium, system-maintenance, implicitly denies possibility/usefulness of change.

Rousseau's own paradox, which has invited so many unfavourable interpretations, that in being forced to obey the law, man is 'forced to be free'.[36] Rousseau's *Social Contract* (1762) begins with an account of an original contract in which each individual renounces his natural liberty in exchange for the equality and conventional liberty which society offers. He foregoes some of his power over himself and gains power or influence over his fellows in exchange — a mutual assurance scheme.

The ideas of the common good and the General Will are central to Rousseau's analysis. Locke's theory began with an individual who best knows his own interests, and the common good is merely the aggregate of all private interests. But for Rousseau, the common good is something which benefits all individuals equally, but may not coincide with their 'felt', personal interests. The General Will, the dynamic, decision-making element in Rousseau's democracy, is defined as that which promotes the common good.[37] The concept is a baffling one, since Rousseau makes it clear what it is *not* but not what it *is*. It is not the will of all individuals added together and averaged out (this he calls the *volonté de tous*) nor is it the will of the majority. Anyone, or any group, might serve as the mouthpiece of the General Will: 'this does not mean that the commands of rulers cannot pass for general wills, so long as the sovereign (i.e. the people) offers no opposition'.[38] In other words, the General Will is not essentially a democratic notion, although Rousseau thought it could best be realized through a direct democracy where the people's sovereignty would act as a safeguard against the imposition of any 'particular wills'. It may help our understanding of the General Will if it is thought of as the 'right answer' to some question, the answer which most effectively promotes the common good. For some questions, we cannot predict who will get the right answer, or how, nor is there any reason to think that individuals collectively could find it better than singly, but as long as the answer is right, the method of finding it is relatively unimportant. The problem with this analogy is that the common good may not be a question with a unique right answer.

The democratic process envisaged by Rousseau consisted of deliberation, then voting. During discussion, individuals were entitled to put forward their private interests, but in the voting process, they should vote for what they considered to be the common good: ideally this would produce a unanimous vote. This seems less hopelessly optimistic when one remembers that Rousseau assumed certain specific social conditions: a small, homogeneous community of craftsmen, whose education and background would be similar and whose interests would therefore tend to coincide. However, he also proposes the expedient of a legislator, who would propose laws for the common good which the sovereign people could accept or reject.[39] Critics view this as an invitation to dictatorship, but it may merely be a practical acknowledgement that a collective body is usually unable to initiate proposals without effective leadership or guidance.

Another important element in the theory is Rousseau's condemnation of 'partial societies' — that is, groups with vested interests which may prove divisive, and stop the General Will from forming. Rousseau probably had in mind the economic monopolies and small privileged groups which manipulated French politics to their own advantage at the time. His fear of factions clearly influenced Madison, and the French revolutionaries. When the Jacobins suppressed the Girondins (1793–5), they cited Rousseau in justification. Thus, Rousseau's position has been condemned as being authoritarian and inimical to free speech. It shocks those who see adversary politics as the watchdog of freedom and the spice of life, and it is certainly anathema to the pluralist, yet, in terms of Rousseau's own logic and his belief in the possibility of a common good, it is sound. In stripping the citizen of self-interest and making him merely a spokesman for the common good, Rousseau foreshadows the worse excesses of totalitarianism, it is argued.[40] But he thought that on entering society the individual gave up some of his selfish pleasures for the infinitely more fulfilling role of moral being and citizen and it is on this elevated plane that he forms part of the General Will, which in turn creates the conditions for private pleasure.

To many, Rousseau's 'democracy' seems to enhance the authority of the state and to pave the way for a totalitarian society, because of his readiness to submerge the individual in the General Will and his denial that private interests should be paramount in politics. This debate has already been discussed in Chapter 8. But it is certain that Rousseau admired and advocated democracy: his idea of the General Will was obscure, perhaps confused, but not malevolent. However, he has been further discredited in the West because of the use of his ideas in Marxism. The classless society achieved after the revolution will, it is said, achieve such a homogeneity of interests that no political opposition or factions will exist. Direct democracy was supposed to operate in post-revolutionary Russia through the workers' Soviets, although this quickly turned into 'democratic centralism', where commands were transmitted *downwards* from the top. Many have seen echoes of the General Will in Lenin's notion of the dictatorship of the vanguard party, acting on behalf of the proletariat: it could claim to be the spokesman for the common good of those still deluded by bourgeois democracy. Ultimately, the common ideal of Rousseau and Marx is unmediated *popular sovereignty*, an idea which horrifies the champions of representative democracy, who fear the untutored instincts of 'the mass' erupting into politics. The people may be wayward and fickle. Holden perceives another danger of popular sovereignty:

Once government is postulated as the complete servant of the people, it is sometimes hard to retain the view of it as a hostile force that has to be kept within strict limits.[41]

So popular sovereignty, paradoxically, unleashes the leviathan of the state. But liberal democrats cannot criticize direct democracy and popular sovereignty for this without a degree of hypocrisy. The average citizen is assumed by such liberals to be sufficiently rational and educated to vote, but nothing more, and they themselves are thus committed to an elitist view of political capacity which could just as well form the basis of an oligarchical theory as of a theory of representative democracy. The fear of the 'mob' dies hard, and the more that theorists separate the roles of citizen and politician, the more they condemn the masses to political passivity, ignorance, and alienation — the very preconditions for a mob! The early liberal-democratic premise that each has rights and interests which merit representation and the later premise that each has a political capacity both entail a form of government based on popular sovereignty; only elitist convictions can prevent us from admitting this. None of these arguments should be taken to imply that communist countries have realized democracy more ideally than has the West: but they suggest that our theoretical repugnance for the Rousseauist–Marxist radical-democratic ideal embroils us in certain inescapable inconsistencies. Evidently, the difference between representative and direct democracy is not merely one of procedure: representation qualitatively changes the nature of the system, and promotes a different ideal from that of popular sovereignty.

The nature of democracy, briefly summarized, is as follows: a postulate that the individual has the right to and the capacity for self-rule entails popular self-government, with consent as the basis of the government's legitimacy. Related ideals are freedom under law, equality of political rights, and the value of individuals *qua* citizens. Representative democracy adds to these the necessary virtue of government accountability and responsibility to the electorate. Radical- and liberal-democratic theories differ over the possibility of a common good, the scope of government, the desirability of plural interests and factions, and the role of the state, but both treat democracy as an ideal, not just a government apparatus, and so neither theory should be taken as primarily offering an empirical account. In each case the ideal must be distinguished from the associated conditions and the mechanisms of democracy such as the secret ballot, which may reflect the spirit of democracy but are really cultural details, separable from the ideal. This brief survey of the main elements of the various democratic theories makes it possible to discuss the conceptual weaknesses of the ideal, and to offer a critique of some of its presuppositions. Foremost among these is the so-called paradox of democracy.

Democracy's Paradox

The democratic citizen frequently finds himself in the position of wanting one law to be enacted, but having to obey a contrary law chosen by the majority; even worse, he votes for the losing party and has to obey its rival. Such events are more than a passing annoyance, and it is essential for the stability of democracy that the citizen should not disobey, revolt or secede whenever this happens. Yet democracy constantly puts the citizen in the dilemma of believing one thing and having to do another. His dilemma can be represented as the irrational state of holding two contradictory moral beliefs: 'X is wrong' and

'X is right if the majority thinks it right' entail that if the majority enacts policy X, it is simultaneously right and wrong for that citizen. The problem is usually expressed as follows: how can the individual follow his own will, yet conform to that of the majority? A number of solutions have been proposed. In general, the citizen who voted for the losing party can console himself that his party may win next time, a consolation that will only be effective in a society with a fair degree of consensus and a low level of inter-party conflict. But the moral dilemma arises more acutely with regard to particular policies, where two principles come into conflict. Wollheim's solution is to say that individuals hold both direct moral principles, such as 'murder is wrong' and oblique, or second-order, moral principles, such as 'what the majority decides is right'. He argues that there cannot be a contradiction between these two kinds of principles, whereas two direct principles could be contradictory, because direct and oblique principles are not 'immediately' incompatible. So the citizen who believes that X is wrong, but is right if the majority wants it, is not irrational or self-contradictory.[42] Wollheim has been criticized for this sleight of hand: the idea of 'immediacy' is alien to logic—either there is a contradiction or there is not. In any case, the postulate of two different sorts of moral principles is unacceptable to many philosophers.

Another proposed solution is that offered by Schiller:[43] the majority rule is a convenient form of decision procedure, he argues. In subscribing to it, we accept it as the best procedure available; this is a *rational* commitment. The obligation which follows from such commitment is not an overriding imperative but a rational or prudential obligation, which cannot override moral principles. Of course, if our moral belief that X is wrong leads us into disobedience, we are endangering the majority principle practically, but we are not in self-contradiction. Equally, we can retain our moral belief that X is wrong and obey the law enjoining us to do X without suffering a moral crisis: the prudential commitment has overridden the moral principle, simply. Schiller argues that a universal rational (non-moral) acceptance of democratic procedure is a sufficient condition for democratic government, which does not demand moral commitment, but his view tends to undermine the idea of democracy as an ethical ideal to which we should commit ourselves morally.

Rousseau's solution to the problem has already been intimated. He asks 'How can a man be both free and forced to conform to wills that are not his own?' Part of his solution deals with the lawmaking process: men can promote their own beliefs in debate but should ignore these when it comes to voting and vote for what appears to be the common good. For this to be a satisfactory solution, we must first believe, as Rousseau did, that the common good can be unambiguously identified. Rousseau's proposal splits the individual into two selves—his private and his citizenly self—and so evades the psychological problem which arises when someone has two contradictory desires. Rousseau's case for why we should obey laws of which we disapprove is that it would be self-contradictory to disobey laws which we ourselves had taken part in enacting.[44] This may carry some weight in a direct democracy, but the representative system interposes so many mediating levels between the citizen and legislation that he could easily undertake civil disobedience (or indeed criminal activity) without feeling the contradiction which Rousseau foresees.

The paradox of democracy can be viewed as a special case of the permanent tension between individual freedom and authority, which is most sharply emphasized under the democratic form of government, which most seeks to promote freedom. In a society like Britain, where consensus on the political system is reasonably strong and political conflicts and controversies fairly muted, the so-called paradox may seem an academic irrelevance. Our society is a tolerant one: doctors who think abortion wrong are not obliged to perform the operation, and people rarely come face to face with the paradox in its acutest, moral form. But in a situation of ideological or minority conflict, Wollheim's solution (if the direct moral principle prevails and determines people's behaviour) might cause a breakdown of democracy, whereas Rousseau's would probably preserve it. The whole debate is therefore crucial for the legitimization of government and the laws, for establishing political obligation and for upholding the majority principle. Which solution to the paradox you prefer depends on how certain you are of your beliefs and whether you value them more than political stability. Those adhering to some system of moral absolutes, such as a religion may provide, may decide to defy the majority, buoyed up by their moral infallibility, while those with a more subjectivist view of ethics may be swayed by the majority's view of what is right, or allow their prudential commitment to democracy to outweigh their moral principles. This suggests why democracy is more at risk and harder to establish in a country with a strong and absolutist religion.

The Problem of Minorities

The paradox of democracy is applicable to individual citizens who by and large find themselves in agreement with the majority and democratic procedure. But what of groups who, because of their race, religion, geographical or economic situation, or moral beliefs (or a combination of these) find themselves permanently in the minority? They are unlikely to agree that majority opinion is right and that its laws are just: more likely, they will begin to question the validity and value of democracy itself. Given the heterogeneity of people in most societies, democratic theory has sought various ways of safeguarding the position of minorities, to prevent this and foster greater justice. In fact, the problem of minorities is the greatest threat to any established democracy, as our experience with the Catholic minority in Ulster shows. The individualistic axiom of political equality, 'one man one vote' which is built into democratic theory as a fundamental ethical principle, upholds majority rule, which is widely accepted as the only practicable method of decision-making, even though it is less ideal than unanimity. A unanimity requirement would, of course, be the ultimate protection for all minorities, even minorities of one, but one would also lead to endless political impasses.

In practice, the position of minorities varies with the political system. The American system, a plurality of minorities, with its emphasis on wheeling-dealing and compromise and consensus, affords some protection, whereas the British 'populist', first-past-the-post electoral system, and the strength of party discipline in parliament, tends to submerge minorities unless they are aggressive and vocal. The easiest case to solve theoretically is that of the 'intense' minority and the indifferent majority. People have preferences of varying intensities, and it would surely be unjust to allow an intense and committed minority to be constantly outvoted by an indifferent majority, if the minority's preference concerned only itself, and threatened no harm to the majority.[45] Thus, most English people are indifferent as to whether to Welsh language is used in Welsh schools and courtrooms, but the Welsh-speaking population feels passionately about this, so their wishes should prevail. (The case is, of course, complicated by the fact that the Welsh speakers are themselves a minority of the Welsh population). Utilitarians solved the problem in the contrary direction, however. They hold that interpersonal comparisons of preference (with regard to intensity) cannot be made, and that everyone should count as one in utility calculations. This would mean that minorities were permanently submerged, however just their cause. So the utilitarian approach leads to evident injustices, but so, on the other hand, would the weighting of votes to benefit minorities, which would undermine the political equality which is the basis of consent and of the legitimacy of democratic government. Mill's proposal of extra votes for the wealthy, for example, seems manifestly unjust. To institutionalize the position of minorities goes against democratic equality, while to leave their cause to the good nature of the majority will in many cases mean that they suffer injustice, or even oppression.

It seems that no theoretical solution to the problem can be proposed that does not threaten basic democratic principles: maybe we can only introduce *ad hoc* constitutional and conventional safeguards as such cases arise. Proportional representation is the most easily institutionalized way of guaranteeing protection to minorities, as Britain's acceptance of PR in Ulster (while it is rejected for the rest of the United Kingdom) indicates. In some parliaments, minorities are guaranteed a certain number of seats, as are the whites in Zimbabwe. Elsewhere, it might be appropriate to give an identifiable minority or interest group a veto over legislation specifically affecting them. Although women are not a minority, it might be appropriate to give women, or women MPs, a veto on legislation concerning abortion and contraception, as the people most closely affected. The problem with vetoes in general, as is shown by the experience of the UN Security Council, is that they tend to prevent any decisions. Sometimes it is possible to remove minority matters from majority control altogether, as when Welsh or Scottish matters are referred to the appropriate Grand Committees which have statutory powers. In the original US Constitution, the slave-owning Southern states were given a veto over legislation concerning slaves, and thus protected at the most fundamental level. This raises the question of which minorities should be considered legitimate, and protected. I can, presumably choose whether or not to be a slave-owner, but not whether to be a Welsh-speaker, black or a Catholic. If minority interests are to be institutionally protected, they should be 'permanent' interests, arising from some unalterable characteristic of the individual and not, for example, economic interests which he has voluntarily adopted. But then, the members of a traditional mining community did not, on the whole, choose freely to become miners . . . All this goes to show that if the principle of protection is conceded, the empirical problems involved in deciding which minorities legitimately deserve protection will be extensive. As a rule, such decisions are taken *ad hoc* in emergencies, which adds to the confusion and does not suggest any general rule which democracies might adhere to.

The case of minorities seems to be a special problem for liberal democracy because it is based on individual interests and political equality and prefers to overlook the existence of interest groups which spoils its individualistic approach. The citizen is primarily seen as a voter, and his interests exist in another sphere, so that no conflict of his political and economic roles appears in the abstract theory. However, liberal democracy's individualistic concerns demand that it should try to solve the problem of minorities since a minority consists of a large number of individuals. Commentators from Tocqueville onwards have deplored the dangers of majority tyranny in practice, but this does not mean that minorities are just an *empirical* blot on an otherwise satisfactory theory. In so far as democratic theory assumes that individual interests are independent, homogeneous, and compatible, it falsifies reality, for all modern societies are composed of groups of unequal size with various, potentially conflicting, interests. Democratic theory is essentially a theory about the peaceful reconciliation of differing interests—even that of Rousseau—and so the existence of minorities should be one of its original premises, a problem to be dealt with theoretically as well as institutionally. Pluralist democratic theory moves in this direction by making minorities the *sine qua non* of democratic government. The institutional protection of genuine minorities is something which the majority owes them, in all justice. But informal safeguards are equally important: minorities should not forget Mill's injunction to them to be informed, active, and articulate in the protection of their own interests. In a society which practices the kind of tolerance of others' beliefs and habits that Mill recommends, minorities would rarely need to seek redress of their grievances in the political arena. So tolerance is one of the most important safeguards.

The problem of minorities seems to call into question the 'one man one vote' principle, which would imply that the majority has the right to dictate to the minority. The principle was asserted, in particular by Bentham, at a time when only a section of the population had political power, and so constituted a radical claim. But this simple maxim cannot constitute the full basis of democracy, for it does not solve the problem of how votes should be aggregated. A complicated voting system—some kind of PR—is needed to make 'one man one vote' true in a representative democracy. Even so, minorities may suffer because much more than one vote is needed to ensure the adequate representation of their views: they also need access to MPs, to the media, and to information. 'One man one vote' implies equal capacity and equal desert on the part of all voters, an idealistic assumption, but ignores the differential weighting which electoral systems tend to give to different votes. Nor does it specify whether the elected representative is to act as a delegate, reflecting the voters' views, or as a true representative. It also treats the limited political sphere as all-important, and ignores the political significance of other factors: economic and social standing lead to inequalities of influence even in the best designed electoral system. In Britain today, the realization of 'one man one vote' through PR would presumably dissolve existing majorities into minorities and radicalize the political system, but even that dramatic change would ignore the other factors which detract from political equality. The conclusion must be that while 'one man one vote' provides a useful safeguard for the individual and emphasises his ultimate importance in liberal democracy, considerably more factors than the vote must be taken into account in order to guarantee political justice for everybody.

Democracy and Liberalism

Despite the frequent yoking together of these two ideas, a number of writers point out the potential incompatibility of the individualistic aspirations of liberalism and the collectivist democratic notion, 'the will of the people'. Analysis shows a number of theoretical conflicts which may be flashpoints in the real politics of liberal democracy. The first problem is that of representation. Liberal ideology assumes the separation of the political and private spheres, and representative institutions achieve this *par excellence*; politics becomes an elite profession, with obvious concomitant disadvantages, but this also leaves ordinary individuals free to pursue their private interests most of the time, except on election day. This is practically convenient, but it complicates and dilutes democracy.

According to Locke, men pursue their own interests through elected governments; according to Rousseau, one person cannot represent another, and democracy should be direct, participatory. Rousseau's view seems philosophically sound. If you could represent me ideally, you would need so much understanding and knowledge of me and my interests that you would virtually be identical with me, in which case I may as well represent myself. However, given the size of nation-states, representation has long been inevitable and various theories have been developed to justify the institution by proving that the individual is in fact properly represented. First, the representative can be viewed as a delegate, who reiterates the views of his constituents and expresses no independent opinion. The view expressed in the *Federalist*[46] was that the representative should be a mere spokesman, made accountable by frequent elections. Marx, in praising the democratic arrangements of the Paris commune, emphasized the delegate role of the representatives, and the electors' power of instant dismissal.[47] The practical difficulties of a delegate system are plain: unless only one issue is at stake, how could the delegate fully represent, or even know, the wide variety of the opinions and interests of his electors? Only where electors had overwhelming common interests as, perhaps, in the Commune, could this begin to work. Even the advocates of the delegate role do not suggest that electors should *instruct* their delegates in detail: the device adopted is rather that of recall, so that the 'spokesman' role really reduces to a system of strict responsibility to the electors.

A different theory of representation is the 'microcosmic' theory, which sees parliament as a microcosm of the nation. Each representative is taken to be typical of a class of persons, whose interests he will automatically promote. This would not be easy to organize, since criteria would be needed to decide which interests are worthy of representation, but some countries have succeeded in composing second chambers on this sort of basis. Theorists have tried to solve the problem similarly: Saint-Simon's ideal parliament was to be composed of scientists, industrialists, and men of letters, these being the most important interest groups in his utopia. In the past, this 'typical' representation occurred haphazardly in Britain: a miner might be elected by a mining community — but it is less frequent as politics becomes more professionalized. In any case, elections are not vital to this form of representation: a 'typical unionist' could equally well be *nominated*, and a system of co-option of those who typify certain interest groups is used by some government bodies. Typical or microcosmic representation, then, is not essentially a democratic idea: indeed it was cited as a justification for the unreformed, pre-1832 parliament. In any elected body a degree of typical representation will emerge spontaneously, since those elected will have certain interests which are representative of those of a larger group in society.

The third theory, always popular in Britain, is that representatives should be accountable but independent, acting on behalf of their electors' interests but using their own judgement. This tradition can perhaps be traced to Hobbes's extreme assertion that the authorization of a representative binds the 'author' (elector) to follow his decisions, but gives him no control over these decisions, and does not make the representative accountable.[48] The case for independent representatives was stated in its classic form by Burke; he admitted the MPs' ultimate responsibility to the electors, but thought that infrequent elections would preserve their independence and ability to act for the public good, and help them to avoid embroilment with the private interests of electors.[49] Behind Burke's reflections lay a faith in the wisdom of the 'natural aristocracy' from whom representatives would be drawn, and a fear of the demagogy and mob rule which might result from anything approaching popular sovereignty. Later J. S. Mill asked 'Ought pledges to be required from members of parliament?' and decided that they should not. The voters' perception of the 'mental superiority' of the candidate should make them tolerant of his acting independently, except on the fundamental issues on which he was elected.[50]

Today, British MPs jealously guard their independence, in line with such arguments, and parliament's long-standing refusal to hold referenda, except in very special cases, is an assertion of its independence and sovereignty — something of a surprise for those who think that democracy means the sovereignty of the people!

Behind the notion of the independent representative lies a number of ideas; the paternalistic aspect is clear in Burke's and Mill's emphasis on the intelligence and wisdom of the representative. The view that representatives should be able to promote the national interest, free of selfish interests, suggests an underlying conception of a common good, more appropriate to 'radical' democracy, and contradicting the Lockean view that a government's duty is the preservation and pursuit of individual interests. In Britain, the strength of party discipline and the theory of independent representatives means that the government only enacts the will of the people in the remotest sense, or not at all. At a fundamental level, representation conflicts with liberal individualism and makes elite government likely, with all its correlative dangers. Only by ensuring maximum accountability of the representatives to the electorate can we avoid such representation leading to a government divorced from the people. (Even if the problem of representation were solved, the British system of adversary politics means that 49% or more people are unrepresented by each government — and governments are usually elected on the votes of 38% or less of the people. Thus, the mechanics of the electoral system can further dilute the democratic elements in a representative system.)

The incompatibilities between democracy and liberalism rest on the clash of two basic principles: the will of the people, and individual freedom. Berlin argues that democracy facilitates the 'positive liberty' of self-government, and, if popular sovereignty is interpreted literally, no limitation on the government's activities is theoretically allowable.[51] In other words, if the people are the sovereign, they can do anything — which would include oppressing individuals. Berlin fears that the paternalistic element in democracy is antagonistic to the liberal ideals of non-interference and minimum government. He argues that the liberal ideal might, in theory, prosper under a non-interventionist dictator: there is no necessary affinity of liberalism with democracy. The ideal for liberalism is 'every man his own legislator', but when Rousseau, Hegel, and Marx attempted to reconcile this theoretically with democracy, liberals labelled them 'authoritarian'. Whether the two political ideals are seen as compatible depends partly on the assumptions made: the postulate that men are homogeneous or classless validates the popular sovereignty of Rousseau or Marx, whereas the belief that they are irreducibly different demands a pluralist democracy with liberal safeguards in the form of individual rights.

Democracy proper requires more individual participation than liberals, who put such a high value on privacy, would countenance. The opposition in Britain to compulsory voting (a very minimal citizen's duty!) is indicative of the way in which the liberal focus on private life undermines the participatory spirit of democracy, as does the representative system. An indirect incompatibility between the two ideals occurs through the mediating idea of equality. Democracy posits and offers a limited, *artificial* equality to all men in the political sphere, *qua* voters, while the liberal value 'equality of opportunity' in the socio-economic sphere sanctions the development of *real* inequalities which effectively destroy the equality of the vote and of other political rights. So, while democracy threatens liberalism, liberalism undermines democracy. Usually it is the radical and popular elements of democracy that are perceived as potentially threatening to liberalism; liberals are happy with the representative system which makes parliament an autonomous elite. But it is not surprising that, despite these theoretical divergences, liberalism and democracy have blended so well historically. Both oppose older, autocratic forms of rule and claim to destroy old social hierarchies. The ideal of tolerance is common to liberalism and representative democracy, although radical democracy is criticized for its potential intolerance. Ultimately, the liberal values life above everything, and so considers peace essential, and democracy is clearly the most promising device for peaceful conflict solution. It is therefore worth suffering the occasional tensions between the two ideals, from the liberal's viewpoint.

Democracy and Truth

The long-standing controversy over what form of democracy is ideal rests ultimately on conflicting perceptions of the relation of democracy to truth. An important axiom of formal logic is the 'law' of the excluded middle, which states that a proposition is either true or false. This impeccable, dichotomous reasoning cannot be transferred directly to the real world, where it is often fallacious to propose two alternatives as if these exhausted the available possibilities. 'Either he is a marxist or he is not' is logically correct, a matter of definition, but 'Those who are not with us are against us' fallaciously excludes various alternatives or 'middles'. The exclusion of intermediate possibilities entails a choice between two propositions which, by implication, encompass between them all the possibilities. This is false in the contingent real world.

The relevance of this to British politics is that our populist democracy has long operated on the covert assumption that there are only two sides to every question, a further implication being that one side is necessarily right. This dichotomous approach to politics has sometimes been blamed on the rectangular shape of the house of commons, which supposedly encourages the two-party system; the 'winner takes all' electoral system also plays its part. Much parliamentary procedure seems to stem from a misapplication of the law of the excluded middle. In voting, MPs are forced to choose between policies presented as dichotomies which exclude other viable alternatives — although these are sometimes dealt with as amendments. 'Either-or' logic, in conjunction with the basically two-party system moulds the form in which policy issues are perceived, and are presented to the public. It also influences our perception of voter rationality: 'Don't knows' are treated as just that, and never as a group of people who might adhere to options which they cannot express through voting. The dichotomous approach has beguiled us into a system of adversary politics, whose shortcomings Johnson exposes in *In Search of the Constitution:*[52] it also causes us to believe that one-party systems, where only one side of any question is — supposedly — put, are undemocratic.

In order to criticize or validate this approach to politics, we have to decide whether democracy deals in truth, opinion or the representation of material interests. If in truth, and if we could be sure of being right, only one side of the question would need to be put, the right side, and a one-party system would be adequate. British democracy actually represents opinions and interests in parliament but, deceptively, the rhetoric of our politics is about truth. Are there in fact objectively right solutions to political questions, or only *preferred* solutions (opinions)? Depending on how we answer this, we can decide what organizational form is best for ascertaining the truth, or reflecting preferences. A caveat is needed about truth. The difficulty of determining objective truths even in science has been discussed, and this book has emphasized the permeation of all political thought and activity by ideological elements. Truth must be established with implicit reference to some epistemology, or theory of knowledge; but rival epistemologies abound. However, some political philosophers dealt with truth as if it were unproblematic, and realizable in politics, notably Plato.

During the Enlightenment, Rousseau and Condorcet based political theories on the assumption that political truths 'exist' and await discovery. Rousseau's analysis of the common good is typical: for any political problem, there is one solution which would conduce to the good of all members of society, the 'true' solution. This depends on his assumption that men's interests are similar. If reality *is* structured like this, one-party democracies are justified, so is enlightened despotism or the rule of Plato's Guardians. For both Rousseau and Condorcet, political truth was fused with moral right. The idea of the common good was also adopted by the liberal T. H. Green, who made it the basis of political obligation. Plamenatz has argued that the idea is fallacious or nonsensical: the idea that two non-identical individuals could share a common good is suspect, and in a self-proclaimedly pluralistic society the notion is evidently false.[53] This discovery is not fatal to the idea, however: in every case there must be an optimal policy which would benefit as many people as possible — if only this could be infallibly calculated! But we might not label merely optimal politics as 'true' or 'right'. Condorcet and, in our own time, Black, have mathematically shown that if each individual has a 51% chance of being right in a decision, the majority has a more than equal chance of being right, which approaches 100% the more nearly the majority approaches unanimity.[54] However, 'being right' suggests that politics is a matter of deciding what is true, which is probably not the case. (This may reflect on the nature of our idea of truth rather than on politics.)

Some political questions *can* be posed so that there is an objectively true answer. When Britain was considering joining the EC, the question asked was whether this would benefit us financially. The only problem was that the calculations made in advance contained too many uncertainties to know whether the answer was 'Yes' or 'No'. Some questions are easier: we can be sure that reducing public expenditure will increase unemployment. The role of politicians is not to discover or verify this but to decide whether it is a good thing. Ultimately, major political questions turn on judgements of value, rather than truth. Can there be a right choice between values, in which case Rousseau's system is still appropriate, or are we merely forced to accept majority opinion on such matters? Modern liberal-democratic theorists have imbibed the logical positivists's view that value judgements are unverifiable, so that no rational method can exist for choosing between them. In the absence of such standards, opinion is the only guide. Liberal-democratic theory makes the simplifying assumption that the vote reflects such opinion, the political consumer's preference. This stipulation is probably untrue in the absence of the conditions built into an abstract model of choice, which state that the voter should have perfect knowledge of all the alternatives, and be offered a full range of choices. In voting conditions of restricted choice, it is mere deception to argue that an expressed preference is anything more than a suboptimal choice, the best of non-ideal alternatives. However, in the absence of divinable political truths and in the realm of unverifiable values, opinion is omnipotent. Most modern theories of democracy assume that opinion and interests are the stuff of politics, and they prescribe maximizing strategies, rather than procedures for determining what is true and right.

The suboptimal conditions under which the voter expresses his opinions must be emphasized, in view of the interpretation of election results in democratic countries (both in the West and in communist states) as a mandate, and as 'the will of the people'. Perhaps, if the presuppositions of the various theoretical models were fulfilled, such a conclusion would be valid. If, as Rousseau assumed, we lived in a small, close-knit society, what we chose might always be the common good. Again, if in Britain we had equal constituencies, proportional representation, a range of parties reflecting all shades of political opinion and MPs who acted as delegates, our elections might indicate the will of the people and so realize the representative democratic ideal. But, given the imperfect conditions, what value or interpretation are we entitled to put on election results? In most cases, this problem is solved by ideological assertion.

Asking whether democratic politics is, ideally, about truth, values, opinions or interests, helps us to highlight the assumptions underlying our own political system. If MPs are regarded as representatives who apply their superior knowledge and intelligence to make correct decisions, the inference is that the purpose of the political system is to discover truth and right. On the other hand, a system of delegation or typical representation suggests that politics is a matter of expressing opinions and interests. It is not surprising to find that recent theories of voting—elitist, cynical but doubtless realistic—argue that voting has a largely *expressive* or therapeutic function, which allows people to express their views and let off steam while politicians and civil servants go about their business of taking decisions, with very little accountability to the electorate. The British government of the day justifies its measures by whichever theory of politics fits best: sometimes MPs are enlightened representatives, deciding what is right (as when they abolished capital punishment despite the fact that majority public opinion was against this), sometimes they are considered to reflect their electors' interests. Because we are, by and large, moralists, government decisions are usually clothed in the language of truth and right which is, in fact, inappropriate to liberal democracy. The liberal outlook emphasizes the importance of individual interests, the variety of possible truths, and the need for tolerance, so that the claim of a democratic system to decide on truth and right is in principle antithetical to the liberal ideal.

Another way of expressing the difference between liberals and other democrats on this matter is that, for someone like Rousseau, the right solution still exists even if politicians fail to discover it, whereas the liberal may consider even a suboptimal solution optimal, in that it is the expression of public opinion. Marxists, like Rousseau, look to politics for the discovery of truth and the establishment of right, arousing deep suspicion among liberals. An idealistic answer to the question of what politics is about is that it *should be* about truth and right while, pragmatically, it still has to take some account of individuals' interests.

The conclusion here is that one's view of the nature of the goal of politics determines the theory of democracy which one opts for.

The Will of the People

This chapter has shown the empirical obstacles which stand in the way of the democratic realization of 'the will of the people'; it also points to the conclusion that the idea itself is theoretically problematic, for the same reasons that 'the common good' is problematic. Whereas a Marxist government, modelling itself on Rousseau's theory, might proclaim that it represents the will of the people, a liberal democracy has to solve the problem of how a general will could be reached by the aggregation of individual wills, a task made even harder by the work of Arrow, which shows that individuals' wishes cannot be satisfactorily aggregated into social choices.[55] Schumpeter attempts a theoretical solution in his 'neoclassical' theory of democracy, which aims to revise the classical democratic ideal, which he defines as:

That institutional arrangement for arriving at political decisions which realises the common good by making the people itself decide issues through the election of individuals who are to assemble in order to carry out its will.

He shows that this definition embodies four fallacious assumptions concerning the common good, the will of the people, rationality, and the existence of definite answers to political questions. He then sets out to substitute a theory free from such questionable assumptions, which centres on *leadership*. Democracy is:

That institutional arrangement for arriving at political decisions in which individuals acquire the power to decide by means of a competitive struggle for the people's vote.[56]

The essence of democratic procedure becomes the choosing of a national executive — a conclusion Schumpeter may have reached by observing the American political scene, which does not necessarily constitute a theoretical insight. The idea of a *manufactured will* replaces the will of the people in his theory, a will created by the leaders who act as persuaders, so that it becomes widely accepted as the will of the people. Other theorists have accepted the need to create an 'artificial will' where people are passive or ill-informed: Rousseau's legislator, and Bentham's, and Mill's informed minorities execute such a task.

The virtue of such a system is that the leaders can take into account the long-term interests which individuals might ignore, opting for immediate gains; its vice is the lack of protection against the self-interest of such leaders. Schumpeter believes he has taken care of this by emphasizing the accountability of leaders through elections, but if the leaders can manufacture a will, they can certainly gain acceptance of policies furthering their own interests. Neoclassical theory reintroduces the risk of manipulative leaders, against which the democratic tradition always struggled by advocating 'the will of the people' as the final arbiter. Schumpeter seems to have abandoned the concept of democracy as a *good in itself*, and dedicated himself to describing what is a reasonably workable form of government, given the size of modern nation-states and our sentimental attachment to democratic formulae; however, he concedes that democracy upholds certain values, which is why it deserves support. But Schumpeter's theory seems, like that of Dahl, to be endowing a descriptive account of Western (more precisely, American) government with a normative value.

The most recent attempt to amend liberal democracy in practice so as to realize the will of the people is the movement for participation which fights against centralization, bureaucracy, and the increasing elitism of politics. The participation movement can be viewed as an attempt to persuade individuals to become in reality the active, rational, informed citizens of Mill's democratic theory, operating not primarily in the narrow political sphere, but within the plethora of groups and organizations in society. In Britain, the Liberal Party's call for regionalism and the recent government attempt to introduce Welsh and Scottish devolution are symptomatic of the rise of the participatory ideal. Participation does not merely denote a higher level of political activity in conventional, established channels, but the intervention of citizens in areas formerly thought to be the province of politicians, civil servants or experts: proposals for industrial democracy and the introduction of Community

Health Councils are examples of such forms of participation inaugurated from above (although the scheme for industrial democracy was rejected by both managers and unions), while the formation of tenants' and neighbourhood associations and other self-help groups are participation initiated from below. The idea of widespread participation challenges various preconceptions of liberal democratic ideology — the primacy of the representative system, and the separation of politics from other parts of life — and might eventually bring about a revision of the theory, although in empirical analysis the phenomenon of participation can comfortably be accommodated within the account of pluralist democracy. Liberalism has always been ambivalent about participation: the individual is paramount, he wishes to protect his interest, he is politically rational and capable, but ultimately he prefers to spend his time on other things, while retaining a notional ultimate control over the politicians. Any growth in the theory and practice of participation could help to make that control more than notional.

Much has been written about the role of 'public opinion' in controlling seemingly intractable political institutions and making them bow to the will of the people. Bryce, in *Modern Democracies* (1921), a comparative study of various democracies, asked 'How is the people to exercise its power?'. 'By voting' is the usual answer, but Bryce argued that 'what purports to be the will of the people is largely a factitious product, not really their will' because of the representative system, corruption and the reduction of all men's opinions, wise and foolish, to the same weight (an anti-democratic point).[57] He argued that public opinion should be an independent factor in the governmental process, operating to control and influence elected representatives. The current ubiquity of opinion polls suggests that this is the rare case where a political theorist's will was realized. However, the addition of public opinion as a separate factor adds little to democratic theory, in which it was always implicit, although we are now able to quantify it (crudely) in practice, which may make it more influential.

This account of democratic theories has shown the fallacy of distinguishing too strictly between means and ends, although such a distinction must be attempted in principle. The idealistic spirit of democracy is constantly modified in the attempt to realize it institutionally, as is shown by the imperfections of the various democracies in the West and East. The analysis has touched on practical problems such as the irresponsibility of institutions, the anomalies of voting behaviour and the problems of representation, which may seem to be procedural matters, because such factors colour and modify our perception of the ideal. None of the ideal versions of democracy is likely to be fully realized because of such practical obstacles. The theory of democracy which we adopt depends ultimately on other ideological beliefs that we hold. A discussion of the various ways in which the democratic ideal has been put into practice is found in C. B. Macpherson's *The Real World of Democracy* (1966), which challenges the Western conviction of the superiority and uniquely democratic nature of liberal democracy. In conclusion it must be emphasized that democracy, in any of its ideal versions, is concerned with the maintenance and extension of human liberty through self-government. However, the ideal needs the support of other ideological beliefs to have substance, since essentially it applies only to the narrow area of mechanisms of government, and the infusion of ideologies often seems to transform democratic theory and practice out of recognition. Ultimately, every theory of democracy seeks to uphold the political equality of men, the value of deliberation, and the exchange of ideas and the resolution of conflict by peaceful means.

Notes

1. See, e.g., J. P. Plamenatz, *Consent, Freedom and Political Obligation*, 2nd edn, Oxford University Press, 1968.
2. Plato, *The Republic* (Trans. H. D. P. Lee), Penguin, 1955, pp.330–1.
3. Aristotle, *The Politics* (trans. T. A. Sinclair), Penguin, 1962, Bk VI, Chaps 2–3.
4. Aristotle, *The Politics*, pp.236–7.
5. Aristotle, *The Politics*, p.239.
6. See p. 175 above.
7. Locke, *Essay*, Chap. IX.
8. Locke, *Essay*, s.119.
9. Locke, *Essay*, s.57.
10. Locke, *Essay*, pp.143–4.
11. Locke, *Essay*, Chap. XIX.
12. T. Paine, *The Rights of Man*, Penguin, 1969, pp.92–4.
13. Paine, *The Rights of Man*, p.133.
14. A. Hamilton, J. Madison and J. Jay, *The Federalist* (Ed. M. Beloff), Blackwell, 1948, Paper X especially.
15. R. Dahl, *A Preface to Democratic Theory*, Chicago University Press, 1956, pp.132–3.
16. J. S. Mill, *Considerations on Representative Government*, Oxford University Press, 1912, p.186.
17. J. S. Mill, *Considerations on Representative Government*, pp.188–9.
18. James Mill, *Essay on Government*, Cambridge University Press, 1937, pp.63–73.
19. J. S. Mill, *Considerations on Representative Government*, Chap. VII.
20. A. Tocqueville, *Democracy in America* (trans. H. Reeve), Oxford University Press, 1946, Chap. XV; J. S. Mill, *On Liberty*, Collins, 1962, Chap. III.
21. Mill, *On Liberty*, pp.243–4.
22. For an introduction to the subject, see T. Bottomore, *Elites and Society*, C. A. Watts, 1964. Also, J. P. Plamenatz, *Democracy and Illusion*, Longman, 1973, Chap. 3 gives an account of the relevance of early elite theorists to democratic theory.
23. J. Ortega y Gasset. *The Revolt of the Masses*, Unwin, 1961.
24. For citations and summaries of the major literature in the elite theory debate, see P. Bachrach, *The Theory of Democratic Elitism*, London University Press, 1968; S. Lukes, *Power: A Radical View*, Macmillan, 1974; and B. Holden, *The Nature of Democracy*, Nelson, 1975, Chap. 6 especially.
25. Bachrach, *The Theory of Democratic Elitism*, p.34.
26. Bachrach, *The Theory of Democratic Elitism*, p.98.
27. Dahl, *A Preface to Democratic Theory*, Chap. 1.
28. B. Berelson *et al.*, *Voting*, Chicago University Press, Chap. 14.
29. G. Duncan, and S. Lukes, 'The new democracy', *Political Studies*, **XI**, No. 2, 156–77 (1963).

30. A. Downs, *An Economic Theory of Democracy*, Harper, 1957.
31. For an account of exchange and transaction theories see S. Waldman, *The Foundations of Political Action*, Little, Brown & Co., 1972.
32. L. Davis, 'The cost of realism: contemporary restatements of democracy', in *Apolitical Parties*, (Eds C. A. McCoy and J. Playford) T. Crowell, 1967, p.198.
33. Holden, *The Nature of Democracy*, p.6.
34. S. Lipset, *Political Man*, Heinemann, 1960, Chap. 2.
35. Rousseau, *The Social Contract*, Dent, 1913, p.78.
36. Rousseau, *The Social Contract*, p.15.
37. Rousseau, *The Social Contract*, Bk II, Chaps I–III.
38. Rousseau, *The Social Contract*, p.20.
39. Rousseau, *The Social Contract*, Bk II, Chap. VII.
40. See Note 12 to Chapter 8 for citations of typical literature on this.
41. Holden rehearses all the typical liberal arguments against popular sovereignty in *The Nature of Democracy*, Chap. 2 and its Appendix.
42. R. Wollheim, 'A paradox in the theory of democracy', in *Philosophy, Politics and Society*, 2nd Series (Eds P. Laslett and W. G. Runciman), Blackwell, 1972. See also B. Barry, *Political Argument*, Routledge & Kegan Paul, 1965, pp.58–66.
43. M. Schiller, 'On the logic of being a democrat', *Philosophy*, **XLIV**, 46–56 (1969).
44. Rousseau, *The Social Contract*, pp.30–1.
45. W. Kendall and G. W. Carey, 'The "intensity" problem in democratic theory', *American Political Science Review*, **LXII**, No. 1, 5–24 (1968).
46. *The Federalist*, Paper LII.
47. *The Civil War in France* in Marx and Engels, *Selected Works*, Vol. 2, Progress, 1969, pp.220–2.
48. Hobbes, *Leviathan*, Chap. 16.
49. E. Burke, *Reflections on the Revolution in France*, Penguin, 1969, p.303ff.
50. Mill, *Considerations on Representative Government*, p.333.
51. I. Berlin, 'Two concepts of liberty' in *Political Philosophy* (Ed. A. Quinton).
52. N. Johnson, *In Search of the Constitution*, Pergamon, 1977.
53. Plamenatz, *Consent, Freedom and Political Obligation*, Chap. 3.
54. B. Barry, 'The public interest', in *Political Philosophy* (Ed. A. Quinton), p.122.
55. K. Arrow, *Social Choice and Individual Values*, 2nd edn, (Yale University Press, 1963, Chap. 5 especially.
56. J. Schumpeter, *Capitalism, Socialism and Democracy*, Allen and Unwin, 1943, pp.250, 269 especially.
57. J. Bryce, *Modern Democracies*, Macmillan, 1926, 2 vols.

Further reading

B. Holden, *The Nature of Democracy*, Nelson, 1975.
C. B. Macpherson, *The Real World of Democracy*, Oxford University Press, 1966.
P. Bachrach, *The Theory of Democratic Elitism*, London University Press, 1968.
J. Lively, *Democracy*, Blackwell, 1975.
J. P. Plamenatz, *Democracy and Illusion*, Longman, 1973.
A. H. Birch, *Representation*, Pall Mall, 1971.
J. R. Pennock and J. W. Chapman, (Eds), *Participation in Politics*, Lieber-Atherton, 1975.

CHAPTER 10

Obligation, Authority, and the State

After considering the political arrangement which most enhances the individual's freedom, democracy, we turn to the aspects of political life which tend to impede his free action and to subordinate him to the 'whole'. In modern society the state is a powerful, objective reality, but it will be shown that authority and obligation are concepts with an important subjective component which determine our attitude to the state: although they operate at the psychological and intellectual levels, they can serve to increase or curtail the state's powers.

Why Should I Obey the Law?

Perhaps the single most remarkable fact about society is that most people, most of the time, acknowledge and obey political authority, however remote it is from their lives, and however much it is against their inclinations or short-term interests. Political scientists explain this phenomenon in terms of our political socialization from an early age,[1] while theorists explain it in terms of political obligation. But the two explanations are compatible, for the process of socialization contains arguments to convince the individual of the wisdom, morality or necessity of obeying his rulers. Such arguments merit close and critical examination, and this will involve discussion of how political obligation is said to arise. It has been remarked that questions of political obligation 'would be likely to occur only to the members of a certain type of society: an individualistic society like that of Ancient Athens or seventeenth-century England'. This is because only in a society where the individual has a lively impression of his own autonomy and personal interests does an inevitable tension arise between his will and the commands of the state. In a strongly hierarchical or religious society, with an ideology which binds the individual parts to the whole, such a divergence rarely occurs.

It might be thought that 'political obligation' is a political philosopher's genie, unrelated to everyday politics and meaningless to the man in the street, yet the notion is crucial both to political theory and to state propaganda.

Theory needs to explain how man is integrated in society and why he accommodates himself to the pressures and demands of his fellow-citizens, even when this is against his interests, or avoidable. Political obligation provides the theorist with a premise of consistent, law-abiding behaviour applicable to any 'normal' situation, and for the state it is useful to be able to assert the general duty of citizens to obey the laws and respect the government, using one of the accounts of obligation provided by the theorists.

Political and moral obligation are closely linked, and some theorists assert that political obligation is always moral. Obligation operates internally, via the conscience, to procure compliance, yet it must also exist externally, objectively, so that others can remind us of it if we neglect it. Moral obligation used to be seen as emanating from absolute moral codes (often religious codes established by God) which had objective existence yet were internalized and acted upon by individuals. Kant's categorical imperative likewise takes an unconditional form which rests on our nature as moral beings. Such moral absolutes confront us as external forces to which we must adapt our thinking and actions. But since the Enlightenment it has been more usual to regard morality as *self-imposed*, which makes it more acceptable to individuals, although none the less universal and binding; promising is sometimes used as an analogy for how moral obligation is self-imposed, although it is a poor analogy in the case of political obligation, as we shall see.[2] With the emergence of the view of man as a rational and independent actor, a model of self-assumed political obligation came into fashion, and this was a watershed in political theory, which had previously ignored the political role of the people. The major contract theories will be stated briefly, and contrasted with the modern account of consent.

Contractual Obligation

Hobbes responded to the need for a secular theory of obligation to replace the unconditional obligation which 'divine right' imposed on the king's subjects. He imagines a pre-social state of nature far from the Garden of Eden, where men are in constant uncertainty, under the threat of violence or sudden death from others. He hypothesizes that to escape from this state of war they would form a society via a 'convenant' to ensure peace and their own survival. But, distrusting each other to keep the pact, they would have to set up a 'common power' above themselves to enforce obedience to it. This power is Hobbes's *sovereign*, authorized to act on behalf of the original contractors. As we saw earlier, Hobbes so defines 'authorization' that the author gives the actor complete power and foregoes the right to instruct him, yet remains responsible for all his actions. Hobbes allocates the sovereign wide, absolute powers necessary for preserving peace and men's lives, and goes on to deduce that, whatever he does, the sovereign cannot injure the subject because this would be equivalent to the subject's injuring himself, and hence absurd. Not surprisingly, Hobbes has been accused of advocating an absolutist state where citizens have no rights except the ultimate right to try to avoid death if the sovereign seeks to kill them (but that, too, is *his* right).[3]

From the conditions which Hobbes postulates, a twofold obligation to the sovereign arises. First, the third law of nature is 'That men perform their convenants made',[4] and this *morally* obliges men to obey the original covenant and abide by its consequences. This means that the obligation to obey is partly externally imposed and partly self-imposed, since the laws of nature exist independently of man's will, but the covenant is a self-assumed obligation. Second, *prudence* commands men to obey because any disobedience will threaten the sovereign's existence and could precipitate a return to the warring state of nature. It is often asked whether Hobbes sees obligation as moral or prudential. Both sorts of obligation appear in his theory, but prudence alone would establish political obligation: since *any* regime is preferable to the infernal state of nature, we are obliged by prudence to obey the sovereign, however tyrannical. But what Hobbes intends to create is *unconditional moral obligation in perpetuity*. Most moral philosophers would repudiate such an extreme conception of obligation—even promises can be broken in some situations—and its political consequences would certainly be disastrous, since it gives *carte blanche* to tyrants.

The position from which Locke challenged Hobbes is that a man cannot give away more power over himself than he himself has: this denies the theoretical possibility of *any* absolute sovereign. Locke also located the origin of government in a state of nature, but for him this was a peaceful, semi-civilized state. For greater security of their 'life, liberty, and estate', men consented to form a political community. The result of this contract was a government whose duty was to protect and further their interests, but the people still remained sovereign. Anyone with 'possession or enjoyment of any part of the dominions of any government' gives *tacit* consent to the government and must observe its laws; by this provision Locke answered more satisfactorily than Hobbes (although not convincingly) the question why the descendants of the original contractors should owe loyalty to the government. But tacit consent itself raises many problems.[5] Importantly, Locke limits the extent of obligation. The community remains supreme and the people can resume power if the government is generally judged to have betrayed its trust. Obligation is thus conditional and is largely prudential, being tied up with the protection of individual interests, although there is the implication that it also rests on our gratitude to the government for protecting our 'estates', so again there are moral elements in the idea. Locke is also emphatic that men must acquiesce in the laws which they will have to obey: 'the supreme power cannot take from any man any part of his property *without his consent*'.[6] It must be remembered that Locke, like other contract theorists, was not describing a historical contract, but hypothesizing about the minimum conditions under which men would have sacrificed their natural liberty, conditions which should logically limit the scope and activities of real governments.

A number of theorists in the eighteenth century pointed out that the real basis of government was not contractual. Hume, Rousseau, and Paine saw existing governments as founded on force or deception,[7] but while Hume saw this as a reason to reject contract theory altogether, Paine and Rousseau contended that real governments should act *as if* they were based on egalitarian contracts. Rousseau considered that society and government would ideally come about through contract when the risks and inconveniences of the state of nature threatened men's survival. The individual would 'alienate' his natural liberty to the community, receiving in exchange 'conventional' liberty.

Each man, in giving himself to all, gives himself to nobody . . . he gains an equivalent for everything he loses.[8]

That equivalent is power over others. Each individual is doubly bound, both as a member of the sovereign power to other individuals and, as a member of the state, to the sovereign. While adherence to the terms of the original contract which creates the sovereign appears partly prudential ('violation of the act by which it exists would be self-annihilation'[9]), the obligation to obey the laws made by the General Will can be characterized in several ways. This obligation is implied in the original undertaking, so it would be imprudent to repudiate it; it would also be irrational, and perhaps immoral, to disobey laws which one had oneself made as a member of the sovereign. Day-to-day political obligation for Rousseau clearly stands or falls with the General Will.

The attempt to determine whether obligation, as viewed by the contract theorists, is moral or prudential is more than a philosophical nicety, for it can be argued that we are entitled to reject prudential obligation when it is to our advantage to disobey, whereas moral obligation is more strongly binding and often partakes of an unconditional nature. This is one of the obstacles encountered by a utilitarian view of obligation, which suggests that someone can disobey the law when this is conducive to his personal utility, a point discussed further below. Contract and consent theory emphasizes the voluntary nature of obligation and thus appeals to cultures which emphasize individuality and free will, but it meets with the difficulty that what has been voluntarily made can also be voluntarily broken: hence, presumably, the introduction of various resistances into the circuit of obligation, such as 'natural laws' enjoining us to keep our promises, which make obligation moral in part, and so unconditional. Contract theory, although widely regarded as obsolete now, is interesting because it describes how *authority* is created out of a situation in which there is only naked *power*, the state of nature. This mirrors the philosophical problem of whether 'ought' can be derived from 'is', and is subject to the same objections. The contract theories rest heavily on the original act of promising, a paradigm way of imposing obligation on oneself, but the contract must logically have taken place via an established institution of promising, which is itself a social institution and could not have existed before society, or been invoked to create society. Similarly, the terms of the contracts turn on men's equal surrender of their natural rights, yet the concepts of rights is itself created by society, and could not therefore be instrumental in the making of the original contract.[10] So there is an insoluble contradiction at the heart of contract theory.

The more modern doctrine of consent avoids many of these pitfalls, since it does not concern itself with the origin of government, but with the ongoing process, and allows us to pass continuous judgement on the justice of governments by giving or withholding consent—in theory at least. The theory is tailored to democratic systems of government where there are established procedures for obtaining consent. Plamenatz takes the somewhat Hobbesian view that X can authorize Y's actions by voting, yet remain 'indirectly' responsible for them, and be obliged to obey them.[11] He argues that in voting we consent to obey *whoever* is elected—that is, we really consent to the rules of the democratic game—and that a vote constitutes a 'promise' of obedience to the government.[12] Any theory of obligation in a democracy must rest on some such argument, yet this is a very strong theory of obligation resting on a very weak act of consent. The elaborate structure of politics means that, although we merely vote for a name or for a short-term programme, we are interpreted as consenting in advance to a multitude of particular acts, many of which do not even appear in the manifesto of the winning party (which in any case, we may have voted against), and also to the system in general. On this theory, to vote is to sign a blank cheque in favour of the democratic system and whatever consequences follow from it in the current election.

Consenting is, of course, an intentional and personal process, yet modern contract theorists take a deliberately objective, standardized view of it: the vote is an act which, no matter what intention underlay it, creates an obligation. Many objections can be made to the wide interpretation of the vote as consent. First, it would scarcely be rational to consent in advance to whatever a government might do, unless it were strictly specified in a manifesto whose terms would not be exceeded. In Britain, protest sometimes arises when governments enact unpredicted measures which are not within its mandate, but doctrines of the mandate equally often present it as a blank cheque which justifies any measures. Should we really be said to consent to long-term aims or to express approval of the whole system when we are only invited to express a view on a short-term programme? For consent to create political obligation, an immense weight of interpretation must be laid on the act of voting: the empirical studies which illustrate the imperfections of voting and voters could be cited against such an interpretation. Again, political institutions, such as representation and parties, remove the act of voting far from meaningful consent. More frequent elections and a delegate system might remove this distance; the Labour Party's recent conversion to the reselection of MPs is a small step in this direction. But ultimately voting in a modern democracy is a passive, acquiescent process and only a strong, positive choice really qualifies as consent. Since we are unlikely to attain the ideal conditions for strong consent, it would be more logical to revise the theory and accept a much reduced concept of political obligation—or abandon it.

Several other objections can be made to consent theory. First, if governments make policy by inaction or 'non-decision-making', the people cannot demo-cratically register their consent to, or dissent from, such imperceptible decisions. A case in point is the neglect by many governments of civil defence, a governmental 'decision' only brought to the notice of the public in 1980 when nuclear war seemed possible and the issue was debated in the media. To assume that the people have consented to the government's inaction in such a case stretches the already elastic concept of consent out of all recognition. Secondly, a theory which bases political obligation on voluntary consent should logically provide an account of what counts as *dissent*, and how people can reject the political system. Plamenatz's account deprives us of any insti-tutionalized way of expressing dissent from the system: abstention is a weak, ambivalent act which will always be interpreted by governors and psephologists as ignorance or apathy, rather than as a principled rejection of all the alterna-tives. In reality, the dissenter can embark on direct action and other forms of protest if his dissatisfaction is extensive, but consent theorists would say that he is then breaking his obligation. The fact that consent, but not non-consent, is defined weights the theory in favour of authority.

Clearly there are inconsistencies in consent theory. Our consent is said to create a political obligation which is self-assumed and so should not be repudiated. Yet people who spend their lives without casting a vote are *also* said to have political obligation, presumably on the grounds of tacit consent, which is really an argument based on gratitude. So there are two different kinds of consent running in tandem which, between them, put everybody under some obligation. Tussman actually makes this explicit: he defects from the idea of active consent altogether (in the face of the facts) but says that 'tacit consent' must be knowing and conscious, a standard only lived up to by a small, aware elite. Nevertheless, *all* are obliged to obey the government since the non-consenting 'clods' are obligated, like children, by the tacit consent of the elite.[13] Plamenatz also confronts the problem—tangentially—by arguing that there must be another basis for obligation as well as consent, for otherwise there would be

in every state, however democratic, a large number of persons (i.e. non-voters) under no obligation to obey its laws . . . no state could perform its proper functions if it contained a large number of citizens exempt from obedience to its laws.[14]

There is a radical error in this argument, since my feeling no obligation *subjectively* does not mean that I am not under obligation *objectively* to obey the laws, nor does it prevent my obeying them out of prudence. But the conclusion is sound, that consent cannot be the sole basis of 'the duty of the governed to obey their rulers'. Most consent theorists therefore reinforce their arguments by citing other sorts of obligation.

The inadequacy of consent theory turns on two problems. The first is that consent theory, like contract theory, rests on a legal or contractual account of obligation which it tries to amalgamate, unconvincingly, with the older tradition that makes political obligation a moral duty. On the latter view, it is binding, perhaps unconditional, while on the former view, the rational citizen would withdraw his consent and repudiate his obligation when it was to his advantage. To this is added the difficulty that not everyone actively consents, so that alternative accounts of obligation have to be invoked to cover non-consenters and dissenters. A theory of political behaviour can accommodate the fact that some people vote while others abstain, but a theory of obligation with universal import cannot be so open. Someone who argues that some people are obliged because they consent, others because they enjoy the protection of the law, can be accused of over-determining the case of the first group, who also enjoy protection and are doubly bound — or else of being bent on laying obligation on everybody, no matter how. In effect, as Tussman argues, there are probably two classes of citizens, the active and the passive, but to say that the former are more 'obligated' because of their political activity and acumen is a moral, not a contractual, argument, with no obvious justification in fact or logic. Perhaps if theorists cannot establish obligation for every citizen on the same basis, consent, they would do better to look for a different, universal source of obligation.

An important question for consent theory is whether we consent to, and have political obligation to, the political system as a whole, to the law in general, to a particular government, or to particular laws, or to a combination of these. Locke provided a tidy answer to this: our contractual obligation is to the political community as a whole, 'society', but we can overthrow a government without endangering society itself, or rejecting our basic obligation, if the government breaks its trust. Otherwise, we are obliged to obey governments and laws to which we have consented. The clarity of this solution diminishes when practical questions are raised about who judges the government to have betrayed the people, and whether objectors to a law are still bound by it. Such questions are theoretically insoluble on this account. Plamenatz's account seems to imply that in voting we assume obligation towards the system, the government *and* the particular laws which it passes. It might be reasonable to interpret the vote as an endorsement of the system, though a different argument would be needed where voting was compulsory. But if you accept the democratic system, Plamenatz says, you also undertake an obligation even to a government you do not vote for — and hence, presumably, are committed to obey its laws. At this rate it would be better not to vote, and have a free conscience. Surely we should be sceptical of these multiple, simultaneous levels of meaning accorded to the vote. Consent theory purports to make political obligation a result of man's free choice, then over-interprets his acts to lumber him with extensive moral obligations. Since, except in rare cases, we never consent to particular measures by voting, it could be concluded that we consent to the general system, and owe it respect, but that our obedience to particular laws is purely prudential, not conditioned by obligation (except for those people who believe that we have a moral duty to obey laws, for reasons other than consent). But this interpretation also fragments consent theory, which must clearly be modified or replaced by some more unified, universal explanation. We now turn to some alternatives.

The Just Government

A number of theorists elude the problem of political obligation by arguing that it exists self-evidently. MacDonald asserts that since political society is essentially a group organized according to rules enforced by some members, society without obligation is impossible. By virtue of being social animals, we are politically obliged.[15] But this makes the concept strongly asymmetrical: we can never deny, or be discharged from, political obligation. This view is reminiscent of that of Bentham, Austin, and other legal positivists who argued that obligatoriness is the essential quality of law. The question 'Why should I obey the law?' is answered tautologously by a definition of law as 'that which must be obeyed'.[16] Arguments of this form would oblige us to obey a cruel despot just as much as a democratic government, and would suggest that the latter is no more legitimate than the former, an implication unacceptable to most people. However, an argument on the same lines has been developed to show that we are self-evidently obliged to obey a *just* government, whether or not we consent to it. The pedigree of this argument goes back to Socrates. When he was under sentence of death and friends tried to persuade him to escape, he replied that men have a duty towards the laws which give them education and a good social life, even to the occasional unjust laws.[17] Recently, Pitkin has developed a 'nature of government' theory based on 'hypothetical consent'. If a government is just, you *should* (hypothetically) consent to it, and are therefore (actually) committed to obedience. A legitimate government is 'one which deserves consent'. There are two general criteria for determining the justice of a government: the justice of political institutions and procedures, and the justice of the government's measures.

Pitkin believes that this formula answers most questions about obligation adequately, although she thinks no definitive answer can be given to the more philosophical question 'Why should I *ever* be obliged?' As she notes, a determined dissenter can reject such pleas as 'it is for the good of the greatest number' or 'most of your fellow-men have consented to it' by saying 'what have these to do with me?', even if he repudiates morality and his own social nature in so doing. Pitkin's account would show that he was, even so, under obligation. But the 'just government' theory actually transfers the difficulties to the meaning of 'justice'. Is the just government self-evidently just? In *A Theory of Justice*, Rawls takes a similar view of obligation, basing it on the somewhat different idea of hypothetical consent which underlies his theory. Fairness requires someone to accept his obligations, Rawls says, when: (a) the institution is just; and (b) one has voluntarily accepted its benefits to further one's interests.[18] Condition (b), a version of the gratitude argument, seems an unnecessary addition to condition (a). As to (a), Rawls stipulates that when the constitution and social structure are 'reasonably just' we are obliged to comply even with unjust laws.[19] He specifies that we should only tolerate injustice if it is fairly distributed between groups 'in the long run' and that we need not comply with laws denying our basic liberties.[20] In his derivation of obligation from fairness and justice, Rawls mingles moral obligation (gratitude) and consent, for the definition of a just government is one to which we *would have* consented in the ideally impersonal and neutral 'original position'. Hypothetical consent is, of course, several degrees weaker than real consent, for it does not constitute an actual promise, but one imputed to me, and so the main weight of Rawls's case rests on this weak link. The injunction to obey unjust laws if the government is 'reasonably' just seems inadequate as a prescriptive principle.

The 'just government' argument avoids some of the conceptual problems of consent theory, and the problem of non-consenters. Our obligation to pursue justice is moral and unconditional. The theory also helps us to distinguish between general obligation to a just regime and modified—or annulled— obligation to particular unjust laws, and allows a theory of disobedience to be formulated without too much inconsistency. The problem of Pitkin's account is that it implies that a just but non-democratic government is still legitimate, although Rawls avoids this pitfall by building a notion of democracy into the idea of the just government. Both theories fail to confront the fact that in a heterogeneous society, ideas of justice will differ (though in Rawls's case, he has already stipulated what justice is): in practice, such differences would be important, and attitudes to the same government could vary.

Among other moral theories of political obligation is that of T. H. Green who, despite his liberalism, sought to make obligation strongly binding. He says that our common humanity and rational nature lead us to recognize a common good, which creates moral and political obligation towards our fellows;[21] to deny this would be to deny our humanity. The state promotes the common good and, hence, is owed obedience. Disobedience is only permissible 'in the interests of the state'. So Green's theory rests on our social nature, which creates an *a priori* moral obligation, rather as the justice of a government in Pitkin's theory creates an external imperative to obey: both theories depart from the voluntariness of consent theory, the idea of self-assumed obligation. Although for Rousseau the law consisted of self-prescribed rules, he fits better in the company of Green than of the consent theorists, for both see society as an association of moral beings who are by their very social nature strongly bound to conformity with the laws.[22] Neither provides satisfactory conditions for the rejection of obligation.

Self-interest and Gratitude

The utilitarians approached the topic of obligation armed with the felicific calculus. In principle, utilitarianism simply enjoins us to obey the state when it is beneficial to us: there can, logically, be no continuing obligation as each case must be considered on its merits. Problems arise depending on whether the individual or the social calculus are used. If individuals merely maximized their own utilities, this would frequently absolve them from obligation and justify them in disobedience, or free-riding, in their own interests. As Pitkin remarks, this would imply that at any time, some individuals would be obliged to obey and others would not — an inadmissibly contradictory situation. On the other hand, the 'greatest happiness' principle would often oblige individuals to obey laws which were contrary to their own interests, to benefit the community. The problematic nature of both these alternatives reflects the permanent difficulty of applying an egoistic moral theory to social matters, including the problem of obligation. Pitkin points out that utilitarianism, which judges according to the consequences of actions, cannot provide a sound basis for future obligation and obedience.[23] No doubt a utilitarian trying to construct a theory of obligation would have recourse to some form of rule — utilitarianism, which recommends that we should obey general rules conducive to happiness, even in a particular instance where they run counter to our individual interest; political obligation could be one such rule.

Undoubtedly a survey which asked the question 'Why should we obey the law?', when it did not meet with blank incomprehension on the part of those questioned, would evoke the reply 'Because the law/the state protects and looks after us'. The argument from gratitude is a profoundly common-sense one, and probably what causes most people to abide by the law when they are tempted to do otherwise. The idea appears in Locke's and Rawls's theory to reinforce the contractual form of obligation, and it may become increasingly popular with theorists as the state intervenes more in our lives and provides us with more benefits. However, the idea of gratitude in the relations of the individual to the state is misapplied. First, we pay for all the benefits that we receive from the state as taxpayers; gratitude is not owed in such circumstances. Second, the argument extends the interpersonal moral relation of gratitude to the state as if it were a moral agent and our benefactor, which is inappropriate, for the state is not a super-person, and exercises no personal kindness in distributing benefits to us, so there is no reason to react morally to its bounty. Gratitude, in any case, leaves several details unexplained: it cannot account for the *origin* of the state's legitimacy because prior to the existence of the state there were no grounds for gratitude, nor can it advise us when our obligation ceases, if the state reduces benefits or protection. It would also justify any form of government, however undemocratic, which protected and nurtured the people. Nor can the problem of individual disaffection be answered by the gratitude argument: what reason for gratitude have disenchanted, unemployed young people? As with the 'just government' theory, there will always be some elements of benefit (or justice) which could be used to justify a generally bad regime, and neither theory indicates how much justice constitutes obligation, or how little annuls our duty to the state. Both theories suffer another basic weakness: justice and gratitude are, largely, matters of individual judgement, and those who feel unjustly treated would only be following the recommenda-tion of the theories if they withdrew their allegiance. But a theorist cannot allow that his theory of obligation is selectively binding, like this, for he wants to posit consistent and universal obligation. Despite its common-sense appeal, then, gratitude alone cannot give rise to an adequate theory of obligation, nor, because of its inconsistencies, should it feature in any more eclectic account of obligation.

A number of other theories could also be cited here such as those resting on natural leadership (our duty to follow the wise) or divine right (our duty to obey God), for each political ideology has its own account of political obligation. Only the anarchist absolves men from it entirely, but he would commend to us a strong sense of moral obligation to our fellows. (This, however, seems more acceptable than the injunction that we should feel a moral duty towards state or government.) Marxist theorists would doubtless use a similar range of theories to justify obligation—consent, justice, gratitude, or a mixture of these. As we have seen, most arguments make obligation partly moral, which is conducive to subjective, internalized feelings of duty which are virtually self-policing, and is therefore a highly efficient, economical way of maintaining public order and keeping down the crime and protest rate. Externally imposed moral imperatives, such as 'the law is that which must be obeyed', are more likely to provoke resentment and resistance than self-assumed obligations—hence consent theory. But consent theories also rely on the general conviction that it is self-contradictory to break a contract, or promise, that you have freely and voluntarily made, so they appeal to personal rationality while invoking moral duty as well. Theorists naturally wish to develop theories of obligation which will show everyone to be obliged all the time (except when good reasons exonerate them, such as gross injustice), since they cannot build a theory of authority or the state on the basis of partial, non-universal obligation. Hence the search for a single, universal source of obligation, and the problems with theories which produce inconsistent or selective obligation. All such theories seem to overlook the obvious prudential reason, the fear of punishment, which usually motivates obedience to law, perhaps because they wish to maintain that political obligation extends beyond mere obedience and connotes feelings of respect for government, and for the system. It is hard to see how such a nebulous form of obligation could be manifested in political life.

Why Do I Obey the Law?

The objectionable feature of theories of obligation is that they seek to establish that we are all obliged unless we can prove ourselves exempted: the odds are heavily weighted against the individual, in favour of obedience and conformity. This may result from a persistent, Hobbesian fear of social disorder breaking out unless obligation and authority are strictly maintained. (However, life would probably go on much the same, even if *all* theories of obligation were suddenly proved fallacious.) I shall now discuss some of the reasons for limiting the idea of obligation, or rejecting it altogether. First, obedience to the law is adequately explained without recourse to obligation. Habit, fear, incapacity to disobey (the non-motorist can hardly disobey motoring laws) and inclination to obey (if one approves of the law) are major reasons.[24] Ordinary citizens only infrequently find themselves in a position where it would be convenient to disobey the law: even then, obedience is probably still the rational and prudent course of action. Criminals are people who think they can benefit from lawbreaking, not those who have conceptually rejected their obligation. The inference of some theorists that obedience is tantamount to an admission of obligation is clearly false. And the fact that the average citizen has no conception of political obligation casts further doubt on the idea. Explaining the maintenance of political systems, Easton invokes the 'reservoir of support', built up over time, for a system or a regime. This behaviouralist concept alone would adequately explain continued obedience and the legitimacy of governments, without the need to explore subjective feelings of obligation.[25]

Secondly, as the foregoing arguments suggest, theorizing on the subject is confused, with no general agreement over the basis or extent of obligation. Our duties to the system, the government, the law in general and particular laws are not clearly differentiated, and the relation between these entities is unclear, so that some theorists would consider disobedience of one law an acceptable act of protest, while others would interpret it as threatening the whole structure of society, as did Socrates. Such confusions make the theory an unhelpful guide to action. Thirdly, most people today in our individualistic society, with its emphasis on free will, would deny that obligation can be unconditional, yet the classic theories are heavily weighted in favour of government and offer no philosophical account of justified dissent, in most cases. Thus, they are asymmetrical, yet any theory which seeks to establish obligation should surely offer a corresponding account of when it can rightly be repudiated. Such one-sided theories may be suitable for societies composed of 'deferentials' but they are unacceptable to members of an active, participatory democracy.

But the idea of obligation is important for political propaganda. It appears in the political socialization of children and in governments' justifications of controversial measures. Obligation itself may not be cited, but consent, justice and gratitude are mentioned as reasons for obedience. Devlin's idea that law is co-extensive with morality is also sometimes invoked to persuade us that our moral duty is to obey the laws.[26] Alternatively, people's natural resistance to the imposition of obligation is overcome by pointing out that they have consented to the law through the democratic process. The aim of such arguments is to promote deference to governments which may not always be just, based on consent, or worthy of gratitude. Hence the need for a re-examination of the theory of obligation to help us to assess the familiar political rhetoric more critically.

Because of the propagandistic power of the notion, obligation is more than an academic issue, even if most people 'just do' obey governments. Although theorists often infer a mental acknowledgement of obligation from the fact of obedience, the inner rebel can be an outward conformist, since there are over-whelming prudential reasons for obeying the law. As has been suggested, the hypothesis of obligation over-determines the explanation of obedience, which can adequately be accounted for by prudence. By contrast, Milgram's *Obedience to Authority* (discussed in Chapter 8) also suggests that non-rational, psychological causes determine deference and obedience. Yet the theorist working within the paradigm of free and rational human action is often unwilling to accept such theses; also, he may wish to introduce a normative element which the behavioural concept of *obedience* cannot support. The process is similar to the complex interpretations of the act of voting in democratic theory: obedience to the law is the tip of a conceptual iceberg which the theorist conjectures must consist of consent, moral duty and other intangibles.

I have dealt with obligation at length because of its important role in binding the individual—theoretically—to the government. The acknowledgement of obligation by the people is said to bestow legitimacy on a government, and the 'fact' of legitimacy is then used to encourage obedience. The puzzle is how *subjective* attitudes (on which obligation would rest, if it existed) can ever confer the *objective* property of legitimacy on a government. It may be that they cannot, and that legitimacy is a figment of the imagination. But Pitkin would argue that the 'just government' is objectively legitimate, by reason of its just and benevolent procedures and policies. This makes legitimacy independent of obligation, which then derives, objectively, from the justice of the government itself, a reversal of the consent argument. Consent theory is clearly of major importance in democracies, for it provides the main justifica-tion of government. Marxists may use the consent argument, but they are also likely to argue that the will of the people creates a just socialist government, which is self-legitimizing. With regard to capitalist society, they would argue that class rule and oppression absolves the exploited classes from any obligation; the theory of obligation is a form of false consciousness. Clearly, the notion of obligation is no less ideological than other concepts. The idea is mainly invoked when the legitimacy of governments or laws is challenged, or an abnormal situation arises, to increase obedience and deference. But also, some conception of obligation is vital for any theorist wishing to assert the right to protest, or the 'obligation to disobey', since he can only properly account for these by contrast with some general obligation.

The concept of obligation has been criticized partly because it is habitually invoked to protect governments and the status quo, and deprived of any critical content, and partly because of the inconsistencies it embodies. In this controversy, we are forced to choose between individual-based justifications which cannot guarantee universal obligation, and state-centred justifications which make obligation well-nigh unconditional. If the concept is to be retained, the best approach would be to develop a more eclectic theory which showed the various possible sources of obligation and concentrated on people's subjective attitudes to government and law, rather than on the objective existence, in some world of intangibles, of obligation. In fact, the concept of authority could assume many of the burdens now carried by the concept of obligation. Finally, the critical drift of this discussion is not intended as a vindication of the ultra-egoist, who considers that he owes nothing to anyone, nor of his friend the free-rider. Indisputably, we have a duty to our fellow-citizens—some would say, to the citizens of the whole world—a duty to make life tolerable for them, in exchange for similar services. Robinson Crusoe, or Rousseau's noble savage, would not have such a duty, but the objective fact of social life creates it. If you prefer to avoid moral terminology, it can be based, ultimately, on self-preservation. However, theories of political obligation have transformed this wide, humanitarian duty into specific duties to particular regimes which we may feel do not deserve our loyalty, or to laws which we often disapprove. Hence the need to examine the justness of a government, *and* whether it represents your fellow-citizens before according it the legitimacy which your acknowledgement of obligation is said to create.

Who Has Power?

The distinction between power and authority has exercised many political philosophers who feel that there should be a sharp demarcation between the two rather than the blurring and merging which typifies them in political life. The approach recommended by linguistic philosophers, that we should study the everyday uses of such terms, leads to endless confusion since people, and even philosophers, use them interchangeably.[27] If we eschew everyday usage, six separate 'ideal categories can be distinguished which run the gamut of the exercise of power in politics:

(1) *Authority*. This attaches to offices and requires a subjectively deferential attitude on the part of citizens to be fully established. Those in authority may have recourse to (2)–(5), however.

(2) *Power*. The general ability to influence others which a politican, office-holder or other politically active individual has.

(3) *Powers**. Particular rights of office-holders, e.g. the police power to search for drugs, the tax inspector's power to inspect bank accounts.

(4) *Coercive power**. The power to make people do things and to punish them if they refuse. This operates according to *rules*, unlike (5).

(5) *Force**. This most accurately describes the use of (4) in an unstructured situation (e.g. during a war or revolution) by a group with a recognizable political identity—the army, a guerilla band.

*A subspecies of category (2).

(6) *Violence.* As suggested in Chapter 6, this is an emotive and pejorative term. But physically coercive and destructive acts by unauthorized people in orderly situations are usually termed 'violence'. This differs from (4) and (5) in that violence does not usually coerce people to do particular things, but forces the authorities to take notice — e.g. terrorist acts.

The guiding principles determining which of these methods a political operator chooses are effectiveness, economy and acceptability. In the case of a government in a 'normal' situation, (1) will be preferred over (2) as embodying all three criteria, and (2) over (3), and so on. In a revolutionary situation, the order may be reversed, with a view to effectiveness. There are many societies where effectiveness and economy are subordinated to other goals such as revenge, or where those in power choose to substitute violence for regulated coercive power — hence the length of Amnesty International's list of torture and other atrocities.

With the boundaries between these various concepts provisionally drawn, it is possible to analyse the concept of power. Power is the ability to cause someone to act in a way which he would not choose, left to himself. At the personal level, we control others by persuading, threatening, provoking, frustrating them: at the political level, the threat of some sanction, the use of propaganda, the invocation of particular powers, are all operations of power. Some political scientists offer models of political power based on interpersonal exchanges and interactions, but these are inadequate to describe the power exercised by groups whose members would have no influence alone, and that created by institutions with rules and norms. Political theory asks questions about what power is and where it lies; the answers are interdependent. Russell defined power as the production of *intended* results: the unforeseen effects of our influence on others cannot be called power.[28] This suggests that power is an *activity*, judged to exist by its consequences, so that power cannot 'lie' somewhere, dormant. Other theorists speak of power as if it were possessed by people or groups, which suggests that it *is* possible to have power without always using it. This led elite theorists to invent the mystifying concept of 'latent power'. On this view, power is an object, rather than a political activity.

It seems that those who usually have power are office-holders and people with special resources which give them political 'muscle'. Sufficient resources may create powerful groups who actually rival the government and become engaged in conflict with it, as the large unions have in Britain in recent years. To dramatize this as a struggle for sovereignty indicates a misunderstanding of the limitations of power without political authority, such as the unions have. Without subscribing to the idea of latent power as a sort of possession, one may say that groups with large resources (of money, manpower, etc.) are *potentially powerful*, meaning that they could exercise power if they chose to intervene. For example, the Church of England here is potentially powerful, but normally stays out of politics. Thus, power seems to be a function both of possession of power-relevant resources, and of activity, so that either criterion taken alone would not adequately account for the variety of power phenomena.

Why, in a normal political situation, can some people exert power over others? The organization of the state establishes certain channels for the enforcement of decisions, and discourages or forbids the exercise of power outside these. Political institutions give powers and other resources to office-holders. In what Weber defines as legal-rational-bureaucratic societies, a description which includes most modern societies, laws and conventions attach both authority and power to *offices*, not to their incumbents. 'The throne is not an empty chair' signifies that the powers and responsibilities of monarchy attach to the throne itself, and to individuals only by virtue of their temporary occupation of the throne. Likewise, the chain of command in the armed forces exists irrespective of which individuals fill the positions, or of their personal merits. In the modern state, the individual's exercise of power has little to do with his physical strength, but everything to do with his role. In the case of those operating outside the formal power structure, it is probably determined by their economic resources: trade unions have no formal place in decision-making but their economic strength enables them to exercise power and influence decisions. In self-defence against such informal — and threatening — manifestations of power, the state reasserts vigorously its 'right' to the monopoly of power in society.

Although the power attached to office comes close to authority, political theory has traditionally distinguished between the two, and separated them conceptually, as a safeguard against tyranny. They also recommend a separation in practice: Plato's Guardians formed a distinct class from the law-enforcing auxiliaries, and Locke advocated a 'balance of powers' between the legislature and the executive, with a view to curtailing the latter's exercise of power by the former's authority as sovereign. But in another tradition, the two are fused: for Hobbes, any such division of labour within the sovereign would have been fatal — 'divide and fall'. In reality, the possession of executive power by an organ of the state usually gives it a certain authority, by accidental or deliberate transference — as in the case of the police. The reason why theorists distinguish so sharply between power and authority and try to show the latter to be supreme is that they see *coercion* as the archetype of political power, a form of power which can easily get out of control and must be resisted on humanitarian grounds. Plamenatz writes

It is a mistake to suppose that power is prior to right and obligation. No man has power unless his right to command is acknowledged by some at least of those who obey him; it is only because they obey him that he has power. All exercise of power is *subject to rules;* it is in principle regular and cannot last long or be effective if it is often arbitrary. [29]

This last remark expresses optimism rather than a necessary truth, for there is unfortunately no logical or practical reason why a regime based on arbitrary and coercive power should not maintain itself for a long time if it is willing to pay the extra cost of such an uneconomic form of rule. Lukes has distinguished between power based on acquiescence or co-operation and power based on coercion:[30] the former is more common in a stable society, although it is clearly important to have a philosophical analysis of the latter, which will enable us to identify and combat abuses of coercive power, and the use of force. Whether power based on co-operation should instead count as authority can best be answered by analysing the latter concept.

What Creates Authority?

Today's authority is the site of yesterday's struggle for power. Experts in jurisprudence describe power as a *de facto* concept, concerning fact or actions, while authority is a *de iure* concept, concerning right. The primary aim of any regime which displaces another by force is to transmute its coercive power into authority, by invoking legal and moral concepts on its behalf, to achieve the deference and co-operation of the people, and to establish its legitimacy in their minds. A government's authority rests both on its legal validity, and on the people's acknowledgement of political obligation which in turn commands their loyalty to government and the laws, hence authority has an objective aspect and an internal, subjective aspect and is incomplete and precarious unless both of these are achieved. Where coercion creates obedience at a high cost in men and equipment, authority can control both the minds and behaviour of individuals at a very low cost, once it is established and accepted.

Authority's objective basis is usually the law. In a democratic country, it emanates from the constitution which expresses the sovereignty of the people and guarantees the legality of the laws, whereas in, say, an Islamic republic it rests ultimately on the divine will as expressed in the Koran. (We cannot ask that this higher law should be validated by further laws without risk of an infinite regression. As Hart has said, the justification of higher law takes the form of a value judgement—a moral code, for example.[31]) In a post-revolutionary situation, the new regime seeks to create authority by enacting a new constitution. This is not difficult, since the law is ultimately self-validating, according to the positivist view,[32] but the regime may have difficulty in persuading people accustomed to an earlier constitution and political tradition to adopt a suitably deferential attitude to its new creation. Probably no revolutionary regime can exist for long when a widely established democratic tradition emphasizes the people's part in bestowing authority, and given that the exercise of coercive power is so much more costly and less effective than the invocation of authority. But authority is hard to achieve if the people fiercely oppose the new regime, and it takes time to create deference. The English Revolution of 1688 was an example of a popular revolution where enough elements of the previous system were wisely preserved—in particular, parliament—for the majority of the people to transfer their loyalty to the new regime and accept the constitutional laws which it passed.[33] In other cases, a new regime may have to be on its best behaviour for a long time before it gains legitimacy in the eyes of the people.

The interaction between power and authority, fact and right, engrossed all the classical political theorists. Machiavelli is notorious for arguing in *The Prince* that a new ruler, perhaps a usurper, who cannot claim a hereditary or religious basis for his position, must become an expert in the exercise of power and the manipulation of the people to survive, using opportunistic tactics and an 'economy of violence'. Authority is thus not essential in the short run although the prince seeks to acquire it in the long term. Hobbes's sovereign is appointed to enforce obedience to the covenant. In so far as the original contractors authorized him, he is in authority over them. But later generations obey the sovereign for prudential reasons, fearing a return to anarchy, so he could be said to be in power over them, rather than in authority. This is particularly true if one ruler is replaced by another, perhaps by force. The new ruler now fills the role of the sovereign who can alone prevent a reversion to the state of nature, and so is still owed prudential obedience. Hobbes's model has the possibly unintended consequence of legitimizing any successful coup and the *de facto* power thereby established. Only if the original contractors' obligation could somehow be transmitted across generations could new sovereigns be proved to have authority as well as power. Doubtless Hobbes realized that legitimacy was an important attribute of any sovereign, but it is not logically required in his theory, because of the emphasis on prudential obedience.

Locke, by contrast, locates authority in the people as the supreme sovereign. Authority and power are delegated in limited amounts to the government, which remains subordinate to the sovereign people. Individuals are, however, bound to accept the authority and obey the laws of a properly constituted government because these are laws to which they have consented. The contract theories especially make it clear that nothing except power exists in a pre-social situation, where men seek to dominate each other and each individual is fully 'the author' of his own actions, and that authority comes about with the creation of society and a division of labour between the rulers and the ruled. We can be fairly sure that a state based purely on power would be less pleasant for the inhabitants, and less efficient, than one based on authority, so that theories about the nature and creation of authority are important: authority may rest on men's subjective attitudes, but it is a concept with a recognizable counterpart in real life, unlike obligation.

Weber's analysis of power in fact offers a sociological explanation of authority. He sees different political organizations as power structures, each with a specific internal dynamic. Three ideal types are distinguishable[34]:

(1) Patriarchal or traditional power supported by traditions and myths.
(2) Bureaucratic power, resting on a rational legal structure and characterized by impersonal rules, and regularities, and authority attached to offices.
(3) Charismatic power, which rests on the leader's personality and is the antithesis of permanent, rule-bound authority.

The notion of charismatic power, also called charismatic authority, upsets political theorists, especially since the rise of Hitler, because it connotes an unpredictable, uncontrollable element which may threaten or supersede the bureaucratic–democratic form of authority which typifies modern Western society. Although it constitutes a negation of legally based authority, charismatic authority essentially relies on the deference of the leader's disciples, for without them he is nothing. Unlike the impersonal authority which characterizes institutions, his authority is entirely personal, and its loss entails immediate loss of the power to influence his followers. Early charismatic leaders were war heroes and divine prophets—today's are demagogues and, occasionally, religious leaders like the notorious Jim Jones. Weber sees charisma as ephemeral, but thinks that it can be routinized 'into a suitable source for the acquisition of sovereign power by the successors of the charismatic hero'. He notes that most charismatic kings had a permanent scapegoat to protect themselves, something recommended by Machiavelli, which suggests that charisma is incompatible with responsibility, whereas legally constituted authority and accountability are inseparable. The scope for charismatic leaders in a stable, pluralist democracy may be small, but we can predict that they will emerge in times of crisis. Whether they are successful, and whether they are a blessing or a danger to society, depends largely on how representative of the people is the government at the time. Weber's concept is useful for the analysis of 'abnormal' or unstable situations, so the concept is not fundamental to 'normal' political theory. The importance of the idea of charismatic authority is that it helps us to see 'normal' authority in perspective.

The *de iure* authority to which we are accustomed rests on a system of rules, usually legal rules, which direct people's feelings of deference to appropriate objects. According to Winch, all social activity is participation in rule-governed activities which 'involve a reference to an *established* way of doing things'. This feature of society gives rise to notions of authority, which Winch defines as 'not a kind of *causal* relation between individual wills but an *internal* relation'. He would consider *power* a causal relation, evidently. He also argues that authority is not a curtailment of liberty since 'to follow an authority is a voluntary act',[35] a conclusion which I would qualify. Even supposing that you freely and rationally decide to acknowledge a government's authority, in choosing to defer to its laws and commands you limit your own future freedom, albeit voluntarily, thus ending up in a state of what has been called 'imperfect rationality', where one chooses rationally *not* to make a future choice.[36] Political authority based on law is crucial to the existence of society, and preferable to the use of coercive power, but we cannot pretend that it leaves the individual paradigmly free.

This leads to certain problems in evaluating the relative merits of authority and power. The individual may feel more contented when he defers to authority than when he yields to power, whether power appears as the exercise of 'powers' or sanctions, or as coercion. Even if he feels that authority does not rest on his full consent, it is pleasanter to accept its ruling, since his actions then seem partially voluntary, than to be forced by the exercise of power to act against his will. Most people accept authority unquestioningly in their daily lives, having internalized the legitimacy of government and the state from an early age. However, it could be argued that a state which inscribes the minds of citizens with ideas of authority and obligation disguises their lack of freedom and that this threatens human liberty more than a state which rules by the use of coercion or force. In the latter case, individuals can at least perceive the state's illegitimacy and the threat to their liberty, and can protest and resist. (Some philosophers argue that captivity of the body is preferable to enslavement of the mind for this reason.) This is why critics of the modern capitalist state, who consider it illegitimate, regret its transformation into a benign welfare state which gains authority in the eyes of the people by its dispensation of social justice and its democratic appendages. Marcuse's revelation that such benign capitalism is based on disguised violence is intended to remove the blindfold of authority and legitimacy from our eyes and encourage us to protect our threatened liberties.[37] His argument imputes false consciousness to the large percentage of the population which genuinely believes the state to be legitimate. A typical strategy for those who believe that the modern capitalist state is based on force, not authority, is to provoke it into showing its hand, so as to expose its true repressive nature. Many left-wing thinkers in Britain today argue that what they consider to be police violence at demonstrations and on picket lines is symptomatic of the force on which the state is based; the more frequently such events occur, the more people will understand how illusory is their liberty in liberal society. One reply to such arguments is that if the people *think* that the state has authority and legitimacy, then it *has*, since these are constituted largely by the people's attitude to it. Nevertheless, people may be deceived into according approval to a government or system not really in their interests. If they can be persuaded to rescind that approval, the state ceases to have authority (except in the legal sense) although it may retain power, for a time. Legal authority without deference is not much use, since it has to be backed up constantly by punishment and coercion. It would be ideal if just states were founded on authority while unjust states always revealed themselves to be based on force and alerted the people who would then overthrow them, but a state's authority in the eyes of the people is not necessarily an indication of its justice. However, each political ideology gives rise to a theory of when authority is justly accorded, by which the authority of existing states can be evaluated. Needless to say, such theories differ.

Power and Authority — Siamese Twins?

The attempt to distinguish rigorously between these two concepts is ultimately doomed to failure. In any normal political situation, and in every state institution, they co-exist and support each other, and between them condition the behaviour of citizens. Mr White pays his taxes because he voted for the government and believes in its authority (1); Mr Grey is reluctant, but pays, being in awe of the general power of the Inland Revenue (2); Mr Brown tries to evade payment but finds particular powers invoked against him, so conforms (3), and Mr Black defrauds the Inland Revenue and is prosecuted and punished (4). (The numbers refer to the types of power listed above.) It is clear that the use of force and violence, (5) and (6), indicate abnormal circumstances where authority has broken down. In the example, in the first three cases the same end result is produced, but each taxpayer is influenced by different aspects of the power–authority nexus so that the combination of both power and authority in a government can be seen to be essential, to minimize disobedience. Authority alone might cut little ice with people where their financial interests were concerned: the tax inspector needs both executive powers and legal sanctions.

To the citizen, the power and authority of an institution seem inseparable, and people commonly regard an institution or an individual as having authority because they know that it, or he, has certain powers. This fact undermines the theorist's attempts to root authority in consent. Political scientists proceed more in accordance with the layman's perception. They ask who takes the decisions on particular issues, and whose wishes prevailed when conflicts of goals or values arise. This analysis omits all reference to authority and to powers as rights. In a typical study, *Power and Poverty*, the authors say 'To regard authority as a form of power is not operationally useful'.[38] The analysis of power has a tendency, as does much political science, to validate whatever it discovers. This is where the theorist's emphasis on authority is vital: assuming that there *are* methods for validly bestowing authority on a just government, the concept is useful for highlighting areas where part of the state has assumed unwarranted powers, and for detecting other usurpations of power. Plamenatz's observation that the rule of power is necessarily short-lived suggests that whenever a divergence of power from authority occurs, the power-holders will seek to legitimize their position by devising mechanisms for establishing their authority. Hence, it is the cases where power and authority diverge that most interest the theorist, and where the normative and critical force of his analysis can come into play.

Much English and American theory about the nature of power is permeated by a conviction of the stability of our own political systems, in which power is usually comfortably legitimized and contained by authority. A situation where this reassuring partnership would cease is that which might occur after the devastation of a nuclear war. Many different scenarios for this have been envisaged, but most concur on the inevitability of strict martial law, emanating from regional centres of government, keeping the relatively few survivors from rioting and looting, and putting them to work. Would the regional governors and their troops have authority in such a situation? Whether authority is based on consent, justice or the interests of the people, the answer is surely 'No', whatever the emergency laws may prescribe. The democratic apparatus would have disappeared, and the governors could hardly invoke the consent of the deceased population, given in the last election where issues were very different.

Nor would the predicted attempts to restore order by force, and communications by directed labour be much in the interests of those trying to survive from day to day, or earn their gratitude. This is just a grim, hypothetical example which suggests that in abnormal situations where authority and power diverge, force will prevail. Without the constraining influence that authority provides, the use of force (unregulated coercive power) is unrestrained, and may be used to promote the interests of the powerful. This illustrates the two-edged nature of authority, which revolutionaries may see only as a means of deluding the population, but which equally acts as a brake on the coercive elements that necessarily underlie government. The retention of an active role in our political thinking for the concept of authority is therefore crucial, although theorists should be more ready to admit and examine its idological role. But, before a final assessment of the importance and interrelation of power, authority and obligation, we must consider the institution to which all three refer, the state.

The State Leviathan

The state consists of the legislative, executive, and judicial branches of government, along with all the institutions to which they delegate powers (including the army, prisons, the media if these are state-owned, and so on). In democratic theory, the powers of the separate parts of the state are delegated from the supreme sovereign, the legislature, and subject to its control. If this were ideally realized, in a democratic society the state would be the servant of the sovereign people, but various factors prevent this being so. The shortcomings of the representative system, already discussed, prevent the elected government from being a sensitive barometer of the people's opinions and desires. Secondly, most state institutions are of longer duration than elected governments, so that they form their own long-term policies and acquire vested interests, which new governments may be obliged to accommodate — the tail wags the dog. Thirdly, delegated powers give some state agencies a high degree of autonomy, not always matched by accountability. The persisting nature of state institutions and the transitory nature of governments means that a newly-elected government tends to merge into and be identified with the apparatus of the state, unless it makes special efforts to remain aloof and control the latter. This conceptual and technical separation of government and state and the theoretical subordination of the latter to the former is important when we are trying to gauge how democratic a country is, how accountable its institutions, and whether the state presents a threat to individual freedom.

What is the nature of the state? Four alternative views will briefly be summarized here:

(1) *The contractual view.* The state derives from the voluntary agreement of men, via the social contract, and its task is to promote the interests of the people as individuals (Locke) or as a collectivity (Rousseau). The government's power, and therefore the state's, is unlimited (Hobbes), or limited by men's

natural rights (Locke), or is constrained to realize the General Will (Rousseau). The hypothesis of the contract thus leads to no *general* conclusions about the nature and powers of the state, as these are deduced from the different original premisses of the various theories.

(2) *The state as arbiter.* A view which reflects the minimal role assigned to the state by classical economists and liberals. In particular, the utilitarians emphasized the neutrality of the state. Its origin is unimportant for its justification lies in its performing satisfactorily its role of negotiator, arbiter, and minimizer of conflict. The state's impartiality is entailed by its moral obligation to care equally for all its members, as utilitarianism enjoins, and to ensure this the state is best subjected to a constitution which enforces this impartiality. On this view, the state is merely the sum of its individual parts.

(3) *The state as organism.* Conservative romantics like Coleridge, but also the anti-romantic Hegel, conceived of the state as an integrated organism, predating individuals, a whole greater than its component parts. Hegel was anxious to oust the contract view and the liberalism based on it. The organic ideal denies the possibility of conflicting interests: it offers a 'natural' foundation for the state. Hegel characterized the state as 'abstract mind' which acknowledges no other absolute principles, such as morality, and is an absolute itself. Hence the omnipotence of the state in his theory. On this organic account there can be no balance of powers and no neutrality in the state, for the state has its own holistic interest, set above those of individuals.[39]

(4) *The state as oppressor.* The Marxist analysis, to which most anarchists would also adhere in principle if not in detail. This sees the state as the instrument of the ruling class, and explicitly contradicts the other three views. The state was not built on a contract but on force and usurpation, and cannot be neutral. The modern state is 'a committee for managing the common affairs of the bourgeoisie' and it cannot be an organic unity because society is an imbroglio of class conflict, of which the state's very existence is symptomatic. 'The state is a product and a manifestation of the irreconcilability of class antagonisms'. Marx also notes that the state is an embodiment of individual interest which is opposed to the interest of the whole community. Marx therefore predicted the withering away of the state in a classless, fully socialist society. This analysis is, by and large, adapted by contemporary Marxists *mutatis mutandis* to the advanced capitalist state.[40]

Evidently, ideological convictions condition our understanding of the state, its origins, and its limitations. Given the Marxist dismissal of the state as a class instrument and the general suspicion of would-be totalitarian 'organic' views, most Western theorists still analyse the state as a neutral arbiter, true to the liberal-democratic tradition. Particularly curious is the neutral tone which such analyses adopt. They seek to define the precise functions of the state, and what distinguishes it from other associations (as if there were a risk of confusion!) but do not question its scope and purposes, perhaps because it is assumed that democratic institutions automatically keep the state within bounds.

A typical approach of this kind defines the state as a system of rules, procedures, and roles, operated by individuals using various methods including coercion. Since this might describe almost *any* system or association, the author goes on to list its five special characteristics:[41]

(a) The state has universal jurisdiction.
(b) The state has compulsory jurisdiction.
(c) Its ends are broader than those of other associations which pursue 'privately conceived ends'.
(d) The state has legal supremacy or sovereignty over other associations.
(e) The state ranks as equal with other nation-states, being 'self-sovereign'.

Clearly, all except (c) are defining properties of the state with which even a Marxist would agree. These criteria identify the state as unique among associations, and this proves its clear, indisputable supremacy and directs citizens' basic loyalty towards the state rather than to other sectional associations in society. Walzer designates the state a 'primary association', distinct from secondary associations such as the church, firms, and interest groups, membership of which also generates duty and loyalty.

Having characterized the state thus, can its existence in this form be justified? We could, after all, imagine societies existing without such an overbearing form of association, such as the anarchists recommended. One justification for the state's supremacy is its claim to promote the common good, a claim regarded sceptically by liberals; the other is the 'arbitral' role of the state which judges between competing claims, considering everyone impartially. One wonders at the immense apparatus required for this modest aim! Implicit in both these justification is the claim that the same ends could not be achieved by looser or narrower associations, a claim disputed, for instance, by Nozick who suggests that a market society, with free entry to and exit from a multiplicity of small communities, could spontaneously fulfil both these functions.[42] For all except those who hold an organic, or similar, view of the state, it must justify its existence in terms of the good which it does to the members of the state. We may ask whether these benefits might not be achieved in other ways, but for those with a view such as Hegel's, the state is a good in itself and an end in itself, and needs no further justification.

For the legal or the political theorist searching for a definition of the state and its rights, the most important question is where *sovereignty* lies, a question complicated by the fact that some talk of *de facto* sovereignty, a seeming contradiction since the idea rests heavily on *right*. Weber, for example, defined the state as having the monopoly of the legitimate use of physical force, and Raphael accuses modern power theorists of equating sovereignty with 'supremacy of coercive power rather than of legal authority'.[43] The *de facto* approach makes it impossible to establish or dispute the state's *right* to such powers, although it makes sovereignty easier to identify empirically. However, this approach is not adopted by theorists, for whom the normative or *de iure* elements of sovereignty are all-important. In most modern theory, the democratic ideal of the sovereign people is put aside (as an irrelevant truism) then the theorist tries to determine to which of the state's organs sovereignty attaches. Law-making is seen as the essence of the sovereign role but this is not always an unambiguous criterion because the lawmaking function can be, and is, divided. The 'problem of sovereignty' in political theory now seems an exceptionally sterile academic debate, however. The democratic theorist can easily say where power *ought* to lie and the focus of analysis should be to discover how the constitution, or political practice, might best ensure that the supreme law-making body is responsive and accountable to the people. The theorist's role cannot be merely to determine where sovereignty lies in particular socities, as this is an empirical matter, but to decide where it should lie. In his analysis of sovereignty, however, the political theorist's prescriptive approach is liable to conflict with the jurisprudentialist's positivist account of where legislative sovereignty actually lies, and since the theorist cannot gainsay positive law, he should shift his activities elsewhere. In the making of constitutions, for example, the theorist could play a useful part, but otherwise he might as well follow Benn's recommendation to discard the concept, with its confusion of multiple senses.[44]

In popular usage, the concept of sovereignty is mainly invoked when other sovereign states seem to threaten a state's supremacy within its own boundaries. Many Labour opponents of Britain's membership of the EC argued against the threat to Parliament's legislative supremacy which it posed: one might note that the case could equally have been based on democratic theory alone since the EEC was not then, and the EC is not now, a democratic organization. Once in the EC, British citizens had to submit to legislation to which they had not consented—a point which still applies as EC regulations are not made by the European Parliament. The exclusive emphasis placed on *parliamentary* sovereignty in such cases by British politicans is symptomatic of their tendency to forget the final sovereignty of the people. Sovereignty is also much debated here when a high court judge makes an interpretative ruling on some point of law which is contrary to the spirit in which Parliament intended the law to be enforced. Lord Denning consistently does this, 'upholding justice against the law', he says. In such cases politicians would argue that the balance of power between legislature and judiciary is being tilted to the detriment of parliamentary legislative supremacy. In constitutional matters like this, the employment of the concept of sovereignty is appropriate, although the political theorist might again better describe the event in terms of the damage caused to the democratic principle when non-elected, non-accountable judges start to make law.

In daily life, of course, the state is an objective reality to which the individual must accommodate himself as best he can, but political theory need not endorse this subjection of the moveable to the immoveable. If a legalistic approach is adopted to the state and its sovereignty, there can be no question but that it is supreme according to positive and/or constitutional law. However, the law only goes a certain way towards establishing a state's authority, and the law can be changed, or overthrown. An equally important factor, as was argued above, is the attitude of the people towards the state — their acknowledgement of its authority, and acceptance of their own political obligation. Although these concepts have often been used propagandistically to justify the supremacy of the state over the individual, new conceptions of them could be devised with a contrary, restraining effect on the state. If our notions of authority and obligation could be refashioned on a thoroughly democratic basis, we would tip the balance which so strongly favours the state back a little towards the individual. Of course, this is a long-term process: even if missionary political theorists could popularize their reinterpretation of the individual's duty to the state, and this was widely accepted, the state would continue to hold the monopoly of coercive power, which it could activate against any radical effects of the conceptual revolution.

For anarchists and Marxists 'the state' was always a dirty word, and now a similar attitude is partly pervading liberal-democratic societies, although its cause is different: the modern interventionist state threatens personal liberty in innumerable ways. 'Convergence theory' argues that liberal and Marxist states are converging towards a common pattern, state socialism, alias state capitalism. The details may differ, but the spectacle of a constantly growing state leviathan is common to both liberal and communist society. This is equally ironic for liberals who remember Mill's injunctions against state intervention and for Marxists who recall Marx's prediction of the 'withering away'. The shared failure of their analyses and ideals should give rise to a different analysis of the nature of the state in advanced industrial society, which will provide different prescriptions from those now available concerning how we can assert the will of the people or the rights of individuals against the state. We have lost control of the modern state theoretically, just as practically we are no longer able to enforce its accountability. Mills's account of the power elite and Galbraith's analysis of the technostructure, were pioneering steps towards a new theory of the state, but perhaps Orwell's account, in *1984* of the three permanently warring superstates with their terrified subject populations cannot be bettered by theory . . . .

A number of factors contribute to the distinct nature of the modern interventionist state. A major factor is the massive advances made in technology which have several consequences. To follow up such advances commercially requires such heavy investment that governments are called upon to finance them, and so become deeply involved in economic enterprise. Where government intervenes, it will also attempt to regulate, hence the need for an increased number of experts called in as aides to government bodies, whose criteria for policy-making may differ from what the people may wish. In particular, the development of nuclear weapons and the arms race, itself an important stimulus to postwar economies, and now a dangerous addiction, necessarily increased the power and scope of government as the military section of the economy under its control became even larger.[45] (We also see Orwell's predictions borne out at the ideological level, as each major power incites its citizens to greater fear and dislike of the opposing power, and to greater loyalty to itself, to justify arms expenditure.) Third, the output of legal regulations necessitated by advanced technology and welfare measures, and by membership of superstates such as the EC, has created and subsequently overloaded large bureaucracies which are only marginally accountable to the people via the democratic process. The heavy involvement of each country's economy in the world economy is another, external, factor which diminishes the controllability of the state: the world economy is not controlled by individual states but it, in part, controls them, often in ways antithetical to democracy within the countries. The stringent conditions attached to IMF loans concerning domestic policy is a common example of such control.

These are hardly original observations — nor, unfortunately, have they yet become commonplace enough in democratic politics to warrant action to curb these developments. These factors are added to, and enhance the increasing elitism and isolation of the political process in liberal democracies. Some parts of the state have escaped the control of the governors, other parts are controlled by them, but the governors themselves are largely uncontrolled. It is a poor lookout for democracy, and one which calls for a re-thinking of our old concepts. Since the possession of authority is essential for the maintenance of the state, which cannot afford to operate in the long term by the exercise of power and the use of force, the way in which authority is conceptualized is important. If political theorists could develop and disseminate a more critical concept of authority, resting on stronger forms of consent and accountability, and a more selective, less deferential account of political obligation which emphasized the right to dissent, they could make a useful contribution to controlling the new leviathan.

Notes

1. R. E. Dawson and K. Prewitt, *Political Socialization*, Little, Brown & Co., 1969.
2. The nature of self-imposed obligation is described in R. M. Hare, *Freedom and Reason*, Oxford University Press, 1963.
3. Hobbes, *Leviathan*, Penguin, 1968, Chaps XIII–XIX.
4. Hobbes, *Leviathan*, p.201.
5. Locke, *Essay*, Chaps VII–XIX. See also H. Pitkin, 'Obligation and consent', in *Philosophy, Politics and Society*, 4th Series (Eds P. Laslett, W. G. Runciman and Q. Skinner), Blackwell 1972.
6. Locke, *Essay*, s.138.
7. D. Hume, 'Of the origin of government', in *Essays, Moral, Political and Literary*, Longman's, Green & Co., 1875, Vol. I, pp.113–7. See also Rousseau, *A Discourse on . . . Inequality*, Dent, 1913, p.205 and Paine, *The Rights of Man*, Penguin, 1969, pp.94, 194.
8. Rousseau, *The Social Contract*, Dent, 1913, p.12.
9. Rousseau, *The Social Contract*, p.14.
10. T. H. Green, *Lectures on the Principles of Political Obligation*, Longman's, Green & Co., 1901, p.66.

230

11. J. P. Plamenatz, *Consent, Freedom and Political Obligation*, 2nd edn, Oxford University Press, 1968, pp.16–18.
12. Plamenatz, *Consent, Freedom and Political Obligation*, p.154.
13. J. Tussman, *Obligation and the Body Politic*, Oxford University Press, 1960.
14. Plamenatz, *Consent, Freedom and Political Obligation*, p.13. The appendix to the second edition modifies Plamenatz's position somewhat.
15. M. MacDonald, 'The language of political theory' in *Logic and Language*, 1st series (Ed. A. Flew), Blackwell, 1960.
16. J. Bentham, *A Fragment on Government* (Ed. W. Wharrison), Blackwell, 1967, Chaps IV–V. The circularity of the account is indicated by Bentham's positivist definition of 'duty': 'that which I am punished by law if I do not do'. The Benthamite view of law was restated more famously in J. Austin, *The Province of Jurisprudence Determined*, London, 1832.
17. Plato, *Crito* in *The Last Days of Socrates* (Trans. H. Tredennick), Penguin, 1969, pp.90–2.
18. J. Rawls, *A Theory of Justice*, Harvard University Press, 1971, pp.111–2.
19. Rawls, *A Theory of Justice*, p.351.
20. Rawls, *A Theory of Justice*, p.355.
21. Green, *Lectures*, pp.124–7. See Plamenatz's criticisms in *Consent, Freedom and Political Obligation*, Chap. III.
22. Rousseau, *The Social Contract*, pp.26, 31.
23. Pitkin, 'Obligation and consent', pp.49–50.
24. For a sociological study which suggests the *practical* reasons why people obey the law see A. Podgorecki *et al.*, *Knowledge and Opinion About Law,* Martin Robertson, 1973. Legal theorists such as Austin and Hart recognise this routine obedience to law when they base law in part on the 'habit of obedience'.
25. D. Easton, 'A reassessment of the concept of political support', *British Journal of Political Science*, **5**, 435–58 (1975).
26. P. Devlin, *The Enforcement of Morals*, Oxford University Press, 1965.
27. This method of analysis is described in T. Weldon, *The Vocabulary of Politics*, Penguin, 1953. For an example of its application to authority see R. S. Peters, 'Authority' in *Political Philosophy* (Ed. A. Quinton).
28. B. Russell, *Power*, Allen & Unwin, 1938.
29. J. P. Plamenatz, *German Marxism and Russian Communism*, Longman's, Green & Co., 1954.
30. S. Lukes, *Power: A Radical View*, Macmillan, 1974.
31. H. A. L. Hart, *The Concept of Law*, Oxford University Press, 1961, Chap. VI, s.1.
32. Austin's famous positivist account of law as the commands of the sovereign backed by force means that no further justification need be sought if there is a determinate, supreme sovereign in a polity. For a modern positivist account of law, see Hart, *The Concept of Law*, Chap. II.
33. The Bill of Rights (1689) placed the monarchy firmly under the law and ensured free elections and free debate in Parliament.
34. M. Weber, *Essays in Sociology* (Eds H. H. Gerth and C. W. Mills), Kegan Paul, 1948, Part II.
35. P. Winch, 'Authority' in *Political Philosophy* (Ed. A. Quinton), p.38.
36. See J. Elster, *Ulysses and the Sirens*, Cambridge University Press, 1979, pp.88–103. Imperfect rationality occurs in a situation where one makes a subsidiary choice which commits one to a future major choice. Thus, voting can be seen by theorists who use the notion of obligation as committing us to certain future actions which we do not yet know and might not choose freely.
37. H. Marcuse, *One Dimensional Man*, Sphere, 1968.
38. P. Bachrach and M. Baratz, *Power and Poverty*, Oxford University Press, 1970, p.33.

39. G. Hegel, *Philosophy of Right* (trans. M. Knox), Oxford University Press, 1952.
40. Marx and Engels, *Communist Manifesto* in *Selected Works*, Vol. I, p.127. See too V. I. Lenin, *The State and Revolution*, Moscow, 1972, p.9.
41. D. D. Raphael, *Problems of Political Philosophy*, rev. edn, Macmillan, 1976, pp.41–53.
42. R. Nozick, *Anarchy, State and Utopia*, Blackwell, 1974.
43. Raphael, *Problems of Political Philosophy*, p.59.
44. S. Benn, 'The uses of sovereignty' in *Political Philosophy* (Ed. A. Quinton).
45. See *Report From Iron Mountain* (Ed. L. Lewin), Penguin, 1968, an anonymous 'hoax' document which nonetheless exposed the truth about the dependence of the US economy on arms production. See also J. K. Galbraith, *The New Industrial State*, Penguin, 1969.

Further reading

S. Lukes, *Power: A Radical View, Macmillan, 1974.*
C. Pateman, *The Problem of Political Obligation*, Wiley, 1979.
J. C. Friedrich, (Ed.), *Authority*, Harvard University Press, 1958.
R. Flathman, *Political Obligation*, Croom Helm, 1973.

CHAPTER 11

Liberty, Rights, and Protest

To renounce liberty is to renounce being a man, to surrender the rights of humanity and even its duties.[1]

The idea of individual liberty* is inseparably fused with the theological doctrine that man has free will, with which to choose good or evil, and that this is the defining characteristic of his God-given nature. The philosophical debate as to whether man is indeed free, or determined, in his actions may be more germane to moral than to political philosophy but which ever viewpoint is taken has consequences for the adoption of political ideals. From the eighteenth century onwards, rationalist philosophers insisted that causal explanations could in principle be given of human behaviour, as of events in the natural world, and determinism became a widespread doctrine. The related precept, that men's characters are formed by their social environment, gave rise to a new generation of utopias in which men were to be made perfect by the perfection of social institutions. Marx's materialist analysis stemmed from the same origins. Darwinism and, in this century, the behavioural sciences continued to foster the determinist view of man despite which liberty remains our most vaunted political ideal in the West. Many philosophers have contended that a crucial element in social life is the assumption that men are responsible for their actions, an assumption only possible in conjunction with some theory of free will.[2] How could a liberal system of justice reward people for their merits, if they were not responsible for their achievements? Many liberal thinkers, like Rousseau, as quoted above, make freedom man's defining attribute. The democratic ideal is posited on people's capacity for free (and rational) choice, and one major quarrel which liberals have with marxists is the latters' 'deterministic' view of man.

*It is an accident of the English language that we have two words for the same concept, 'freedom' and 'liberty'. They are treated as synonyms in the discussion which follows.

We are unlikely ever to prove the case for free will or that for determinism; in any case, most philosophers do not hold man to be totally *determined* or totally *undetermined*. It is possible to specify the determining factors such as conditioning, which limit our *choices* but to hold that we still have a degree of *choice*. The degree of free will or causation attributed to human action in a political theory is clearly all-important in deciding how political behaviour is explained and what political values are pursued. Thus, the philosophical assumptions made about free will, although this is not primarily a political question, will set the parameters for an ideology. But when liberty is discussed in political philosophy what is referred to is not so much the individual's capacity for freedom as his 'objective' freedom, defined as freedom from coercion or restraints and freedom in terms of opportunities.

With all due respect to anarchists and libertarians, the idea of *absolute freedom* is a chimera, unattainable by man in society, which is essentially a system of shared norms and mutual restraints. Most of the activities which make life worthwhile—friendship, marriage, belonging to a group—depend, as has been said, on self-imposed obligations or promises which restrict our freedom but enrich our experience. So the concept of absolutely free man, untrammelled by laws or morals and unimpeded by the actions of others, cannot function in political argument, even as an unrealisable goal. The focus of argument must instead be whether particular ideologies or political systems *extend* the range of choice and *diminish* interference: that is, the concept must be viewed relatively. Berlin, discussing J. S. Mill, distinguishes between *negative liberty*, freedom from interference, and *positive liberty*, 'the freedom which consists in being one's own master',[3] which he connects analytically with self-government. The potential conflict between the two which Berlin claims to find has been disputed, but his distinction reflects an obvious truth, namely, that there is a category difference between my *rights*, which prevent my being interfered with in specific areas, and my *opportunities*, including the widest opportunity of controlling my fate through self-government, which vary according to social context—even if the negative and positive forms of liberty constantly interact. Both must be considered in answering the question 'How free am I?'

The accounts of liberty given by liberal political theorists have changed over time, according to the source of threats to individual freedom. In the seventeenth century, freedom of religious belief was very important and dominated discussion. In the eighteenth, freedom from the arbitrary will of despots was crucial, and freedom was viewed in constitutional terms. In the next century, J. S. Mill argued for freedom from the tyranny of public opinion and the moral conventionalism of Victorian society, while in this century freedom for nations ('self-determination') and freedom *from* 'the system' have been among the demands. Positive freedom is even more dependent on context than negative freedom, for each social and technological innovation creates possibilities which people may then claim as rightful opportunities necessary to their self-fulfilment. A government which now restricted car ownership would be said to be curtailing people's positive freedom: a similar argument is used concerning the expensive medical equipment which could save lives but which the NHS has insufficient funds to make available, such as body scanners. In a progressive, stable society, then, positive liberty is cumulatively extended: a hundred years ago in Britain, primary education was the norm, now free higher education is (supposedly) available for all those suitably qualified. Whatever its spiritual drawbacks, affluence increases positive liberty in such ways.

Varieties of Freedom

Just as ideas of liberty depend on social context, the accounts of liberty elaborated within different ideologies vary considerably, as Part II has shown. These will now be briefly recapitulated. According to liberals, liberty is intimately connected with law. All are subordinate to laws to which they have freely consented, and so are equally free. As Locke said, 'freedom of men under government is to have a standing rule to live by, common to every one'. Locke's conception also had an economic dimension, for he emphasized man's natural right to appropriate property and to sell his labour; according to Macpherson's interpretation, such early liberal freedom was, effectively, the power to enter into contracts in a system of market relations. With regard to government, Locke said that men's lives are owed to God, and they are not free to enslave or kill themselves: therefore they cannot logically consent to arbitrary governments, which might do just that. His definition of the task of government as the preservation of natural rights emphasized the limited role of government and the extent of personal liberty in liberal society. Later, when the broad principles recommended by Locke had been constitutionally established in some countries, liberal theory focused on specific political liberties. Mill advocated freedom of thought, discussion, religion, and assembly against contemporary laws which threatened such rights. He also asserted that society had no right to force its moral views on the individual. His famous principle, that society is only entitled to interfere with the individual to protect its members from direct material harm, set a parameter for liberal thinking which is still observed. Mill also defined freedom in the positive sense as the freedom to develop as an autonomous individual through political self-determination and education, although Berlin argues that this may conflict with the non-interference principle. 'Both are ends in themselves. These ends may clash irreconcilably'.[4] Berlin is clearly right: each new government power which theoretically extends self-government may curtail individual liberty. Likewise, each new policy to improve the quality of life and the range of opportunities entails further interference. The right to education has been associated with compulsory education (even if for the best of reasons, as advanced by Mill): the right to social welfare benefits is accompanied by a duty for claimants to provide information about their private lives. This is a continuing problem for liberals, but most would prefer the exchange of some privacy and independence for security and opportunities to a return to the reign of market forces.

The socialist view of freedom has also been discussed: freedom is seen as self-realization through creative work and leisure, which need not entail a wide range of choice, if individuals are given opportunities suited to their talents and needs. The early socialists' criticism of 'bourgeois' political rights, that they were useless to the majority of the people who had no economic freedom, still holds good in the many third-world countries which maintain a veneer of democracy in conditions of acute poverty — India springs to mind. So economic freedom is basic for socialists. But many Western socialists insist that political freedoms such as Mill advocated are valuable, and should be retained alongside socialist welfare measures. The socialist conception of liberty rests on a more deterministic view of man than that of liberals, and outlaws the connection between choice and freedom: it does not entail that state power should be minimized, but does entail the abolition of economic exploitation, the outstanding obstacle to creative self-realization and material sufficiency.

There is another approach to freedom, which appeals to authoritarian thinkers of both right and left, the paradoxical conception of *freedom as obedience*. The doctrine that freedom is doing what you ought to do, or are told to do, is foreshadowed in Christian accounts of God, 'whose service is perfect freedom'. Rousseau is associated by his critics with this way of thinking because he defines freedom as obedience to the General Will. 'Each, while uniting himself with all, may still obey himself alone, and remain as free as before'.[5] Each individual in a society of n people submits to the wills of $(n - 1)$ individuals and in return has a fraction of power $(1/n)$ over the same number — although this is hardly the same as obeying only himself! The problem is glossed over by the idea of the General Will, which Rousseau defines as what each would really will if he could divest himself of his selfish interests. The deviant who is coerced into obeying the law is 'forced to be free', therefore. Freedom is also characterized as obedience to self-prescribed laws by Hegel, for whom the state's political power is the 'externalization' of the individual's will. The individual identifies with the state and thus reconciles outer submission with inner freedom.[6] Such 'mystical' views of freedom arouse the strong suspicion of liberals: although they share the formal assumption that freedom is obedience to self-prescribed laws, since freedom without law is inconceivable, liberals repudiate intangible entities such as the General Will, and describe the visible mechanics of freedom in terms of submission to the will of the majority, where everyone has previously agreed to majority rule. The doctrine of freedom as obedience is most often espoused by thinkers who believe that there can be certainty about what is right or who is to be obeyed. Rousseau defined the General Will as political truth, while Hegel saw the state as the realization of Spirit; the Christian view of obedience rests on similar certitude. The organic view of society leads to parallel conclusions: the whole is greater and wiser than the parts, which must subordinate themselves to it. But those who doubt the possibility of such certainties consider it dangerous to define freedom as the submission to absolutes. Liberals detect the doctrine of 'freedom as obedience' at work in left-wing societies, on Rousseau's model, and in right-wing states, influenced by the Hegelian view.

It could be said that the liberal conception of freedom is chiefly concerned with the individual's intellect and conscience, that of socialists, with his material wellbeing and that of 'authoritarians' with his soul. But in this century, developments in psychology have given rise to different conceptions of man and of freedom. The behaviourist psychologist Skinner has recently developed a critique of freedom based on determinism.[7] He argues that all living organisms are constantly acted on by the environment, including man. Behaviour patterns are established according to whether the (social) environment responds with positive (pleasurable) or negative (aversive) 'reinforcement' to their actions. Although he drew his conclusions from experiments on rats and pigeons, he applied the theory of reinforcement to man in society, arguing that the 'contingencies of reinforcement' are manipulated by controlling institutions like the state. In earlier times, the forms of control used were 'aversive and conspicuous'—coercion and brutal repression—and in response individuals developed 'countercontrol' devices. (Countercontrol is the self-defence mechanism by which an organism tries to reduce the control of the environment.) One such device was the doctrine of freedom. However, in modern society the controls employed are *inconspicuous* and *non-aversive*—persuasive ideology, inducement, and covert manipulation. The result is that men feel themselves, illusorily, to be free, in the absence of visible coercion. 'The feeling of freedom becomes an unreliable guide to action as soon as would-be controllers turn to nonaversive measures'. Skinner recommends that we abandon the notions of human autonomy, freedom, and dignity, since these are deceptive political ideals, given our status as determined organisms, and that we substitute another value, 'the survival of cultures'. The upshot of Skinner's analysis is that freedom is a chimera: men will always be controlled, and the most we can hope for is non-aversive, inconspicuous controls.

Skinner's method of generalizing from the laboratory to society, from animal to man, and his conclusions, have been strongly criticized,[18] but his arguments are in some ways revealing. He rightly shows that we do not use 'freedom' consistently but employ it to emphasize our likes and dislikes, depending on whether or not we perceive the controlling mechanisms. His analysis makes clear the difference between the subjective and objective aspects of freedom: we may feel ourselves to be free because the controls are hidden and yet, objectively, be unfree. But it is hard to accept the totally deterministic view of man, or to agree with the Darwinian ideal of the survival of cultures, which seems to brook no distinction between good or bad cultures. An unsolved problem in Skinner's analysis is that of who controls—or reinforces—the controllers, who are equally determined.

Fear of the 'hidden persuaders', implicit in Skinner's work, is typical of modern social thought, stemming from our sophisticated understanding of human psychology and from the new, subtle means of communication, persuasion and control which high technology generates. One consequence of these developments has been more subtle analyses of freedom. Marcuse's theory serves to illustrate these. He argues that toleration is a form of assimilation which produces 'threatening homogeneity'; by permitting protest within a given orthodoxy, the liberal establishment removes the capacity for protest. Following Freud, Marcuse analyses the repression of the sexual instinct, Eros, which Freud had seen as essential to the maintenance of civilization. Capitalism rests on the 'performance principle' (the opposite of the 'pleasure principle') which imposes delayed gratification, and transforms libidinal energy into productive labour. At least in the past, sublimated sexual energy could be diverted into protest, but in the permissive era, 'repressive de-sublimation' occurs, and sexual gratification can be achieved directly. What seems to be the substance of freedom is thus inimical to it, for the current state of permissiveness provides 'satisfaction in a way which generates submission and weakens the rationality of protest'. Also, by making men work longer than is necessary with automation, capitalism achieves the 'surplus repression' of men's energies, leaving them no leisure to act politically. The other threat to freedom identified by Marcuse is 'the closing of the universe of discourse', the manipulation of language by the media and the system to foreclose the possibility of radical thought and protest, and prevent people understanding their true alienation. Theoretical language is gradually ousted and people are obliged to express their grievances in a concrete, factual vocabulary: this makes complaints easier to remedy superficially, and masks the true social malaise. Marcuse is concerned about the all-embracing nature of tolerant, pluralist society, with its bribes of affluence which remove the will to attack the system as a whole. His recommended solution is *liberation from the system*, the destruction of repressive institutions and the achievement of private autonomy. Although Marcuse is usually considered a Marxist, his utopia of personal and sexual freedom is closer to the anarchist ideal.

The barrage of eclectic, often incompatible arguments which Marcuse directs against the system are highly contentious and take us far from the philosophical analysis of liberty, but they constitute an important warning. Freedom is not confined to the sphere of personal and civil rights, and today it is threatened from many quarters, especially by the economic system and by the control and manipulation of information. Yet contemporary liberal society is clearly not based on the extensive, direct repression of a police state. The diffuseness of the controlling devices makes it hard to argue that we are the victims of a conspiracy of rulers acting in their own interests. Marcuse, Illich, Galbraith, and other radical thinkers go beyond the crude conspiracy theories and allude to the complex, all-embracing, supra-individual *system* which pervades and dominates Western societies, despite their appearance of loosely-woven pluralism.

The system develops its own momentum towards expansion and self-perpetuation irrespective of the individuals operating it, who become subordinate to its goals. This is not beyond belief: Weber, writing on bureaucracy, analysed a similar phenomenon in the narrower context of administration. Whereas the terms 'liberty' and 'rights' suggest something institutionalized, permitted within the system, Marcuse's prescription for freedom, 'protest', 'the Great Refusal' and 'liberation', connote the rejection of the system itself.[9] How he thought this could be achieved remains obscure, but thanks to Marcuse the idea of liberation has become a key idea in radical thought: it connotes both the act of gaining freedom from hidden oppression *and* the subsequent experience of self-realization outside the system. Thus it is a wider and more evocative concept than that of rights, which are necessarily given *within* the system, and a more inspiring one in the age of disillusion.

Freedom and Illusion

Common to the modern critiques is the belief that we can be deluded about the extent of our freedom. Can I think that I am free, yet not be free? Marcuse and Skinner would say 'Yes', because people can be tricked by the possession of formal rights and the language of liberty into ignoring the multiplicity of devices, including ideology, which predetermine their choices and ways of thinking. Certainly, feeling free can be an illusion, though a pleasant one, and philosophers have often pondered the case of the 'happy slave' who believes himself to be free. Should he be disabused, and made wretched, so that he can struggle against his enslavement? Philosophers like Godwin think he should, so central to their idea of human life are the notions of freedom and rational knowledge. Marcuse's warning is, precisely, a re-statement of this view, intended to undeceive the happy slaves of capitalism, and it has evoked the hostility which the slaves might feel towards their 'benefactors'. A common response to those who seek to liberate the unwittingly oppressed is 'I *feel* free — so leave me alone.' Whether Marcuse's analysis of our illusion of freedom is accurate remains a matter for personal and, inevitably, ideological judgement. Of course, I may also believe that I am free because of the absence of apparent restrictions, and not realize that every 'free' choice that I make: (a) is causally determined by my personality and environment; and (b) restricts my future choices. Political theory cannot do much about this aspect of the human predicament, but recognition of it makes us aware that the idea of freedom as an absolute possession is an illusion. Policy may be directed towards minimizing the restraints on individuals and maximizing their opportunities, but it cannot make them free in themselves if they do not know how to utilize freedom. For this reason, some thinkers distinguish *latent* from *actual* freedom.

Freedom itself is not an illusory concept, but it embraces such a tangle of subjective and objective, personal and public elements that a search for a final definition is doomed. In the political sphere, latterly, freedom has been equated with particular liberties to act or think. In some countries these rights are enshrined in a constitution while in Britain they mainly exist in the spaces between the laws—which are shrinking. The possession of specific liberties cannot *make* us free, but they help us to exercise our freedom, and their absence would render us more susceptible to oppression. Such liberties operate as elaborations of the generally accepted principle of freedom in changing social circumstances. New rights are constantly demanded in the context of new exigencies. The freedom not to have one's telephone tapped, not to be brainwashed by subliminal advertizing, and a woman's right to choose whether to bear children, are all freedoms demanded or established as a result of technological or medical innovations. Although particular freedoms do not add to a free society, and they are often abrogated in emergencies, they do offer a rudimentary yardstick for measuring freedom: other criteria, such as the calibre and intellect of the people, which Mill proposed, are too vague.

The major debates about the nature of freedom have taken place within liberal thought, where it remains the highest political ideal. Liberty as an ideal is inseparable from an individualistic ethos: the concept of 'collective' freedom is different from, although parasitic upon, the idea of individual freedom. A people may have the right to self-determination, but this collective freedom could actually impose a rigid obligation on individuals to subordinate themselves to the whole. In liberal terms, a free society is one where each individual is equally free, and this is achieved by giving identical rights to all, although some may be materially unequal and, hence, less free despite these rights. Both liberals and anarchists emphasize that freedom for each is bound up with freedom for all, and would argue, for different reasons, that freedom entails equal freedom. Unfortunately, experience does not bear this out. I can often make myself freer at the expense of others; societies have existed with remarkably free rulers and oppressed masses. I think we cannot say that it is part of the meaning of 'freedom' that it should be equal for all, but it *is* a condition for justice that if some are free, all should be equally free: political freedoms and other rights must be equally distributed. So what seems to be an individualistic ideal has a social dimension.

Freedom as the individual's right to non-interference is a weapon directed both against the state and against his fellows. A vexed question is whether paternalistic intervention by the state or other individuals is ever permissible. Mill stated unequivocally that a government may not interfere to prevent someone harming himself: no compulsory cure for the alcoholic, no law against suicide. However, he admitted that 'self-regarding actions' which also harm others could be restrained. The habitually violent drunkard could be punished for drinking, and someone who 'through idleness' neglected to care for his family could be forced to carry out his obligations—though presumably he could not be made to work for his own good.[10] Since all our self-regarding actions may harm someone indirectly, if not directly, there must be an arbitrary cut-off point to limit state interference in such cases. This line is not drawn consistently in Britain today. Possession of dangerous drugs for personal use is a crime, not because the use of drugs is not self-regarding, but largely for paternalistic and moral reasons. In the case of self-regarding actions outside the scope of morality, the operative criterion seems to be whether they cause a nuisance to the state. When crash helmets were made compulsory for motor-cyclists, the major reason cited for state interference was the cost to the state of serious accidents or deaths, in terms of medical care and sickness benefit (for which the injured presumably paid their insurance contributions) and '*lost production*'. Mill would hardly have approved of such reasons. By contrast, the law legalizing private homosexual acts between consenting adults constituted an acknowledgement that such acts were purely self-regarding and not the state's concern. Although it is unlikely that any general principle restricting state action will be agreed upon, we can analyse—and oppose—interventionist legislation according to whether it is proposed for paternalistic reasons, for moral reasons, or to prevent harm to others: only the latter seems to justify interference in private actions.

The question about paternalism also arises when there are questions of long-term good. May a government, because it 'knows best' contravene the people's immediate, expressed preferences in order to promote their future good? Despite his repugnance for state interference, Mill thought it acceptable for education to be made compulsory on these grounds, and for 'advanced' countries to colonize 'savage' peoples in order to civilize them. Many government actions override people's short-term preferences to promote the general and long-term good—that is, there are inevitably both collectivist and paternalistic elements inimical to freedom in all government action, whether in embarking on a defence programme or in engineering short-term economic recessions for long-term prosperity, or in making people pay for a pension scheme. If this is not legitimate, then the case for government disappears altogether.[11] Philosophical accounts of liberty sometimes proceed as if all decisions and actions were simultaneous and all considerations short-lived, but politics is necessarily a long-term enterprise and necessarily involves some paternalistic actions. The best that people in a democracy can do to preserve their liberty against unwanted paternalistic incursions is to hold frequent elections and vocalize their discontent with such policies. The problem with the liberal idea of freedom is the sharp distinctions drawn between public and private, government and people (inappropriate in a truly representative democracy?) and the self and the 'other' (as if the individual could exist in society autonomously!). The realm of action is less clear-cut than these philosophical categories suggest, and all but the most trivial actions bring us into contact with others, or with the state, or society at large. An action innocent in one context is harmful in another. Since laws cannot cover all eventualities, the best way to guarantee personal freedom of action is the establishment of rights which the individual can invoke if the government or other individuals interfere unduly. The analysis of rights is thus a necessary part of any discussion of liberty.

The Rights of Man

The rights of man rest on the fundamental premise of the right to life, stated as the right not to be deprived of life by other men or governments, and as the right of those living to reasonable conditions for life. Traditional liberal accounts of rights rest on the idea of a pre-social state of nature and the myth of a social contract. Locke said that the task of government was the protection of man's natural rights to 'life, liberty and estate (property)', a view restated in the American *Declaration of Independence.* Paine's classic text, *The Rights of Man*, draws on this and on the claims of the French revolutionaries. He argues that government could only have arisen originally through a contract between men so that, theoretically, constitutions have priority over governments. Every civil right is a natural right exchanged. Equal rights attach to each individual by virtue of his existence. Discussing the French *Declaration of Rights*, Paine says that the first three points are fundamental:[12]

(1) Men are born and always continue free, and equal in respect of their rights. Civil distinctions, therefore, can be founded only on public utility.
(2) The end of all political associations is the preservation of the natural and impre-scriptible rights of man . . . liberty, property, security, and resistance of oppression.
(3) The Nation is essentially the source of all sovereignty; nor can any INDIVIDUAL, or ANY BODY OF MEN, be entitled to any authority which is not expressly derived from it.

All other rights proceed from these, including political liberty, the limitation of law, the minimization of government, freedom of speech, justice in taxation and everyone's right to choose their government.

Natural rights theory rested on the hypothesis of a pre-social code of natural law, and was widely challenged in the eighteenth century. The critics of natural rights theory came from all parts of the political spectrum. Burke maintained that such absolute and inviolable rights were impossible in society, which is organic, evolving, and hierarchical. Only the rights prescribed by custom could be admitted. Bentham attacked natural rights both as a legal positivist and as a utilitarian. Such rights were 'nonsense upon stilts' and 'anarchical fallacies' — metaphysical entities which threatened to supplant the authority of law. Nothing not established in positive law could claim to have a higher status than the law itself: the only real rights were positive, *legal* rights, established after the creation of the social and legal systems. Such rights could therefore not be natural. Utilitarianism also could not accede to the existence of such rights as absolutes or ends in themselves, lest they should claim priority over the supreme principle of utility. Mill later modified utilitarian theory to admit the existence of rights and reconcile them with utility. A further widespread criticism of natural rights was that they paradoxically impute a quasi-legal system to the supposed state of nature, since rights themselves are a legal concept.

Marx attacked the *Declaration* 'of the so-called rights of man' on the ground of its bourgeois content.

None of the supposed rights of man . . . go beyond the egoistic man . . . an individual separated from the community . . . wholly preoccupied with his private interest.[13]

He argued that the bourgeois state abolished inequalities of wealth, class, and birth 'in its own manner' — deceptively — by giving each man the vote, an abstract right, while outside this narrow political sphere inequalities abounded. As to the *Declaration*, *liberty* separates man from man, making him an 'isolated monad', limiting his responsibility to his fellows. *Property* is 'the right of selfishness', *equality* is man's right to be treated, without discrimination, as a self-sufficient monad, while *security* 'guarantees egoism'. Bourgeois man has in theory no communal existence or duties as a citizen: these rights all facilitate his 'withdrawal' from society, allowing him to exploit his fellows without guilt. Most dangerously, these political rights establish an ilusion of equality amidst genuine inequality and oppression, just as democracy disguises the repressive and partisan nature of the state. Hence the irony of the liberal claim that government's task is to preserve rights: the state abrogates them by its very nature. Human rights are therefore part of the ruling ideology, part of universal false consciousness. Although the French Revolution had produced the *Declaration*, it was drawn up by members of the bourgeoisie, the ultimate beneficiaries of that revolution. While there is some truth in Marx's view that political rights create a formal, illusory equality which disguises the true state of society, this is not a sufficient reason for trying to abolish those rights so that the state can be seen as the source of oppression. But some revolutionary strategists advocate tactics to provoke repressive state action and the rescinding of rights, to hasten the cataclysm. However, many Western Marxists accept such rights as instrumentally useful in the pursuit of their goals, and would defend them, with the qualification that they do not constitute *real* equality or freedom.

Human Rights

In the present century, as the conception of rights based on natural law and social contract was no longer tenable, 'natural rights' gave way to 'human rights', which are said to attach to every being by virtue of his or her humanity and right to dignity, independence, and equality of respect. Such assertions are justified by Kantian forms of mortality which enjoin equal respect for all men as an absolute. Like the idea of liberty, that of rights evolves according to contemporary events and exigencies. Among the root causes of the First World War were nationalism and the problem of national minorities in large states. After that war, countries joining the League of Nations, whose territory or population had been changed by the war, were obliged to sign treaties or declarations protecting their minorities with respect to freedom of religion, the use of their own languages, the right to education, and similar matters. These provisions particularly affected the countries of Eastern Europe and the Balkans. Contraventions could be brought to the League, although this procedure and the guarantees were not very successful. The principle of self-determination of nations, which dictated no interference in nation's internal affairs, was also accepted — a collective equivalent of the individual's right to non-interference. But the Second World War proved how poor a protection against powerful predators were national and individual rights, and how impotent was the League to enforce them.

Nevertheless, a further attempt was made to get worldwide acknowledge-ment of man's dignity and rights under the aegis of the United Nations in the 1948 *Universal Declaration of Human Rights.* This reasserted the now familiar rights and some new ones — the right to life, liberty, property, equality before the law, privacy, fair trial, religious freedom, free speech and assembly, to participate in government, to political asylum, and the absolute right not to be tortured. Also, largely at the insistence of the Soviet bloc, various economic and social rights were included: the right to education, to work, to equal pay, to an adequate standard of living, and paid holidays. Western negotiators regarded these as qualitatively different from the other rights, being *ideals* rather than moral claims. This ideological division of opinion reflected the distance between the liberal and the communist view of liberty. In practice, communist states tend to ignore many of the first set of rights but guarantee social and economic rights, while capitalist countries do the reverse. This raises the question whether the *Universal Declaration* has any significant moral or legal status in the signatory countries. Some countries wished it to be incorporated in the positive law of each nation and so be enforceable in the normal way, but the USSR and other countries opposed this, and doubtless few states would have been willing to accept the wide responsibilities which incorporation implied. It was also asked whether the *Declaration* might not be given the status of international law, but this was problematic as the latter deals with nations, not individuals. At present, the European Court of Human Rights may hear individual cases, but its judgements are not legally binding on governments. Likewise, the recent Helsinki agreement on rights is only enforceable 'morally' (a contradiction in terms), by states bringing pressure on each other to observe it — mainly, pressure from the West on the USSR.

These brief details of the recent history of human rights serve as a background to consideration of the questions raised by philosophers about such rights, such as 'Who should count as human?', 'What are the *basic* human rights?' and 'What is the status of such rights?' Human rights derive from our nature as human beings, so their content depends on our definition of humanity. Because man is corporeal, he has a right to life, freedom from pain and torture, and to sustenance. Because he is rational and thinking, he has the right to freedom of thought and conscience, and so on. As Cranston observes, such rights can only be minimal because they are generalized so as to apply to all.[14] The point of this universality is, of course, to prevent victimization of supposedly inferior races or individuals. But it has recently been asked whether the restriction of rights to the human race is not human chauvinism. Animals too have bodily needs and feel pain (and, for all we know, think in some way) and so could be said to deserve the same treatment as human beings in many respects. An increasing number of philosophers have advanced the case for animal rights, partly as a protest against the experimental use of animals, partly as a philosophical demonstration that we cannot complacently draw such a clear line between ourselves and other species.[15] It has also been argued (seriously) that sophisticated computers fulfil the criteria for thinking beings, and may have certain rights. These examples are often contested because the notion of human rights seems to rest on an intuitive recognition of others as, approximately, our equals, a condition not fulfilled in such cases, but there is a good case for arguing that some of the rights which men attribute to themselves should be accorded to all living things. Science fiction often speculates on how we would treat intelligent beings landing here from elsewhere in space, but the more interesting question with regard to rights and morality is how they, the superior form of life, would treat us . . . .

In principle, a catalogue of human rights should not be too long, nor determined by a particular cultural outlook, for human rights specify the minimum conditions for human dignity and a tolerable life anywhere, at any time. However, as the length of the Declarations grows, they contain more and more political rights, most of which reflect liberal-democratic ideology. It could be argued that these are really *civil* rights established in certain societies but not sharing the universal qualities of human rights and not obligatory for all societies. Alternatively, the very idea of a decent human life may include the right to participate in choosing a government and so to control one's destiny. If this is so, human rights do not stop at the satisfaction of man's corporeal and intellectual needs, but are a seamless web, covering the political, social, and economic life of man. It is hard to choose between these arguments: the liberal desire to fuse political and human rights suggests an element of moral imperialism, but the acknowledgement implicit in this of man's political nature is an important assertion. Precisely the same may be said of the economic and social rights added to the *Declaration* on the insistence of the USSR. If all the points of the *Declaration* were realized in one country, utopia would be achieved.

The question of the *status* of human rights is closely linked with that of their enforceability. Such rights are not established in law in many countries, so they cannot be regarded as legal entities or 'possessions' in a legal sense. Human rights are, essentially, *moral claims* to certain kinds of treatment for all human beings, and such claims are only enforceable through conscience, unless they are made law. The issue is obscured because rights are sometimes spoken of as if they were *facts*, to give them greater rhetorical force: 'men are free and equal'. They are presented as analytical truths about human nature for the same reason: man, defined as a free being, necessarily has the right to be free. The philosophical status of human rights is sometimes likened to the status which Kant gave to moral propositions: they are 'synthetic *a priori*' statements. That is, they have an *a priori*, absolute application to all human beings because they derive from the definition of a human being but, paradoxically, they are also 'synthetic' because they refer to the contingent, real world and are not mere tautologies about man. Whatever their precise analytical status, which is controversial, statements about rights are normative and prescriptive and empirically unverifiable, hence Bentham's dismissal of them as nonsense, and the suspicion of their status among logical positivists who regard moral and other unverifiable statements as being outside the realm of fact, mere statements of preference.

Rights, then, are essentially part of morality, but are often referred to in quasi-legal terms, to make them seem more authoritative. Plamenatz defined them as follows:

a right is a power in the exercise of which all rational beings ought to protect a creature, either because its exercise by him is itself good or else because it is a means to what is good.[16]

He later added that someone has a right when no-one ought to prevent him from doing something, or refuse him some service that he needs. His definition, quite properly, links rights to a notion of *human good*; it also brings into prominence the obvious truth that every individual right also creates a duty for other individuals and/or for the state. My rights impose an obligation on everyone else to respect them, and vice versa. There can be no objection to this limitation of freedom as long as rights are acknowledged to be equal and universal. The interplay of reciprocal rights and duties is the basis of most moralities although some moral codes said to emanate from higher sources, such as the Ten Commandments, seem to create only duties: how could man claim rights from God? According to Plamenatz, a right may even justify demanding a service from someone else. If we claim human rights for ourselves, then, we are logically bound to accept our duty to observe similar rights for others, without considering this an infringement of our personal freedom. Only the solipsist could want a world in which he had rights but no reciprocal duties.

Philosophers argue that moral injunctions must observe the axiom that '"ought" implies "can"': that is, I cannot be morally required to do something that I am unable to do. Similarly, rights should not, they say, impose duties which are beyond individuals or states in practical terms. Some would argue on these grounds that the economic and social rights advocated by communist countries are illegitimate or vacuous since the preconditions for realizing the right to work, or the right to an adequate standard of living simply do not exist in many countries. The answer is that rights differ from moral imperatives in the following respect: when we say that the unemployed in an impoverished country have the 'right' to a living wage, we are stating a political recommendation, not an imperative but an ideal, in the form of a right. Like other rights claims, this refers implicitly to an idea of the Good Life. However, because such ideals are conditioned by ideology, rights claims of this kind are often highly controversial and open to dispute by the states against whom they are asserted.

Can a hierarchy of rights be identified, showing that certain rights are more basic and less ideological than others, and therefore merit universal application? Hart's argument that the fundamental right is the equal right to be free might be used as the basis of such a hierarchy. But this vague, liberal formula would need to be translated into more concrete terms before it could form the basis of a code of rights, and the translation would be controversial. The rights which Amnesty demands—the right to a fair trial, the right not to be inhumanely treated or executed—seem to be the most basic rights pertaining to social life, although even these reflect certain recent cultural and moral developments and so might not properly be called basic and universal. *If* we could clearly distinguish basic, universal rights from secondary rights (defined as 'ideological' or 'cultural' rights) it would follow that countries could require each other to observe the basic rights but should not interfere in the matter of secondary rights which are culture-specific, a matter of choice. But this distinction, which is hard to make philosophically (some of our most basic rights would have been disputed by slave-owning societies), would probably be rejected in any case by countries eager to export their own values. The West habitually tries to make communist countries implement the rights which are probably cultural, but which liberal ideology holds to be universal, rights of free speech and protest. And with the revival of 'revolutionary' orthodox Islam in many Middle Eastern countries, Westerners have been quick to pass judgement not only on the revival of traditional punishments such as death by stoning (which contravenes the 'basic' injunction against cruel punishments) but also on the treatment of women. The Islamic countries say that this is an internal matter bound up with religion, morality, and culture, while we consider it a violation of a basic, universal right, the right of women to be treated with dignity, as free beings, and to have the same rights as men. In short, even if the worst evils such as torture and coercion could be eradicated by the enforcement of basic rights worldwide, while such cultural differences persisted disputes about what other rights should be observed would continue, with countries taking a missionary stance in favour of the rights favoured by their ideology and culture.

Some right-wing thinkers are given to speaking of rights as 'privileges'. Since rights are a major defensive weapon against autocratic governments and the hypertrophy of states, it is important to refute this conception, which deprives rights of their political force. The connotations of 'privilege' are as follows: first, that it is something which a limited number of people have, second, that it can be taken away, third, that it is given from above and fourth, that it is somehow earned or deserved. By contrast, human rights first of all attach equally to all human beings. Second, rights cannot be 'taken away':

even when they are contravened, they remain valid moral claims. Third, such rights are, in principle, given by the people to themselves, democratically. Fourth, such rights are not earned because they are *a priori* rights—even if elitist governments have sometimes extended legal rights to the people as a reward for 'good behaviour'. If we say that Westerners are 'privileged' to have so many rights, it is far from an assertion that we wish to guard these privileges from the people of other countries. Rights, unlike privileges, are not scarce goods, since they can be created easily and often costlessly, so that the element of competition implied in the term 'privilege' is not present in rights. Nor should we feel *beholden* to a state which allows us extensive rights, for the reasons just mentioned. In fact, the language of rights and their function in political practice both necessitate that they should always be asserted as *rights*, not petitioned for as privileges given from above, which might be rescinded. This sometimes involves the anomaly of asserting as facts what we really know to be moral claims, or ideological preferences, but this tactical rhetoric is necessary in the endeavour of individuals to extract humane treatment from states.

Special Rights for Women?

Before leaving the topic of rights, I shall discuss briefly the question of women's rights, both because of its current importance and as a way of considering generally the status of the special rights claimed by particular groups or minorities on the basis of their own special characteristics. Claims for women's rights, black rights, gay rights, and rights for the disabled have all been heard recently. Because human rights belong to all individuals by reason of their humanity, there are no grounds for denying them to people placed in a particular category by certain, 'permanent' characteristics such as race, sex or handicap. Nevertheless, in the past women were denied the political and property rights considered basic in liberal society because they were considered unequal, being supposedly inferior to men in terms of intelligence and judgement. (Suffragettes pointed out that this bracketed them with criminals and lunatics.) The case for equal civil rights rested, naturally, on the contention that women were equal to men in all relevant respects. I speak of 'civil rights' here because, although some civil rights such as the right to property were counted as *basic* human rights by liberals, they were simultaneously—and inconsistently—viewed as resting on certain criteria, which women did not fulfil. The extension of such rights to women was an admission of their equality in all relevant respects. Undoubtedly, the achievement of 'bourgeois' rights by women was crucially important, although some feminists now denigrate it because such rights did not alter other fundamental inequalities.

However, the terrain of the debate on women's rights has now shifted. A group of individuals with full human and civil rights may nevertheless consider that its members have special characteristics which entitle them to additional, special rights. The Women's Movement now concerns itself with such needs. Opponents of the movement criticize this as a search for what they consider special privileges, since women now have equal basic rights in most Western countries. But the claim to special rights because of special needs or disadvantages should not be viewed as a demand for privileges. Rather, it is a demand for compensating measures to overcome these disadvantages and bring the members of the group up to full equality with other people. Thus, a woman's right to maternity leave, which some men regard as an unwarranted privilege, is intended to put her in the same position as men with regard to security of employment. The childbearing capacity gives women special needs. It may also be that women's lesser physical strength is a reason for giving them special rights: perhaps, to protect themselves against sexual and other attacks, women should be permitted to carry defensive weapons (which, if carried by men, might be termed 'offensive') which allowed them to feel as free to go about the streets as men do. In fact, this special need is not acnowledged, and women in Britain and the USA have been prosecuted for carrying such 'weapons' of self-defence as pepper-pots and dye-sprays. But such a right is not an unreasonable demand in view of women's vulnerability to attack. Special rights, then, are not privileges, but rights which ensure that all members of the community can enjoy their basic rights fully and equally. Special rights are the elaboration of the spirit of human rights in special circumstances.

Nobody disputes the rights of the disabled to disability allowances and other special treatment according to their manifest needs. But the criteria for special rights are widely disputed in the case of women and various other minority groups, even when their distinguishing characteristics are just as permanent as those of handicap. 'Special rights for blue-eyed brunettes, next?' is the *reductio ad absurdam* of special rights: but this objection is invalid, for special rights are not the thin end of the wedge. The kinds of characteristics and the needs and disabilities which make special rights appropriate are, by and large, intuitively obvious to any reasonable person, even if there is disagreement on the degree of compensation which they warrant. Special rights are justifiable on the grounds that they are necessary for the enjoyment of basic rights for a certain group, and that without the compensation which they provide human equality would be meaningless.

More contentious than special rights is 'positive discrimination', which Americans call 'affirmative action': the giving of 'privileges' to certain groups to correct their particular disadvantages *or* to compensate for unfair discrimination against them in the past. While special rights are also a form of compensation, we could attempt to draw a line—with difficulty—between bringing people up to the same level as others, and giving them unfair advantages. It may seem acceptable that a firm should make creche facilities available to encourage working mothers to apply for jobs there, whereas many people would find it unacceptable if the firm earmarked a percentage of jobs for women and turned away better qualified male candidates. In this case, men might fairly claim that the quota system detracted from their chances of getting a job, and hence contravened their rights. To this objection, it could be replied that, given the greater difficulty experienced by women in finding jobs because of various prejudices, the quota was justified for egalitarian reasons. The firm might, alternatively, claim that the quota system is positive discrimination to rectify historical injustices experienced by women in the past. (Some US universities reserve places for blacks partly on these grounds.) Needless to say, the generation of past women who have been treated unjustly can never be compensated and, as we have seen in other examples, the principle of correcting past injustices leads to both conceptual and practical problems, and is best avoided. It could be said that the first measure (creches) established equality of opportunity to compete for jobs while the second (the quota) established a more substantive equality of treatment. Liberals object to this because it undermines competition and equal opportunity. The disagreement is ultimately ideological: what does equality mean? Given the hostility to positive discrimination in liberal society, it is only likely to be considered in cases of long-term grave injustice, perhaps as a temporary measure or a gesture of goodwill, in the expectation that in the long run women will get positions on their own merits, when prejudices against appointing them are broken down. But the antagonism created by such measures may sometimes outweigh their benefits (as we see even with the legislation prohibiting racial discrimination in employment). In most cases, the righting of historical injustices across generations is best not attempted — justice and equal rights for the living is the best that can be hoped for in an imperfect world.

The arguments valid for women can be extended to all groups who are genuinely disadvantaged by some generally agreed criterion. The principle which should direct policy in a just society is that basic human rights (although, as we saw, this concept involves problems) should be given to all, special rights should be allocated to those with special needs and temporary, 'extra' rights may be given in the form of positive discrimination in exceptional situations.

Rights and Liberty

A final question is whether rights are, or should be, inviolable. It would be nice if they were. But nearly all rights theorists agree that 'reasons of state' and emergencies take priority over right. Habeas Corpus, the most fundamental individual right in the British legal system, has regularly been suspended in wartime and other emergencies — most recently in Ulster to facilitate the internment of republican supporters (1971). The UN Declaration conceded that some rights are subject to limitations prescribed by law which are 'necessary to protect public safety, order, health, or morals, or the fundamental rights and freedom of others'. Even Bills of Rights can be amended. The usual justification for the abrogation of rights is that the state is acting for the immediate or long-term good of the community. The validity of such claims, especially claims citing the 'national interest' in peace time, is often hard to establish, or dubious. Of course, cases are conceivable where some individuals' rights must give way in the interests of justice for others — for example, the limitation of property rights to ensure a fairer distribution — but in such cases the good envisaged is more demonstrable than in cases where 'reasons of state' are cited. The legal philosopher Dworkin argues for the inviolability of rights,[17] but even if all rights were established in positive law, they would be no more inviolable than the law itself. But as moral claims are in principle inviolable, so the violation of rights must always form the basis for a serious moral and political challenge to any state.

Rights are the guarantors of liberty, specific freedoms which, when legally enforced, institutionalize humane morality and tolerance. The language of rights also has an international dimension which legal principles do not, and can be used to propagate humanitarian ideals beyond national boundaries. Rights establish a minimum degree of liberty in society, although personal liberty extends beyond formal rights, of course. Because of these advantages, it is often asked whether Britain should follow other countries in having a Bill of Rights. Given that all laws, including constitutional laws, can be repealed, this could not guarantee absolutely the security of such rights. Nor, *in extremis*, would it prevent a government from contravening those laws. But the purpose of a Bill of Rights is to give governments pause when they are tempted to take coercive measures, and also to ensure automatically that new legislation does not contravene established rights. In both respects a Bill of Rights would be an improvement on our present position, notwithstanding the arguments of those who think that our unwritten constitution is the acme of perfection.

In order to assess the degree of freedom in society, we should consider the following factors:

(1) The negative and positive liberties generally available to citizens, and the balance between them.
(2) The extensiveness and intrusiveness, actual and potential, of the laws. (In Britain, laws against obstruction and conspiracy can be extended almost *ad hoc* to cover nearly any behaviour, so the wording of the statute book is not the only relevant factor: implementation must also be examined.)
(3) The role which the people play in promulgating laws; that is, the extent to which the laws are based on democratic consent, and the responsiveness of the government to the people's wishes.
(4) The existence of specific legal rights, such as those listed in Bills of Rights, which represent semi-immovable bulwarks of liberty for the people against the state.
(5) The degree to which the people *feel* free, and understand and discuss freedom, and defend it when under attack. Though feelings of freedom can be illusory, such feelings in conjunction with real freedoms are an

important part of the subjective and objective components which together constitute freedom in society.

The sections which follow on tolerance, protest, and revolution take up the question of the individual's and the people's rights to act in specifically political contexts against the state and the laws.

The Climate of Tolerance

To tolerate is to endure something of which one disapproves, *voluntarily*, that is, when one has the power to change it. A paradigm case is that of a democracy where the majority tolerates irritating, maybe offensive, behaviour by a minority, which it could easily outlaw, in the interests of social harmony. Also, of course, tolerance is exercised in interpersonal and non-political situations. Society may adopt tolerance as a *value* for several reasons. First, because in particular cases tolerance is less objectionable than the alternatives: we tolerate political extremists because we are not willing to condone their persecution, or the suppression of a political viewpoint.[18] Second, tolerance is a necessary consequence of any morality which enjoins us not to use human beings as means to our ends. If I seek to prohibit someone's behaviour merely because it offends me, I am treating him instrumentally, ignoring his right to equality of respect, whereas if his behaviour violates my rights I am justified in putting an end to it. Third, we may tolerate those who hold and express different beliefs and ideas as a consequence of being unsure that our own beliefs or knowledge are infallibly true.

The doctrine of toleration first developed with respect to religion and was later applied to political belief. Religious toleration may be based on the view that no sect has a monopoly of truth, since there is no known method for proving one particular conception of God to be right, therefore all must be tolerated. It may also be practised for the reason already mentioned, that one morally objects to the forcible conversion or punishment of heretics, even though one hates heresy: tolerance is then accepted as the lesser evil, not as a principle in its own right. Political tolerance rests on the similar view that there can be no conclusive proof or disproof of the truth of political ideas. Since values and ideologies are unverifiable, we cannot choose between them officially, although we may espouse them personally. Political tolerance could also be asserted on the egalitarian basis that, if all men are assumed to be of equal worth and dignity, their opinions are also of equal worth, and must not be suppressed: liberalism admits this in assuming each man to be an authority on his own interests. Evidently, tolerance is a political ideal well suited to liberal ideology and the pluralist form of society which fosters a variety of beliefs and values. On the other hand, a totalitarian state, committed to certain political *truths*, would be inconsistent if it tolerated rival doctrines, since these would necessarily be false. Tolerance is therefore usually found in conjunction with liberal democracy, pluralism, and an empiricist theory of knowledge, which concedes that we can never establish truths conclusively, and must admit an element of doubt.[19]

Tolerance in politics is mainly linked with freedom of thought and expression, but in social life the toleration of *behaviour* is also important. Directly harmful behaviour is prohibited by law — which can be said to tolerate everything which it does not prohibit — but some actions which people find offensive are permitted by law, such as 'deviant' sexual behaviour. Mill argued passionately that people should not inflict their moral beliefs on others by legal means, or seek to prevent them from acting 'immorally', since being morally offended does not constitute material harm. In practice, the law has often come down on the side of 'public decency' (the side of the morally offended), especially in sexual matters, despite the fact that passers-by can avert their eyes from the windows of sex-shops or other unseemly sights, so that moral offence is often a self-inflicted injury.

Cases of moral and political intolerance are often parallel because both rest partly on outrage, partly on a paternalistic impulse. In a democracy which tolerates all ideologies in theory, political groups are sometimes banned or denied free expression because their doctrines are inimical to democracy. When this is justified on the grounds that they might convert the foolish and so threaten the democratic system, the reasoning is paternalistic, like that behind banning pornography in case it corrupts the unwary, or 'public morals'. Political intolerance for such a reason is clearly anomalous in democratic systems, which assume political acumen and rationality on the part of their citizens. An alternative justification for banning such groups is that their own ideologies would, in practice, abolish tolerance: by being intolerant themselves, they forfeit the right to tolerance. This be-done-by-as-you-would-do reasoning is supported by more sophisticated moral theories about the necessary universalizability and reciprocity of moral principles. But to decide when to apply the principle that the intolerant must not be tolerated involves making judgements about people's beliefs, which may be mistaken. Should Marxists be refused academic jobs, which allow them to propagate their ideas, because such ideas, if realized, might — it is not certain — be intolerant? The virtue of tolerance is, precisely, that it saves us from having to make such judgements. The application of 'reciprocal logic' against the intolerant produces a discriminatory situation in which some people's rights and views are suppressed, and this cannot easily be squared with the liberal support of individual rights, however much poetic justice there may be in it. For this reason, most liberals would probably advocate that we *should* tolerate the intolerant unless they attempt to put their views into practice and threaten the freedom of others.

A different justification for banning certain ideas or ideologies is that they are *harmful*, though not necessarily intolerant or antithetical to democracy. We might decide that ideologies claiming that women, blacks, Jews or other groups were inferior were directly or indirectly harmful to those groups and should be suppressed. The 1965 and 1976 Race Relations Acts banned 'threatening or insulting words' intended to 'stir up hatred' against any race on the grounds that such words were likely to cause material harm to individuals or social disturbance. In this case, priorities are reversed: tolerance is suspended because its consequences would predictably be worse than those of intolerance. A problem here is that predictions of harm are uncertain: also, that people differ over what counts as harmful. (Some people wished to ban a recent book on the cultivation of cannabis because it was 'harmful'.) Many champions of the freedom of speech have in fact complained about the restriction of rights by the Race Relations Acts, but this is surely a paradigm case of restricting some people's rights to preserve even more important rights for others. Different reasons for intolerance or censorship will usually be given according to one's ideology. A right-wing thinker might give the paternalistic justification, while liberals are more likely to choose the second or third reason.

Tolerance as a political doctrine is an important part of liberal thought but in any but the most stable and consensual situation it presents liberal-democratic society with dilemmas which are theoretically insoluble, there being no *right* answer to questions such as 'Should we tolerate the intolerant?'. Perhaps the theoretical solution lies in treating tolerance strictly as a subordinate and instrumental value, in contrast to those liberals who view it as good in itself and therefore find themselves with clashes of ideals. On the instrumental view, tolerance would have to give way when primary values such as social justice were at risk—although no doubt tolerance is, normally, conducive to justice—and where individuals' lives were threatened.

The diverse practical solutions attempted often result in the erosion of tolerance. The British way has normally been to tolerate the *existence* of political parties hostile to the system—except, because its aims are 'treasonable', the IRA—but to deny them the facilities for assemblies and demonstrations, by means of the local authorities or the police, when material harm is feared. Rumour also has it that life is, informally, made difficult for members of such groups. This compromise vitiates our ideal of tolerance and gives those concerned a rightful grievance: it would be preferable if the grounds for *not* tolerating groups or doctrines were made clear, then applied consistently.

The fragility of the ideal is not a good reason for abandoning it, but rather one for strengthening our understanding of what it entails. The enforcement of human rights is partly an enforcement of tolerance—the tolerance of some for others' non-conformist actions within certain limits, or tolerance by the state of such actions. As was said earlier, tolerance is in principle *voluntary* forbearance, but there are instances of enlightened (and paternalistic) parliaments causing people to become tolerant by means of legislation: liberalizing the laws on homosexuality has surely had that effect. Tolerance is not, alas, instinctive, but it rests on attitudes, and these may be altered by means of law, sometimes. It is, despite the problems discussed here, an important instrument in maintaining liberal-democratic society and freedoms.

The more tolerant a society which contains diverse opinions and cultures, the fewer the grounds for protest. And, presumably, the more leeway protestors have for voicing their grievances, the more moderate will be the forms of protest which they choose. A tolerant society, then, is committed to tolerate forms of protest not prohibited by law and those established as rights. But is such a society bound to be tolerant towards illegal forms of protest? This will be debated in the following sections.

The Right to Protest

The question at issue is to what extent the individual in a democratic society may rightly protest against laws and policies with which he disagrees. May he embark, as an individual, or as a member of a minority group, on acts of civil disobedience ('direct action') to change such laws, to which he has, in theory, consented, or should he wait to express such protest in the next election, since these laws are, again in theory, the expressed will of the majority? In liberal-democratic societies, the awareness that majoritarianism is an imperfect system and that discontented minorities do exist, has created a fairly lenient attitude to protestors, who are not treated as common criminals when they break the law. Political theory has an important contribution to make in the establishment of the right to protest, since it can define the limits of permissible direct action.

Civil disobedience may be defined as a principled, purposeful, and public disobedience of the law: *principled*, because it does not result in selfish gain (looting shops is not an acceptable form of protest), *purposeful*, because it is undertaken in order to change particular laws or policies (but not the system in general), and *public* because publicity for the cause is the aim of protestors, and clandestine action cannot achieve this. Fourthly, the protestor must accept the *punishment*, if any, for his lawbreaking. Clandestine law-breaking for selfish ends can only be viewed as criminal, while direct action aimed at overthrowing the system (discussed later) must be classified as revolutionary, and its perpetrators usually try to avoid punishment. Protest which takes institutionalized forms—peaceful demonstrations, lobbying MPs—does not enter this discussion as individuals have an established right to take these forms of 'indirect' action.

Civil disobedience can either take the form of breaking the law being challenged—refusal to fill in census forms by those who object to censuses, for example—or breaking unrelated laws to gain publicity for the protest—occupations actually infringe trespass laws, but call attention to other grievances. So comprehensive is our network of laws that most protestors find no difficulty in infringing them, even unintentionally. Civil disobedience need not cause a public nuisance, but the greater the nuisance, the greater the publicity. At present, I shall consider cases where no-one is harmed by the protest, and only legal or state supremacy is slighted.

Civil disobedience occurs for moral or political reasons. *Moral protest* results when a citizen's moral and political values come into conflict and he gives a higher priority to his moral beliefs. The pacifist who prefers prison to fighting does this. Moral protest is usually an individual activity, often undertaken without missionary intent, even if many individuals protest simultaneously in the same way. (If pacifists united to persuade others not to fight they would doubtless be tried for a treasonable conspiracy.) *Political protest* is usually concerted action, sometimes undertaken because a particular law or policy is seen as unjust, sometimes because the government's decisions are disputed. If such protestors are not to be regarded as common criminals, under a normal application of the law, their position needs explicating theoretically. How protest is regarded depends very much on how the citizen's political obligation is conceived.

Hobbes's view of obligation as unconditional leaves no room for the right to protest. But Locke argued that 'the people' had the right to resist a regime if its measures threatened them, contravening the rights which it was appointed to protect. Locke's theory deals with the 'dissolution' of governments and gives little guidance about resistance to particular laws. In the nineteenth century the American, Thoreau, argued that where unjust laws exist men should not wait to persuade the majority to alter them, but should disobey them individually. He was himself imprisoned for non-payment of taxes which he withheld because he disapproved of the Mexican war.[20] In such cases, *right* action is revolutionary, he said. While democracy has merely increased 'true respect' for the individual, civilization will finally acknowledge him as a 'higher and independent power'. Thoreau's argument for disobedience was thus primarily moral.

Probably the most important justification of the right to disobey is that of Mahatma Gandhi. Although he was seeking to oust the British from India, his theory of *Satyagraha*, 'holding on to truth', can also justify more limited protest in democratic countries. Satyagraha enjoins us to disobey evil laws, as a moral duty, 'hence Satyagraha largely appears to the public as Civil Disobedience or Civil Resistance'. Gandhi offered a political as well as a moral justification for protest.

I wish I could persuade everybody that civil disobedience is the inherent right of every citizen. He does not give it up without ceasing to be a man.[21]

Gandhi, once a prosperous lawyer, pointed out that resisters are 'the real constitutionalists' for, in disobeying and accepting punishment they are, in a sense, *obeying* the law. He recommended that resistance should be active, since passive protest appeared as a sign of weakness, civil not criminal, 'sincere, respectful, restrained, never defiant', overt, and that it should be undertaken by otherwise law-abiding citizens. The resistance movement which he led in India followed these precepts and was finally rewarded by national independence. But for Gandhi, the right to resist did not end there: he defined self-government as a state where the whole population had gained the capacity to resist a government abusing its powers. Gandhi's theory, then, asserts that injustice always justifies resistance, so that political protest is fundamentally moral, and can take place equally in a non-democratic or democratic state.

A more recent book by Walzer[22] contends that the right to resist is inherent in the pluralistic nature of democratic society. Society consists of 'primary institutions', in particular, the state, and 'secondary institutions' such as the Church, trade unions, and political parties, of which membership is voluntary, unlike membership of the state. Because we opt into these, our commitment is greater than that to the state. Our adherence to the secondary institutions may clash with duty to the state, laying on us an *obligation to disobey*. If a revolutionary party wishes to supplant the state, its members are, because of their voluntary commitment, 'obliged' to support the revolution. Walzer has thus turned consent, on which democratic government is said to rest, against the state by showing that in pluralist democracy our consent and commitment to other institutions is stronger and more active, and justifies disobedience. It is doubtful if any state would accept Walzer's theory, but he provides a respectable justification for the use of protestors. He also argues that in a democratic society, citizens have the right to protest against injurious, anti-democratic institutions *with all necessary force*, and justifies a notorious strike against General Motors on these terms, the latter being an anomalously authoritarian organization within a democracy.

The most famous argument *against* civil disobedience is that attributed by Plato to Socrates in the *Crito*. Socrates, unjustly convicted, and awaiting execution, argued that if he were to escape it would harm the laws the constitution of Athens; also, that one incurs a debt of gratitude for being nurtured and protected by one's country so that violence against it is a sin. Furthermore, the citizen who does not leave his country thereby makes an undertaking to observe the laws. A disobedient individual thus defies the laws trebly—as his parents and his guardians, and by breaking his own promise. Socrates did not admit even the right to disobey unjust laws, for he equated a single act of disobedience with, potentially, the destruction of the law itself— a common argument against protest, although not a sound one, like most 'thin end of the wedge' arguments. Implicit in his position is the view that we are obliged to obey the laws on three grounds: gratitude, consent and morality.[23] In modern democracies, the arguments against protest are simplified to two: first, that the individual has consented to the democratic system and should obey laws made by the majority, and second (more pragmatically), that democracy provides the means for peaceful change and for persuading the majority to share one's views so that direct action is never justified.

The philosophical justifications for protest *qua* disobedience are most controversial where there is a clear *prima facie* obligation to obey because the government is democratic or because its laws are just, or both. In a country with an unpopular, unjust, undemocratic government, such arguments would not be needed to convince others that the protestors were right. Some theorists argue that we are always obliged to obey just laws, even when passed by non-democratic governments, but both liberal and radical democrats would doubtless reply that the absence of democracy was itself a sufficient injustice to warrant protest. The stronger one's conception of political obligation, the less likely one is to concede a right to protest. If political obligation is thought to rest on consent *and* justice *and* gratitude, the chance of justifying protest is small, since it is unlikely that a government could break all three conditions simultaneously. But theories of the state and obligation which allow no scope for protest are incompatible with the view of man as a rational, moral, political being and can be criticized as authoritarian. A theory of obligation resting on consent is probably most accommodating of a right to protest.

The Scope of Protest

The main purpose of a theory of protest is to convince non-protesting citizens that the protestors' behaviour is justifiable, and not merely criminally or socially destructive; it can also help the discontented to decide whether their grievances merit disobedience, or whether they should be pursued through the 'proper channels'. The general justifications for protest have been set out above, but the scope and form of protest permissible in democratic society, and the cases where protest is appropriate, must be carefully specified.

Macfarlane suggests the criteria which should govern political disobedience, writing from a liberal standpoint and assuming that we have got a general obligation to obey the law.[24] He argues that justifiable disobedience must successfully answer four questions:

(1) *What cause does the disobedience serve?* This must be shown not to be purely selfish, but reasonable and just.

(2) *Why does this cause demand 'rejection of one's obligation to the state and its laws'?* Here the protestors must show that other means have been exhausted, or are for some reason inadequate.

(3) *Do the means chosen further the cause?* This question is to rule out 'overkill' and inappropriate forms of action. Some relevance between the means of protest chosen, and the cause, must be demonstrated.

(4) *Do the consequences justify the protest?* The protest should not aggravate the situation. It is impossible to give an answer to this question, since it involves prophecy. Governments may react in a hostile or conciliatory fashion to protest: success is never guaranteed. Perhaps this is a question for the protestor's own conscience. We can construe it as asking 'Do the ends justify the means?'

It is doubtful if Macfarlane's questions would deter 'fanatics', but they could act as a guide for would-be protestors, or as a yardstick by which citizens and governments can judge whether protest is reasonable and deserves sympathy.

If we assume with Thoreau, Gandhi, and others that everyone has the *right to protest*, when is it *right* to protest? What conditions should obtain? To answer this will, indirectly, involve giving general answers to the questions above. In a democratic system, the right to protest clearly does not justify protest designed to favour oneself exclusively, protest aimed at destroying the system, or protest which seeks to circumvent the majority's will because one happens to disagree with the election result. The protests made by individuals on moral grounds, justified by commitment to higher principles, stand on their own and do not require further consideration here. The form which protest usually takes in democracy, given that the majority's will can be enacted by legitimate, parliamentary means, is protest by minorities. These minorities can be classified as *permanent minorities*, marked out by some fixed characteristics such as race, creed or language, and *opinion minorities* who come together because their members share some opinion. Permanent minorities may feel that their special needs are not being catered for (for example, the Welsh speakers who want their own TV channel) or that they are being victimized because of their special characteristics. Because they are outnumbered, and because their special needs are unlikely ever to gain sufficient attention or support among the majority, they may conclude that civil disobedience is the only way left to get their cause recognized and remedied.

In the USA, such minorities may gain satisfaction within the system, since policies are passed in Congress by coalitions of minorities who trade reciprocal support. This does not help the marginal groups who have no formal representation. In some countries minorities of this kind have constitutional protection, but in Britain no such protection exists and the electoral system militates against anything but majority concerns becoming election issues or reaching party platforms. The majoritarian system can literally *oppress* permanent minorities, who therefore, having failed to get attention in Parliament, feel that they are justified in taking direct action. Their vindication is that they will never win over the majority, which is probably apathetic, even actively hostile, to their cause. Opinion minorities are usually formed to challenge particular laws or policies and are not permanent in composition, nor are their members personally oppressed in many cases. Failing to recruit adequate support from the majority by conventional recruiting methods, or to get parliamentary attention, they may resort to direct action to publicize their cause and attract support: for example, those who contest blood sports have sabotaged hunts, and anti-vivisectionists have stolen laboratory animals and defaced the houses of well-known scientists. In such cases it is often argued that they are abusing the right to protest, since they should try to convert the majority to their opinion, and so enact their policies: they are not in a fixed or permanent minority, and should abide by the democratic rules.

However, political circumstances are infinitely variable, and any generalization about when protest is right or wrong is vulnerable to endless counter-examples. In the pure theory of democracy, a non-oppressed, non-permanent minority would be wrong to take direct action against the will of the majority expressed through the government. But in real, imperfect democracy, opinion minorities are not usually in confrontation with the majority, who may even tend to favour their views, but with the government, the Establishment, and the system — for example, the shortage of parliamentary time for dealing with non-government business. Civil disobedience may thus be a fitting form of challenge to a government which has little claim to embody the will of the majority in any case. Many protests are better viewed as a section of the people acting against a government which protects its own interests, rather than as a minority acting against the majority of their fellows.

The examples given so far have been of minorities wishing for policies to be enacted or altered and undertaking direct action for publicity purposes. Protest equally encompasses direct disobedience of laws which seem to victimize a minority, or contravene the moral beliefs of a group. When the law making crash-helmets compulsory for motor-cyclists was passed, the Sikh community, whose members could not fit helmets over the turbans which their religion obliges them to wear, complained that the law discriminated against them because of their religion. They refused to wear helmets, and some Sikhs were arrested dozens of times and even imprisoned for breaking this law, until Sikhs were made exempt. This was a paradigm case of disobedience — breaking the law and paying the penalty — and also an interesting illustration of the problems of making acceptable laws in a mixed community. Law has to be made to fit Mr or Ms Average Citizen, but the more heterogeneous a community becomes, the more exemptions there must be, or the more protest.

The most famous cases of civil disobedience have involved minorities deprived of civil or legal rights, such as blacks in the South of the USA. Such cases are clear-cut (as far as anything can be in politics) and wholly justifiable. I would also say that a permanent minority with full political rights is still justified in civil disobedience if the majority oppresses it in other ways or denies it the satisfaction of its special needs, when these can reasonably be met. (It would be unreasonable for the Welsh to demand Welsh-language TV if this would bankrupt all the other television networks. In most cases where financial resources are involved, some compromise which shows willing should probably be accepted as reasonable.) As to opinion minorities, it would be most in keeping with the spirit of democracy if they sought to persuade without direct action. However, the imperfections of the system make the use of other methods understandable. Many other permutations of protest could be discussed, some justifiable, others not, but these examples at least suggest that theories of protest must be considerably elaborated to cover each individual case. One further important case is that where an informed opinion minority tries to change a major government policy between elections by disobedience. Tussman argues that consent is in fact an act of the conscious minority, with the majority, the 'clods' merely acquiescing. On this basis he concludes that if the aware, consenting elite dissents, its wishes should prevail over those of the unthinking clods and be acceded to by the government. Hence he justifies elite protest, in effect, on the basis of superior wisdom — a view that majoritarian democrats would reject.

The right to protest is said to derive partly from the injustice or immorality of the laws or policies in question. But 'unjust' and 'immoral' are themselves disputable categories, and some groups will always consider unjust or wrong what the majority finds just or right, because of ideological or moral differences. Theories of protest cannot solve this problem: they can only state that the *bona fide* protestor is one who believes that injustice is being done or that his moral principles are being violated, and so has the right to protest, whatever his principles.

It might be thought that the use of the phrase 'the right to protest' is ironic, since all the theories insist on the duty to accept punishment for disobedience. If the protestor disobeys and pays the price, where does *right* come into it? The protestor's right is really that his law-breaking actions are justifiable in his own conscience, and that they will be interpreted by his fellows and the government as principled political activity and not as crime or sedition — by contrast with the treatment of dissidents in communist countries, for example, where such a right is not acknowledged and dissidents are treated like criminals or traitors. The case against admitting a right to protest rests partly on the vulnerability of the theories of protest, which encounter endless contradictions and cannot give absolute guidance as to when protest is, or is not, right. A number of pragmatic reasons are also cited for denying such a right: 'law-breaking always leads to violence, and violence begets violence', 'law-breaking endangers the democratically elected government', 'some protestors are just criminals, acting out of self-interest', 'protest disrupts the fabric of society' and 'breaking one law brings the law itself into disrepute'. The truth of such generalizations can be debated *ad infinitum*, but the 'practical' case for accepting the right to protest rests on the view that a democratic society is strong enough to absorb dissent, that the majority can be mistaken and that the government often does not represent the will of the majority in any case. More deviously, governments may think that by allowing moderate, if inconvenient, protest, they defuse wider, more fundamental discontent.

The theories of protest reviewed do not condone violence because the individual's right to protest must in a democracy be circumscribed by others' rights. The condemnation of violence is based on a separate value-judgement from that which condemns civil disobedience on the grounds of social disruption, but the two forms of action are often conflated because in practice civil disobedience can lead to violence. Some condemn *all* direct action as being potentially violent, especially those who consider that damage to property is a form of violence. Others argue that threats are a kind of violence, and that disobedience, which is a threat, is therefore violent. To avoid outlawing protest entirely, the first step towards authoritarianism, we need to make a sharp distinction between potential, implied, and covert violence and *real* violence, which actually hurts people. Protest involving real violence is not admissible in a democratic society because it offends the spirit of democracy, which is decision by debate and persuasion and the peaceful resolution of conflict. In liberal democracies it is doubly condemned because of the transgression of the liberal values concerning individual life. However, violence is not a special, unique form of political action (contrary to common usage); it is a *mode* which political activity may take. Law-breaking and revolution may be violent, or not. But for most people violence is strongly associated with those who seek to overthrow the political system, and all consideration of revolution is complicated by the fact that a revolution whose aims seem reasonable, even just, will be widely viewed as evil if its methods are violent. The arguments about violence were discussed in Chapter 6, and here I shall merely consider whether the right of protest can be said to extend to a 'right of revolution'.

The Right of Revolution

The possibilities for political action lie on a continuum which stretches from obedience through tolerated non-conformity, conventional protest, direct action, non-revolutionary terrorism to revolution, a decisive rupture of the existing system. A system based on a democratic ideology can usually survive all forms of behaviour except the directly revolutionary. Within such a system, therefore, there cannot be a 'right of revolution' for individuals or groups by definition. Since each ideology supports a particular political system, there can be no way of justifying a total social revolution in terms of the ideology and the system which it would destroy. When Locke asserted the right to resist a government, the grounds were that the government had transgressed the principles justifying its existence—in other words, the government itself was destroying the political system and the people were entitled to act to preserve the political form based on their previous consent. Locke justified a change of regime, rather than a revolution, a change which would take place within the dominant ideology. For liberal democrats a true revolution is an unjustifiable breach of democratic procedure, condemned both for that and for the violence and coercion it entails. But whether the dominant ideology in a country is liberal democratic, communist or right-wing authoritarian, revolutionaries will not be able to establish their right to act in terms of that ideology, or to justify their revolution to the part of the population which adheres to it. It is not unknown for a group to oust a regime in order to pursue established political doctrines more vigorously—this is similar to the situation Locke envisaged—and changes of regime in countries ruled by military juntas are sometimes justified in this way, but this is not a revolution in the usual sense, which connotes a destruction of the system.

The reasons for revolution advanced by Marxists and anarchists have already been discussed, but these related to particular contexts. If a general right to revolution is to be asserted, we must step outside the major ideologies and look for general justifications derived from justice and morality, although these too will not be free from ideology. A justification of revolution must vindicate the violence, dispossession, and coercion which it entails: if a revolution takes place in a democracy by the majority of the population voting for a different political system, no norms have been violated and no justification is needed. The justification of a general right to revolution in defiance of the ballot box might run as follows: revolution is justifiable when carried out by the majority against a regime and/or a political system which exploits and oppresses the majority. This principle may be extended to include revolution by the minority in the interests of the majority, provided that the majority lends its support to the minority during or soon after the event, thus validating the claim that it is in their interests. This formula assumes that the majority is fairly large: the rights and wrongs of a revolution in a country divided 50:50 or 49:51 would be infinitely debatable. This proposed justification evidently countenances the suppression of the former minority. This is admissible because, since judgements about the relative worth of individuals are invidious and impossible, individuals must be assumed equally worthy, so that the only operable criterion is the numerical one, the wellbeing of the majority. Against such a revolution, supporters of the minority group could argue that they deserve their privileges because of special merit, virtue or wisdom, or that they were in fact ruling the majority better than it could rule itself—the paternalistic argument. The arguments for and against popular revolution typically rest on different doctrines—egalitarianism and elitism—and the choice between them is an assertion of fundamental values. But if the majoritarian or popular view is accepted, it could be used as the basis of a general right to revolution. The contexts in which it applies are, of course, far less black-and-white, since most regimes justify themselves in terms of some imagined majority interest. The right of revolution will not satisfy those who hold the sanctity of life or the inviolability of property as the highest good, for to them no revolution could ever be validly justified. But the inconsistency of such absolutes has been suggested elsewhere.

It can be objected that real revolutions actually take place without the blessing of such theoretical justification: rights and actions in such a case are unrelated, theory is irrelevant to practice. However, for a revolutionary regime it is crucial to justify its takeover theoretically and so to legitimize itself in the eyes of the population—unless it wishes to keep order by force in the long term. Also, in gaining acceptance by other states, the rightness of its revolution can be an important factor. Mendacious justifications are not uncommon, and new regimes, like old regimes, invariably explain their actions in terms of the interests of the people—even out-and-out dictatorships. However, informed citizens and observers can usually judge such claims to be approximately true or false: if true, the rightness of the revolution according to the general principle should hasten the acceptance of the regime abroad, and loyalty to the system at home.

Those who condemn all revolutions *a priori* because of the violence involved are relatively few. More often, particular revolutions will be condemned or condoned according to whether one approved of the displaced rulers and approves of the new regime ideologically. Terrorism is often judged by the same lights. But there is another standpoint for judging revolutions, that of the disembodied observer with a theory of history. To thinkers such as Machiavelli and Hegel, social change, disruptive or disastrous as it may be for individuals, is a recurrent and necessary event in world history, the necessary condition of progress or of the realization of the World Spirit. Such views are best expressed at a comfortable distance in time and space from the revolutions in question, and could hardly be used to vindicate revolution to its victims. And, although some revolutionaries justified their work rhetorically in holistic terms as the purging of social impurities and the march of civilization, the reasons they offer to their future citizens are grounded not on metaphysics but on the concrete benefits which the revolution will achieve. The 'march of progress' justification of revolution makes no reference to individual or collective wellbeing, and is suspect for this reason and because, as a principle, it has only particular application and is subject to the same criticisms as non-universalizable moral rules. Commentators may interpret revolutions far away in time and space as progressive while staunchly opposing similar movements in their own back-yards.

It seems, then, that the right to revolution is one which belongs to individuals collectively, but not one which can be established in the constitution of a country — although democrats might say that the right to vote was a right to make minor revolutions. The right to revolution is a moral claim, based on the right to self-defence and on an ideal of human good, 'the wellbeing of the majority'. Revolution is undoubtedly the most difficult moral and political problem with which political thinkers must grapple: it is also guaranteed that one theorist's solution will displease most other thinkers. But I would argue that the general principle set out above would offer some guidance for assessing revolutions in whatever kind of society they arose.

I am painfully conscious of having left volumes unwritten on the subject of liberty, rights, and protest. These topics and the general subject implicit in them, the position of the individual *vis-à-vis* the state and other individuals, have been discussed largely from the viewpoint of liberal theory and the problems of a liberal-democratic society, because such subjects dominate the writings of political theorists within the liberal ideology. Today, arguments about individual freedom have a double function to perform: they must try to convert non-liberal societies to the liberal scale of values and also they should be revived within liberal societies to check the rise of state power and the elitist institutions which flourish within democracy. Awareness of such arguments and of our rights as inhabitants of liberal society is therefore essential not only for thinking about, but for living in modern Western society.

Notes

1. J.-J. Rousseau, *The Social Contract*, Dent, 1913, p.8.
2. See P. Strawson, 'Freedom and resentment' in Strawson, *Studies in the Philosophy*

of Thought and Action, Oxford University Press, 1968 and I. Berlin, 'Historical inevitability' in Berlin, *Four Essays on Liberty*, Oxford University Press, 1969.

3. Berlin, 'Two concepts of liberty' in *Political Philosophy* (Ed. A. Quinton), p.149.
4. Berlin, *Four Essays on Liberty*, p.xlix.
5. Rousseau, *The Social Contract*, p.12.
6. G. Hegel, *The Philosophy of Right* (Trans M. Knox), Oxford University Press, 1952, Part 3 (iii) and *The Phenomenology of Spirit* (Trans. A. V. Miller), Clarendon Press, 1977, s.371.
7. B. F. Skinner, *Beyond Freedom and Dignity*, Cape, 1972.
8. See, e.g., Noam Chomsky's attack on Skinner's theory in the *New York Review of Books* Dec.–Jan., 1971/2. See too H. Wheeler (Ed.), *Beyond the Punitive Society*, W. H. Freeman, 1973.
9. H. Marcuse, *One Dimensional Man*, Sphere, 1968; *Essay on Liberation*, Penguin, 1971.
10. J. S. Mill, *On Liberty*, Collins, 1962, p.230.
11. Contemporary 'libertarians' recommend the abolition of all taxes and State services, since they reject the case for paternalism and that for collectivism. Nozick could be taken as their theoretical representative: see *Anarchy, State and Utopia*, Blackwell, 1974.
12. T. Paine, *The Rights of Man*, Penguin, 1969, p.166.
13. K. Marx, 'The Jewish Question', in *Early Texts* (Ed. D. McLellan), Blackwell, 1971, pp.101–4.
14. M. Cranston, *What Are Human Rights?*, Bodley Head, 1973.
15. T. Regan and P. Singer, *Animal Rights and Human Obligation*, Prentice-Hall, 1976.
16. J. P. Plamenatz, *Consent, Freedom and Political Obligation*, 2nd edn, Oxford University Press, 1968, p.82.
17. R. Dworkin, *Taking Rights Seriously*, Duckworth, 1977, Chaps 6–7.
18. P. King, *Toleration*, Allen & Unwin, 1976, pp.23, 35.
19. Mill, *On Liberty*, Chap. 2. Mill's justifications for toleration were discussed in Chapter 3 above.
20. H. D. Thoreau, 'Civil disobedience' in *Walden* (Ed. J. Krutch), Bantam, 1962, pp.85–104.
21. W. Reys and P. Rao, 'Gandhi's synthesis of Indian spirituality and Western politics' in *Political and Legal Obligation*, (Eds J. R. Pennock and J. W. Chapman), Atherton Press, 1970, p.449.
22. M. Walzer, *Obligations*, Harvard University Press, 1970.
23. Plato, *Crito* in *The Last Days of Socrates* (Trans. H. Tredennick), Penguin, 1954, p.89ff.
24. L. J. Macfarlane, *Political Disobedience*, Macmillan, 1971.

Further reading

J. S. Mill, *On Liberty*, Collins, 1962.
R. Dworkin, *Taking Rights Seriously*, Duckworth, 1977.
R. Flathman, *The Practice of Rights*, Cambridge University Press, 1976.
D. D. Raphael (Ed.), *Political Theory and the Rights of Man*, Macmillan, 1967.
M. Walzer, *Obligations*, Harvard University Press, 1970.
A. Carter, *Direct Action and Liberal Democracy*, Routledge & Kegan Paul, 1973.
P. Singer, *Democracy and Disobedience*, Clarendon Press, 1973.

CHAPTER 12

Social Justice and Equality

Justice is the highest goal of political life, yet it is *injustice* which dominates political debate. The reason is that it is easier to identify and to deplore injustices than to define precisely what is lacking in an unjust situation, or what an ideally just situation might be like. Injustice often appears as a departure from an equilibrium of which we approve. In political argument, justice is usually said to be the property of a *distribution* of something — of goods, but also of 'bads'. Some form of social justice is the ultimate aim of political ideologies. But many people associate the term primarily with justice in the legal system, the punishment of malefactors. Here, legal justice will be treated as a concept parallel to that of social justice, concerning the retributive distribution of pains and penalties to the guilty: what both concepts have in common are the ideas of due process, impartiality, and distribution according to appropriate criteria. Also, both operate in the context of *scarce goods* which have to be appropriately distributed. What economists call 'free goods' such as air and sunshine do not have to be distributed according to just principles — yet.

Different ideologies produce radically different theories of justice. For Plato, justice was not based on desert, nor on 'giving every man his due', but signified a 'just proportion' between the various parts of society whereas Aristotle proposed a definition which rested on individual desert and departed from Plato's more holistic view. Many conservatives would regard a hierarchical distribution of goods and privileges as just, or even as divinely ordained. For liberals, distribution according to merit, based on equality of opportunity, is the ideal, while socialists strive for justice based on need and fundamental equality. While Bentham and James Mill defined justice as the impartial application of rules, they and other utilitarians considered that, in principle, justice should be treated as a secondary rule, and subordinated to utility: many other theorists, including 'rule utilitarians' see justice as an end in itself. As this wide variety of definitions suggests, justice is a flexible term, which is stretched to fit almost any idea of the good. Any analysis intended to produce an authoritative definition of the idea is therefore doomed to fail, or to be challenged or superseded. The intention here is to assess the merits of the various theories of justice and to examine the conceptual problems surrounding the ideal itself, no matter what content we give to it.

Most modern works of political philosophy start by asserting that justice is a property of *situations* or outcomes, thus avoiding the questions which vex moral philosophers, such as 'Who is the just man?' and 'Can I have a just intention if the outcome of my act is unjust?'. These are questions of private, not political, virtue. But when we treat justice as a property of situations, we must also remember that situations are brought about by human *actions*, which cannot be exempted from questions of justice. Indeed, some philosophers consider that justice is located in the actions or procedures which bring about outcomes, and therefore define it essentially as the impartial application of rules. Ultimately, the two stages are inseparable. First of all, we need to examine the possible methods of distribution which might operate. Logically, any distribution must either be equal or unequal. *Equal distribution* is a simple, numerical form of allocation under which everyone gets an equal quantity of goods irrespective of his personal characteristics — or, in the case of indivisible goods, such as the vote, everyone gets one unit. The outcome of an equal distribution can therefore be specified in advance. This is the least problematic method of distribution but, unfortunately, it is not applicable to most social situations. *Unequal distribution* implies that some individuals are favoured or privileged: an extreme case would be where one individual monopolised the whole of a commodity, and others got none. Unequal, or selective, distribution takes place according to some criterion which relates the goods distributed to special characteristics of their recipients. But a sub-species of unequal distribution is random distribution, where no special criteria are involved, and the outcome is not predictable in advance — for example, a lottery. Both selective and random methods produce unequal distributions which are not unjust if the proper criteria have been observed, and unequal distributions are in many cases intuitively more just than equal distributions. Nobody would dispute that health care should go to the sick rather than the healthy. But if the wrong criteria are chosen, the outcome will be unjust. Our society holds that nepotism is an irrelevant and wrong criterion for the distribution of top jobs, just as social status or wealth are irrelevant criteria for the allocation of medical care or university degrees. Random distribution is the most equitable method in some cases, however. It may be the the fairest way of apportioning risk between individuals, and has traditionally been used to select people for dangerous missions. It might also be seen as a fair basis for distributing a limited number of luxuries after everyone's basic needs have been satisfied.

The Criteria for Justice

From these preliminary observations, it is clear that what is all-important in constructing a theory of justice is the criterion chosen as appropriate for determining a distribution. Three major criteria are usually offered, *equality, merit,* and *need.* Since the eighteenth century at least, when the doctrines of human equality and the rights of man were firmly established in political thought, *equality* has been a fundamental presumption in theories of justice. All men are equally deserving unless, or until, proved otherwise. Equality before the law gradually became a tenet of reformed legal systems, replacing older systems in which different grades of citizen were tried in different courts and had different legal rights. However, a belief in equality does not necessarily lead to an egalitarian theory of justice, since the conviction that men are in some basic and abstract sense equal can co-exist with the principle that because men also differ in certain ways they merit different treatment. What equality requires is that equal cases should be treated equally: as Aristotle maintained, it is as unjust to treat unequals equally as to treat equals unequally.[1] Certainly, some notion of equal treatment must reside in every theory of justice: a god who strikes down one sinner while another prospers is regarded as unjust. It may be that we have an intuitive perception of equality—young children rapidly learn to call unequal treatment 'unfair', although perhaps this is the result of early conditioning rather than any innate idea of respect for equals! Equality, then, may play a part in a substantive theory of justice, requiring as egalitarian a distribution of goods as possible, as Babeuf demanded in his *Manifesto of the Equals*, or it may operate as an ordering principle at the secondary level, requiring that, as a matter of 'due process', equal cases should be treated alike, in law and in the distribution of goods, according to the other criteria chosen. More will be said of equality as an ideal in its own right at the end of this chapter.

While a thoroughgoing egalitarian theory of justice would hold that each man deserves as much as the next because of his equal humanity, theories of justice based on *merit, desert* or *entitlement* distinguish between men and justify differential rewards. (Although 'merit' suggests contribution to society, 'desert' moral worth and 'entitlement' something built up historically and legally established, all three criteria function in a similar way and are often interchangeable.) Such theories fall into two broad categories, those which hold that men's moral worth or intrinsic virtues and talents deserve reward, and those which argue that reward should be linked to an individual's contribution to society. In either case an intangible connection has to be postulated between the individual's merit and his reward—as in the theory of retributive punishment, but in reverse—and this in itself is philosophically dubious and practically questionable. Philosophically dubious because there is no *necessary* or *a priori* link between my moral virtue and, say, the amount of wealth which I should be given—the two are incommensurable—and practically so because my reward must, surely, be modified according to circumstance: if others have less than enough, I cannot justly claim a reward commensurate with my own outstanding contribution to society. But the idea that social justice is based on merit, measured by contribution, is the mainstay of the liberal theory of justice, based on the assumption of equality of opportunity, the assumption that everyone has, in the first place, an equal chance to make a contribution and so to deserve his reward.

Historically, the idea of merit played a progressive role, challenging and superseding the idea that people were entitled absolutely to whatever they happened to inherit or acquire—the rich to their wealth, the poor to their poverty—and when merit, interpreted as contribution, becomes the major criterion of justice, a social element is introduced, the idea that those who contribute most to society deserve most. On this criterion, those who allow their talents to lie fallow deserve no more than those who have no talents. Although our system of income distribution rests in theory on this criterion, it is practically very hard to determine exactly what someone's contribution to society has been. The self-made man's wealth rests partly on the labour of his employees, partly on technology and social conditions to which many others have contributed and partly on the fluctuations of the market. His own real contribution may have been minimal compared with these factors. Again, those in high positions who are said to make key contributions to society and so to deserve the highest rewards, presumably gain immeasurable satisfaction from their work and their power and these should, but usually cannot, be taken into account in deciding their just reward.

It is usually considered that the criteria of merit and need are diametrically opposed and give rise to antithetical theories of justice,[2] namely liberal and socialist theories. A theory of justice based on *need* presupposes everyone's humanity and equal rights to have their needs satisfied irrespective of their merits, as is suggested by the socialist maxim 'From each according to his ability, to each according to his need'. Again, philosophically it is hard to *prove* that the very fact of being alive and living in a particular society, entitles one to help and succour from one's fellows in the satisfaction of one's needs. However, it might be agreed by theorists of most persuasions that human beings have, *a priori*, equal rights to respect, dignity, and freedom, and it can further be argued that they cannot enjoy these if their basic needs remain unsatisfied. The practical problem in delineating a theory of social justice based on need is to decide what shall count as needs. The minimal income needed to keep a British citizen above the poverty line would make an Indian or Vietnamese relatively rich. While we would accept that good health is a universal need, the standards of medical care considered adequate vary considerably from country to country and the definition of a decent standard of living is even more nation- and culture-specific. While it may be possible for each society with socialist aspirations to define and achieve a certain level of need–satisfaction, this does not remedy the great injustices in a world where many people's most basic needs remain permanently unfulfilled. A system of payment according to need has the disadvantage that outstanding individual contributions may go unrewarded—the bad worker with several dependants would earn more than the productive single worker—but it would be possible to devise a system of distribution which took into account people's needs and, when these were met, reflected their individual contributions—providing, of course, that resources were more than adequate to meet everyone's basic needs.

A theory of justice based on need reflects a fundamental idea of human equality and happiness, whereas that based on merit rests on a premise of the differential worth of individuals. Both are metaphysical notions not open to empirical proof, and one's acceptance of one or the other must rest on a value judgement. And although the ideas of need and merit have overtaken that of moral worth as a criterion for justice, there are still those who would answer 'No' to the question 'Does the evil man deserve to be happy?'. The theory implied in the latter position poses insuperable problems for any system of social justice, since there is no foolproof way of sorting out the sheep from the goats which could serve as the basis of social policy. This is no doubt why the just man traditionally gets his reward in heaven.

None of the criteria proposed, equality, merit or need is problem-free. Desert in the sense of moral worth is hard to measure, merit *qua* contribution may be unintentional or accidental and both criteria may run counter to men's basic needs. Need itself is hard to define, and it is debatable whether a system of social justice should or should not try to abolish *relative deprivation*, which is the sense of deprivation we get when we see others who are better off than ourselves, even if our own basic needs are met. Furthermore, even when we agree about the criteria for distribution, we may well disagree over the nature of a particular case. For example, having decided that women deserve equal pay with men for equal work, we may dispute whether their work *is* equal in particular cases. How a particular criterion should be applied is often hard to decide. The difficulty of choosing between the criteria or deciding a permanent order of priority between them has led some theorists to adopt the 'intuitionist' approach to justice. The intuitionist, in Rawls's words, 'maintains that there exist no higher order constructive criteria for determining the proper emphasis for the competing principles of justice',[3] and holds that there is a plurality of first principles. The intuitionist would therefore contend that the relevance of need, merit, and equality had to be weighed afresh in each case where justice was at stake. But in social policy this approach could lead to confusion and to injustice, in that like cases would not always be treated alike. So it is practically and politically necessary to decide on a dominant criterion, or on constant priorities between the criteria.

Although the criteria for distribution play an important part in any conception of justice, it is clear that justice cannot be said to be *identical* to its criteria. Justice is not solely the satisfaction of need or the reward of merit. But if justice is said instead to be a second-order principle such as due process or fairness in the application of the appropriate criteria in the appropriate case, it is reduced to an insubstantial, ordering principle which cannot give us any advice on how the ideally just society should be organized. There have been many attempts to produce substantive theories of justice, most recently that of Rawls which is discussed below, but these differ considerably, according to the other ideals to which the theorist adheres. Justice has always been, as democracy is today, a hurrah-word. Nobody advocates a utopia which he would characterise as unjust, and so there is certainly a risk that the meaning of the term will be reduced to mean anything of which the speaker or writer approves. While people are quick to point to particular abuses in society as unjust, they are slower to say what form of just organization should replace them. In so far as it is possible to attempt a general definition of justice on which all would agree, we have to stick to the secondary level and define it as an ordering principle which enjoins us to treat like cases alike and, as that implies, with due process, or non-arbitrarily, according to the agreed rules, whatever they may be. Thus we arrive at the paradox that according to this formal definition it is possible to administer unjust laws justly: although the fact that due process is used does not make the laws or the society just, it is a shade more just than if those laws were themselves unjustly administered. The ideal is, of course, to have just laws justly administered, but in order to see what such a just society might be like we need a substantive, first-order conception of justice which will in turn rest on value-judgements and ideological convictions. A consideration of the particular conceptions of justice developed within various ideologies will demonstrate what such a substantive view might be like.

Liberal, Socialist, and 'Natural' Justice

Liberalism takes social justice to consist in distribution according to merit or contribution in a society where there exists a basic equality of opportunity. Given the natural inequalities of talent and inherited and otherwise constituted inequalities of wealth and power, the latter requirement has caused liberals to accept the need for limited state intervention to produce equality of opportunity by means of universal health care and education and other welfare measures. Some non-monetary goods such as rights are distributed equally in liberal society, on the supposition that men are broadly equal in certain respects. Thus, the vote is distributed to each citizen and the duty of jury service is distributed by rota (which in itself is an egalitarian form of distribution) on the assumption that all have an equal sense of fairness and an equal capacity for judgement — although in point of fact jury service used to be limited to householders which suggests that there were doubts about this. The liberal adherence to the idea of the 'just meritocracy' is therefore modified in important respects by more egalitarian considerations, but the dominant idea is that in liberal society the meritorious will be justly rewarded. In this respect it is interesting that the great proponent of the free market, Hayek, who calls himself a liberal, admits that the interplay of market forces by no means leads to a just outcome. To achieve a merit-based system of justice would therefore, presumably, require a measure of government intervention and economic regulation as well as the welfare measures needed to achieve equality of opportunity. In reality, the absence of equality of opportunity means that the system based on merit tends to reinforce the underlying inequalities of liberal society.

In *A Theory of Justice* (1971) Rawls propounded a covertly liberal conception of justice based on a contractual view of society which harks back to Hobbes and Locke. He hypothesizes a pre-social or a-social 'original position' in which people would try to decide consensually on the form of society which they would all agree to live in, whatever their station in life. The presumption is that they would choose, and agree to maintain, a paradigmly just society, under the sterile conditons for impartial choice which Rawls posits. Rawls makes various assumptions about these individuals: they are 'mutually indifferent' (that is, neither hostile nor friendly to each other), they do not suffer from 'envy' (feelings of relative deprivation) as long as they are satisfied in their own terms, and in agreeing on a form of society they all seek to maximize their own interests—interests which Rawls defines as 'primary goods', namely 'rights and liberties, opportunities and powers, income and wealth'.[4] Apart from these propensities, which Rawls takes to be value-free and uncontentious, these people are ciphers. They exist behind a 'Veil of Ignorance' which prevents any of them knowing particular details about his own talents, ideals or what his place in the future society might be. The purpose of this device is to get behind people's vested interests, to see what sort of society we would choose if we had no idea of our future place in it. The society chosen in these impartial circumstances would, by Rawls's definition, be just. In earlier versions of his theory, he referred to it as 'justice as fairness' because he argued that the conditions of choice depicted in the original position were ideally fair and would necessarily lead to just choices.

Rawls concludes that in these circumstances each man will choose a kind of society which minimizes his possible losses, making sure than even the worse-off person in that society is not too destitute in case *he* should turn out to be that person. He calls this the 'maximin' principle, since it maximizes the minimum welfare. The choice of this strategy reflects another of Rawls's basic assumptions, that men are not risk-takers, and will therefore choose the safest option. On such a principle, no-one would choose to live in a slave-owning society since he would not risk being a slave despite the gamble that he might end up as the slave-owner, living in luxury. Taking the maximin principle into account, and the definition of primary goods that he gives, Rawls asserts that such individuals would logically choose the following two principles of justice:[5]

(1) Each person is to have an equal right to the most extensive basic liberty compatible with a similar liberty for others.
(2) Social and economic inequalities are to be arranged so that they both: (a) reasonably expected to be to everyone's advantage; and (b) attached to positions and offices open to all.

Clarifying the second principle, Rawls says that 'equally open' must mean that equality of opportunity reigns, levelling out natural differences of talent as far as possible. Rawls, incidentally, denies that he is justifying meritocracy, but this is potentially a merit-based system. He defines 'to everyone's advantage' in terms of the 'difference principle' which stipulates that a gain for anyone in society must contribute to the expectations of the worst-off person in society (and hence, presumably, to the expectations of all those above him too). He himself regards this as an egalitarian principle which would prevent the growth of a wide gap between the welfare of the better-off and worse-off members of society but, as critics point out, it is a slim safeguard.[6] The rich can always claim that in increasing their wealth considerably they are contributing marginally to the welfare of the poorer members of society, for example by increasing their chances of employment and by generating a demand for goods, but this will not produce an egalitarian, but an increasingly stratified society. The first principle of justice has priority over the second, Rawls states: 'people will only agree to limit liberty for the sake of liberty, not for the sake of economic advantage'. However, he concedes that this condition only holds for societies where a certain basic level of material satisfaction has been reached: in very poor countries liberty might justifiably be restricted to further the wellbeing of the people. The economic level at which the first principle gains priority is not, however, made clear, although clearly the West has reached it. The rest of Rawls's long work elaborates the consequences of his conception of justice for social and political organization, and the result looks very like a Western, liberal-democratic society.

Rawls has been criticized from the right for being too egalitarian and from the left for being insufficiently so. But his is a typically liberal model of justice. By taking the individual and his preferences as the motivating force of the model, and asserting that liberty is a primary good, he biases the outcome towards a liberal, laissez-faire society, and although he claims that the two principles of justice merely chance to be liberal and follow necessarily from his original, ideologically impartial premises, these premises are themselves those of liberal ideology. In this respect the assumption of lack of envy is crucial, for if the men in the original position knew themselves to be envious, they would take steps to minimize the differentials of wealth and wellbeing with something stronger than the difference principle, to avoid the risk of relative deprivation. Rawls proposes that any society or institution can be tested for justice by asking if it lives up to the two principles but their abstractness makes such testing difficult. It is invariably easy to demonstrate that a social arrangement is to everyone's advantage by taking a limited field of alternatives for comparison. It is better in capitalist society to have businessmen investing and increasing employment prospects while they enrich themselves than to have businessmen taxed so heavily that they have no incentive to invest — but this presupposes that there have to be investors, that capitalism is the only conceivable economic order. In other words, the phrase 'to everyone's advantage' does not specify what comparisons are to be invoked: if the test is made on the basis of an underlying acceptance of a given form of society, the status quo is likely to be found to be to everyone's advantage.[7]

I have cited Rawls's theory as an exemplar of the liberal view of justice, yet his two principles are not *substantive* in the sense that they state that justice is one thing or another. Rawls himself calls this a *procedural* theory of justice, arguing that:[8]

pure procedural justice obtains when there is no independent criterion for the right result; instead there is a correct or fair procedure such that the outcome is likewise correct or fair, *whatever it is.*

If the two operational principles of justice are followed, then, the outcome will necessarily be just, and good, although the phenomenology of the just society cannot be specified in advance. There is certainly some justification for taking a procedural approach to justice in the complex real world, where the size of the population and variability of relevant factors make it impossible to specify what each individual should justly have. But in calling his theory of justice 'procedural', Rawls seems to bestow on it an aura of impartiality, whereas the procedures he specifies are designed to further a particular form of society which is implicit in the original assumptions which conceal liberal ideals. Although he claims to build a theory of what is good on his account of what is just, or right, he in fact starts out with an assertion of the primary goods which determines his view of justice—as do most theorists, since it is scarcely possible to separate our conception of what is good for human beings from what we think is right and just for them. Where Rawls is at fault is in presenting his theory as a structure of objective argument, when the presuppositions are largely those of liberalism.

The socialist principle of distribution, 'to each according to his needs', is no less procedural than that of Rawls, but the value judgement which it embodies is patently visible. The socialist conception underwent some transformations before it fixed on need as the dominant criterion for justice. The early socialist disciples of Saint-Simon followed the principle 'from each according to his capacity, to each according to his works', which seems nearer to the merit-based liberal conception. Marx too, in analysing expoitation and in claiming that under socialism labour would be paid the full value of its product, might be said to be making implicit reference to a contribution-based theory of justice. However, what he deplored was the real effect which this unjust system of reward for contribution (in a society which purported to distribute rewards according to merit) had on the labourer, whose humanity, dignity and self-respect were threatened and who, as a result, could scarcely satisfy his own material needs. And to claim that labour should not receive less than its just rewards under capitalism is not equivalent to asserting that under socialism social justice will be based primarily on merit.

Although, as was argued in Chapter 5, socialists hold equality to be the major political ideal, the other criteria also play a part in socialist justice. A socialist ordering of the criteria which determine social justice might be as follows: *need* should prevail as the dominant criterion for ordering the distribution of material goods, and opportunities appropriate to talents, with the proviso that equal needs and talents must be treated equally. *Equality* would be invoked in the many areas of life where need is not paramount, and also where the equality of men's needs and capacities can be assumed, as in the field of political and personal rights. Thirdly, *merit* may determine the distribution of any surplus of goods when basic needs are satisfied — for example, a bonus or incentive scheme might operate once all workers had achieved a satisfactory standard of living. Merit could also properly operate when goods which are irrelevant to needs are to be distributed: the socialist utopian Fourier proposed a complex scheme for the award of honours, worthless but gratifying, to the inhabitants of his utopia. Merit would also have to prevail in the distribution of *jobs* in any socialist society with a highly specialized industrial economy, so that the most skilled workers got the jobs to which they were best suited, for efficiency's sake. However, some socialists have envisaged reversion to less complex economies, and even the abolition of the divison of labour, which would mean that anyone could pursue any occupation, or indeed several at once, and would eliminate merit in the distribution of work. Finally, a socialist society might justly use a random or a rote method of distributing extra goods or positions when all needs are met. This method would also be appropriate for recurring duties. Owen thought that the governing positions would be allocated by rote in his ideal communities, which would have the desirable result of de-professionalizing politics and putting each individual in command and under someone else's command on a regular basis, thus preventing despotic behaviour by the rulers. Evidently, the socialist theory of social justice is, like that of liberals, a blend of the major criteria which are commonly thought to bear on justice. A socialist who insisted upon distribution solely on the basis of equality would encounter anomalies as would one who insists that jobs should be allocated purely on the basis of need or preference. It is the ordering between the criteria which is crucial.

One more, limiting criterion might be added to the socialist view of justice, a stipulation that the differentials between the amounts of goods given to individuals should be as small as possible, or should at least be confined within a given range. In other words, having established a welfare minimum via the concept of need, a welfare maximum should also be set, to prevent large differentials of wealth growing, and breeding resentment when those at the lower end of the scale perceive that they are relatively deprived. This sort of limitation is hinted at in Rawls's difference principle, but only half-heartedly, as he does not acknowledge in his model that men feel envy, or compare themselves with others. Since he does not stipulate that the wellbeing of the better-off and the worse-off should grow in the same proportions, the difference principle would not have the effect of minimizing differentials, and could encourage them. It might be thought deplorable that even a socialist society should have to consider the factor of human envy and the socio-psychological problem of relative deprivation, but presumably until the utopia arrives in which everyone is satiated with personal satisfaction, interpersonal comparisons will be made.

The USSR has failed to check the growth of considerable differentials of income and privilege,[9] and is often condemned in the West as not being truly socialist for that reason—with some glee, as this seems to bear out the capitalist conviction of man's natural competitiveness and acquisitiveness. Many writers outside the socialist school have also condemned wide gaps between wealth and poverty as sources of social divisiveness and injustice. Rousseau stipulated that no man should be poor enough to have to sell himself or rich enough to buy another in his ideal community, while Godwin proposed regulation in an anarchist society to prevent the growth of vast wealth, by analogy with the 'sumptuary laws' which regulated expenditure and restrained excess and ostentation in earlier societies. So the concern with vast differences of wealth and the danger of relative deprivation is not purely a socialist obsession, although the elimination of such dangers must be a major concern in the delineation of a socialist theory of justice.

For the purpose of comparison, a third view of justice which is, broadly speaking, conservative, should be mentioned. This is the idea of 'natural justice', discussed in Chapter 1, which is firmly rooted in the minds of many people who would have no interest in discussions of equality, need or merit. As has been said, there is no justice in nature, nor injustice, the concept being one which men have invented in an attempt to regulate each others' social activities. In political argument natural justice is invariably invoked to exclude a group of people from something to which the others feel themselves exclusively entitled. Belonging to a country which happens to find offshore oil off its coast does not in fact make it naturally just that you should have the exclusive use of that oil—as members of the EC are constantly trying to convince Great Britain—although the ease of access ('possession is nine points of the law') means that in most cases countries will benefit from such resources and, *a fortiori*, from the resources within their own territory. Presumably on the same grounds, the fact that I am born in a country does not give me a greater moral right to live there and enjoy its benefits than someone who may wish to emigrate to that country—although it invariably gives me greater *formal* rights in the form of a passport and citizenship. Likewise, the fact that I am lucky enough to live in a materially affluent society does not make it *just* that I should prosper while others, elsewhere, starve, even if this state of affairs is 'natural' (in the sense of 'unplanned'). Accidents of birth and location are not a proper foundation for justice, which is a social, artificial concept, but while the world is divided into so many rival units, the possibility of any universal, humanitarian principle of justice operating globally is excluded, and many people will continue to think of the accidents of their birth as their birthright, sanctioned by natural justice.

I have called the dogma of natural justice 'conservative' because it appeals to the innate conservatism in most of us, the desire to keep things as they are. It can hardly be called a theory because it has no clear abstract principles or justification, and so no defence against counterclaims posed by those with other views of nature's intentions. It appeals to us to maintain the status quo and rests on *faits accomplis* such as the possession of inherited wealth. If an advocate of natural justice is reminded of the fact that there is now a large 'immigrant' population which was actually *born* in Britain, a fact with the same 'natural' status as the fact that he himself was born in Britain, he will have no second criterion by which to distinguish between the naturalness of the first and the second case. He may, of course, argue that the two facts have a different historical basis and that his historical entitlement to live here is greater than that of a second-generation immigrant: recent legislation on citizenship which tries to make precisely such a distinction has been shown to be conceptually confused, and radically unjust. The notion of historical entitlement is a mainstay of the doctrine of natural justice, and has sometimes led to the compulsory explusion of whole groups from their adopted homes, sometimes to the repatriation of others in 'historic' homelands. A just social policy simply cannot take into account historical events outside a relatively short time-span — say, one or two generations — without doing grave injury to the living.

Natural justice cannot be admitted as a theory of justice, then, because it suffers such convolutions and self-contradictions in order to prove that what the propounder thinks is right is naturally just. There is no obviously correct way in which the criteria of naturalness or historical entitlement should be applied. In addition, the doctrine of natural justice is usually propounded self-interestedly by the 'haves' against the 'have-nots' (although when the 'have-nots' use it against the 'haves', it is no better founded), and so it could hardly gain any general credibility as a theory of justice, since impartiality is an important element of any such theory. Although natural justice is a fundamentally fallacious account of justice, it is interesting to see that Locke's view of how property came about in the state of nature is akin to the idea of natural justice. According to Locke, God gave the world to men in common but they, by 'mixing their labour' with the raw materials of the natural world, could appropriate it, in particular by tilling and enclosing land. The object appropriated was then justly theirs, according to natural laws, provided that they observed nature's injunction not to appropriate more of anything than they could use — a natural limitation which disappeared when money was invented.[10] The difference between Locke's theory and the version of natural justice discussed above is that the latter entirely omits the idea of *earning the right* to appropriate something, and argues as if mere birth or geographical proximity created certain rights. In the modern context, where it is utterly divorced from any theory of natural law, the idea of natural justice is an anachronism and a prejudice which should be challenged whenever it is proposed as a justification for some privilege or act of expropriation.

Retributive Justice

Before returning to the general consideration of justice, something must be said about retributive justice, which operates in penal systems. Just as social justice is, according to some, the distribution of goods in proportion to merit, legal justice can be thought of as the distribution of harm in proportion to demerit. The criminal is said to deserve his punisment: some theorists even speak of the criminal's 'right' to punishment. In some theories of retribution, punishment is appropriate to the criminal's moral iniquity, in others, to his infliction of harm on society (a sort of negative contribution). These two rival accounts parallel those which emphasise moral worth and merit, respectively, in social justice. Both theories resolve the problem that misdemeanours and punishments are, by and large, separate and incommensurable, by imputing responsibility and hence guilt to the individual. This responsibility for his moral character and/or for his actions is said to form the bridge between the crime and the punishment. 'Poetic justice' usually denotes retribution in the same kind as the crime—an eye for an eye—and retribution also has close associations with revenge and mere retaliation, but is distinguished from them by the necessity of firmly establishing guilt, and by the fact that legal justice is dispensed according to due process and, in a democratic country, by laws to which everyone has supposedly consented.

During the last century or so, the idea that men's characters and actions are determined by social conditions has pervaded our penal system and modified the concept of responsibility. Such a theory can broadly be referred to as deterministic. In the eighteenth century, theorists like Beccaria and Godwin argued that it was not the criminal who was responsible for his crime but society collectively, [11] and utopias were invented on the supposition that in ideal social circumstances crime would be entirely eliminated. According to the determinist view, whether criminality is caused by environmental factors, or, as theorists like Eysenck argue, by hereditary factors, it is unjust to punish the criminal *retributively*, as if he had committed his crime of his own free will. The most that can be justified is to punish him: (a) to protect society by segregating him; (b) to deter him (causally) from committing the crime again; (c) to reform him; or (d) to make an example of him which will deter others from similar crimes. These four, qualitatively different justifications have given rise to four separate accounts of punishment, all of which are challengeable on both philosophical and practical grounds (which there is no space to discuss here) but which at least avoid the two problems inherent in retribution, that of responsibility and that of whether society has the right to pass judgement on an individual, let alone to treat him inhumanely because of such a judgement and deprive him of freedom and dignity.

The dispensation and vindication of criminal justice cannot therefore be separated from the general conception of social justice which prevails. A society which holds that the successful man is responsible for his success and so deserves his reward is also likely to hold that the criminal is responsible for his crime and merits his punishment. A society which believes that intrinsic moral worth should be rewarded will also seek to punish moral iniquity for its own sake, even beyond the degree merited by the crime committed. By contrast, an ideally socialist society should acknowledge fully the environmental causes of crime and only punish criminals as far as prevention requires it. But from what we know of Soviet judicial processes a retributive element persists, incongruously, with individuals being blamed rather than social circumstances. It is perhaps as unlikely that any society could forego some notions of guilt and retribution in its penal system as that it could entirely forego the idea of merit in social justice, for ultimately most political ideologies, and systems, operate on a mixture of free will and determinist assumptions.

The institutions of criminal justice have contributed something to theories of social justice, namely, the ideas of due process and of equity in the dispensation of justice, which are equally applicable and relevant to the allocation of goods and opportunities in society as a whole. The Rawlsian idea of justice as a procedure rather than an outcome is also parasitic in its form on the judicial process where the outcome, or verdict of a trial is not specifiable in advance, but the proper and fair procedures for reaching a verdict can be specified. But as with any distribution, the procedure and outcome may differ in their degree of justice: perfectly fair trails have resulted in verdicts which were later found to be unjust, and the same can occur in procedural social justice. When considering distributive justice, we need to bear in mind the legal model but not to over-emphasize the parallel since the persistent emphasis on guilt and retribution, despite the efforts of penal reformers, makes it an unsuitable model for the allocation of social goods when other considerations have also to be borne in mind.

What is Justice?

Justice is a moral as well as a political concept, which, according to the moral philosopher, can be applied to any or all of the three stages of action—to the intention, the act, and the result. Justice at one stage rarely guarantees justice at another, hence we have problem cases like that of Robin Hood, whose intention of increasing the happiness of the poor (by robbing the rich) was doubtless just and benevolent. Some would say that the *outcome* of his action was just, some would not, but most would agree that his favourite *procedure* was unjust. Only in the simplest case can a just procedure be specified which is sure to lead to a just and predictable outcome, the case which Rawls calls 'perfect procedural justice'.[12] This is exemplified in the division of a cake between two (or more) people. If the principle '*I* cut, *you* choose' is followed, the outcome will always be a fair, equal division of the cake. However much the cutter's intention might be to take the largest share himself, he is obliged to divide the cake equally to avoid the certainty that an unequal division will mean that the smallest slice is left for him, the last to choose. In the seventeenth century, this principle was put forward in Harrington's *Oceania*, and gained the name of 'Harrington's Law', and it remains of great interest, being relevant to political and other decisions and the making of contracts. But unfortunately this simple principle of social justice cannot be the foundation of social policy, for those who cut the cake are not those who eat it, and vice versa, owing to the elite nature of governments. But a society where government was by rote, as Owen suggested, would to some extent realize the virtues and the safeguards embodied in Harrington's Law.

One's choice of an ideology and of a theory of justice depend on one's moral outlook: this in turn also determines whether one locates justice in intentions, acts or outcomes. A moralist concerned with individual responsibility and virtue might look for justice in intention and action and tend to disregard *results*, which are never entirely predictable, as long as the two former components were just. But intention is notoriously difficult to establish in criminal trials and far harder in the case of political action. In any case, nobody would seriously justify a bad political system or an unjust society on the grounds that the ruler's *intentions* were good, even if that were cited as a mitigating consideration. Orthodox utilitarians took account primarily of the *outcome* of action and thus avoided these problems: if the outcome maximized social utility it was said to be just. But this ignored the fact that social utility could be increased overall by actions which were, by conventional criteria, unjust, as in the case of Robin Hood. The example always quoted against utilitarians is that, in the case where society's utility would be increased by the killing of an innocent scapegoat, their theory would permit this gross injustice. To avoid this and other contradictions, J. S. Mill and others, known as 'rule utilitarians', introduced action-guiding rules to be followed in pursuit of utility: foremost among them was the rule of justice.[13] This avoided various discrepancies but diluted Bentham's injunction that utility was the absolute principle by which everything should be judged. Mill's amendment shifted the emphasis from the outcome to the act, which would be assessed according to whether it accorded with justice.

A theory of justice applied to existing situations (outcomes) is implicitly passing judgement on the results of past *actions*, viewing them in the light of their results. When new reforms are proposed to rectify an unjust situation, the theory must scrutinize the justice or otherwise of the proposed action as well as that of the intended outcome: that is, in assessing political policy and other activities with respect to justice we have to take into account both means and ends. The question often arises whether a *prima facie* unjust means may be employed to achieve a just end, particularly with reference to redistribution, violence, and revolution. Can injustice be committed for justice's sake? To avoid the censure of those who would say it cannot, because justice, like rights, is to be viewed as inviolable, the reformer or revolutionary will usually allude to the injustices of the existing situation—the wealth to be redistributed has been gained by exploitation of the poor, or those who propose political violence are themselves being unjustly repressed and coerced. In the end, one has to make a calculation of where the greater justice lies although, since outcomes are unpredictable, there is always the risk that taking unjust action will still not result in greater justice. Consciousness of this fact should not, however, turn into a general justification for quiescence or inaction. Rawls offers an alternative solution to this dilemma which is tempting because it avoids the necessity of weighing means against ends and calculating the incalculable: he suggests that if we cannot be sure of the outcome we should specify a just procedure, and keep to it. But this assumes that the existing situations to which the procedure will be applied are not themselves grossly unjust: and, as was suggested above, Rawls actually builds his own preferred outcome into his two procedural principles. Those who advocate viewing justice procedurally (and therefore limiting the scope of proposed reforms by this procedure) usually do so because they have already attained a state of society which they regard as just, and have specified procedures which perpetuate it. In other words, procedures tend to grow out of an established social system which they reflect and support. The second-order components of justice, fairness and due process, cannot alone create a just society if it does not already exist, and they may reinforce existing injustices, although they can prevent certain other injustices being perpetrated.

Many important debates arise in connection with social justice, which forms the stuff of contemporary political argument. Can justice exist without freedom? Rawls's theory suggests that it certainly cannot, as does liberalism in general, for the liberal theory of justice is commutative, based on free exchange.[14] But there is no reason to think that justice differently defined could not exist in a society which was unfree by liberal standards. Everyone could be equally subordinated to the whole by due process in the interests of greater material and moral wellbeing for all, as Rousseau suggests. Justice implies a comparison between equals, but if in some society equals were equally unfree it could not be said to be unjust on those grounds alone. The charge of injustice is only appropriate when some equals are less free for no good reason. It is really when 'justice' is treated as synonymous with 'good' that there is said to be an essential link between freedom and justice by those who consider freedom a vital part of the Good Life. Certainly, in an ideal society people would be free *and* justly treated, but in imperfect society freedom must sometimes be curtailed for the sake of greater justice, while justice as a distributive and ordering principle can still operate in the absence of a high degree of personal freedom.

Ever since the industrial revolution made material affluence seem possible in a not-too-distant future, philosophers have wondered whether problems of social justice might not disappear altogether if a state of superabundance were achieved. If everyone had more than enough, what grounds for complaint could there be, even if some still had more than others? From the utopian socialists to quasi-utopians such as Marcuse, the prospect of abundance has provided a convenient hypothetical solution to problems of distribution — even if that prospect is now receding, and has never existed for most of the world. But, although social justice mainly concerns itself with the distribution of *scarce* goods, theorists have pointed out that in any society, however abundant, there will always be 'positional goods', which remain scarce and will have to be distributed justly. Not everyone can win a race, even in utopia, or be Prime Minister, or live in a secluded country cottage. Perhaps ideally such goods would be distributed to those who volunteered to forego some amount of material goods instead of, as so often, to those who are already well supplied. Certainly, some principles for distributing positional goods would be needed in a situation of abundance, where feelings of relative deprivation might shift to the possession or lack of positional goods. It seems, then, that the concept of justice will be with us as long as society lasts, however cornucopian the latter becomes.

Nations and Generations

Whether there should be justice in the allocation of goods between nations was not seriously debated before the present century, when the emergence of so many new and impoverished nations make it an urgent question. According to Singer's 'humanitarian' theory of moral responsibility, the individual has an unlimited duty to help other human beings if it is within his power so to do, even to the extent of reducing himself to bare subsistence level, in order to give to them.[15] (Many would repudiate this logic, being unable to endure the consequences of such a theory, which suggests that we should either reduce ourselves to poverty or suffer constant, overwhelming guilt.) Likewise, if the same principle of moral obligation is said to apply to nations, most nations would be bound to repudiate it, for it would require the depletion of their own resources and the reduction of their citizens' standard of living for the benefit of distant peoples with no well-established claim on their goodwill. Nevertheless, even if the unlimited obligation of Singer's theory is repudiated and some concept of limited altruism replaces it, we cannot regard each nation-state as an enclave where justice reigns, set in a world where, generally, justice is constantly denied. Justice, however it is conceived, can logically take no account of nationality but enjoins equal treatment of all equal human beings, everywhere. The enormity of the task which this proposition entails baffles even philosophers, let alone politicians, but the focus on aid to the developing countries (two-edged though it is) indicates some acknowledgement of the industrialized countries' responsibility to share the world's resources more justly. The Brandt report makes the duty quite clear, although little action has been taken on its basis. The case for international redistribution has been complicated, and not always strengthened, by the argument that the colonial countries owe restitution and reparations to their ex-colonies. Questions of historical guilt across generations and between nations are as contentious as those of historical entitlement: but to base the case for international redistribution on the fact that it is grotesque for some to live in luxury while others die of malnutrition gives it an inexorable and persuasive logic—except perhaps to those who think that this, too, is natural justice.

The question of 'justice between generations' has also been widely debated of late, since Rawls's assertion that men in the 'original position' would agree to a 'just rate of saving' to cater for and improve the lives of their descendants.

Many philosophers joined in the discussion of whether we could have *duties* towards future, as yet non-existent generations, and whether we should allocate goods justly between ourselves and them.[16] This is not merely an intriguing puzzle for philosophers, however, as various practical dilemmas of social policy must be resolved by assumptions (albeit covert ones) about the nature of our duties to posterity. For example, whether we continue to reinvest in and renew our industrial base, or go on a prolonged and terminal spending spree is a vital question for the people of Britain at the moment. Whether we have a duty to preserve the world's exhaustible resources for our descendants or a right to exhaust them over the next generation or two—as it is predicted we shall—is a question of global importance. How we should treat the elderly in society (who presumably impoverished themselves to some extent to provide a brighter future for us, and to pay for their own pensions) is another vexed question, becoming more prominent as the population ages and inflation erodes life-savings. All these are problems of cross-generational justice.

Laslett has argued that we have duties to near-future but not to distant-future generations, and no duties to past generations, except, of course, to those still living. How could such a cut-off point between the near and the distant future rationally operate? The gaps in Laslett's argument show up the complexity of the issue. His case is based on the view, mentioned above, that justice requires us to further the wellbeing of any human being *'actual or potential'* (i.e. including future beings). Does this mean that we actually have a duty to produce as many children as possible so that we can further their wellbeing? The concept of a potential human being is unworkable in theory and in practice, as the controversy over abortion has shown. Rawls is nearer the mark than Laslett, perhaps, when he says that men in the original position would see themselves as possible parents in the future society and would therefore choose to provide for the welfare of all children under the rubric of justice: this argument for cross-generational justice clearly rests on a very different basis from Laslett's view of unlimited responsibility—that of natural affection. In summary, although the debate is far too complex, and too emotive, to summarize, it can be said that while our duty to living generations, older and younger, can be clearly delineated on the basis of conventional theories of justice, our duties to unborn generations cannot rest on justice defined via merit, equality or need (for all we know, they may be undeserving, or inferior to ourselves, and if we are too careless with nuclear weapons they may not exist at all) but must rest on a conception of society and humanity as continuing entities, whose preservation has an absolute value. This is a value-judgement that has no special connection with the idea of justice, and which not everyone would make, even at the risk of being called traitors to humanity if they do not. Justice is essentially concerned with existing situations and with the living, and the marginal overlap between them and the recently dead and the soon-to-be-born.

It is the strong moral element in the concept of justice that makes it such a powerful political ideal, but which also creates the danger that anything viewed as morally bad will also be described as 'unjust', as if the words were mere synonyms. Perhaps nothing which is morally bad can fail to be unjust, since it consists of treating others as less than equal or as means to our own ends, and thus ignoring the injunction to treat equals equally which justice makes. But the political concept of social justice has a more limited application than morality does, and what is unjust in society as a whole is not necessarily the result of morally bad actions by individuals. The *ordering and regulative* nature of justice was stated by Plato, for whom justice denoted a due proportion and harmony within society, or a healthy balance between the various faculties of the individual: the just society is the internally harmonious society and the same is true of man[17]. This view is significantly wider than the modern, individualistic and consumption-orientated view of justice, which concentrates on who gets what, for Plato emphasizes the interrelations of individuals and society, which is largely ignored by the liberal theory of justice, although implicit in the socialist and conservative views. Perhaps future speculation on the subject should take account of the social dimensions which Plato extols.

A fable by Borges, *The Lottery in Babylon*,[18] helps to clarify a common conviction about the nature of justice. In the mythical Babylon of which he writes, the citizens cast lots every sixty days to decide what their role in society should be for the next two months. One may draw the lot of a convicted murderer, and be executed, another may be in command of the army, another a slave, and so on. After two months the lots are cast again, and the shuffling recommences. In describing the origins of the custom, Borges says that it started in a small way, but then people became so addicted to the stimulating uncertainty and variety that they demanded the extension of the lottery to all aspects of life. Formally, the Babylonian system is reminiscent of Rawls's procedural model, but the men in the 'original position' in Babylon are *inveterate risk-takers* and ask for no future safeguards for themselves. The justice of the system lies in the *process* of the lottery alone, since some of the institutions of Babylon are clearly cruel or unjust. Most people would not willingly live in this Babylon, nor would they consider it the epitome of a just society although, procedurally, it is so, and this suggests the extent to which our desire for justice is linked to a desire for the regularity, orderliness, and security, which due process and equity bring into our lives. Likewise, social justice is valued for its importation of these same qualities into the distribution of goods. This is why the best antonym of justice is 'arbitrary' and why, while ideologists of various persuasions disagree about the criteria for dispensing social justice—and such disputes are important for political life—none seriously questions the place of justice among our political ideals, although no other political ideal remains similarly unchallenged.

Justice and Equality

Cursory observation of society shows us inequalities of age, ability, sex, intelligence, education, social, and economic position. Why then, when it seems to be a lost cause, is equality so important a part of political theory and ideology? From what has been said already, it is clear that justice is intimately connected with equality in the sense of 'fair and non-arbitrary treatment of equals', although it does not require a substantive equality between individuals. Equality is the first assumption of morality: we act morally towards others because we assume that they are equally sensitive, equally vulnerable and equally worthy of respect in some formal or abstract sense, even when there are visible differences in the sensitivity and worth of particular individuals. If the people in a certain group are defined as inferior, the requirement to act morally towards them is, some would say, annulled. Genocide, and the oppression of particular groups or races, has usually been justified by redefining such groups as sub-human, unworthy of moral respect. The assertion of the ultimate equality of all human beings operates as a defence against such treatment. The equality of mankind, and policies based on it, have sometimes been justified on the empirical grounds that men resemble each other in more ways than they differ, yet it could be said that even casual observation defeats this assertion—what do we notice if not the differences between individuals? However, from the point of view of a dog or insect no doubt the similarities are far more striking than the differences. The abstract hypotheses which political philosophers sometimes construct, in which all men are identical and equally wise, moral, autonomous, etc., obviously dictates that justice should consist in the substantively equal treatment of all. But the natural and artifical inequalities which exist outside philosopher's models demand a justice based on carefully structured *unequal* treatment, devised so as to remove injustices and to compensate for natural disadvantages. Theories of justice, as we saw, need to stipulate the kinds of inequality which make unequal treatment inappropriate—inequalities of ability, need and merit, for example. Therefore, although we perceive intuitively that it is wrong for a judge to treat similar cases differently, and that a just distribution should be equal in the absence of other considerations, numerically equal treatment is not in itself a *sufficient* condition for justice and may even run counter to justice, although the fair or equable treatment of all is certainly a *necessary* condition.

Some speculation on the causes of inequality is essential to any consideration of whether equality should itself count as an independent political ideal, and how it should function in a theory of justice. Hobbes imagined a pre-social state of nature in which men had a natural equality of experience and 'prudence' (reason) and an approximate equality of strength.

From this equality of ability ariseth equality of hope in the attaining of our ends.[19]

The serpent enters paradise via the scarcity of resources: if two men both want the same thing, and have 'equality of hope' of attaining it, they become enemies. They also, said Hobbes, try to preserve themselves by anticipatory violence against others; furthermore, they desire distinction, the estimation of others, and will extort it 'by damage' if necessary. Thus, approximate natural equality leads, paradoxically, to a war of all against all and the subjection of some by others. Rousseau also sought to explain how the equality existing between happy savages in his mythical state of nature declined as societies were formed. He too pinpoints the desire for distinction as a major cause, along with the inequality of talents which created inequalities of property. Worst of all, social distinction became attached to the possession of property, producing rivalry, ambition, and greed.

All these evils were the first effect of property, and the inseparable attendants of growing inequality. [20]

So Rousseau too suggests that inequality is not natural, but is imposed by circumstance and, more precisely, by society. 'Man is born equal but everywhere he is in chains'.

Rousseau's hypothesis that men are equal in a pre-social state, or at birth, is tantamount to asserting the abstract equality of mankind, which other eighteenth-century writers such as Paine did more prosaically. However, one need not believe that equality is mankind's original state to believe that it should be a political goal, and today most writers avoid speculating about man's natural state. However, it is possible to acknowledge the presence of inequality in society without condemning it. Why, then, did Rousseau, the socialists, and the anarchists abominate it? The first, practical reason was the *overt social misery* resulting from inequality in combination with scarcity, which they condemned on humanitarian grounds. Second, inequalities of wealth and privilege lead to *inequalities of power* and to *dependence* and the subordination of some to others' wills, which deprives them of dignity and autonomy. Rousseau thought that such dependence had come about through the need for joint economic activity, Godwin argued that an unequal accumulation of property leads to 'servility, dependency and domination', while Condorcet noted that educational inequalities lead to the dependency and helplessness of the individual. Post-Enlightenment philosophers merely elaborated these basic criticisms. The list could be extended, but enough has been said to show that social inequalities are not condemned *a priori* by such philosophers, but because they violate other ideals—the enjoyment of a happy, independent, worthwhile life, to which all individuals are equally entitled by virtue of being human.

The champions of inequality defend it not by denying the latter assertion, for this would run counter to the dictates of most religions and moralities, but by emphasizing the functional usefulness of inequality in society, which supposedly benefits everyone. Mandeville argued that inequality produced talent, endeavour and art in *The Fable of the Bees*, and Hume concurred. Later, Kant argued against Rousseau that 'inequality is a rich source of much that is evil, but also of everything that is good'. Social Darwinism, which asserted that the 'survival of the fittest' principle should operate unimpeded in society as in nature gave a new impulse to the inegalitarian cause, with its postulate that some individuals are inferior and that to protect them or compensate for the deficiencies weakens the calibre of society as a whole. Nature abhors equality: 'progress through inequality' was the message. Finally, modern pluralist theories which rejoice in social differences can easily be converted into a defence of inequality. Such defenders of inequality usually justify it by reference to holistic criteria such as 'the quality of life (quality not equality!)', 'the survival of cultures', 'the advance of civilization', for the simple reason that it cannot be satisfactorily justified on individualistic grounds, given that it implies the oppression or even sacrifice of some individuals for others, or for the social whole. Other inegalitarians simply defend social inequality as the just reflection of the genetic differences between individuals, thus implicitly abandoning any conception of their equal worth or equal right to a satisfying life. The assumption that inequality is a natural, permanent phenomenon leads to political theories vindicating hierarchical or elitist forms of society, or justifying meritocracy.

Apart from the argument that inequality strengthens and embellishes the social whole which seems always to be directed *de haut en bas* (would Spencer have agreed to be weeded out if he was discovered to be genetically inferior?) there are several arguments used to demolish egalitarianism by pointing out its shortcomings — these, indeed, are more commonly employed than outright defences of inequality. The first is that we shall never achieve real equality because of the prevalence of natural inequalities and of other human factors such as social envy and greed. This is like saying 'You'll never get 100% in this examination, so don't bother to enter for it' — the fallacy is self-evident. Second, it is argued that egalitarian policies always mean 'levelling down, not up'. This is factually misleading because in any redistribution process some are levelled down, others up. Historically, some socialist revolutions have reduced everyone's living standards for a time: on the other hand the Chinese population is clearly much better-off today than before 1949. To answer this argument in the factual terms in which it is proposed, the egalitarian can argue that in most cases those levelled down are a small minority, so that on any majoritarian principle the levelling up more than compensates in society as a whole. A third argument misdirected against equality was termed the 'tadpole argument' by Tawney. Although many tadpoles are hatched and few survive to become frogs, the fact that a few survive is said to justify nature's enterprise. Similarly, some people justify our unequal society (Tawney was writing a study of Britain in the late 1920s[21]) by the fact that exceptional individuals can rise above it. In India, the 'Bombay-beggar-turned-millionaire' myth may comfort or even inspire the poor, but it is scarcely a *justification* of the hierarchical system there. The argument that equality conflicts with freedom has already been discussed in Chapter 5, and shown to be untenable. In short, the arguments offered against egalitarian policies are essentially weak or fallacious, and usually quite tangential to the basic justification of egalitarianism. This tangentiality is not accidental — for to challenge the moral tenet of human equality of worth is to open a Pandora's box of amoral arguments.

Tawney said that to postulate equality as a *fact* about men's characters and intelligence is untenable, but as a value-judgement it is acceptable. Socially, politics should operate to produce equality of circumstance, institutions and way of life, and although complete equality is not attainable it should be the aim. This is as good a statement of the egalitarian position as any, and neatly demonstrates that when an egalitarian proclaims 'All men are equal' he does not delude himself that this is a fact, but proclaims it as an aspiration. Egalitarian policies in the West have usually been associated with left-wing ideology and the critique of property, but other cultures provide good reasons for aspiring to a more equal society. In *Coming of Age In Samoa*, Mead describes how the Samoan community discourages precocity and outstanding enterprise or achievement, and is more charitable towards the lazy and the stupid than to over-achievers. This 'levelling down' attitude produces social peace and harmony and, it would appear, in many respects a happy and satisfying way of life. Westerners should ask themselves how far the naturalness and inevitability of inequality may have been magnified by an ideology which upholds an economic system whose very essence is division of labour, specialization of function, and large disparities of wealth.

Equality, then, is an ambiguous term. It can be invoked as a substantive or absolute principle which specifically determines the outcome of a distribution: one-man-one-vote, or a uniform distribution. *Equality of treatment* and *equality of opportunity* are both second-order, procedural principles which determine methods of distribution but not particular outcomes. In one form or another equality is invoked by every theory of justice, if only in the form of equity and due process, for only thus can anyone be sure that their case will be treated on a par with others. An account of equality is thus central to any theory of social justice, but the establishment of equality as an end in itself depends on one's ideological standpoint.

Theoretical analysis can only take us to the threshhold of justice, which it analyses as a second-order, formal (insubstantial) principle. At that point, we need the values which ideology supplies to make the ideal substantive, and to step across into the Just Society. In this respect, justice illustrates best of all the ideas or ideals discussed in this book the intimate relation between political ideas and ideologies, and the impossibility of understanding either in isolation.

Notes

1. Aristotle, *The Politics,* (Trans. T. A. Sinclair), Penguin, 1962, pp.73-7, 236-40.
2. But William Galston argues that need and desert *are* compatible in *Justice and the Human Good*, Chicago University Press, 1980.
3. J. Rawls, *A Theory of Justice*, Harvard University Press, 1971, p.34.
4. Rawls, *A Theory of Justice*, p.92.
5. Rawls, *A Theory of Justice*, p.60.

6. For a sustained criticism of Rawls see R. P. Wolff, *Understanding Rawls,* Princeton, University Press, 1977)
7. This is shown by W. G. Runciman's application of Rawls's test in *Relative Deprivation and Social Justice*, Routledge & Kegan Paul, 1966, PartIV.
8. Rawls, *A Theory of Justice*, p.86. Emphasis added.
9. D. Lane, *The End of Inequality*, Penguin, 1971, Chap.4.
10. Locke, *Essay*, Chap. V.
11. W. Godwin, *Enquiry Concerning Political Justice*, (Ed. K. C. Carter), Clarendon Press, 1971, Bk VI. Godwin also cited the earlier humanitarian arguments of C. Beccaria, *Dei Delitti e delle Pene,* 1764.
12. Rawls, *A Theory of Justice*, p.85.
13. J. S. Mill, *Utilitarianism*, Collins, 1962, Chap.V.
14. W. B. Gallie, 'Liberal morality and socialist morality', in *Philosophy, Politics and Society*, 1st Series, (Ed. P. Laslett), Blackwell, 1956.
15. P. Singer, 'Famine, Affluence and Morality', in *Philosophy, Politics and Society*, 5th Series, (Eds P. Laslett and J. Fishkin), Blackwell, 1979, p.23.
16. P. Laslett, 'The conversation between the generations', in *Philosophy, Politics and Society,* (Eds P. Laslett and J. Fishkin).
17. Plato, *The Republic*, (Trans. H. D. P. Lee), Penguin, 1955, Part 5.
18. J. L. Borges, *Labyrinths*, Penguin, 1970.
19. T. Hobbes, *Leviathan*, Penguin, 1968, p.184.
20. J. -J. Rousseau, *A Discourse . . . On Inequality*, Dent, 1913, p.203.
21. R. H. Tawney, *Inequality*, Allen and Unwin, 1913.

Further reading

D. Miller, *Social Justice*, Clarendon Press, 1976.
D. D. Raphael, *Justice and Liberty*, Athlone Press, 1980.
J. Rawls, *A Theory of Justice*, Harvard University Press, 1971.
J. Wilson, *Equality*, Hutchinson, 1966.
W. Galston, *Justice and the Human Good*, Chicago University Press, 1980.

Index of Concepts and Proper Names

Italic page numbers refer to main entries.